This is No. 844 of Everyman's Library. A list of authors and their works in this series will be found at the end of this volume. The publishers will be pleased to send freely to all applicants a separate, annotated list of the Library.

J. M. DENT & SONS LIMITED
10–13 BEDFORD STREET LONDON W.C.2

E. P. DUTTON & CO. INC.
286–302 FOURTH AVENUE
NEW YORK

Everyman, I will go with thee, a
In thy most need to go by

EVERYMAN'S LIBRARY
EDITED BY ERNEST RHYS

POETRY & THE DRAMA

MINOR POETS OF THE
EIGHTEENTH CENTURY
EDITED WITH AN INTRO-
DUCTION BY HUGH
I'ANSON FAUSSET

THOMAS PARNELL, born in 1679 and died in 1718.

MATTHEW GREEN, born in 1696 and died in 1737.

JOHN DYER, born about the year 1700 and died in 1758.

ANNE, COUNTESS OF WINCHILSEA, married Heneage Finch, fourth earl of Winchilsea, and died in 1720.

MINOR POETS OF
THE EIGHTEENTH CENTURY

PARNELL, GREEN, DYER &
ANNE, COUNTESS OF WINCHILSEA

LONDON: J. M. DENT & SONS LTD.
NEW YORK: E. P. DUTTON & CO. INC.

INTRODUCTION

To Matthew Arnold the eighteenth century was an "age of prose and reason"; to Von Hügel it was vulgar, "a purely *this*-world affair," while Count Keyserling has described it as the period of Europe's utmost perfection so far attained. The truth which lies behind these contradictory judgments has yet to be formulated. But it is already clear that our attitude to the eighteenth century is in process of readjustment, and that the verdict of the nineteenth century is now before the twentieth for revision. That verdict, so far at least as English poetry was concerned, echoed and codified the revulsion of the Romantics. For those who felt themselves heirs to the "bright tradition of the golden age" there was inevitably no lustre in silver and no virtue in Reason unless she was intent

> on making of herself
> A prime enchantress.

For them poetry was "like love, a Passion." It shattered "the surfaces of artificial life" and the pride of "self-applauding intellect," while Keats with all the force of an imagination eager to

> prepare her steeds,
> Paw up against the light and do strange deeds
> Upon the clouds,

uttered his famous protest against those who

> went about,
> Holding a poor, decrepid standard out
> Mark'd with most flimsy mottoes, and in large
> The name of one Boileau.

The Victorians, however, had less excuse for being unjust to the eighteenth century. Most of them drew back in alarm from the strange deeds which the Romantic imagination had done upon the clouds. It was rather the new sensibility which they cherished and cultivated and moralised with a cautiousness that preferred the choice pleasures of security to the creative hazards of that Liberty, in whose name terrible, as well as sublime, things had been done.

Yet though they deprecated the extravagance of the

Romantics, they were too close to them in sensibility, as they were in time, to do justice to the eighteenth century.

We can see now that the new discoveries in feeling and sensation, which the Victorians inherited from the Romantics, were but elements in an extension of human consciousness, that indeed the whole problem which the Romantics tried to solve was the reconciling of liberated feeling and sensation with reason, and their unifying in imagination. But this problem, upon which the Victorians compromised, had its roots in the eighteenth century, although its poets, with the exception of those few who were haunted by melancholy or mania, had little inkling of the distractions in which it was to involve those who strove to solve it. Nevertheless that inner conflict between the instinctive and the rational life, which has become the typical malady of modern civilisation, had begun to vex the soul of the age of Reason. And the pleasure and interest which we can derive from these poets to-day lies not only in the balance that they achieved by accepting limits, of which we can wistfully appreciate the advantage, while admitting that they had necessarily to be overstepped, but in their gradual abandonment of those limits, and the gradual infusion in their experience of feelings, sensations, and ideas which were to disturb profoundly, as they were also to enrich and transform, both English poetry and human sensibility.

Viewed from this standpoint the poetry of the eighteenth century has a double appeal. It is both an expression of cultured and very English sobriety, of sanity untouched by fanaticism, and of social elegance, and it trembles with the first vibrations of a new life of vast potentialities. It is a model of the limited integrity which may be achieved by the acceptance of standards and the prescribing of experience, and it is prophetic, however faintly, of the disintegration which was to accompany the effort to realise more creative values, that hunger of the imagination which, in Dr. Johnson's words, "preys upon life," because it demands a deeper reality than good sense can provide. To those, in fact, who study eighteenth-century poetry sympathetically such critical catchwords as "the tyranny of Pope," or "the domination of the heroic couplet," must appear not only superficial, but definitely misleading. And the perpetuation of such flimsy mottoes can only be explained by the fact that many critics have approached eighteenth-century poetry with a preconception that what virtues it possesses are those of style, and of a style existing rather in its own right than as the expression of a particular experience of life. Admittedly there is on the surface some justification for such a view, and inevitably the Romantics exaggerated it with all the self-engrossed ardour of revolutionaries. Wordsworth, for example, wrote with a recklessness which he too soon outgrew and a disregard of his own considerable debts to the poets whom he depreciated—"Now it is remarkable that, excepting the *Nocturnal Reverie* of Lady Winchilsea, and a passage or two in the *Windsor Forest* of Pope, the poetry intervening between the publication of the *Paradise Lost* and *The Seasons* does not contain a single new image of external nature."

To refute this assertion would demand both extensive quotation and a consideration of what a "new image" really is. There is, indeed, a sense in which Wordsworth, despite his exaggeration, was right. The characteristic temper of eighteenth-century poets was not imaginative in the sense given to Imagination by Coleridge when he contrasted it with Fancy. Their "Reason" was Coleridge's "Intelligence." It was a logical, not an intuitional, faculty. But within the bounds of conscious self-awareness and self-respect, of bright observance and fresh invention, it was often original. Wordsworth's criticism, however, was essentially directed against their use of a conventionally poetic diction. And, admittedly, most of the dead-matter in their poetry is the result of such diction. But there is far less of it than is generally supposed, nor is it always deadly. If the use of stock epithets were necessarily deadly, the poetry of Homer would be strewn with verbal corpses. And to-day when Mr. James Joyce and other ultra-modern poets have carried the theory of original diction to such a point that we have to learn their private and esoteric language if we are to understand their meaning, we may well regard more tolerantly those who were content to accept the idiom of their age. And although the language of a great poet never dates as that of eighteenth-century poets often does, their idiom is only valueless when it fails to reflect a personal, as well as a contemporary, standpoint. And the interesting fact about much of the condemned formality of eighteenth-century poetry is that it reflected not only a fashion in diction but a personal temper.

The "antithesis," for example, which we are apt to dismiss as merely a structural convention, was something more than a trick of diction. It was the verbal equivalent of an ideal, superficial and self-regarding as it may seem. That ideal was the ideal of "the mean." To balance one impulse by its opposite, enthusiasm by good sense, generosity by prudence, desire by discretion, and so preserve a mastery over life and an assured poise in yourself—that was "The Choice" of John Pomfret and of many of his contemporaries. Because, in Matthew Green's words,

> Experience joined with common sense,
> To mortals is a providence,

they qualified every feeling, every impulse, every taste. For they felt that indulgence led to excess, and that in excess the individuality was dissipated. They were self-regarding, because they desired above all things to possess themselves.

And just as in civilisation they saw only a small and privileged citadel of culture in a brutish world, so they conceived of poetry as a pattern of good-sense and elegant sobriety, imposed upon the rebel instincts.

This attitude to life may not command our admiration to-day, but it deserves our respect. To make even an imperfect art of life is so difficult that in our hasty times most of us have given up the attempt and live, both in the realm of ideas and of fact, from hand to mouth.

But in the eighteenth century men could still aim at poise and completeness, and although their aim lacked the tension for the most part of supreme endeavour, their serenity, increasingly disturbed though it was by moodiness and melancholy, is a proof that they realised it.

As Cowper, whom no one could consider a meanly self-regarding man, was to write,

> To find the medium asks some share of wit,
> And therefore 'tis a mark fools never hit.

And we have not yet so outgrown our animal inheritance that we can afford to scorn an attitude which accepted Judgment as the

> umpire in the strife
> That Grace and Nature have to wage through life.

We may, however, question its adequacy. And in so doing we shall but follow the example of these poets themselves, who, as the century advanced, lived with less and less certainty by the belief that

> If Reason rules within, and keeps the Throne,
> While the inferior Faculties obey,

happiness was assured. Even in the early years of the century it was not an unquestioned belief. We find Prior, for example, applauding in his charming *Jinny the Just* one whose

> Will with her Duty so equally stood
> That seldom oppos'd she was commonly good,
> And did pritty well, doing just what she wou'd.

But while a balance of impulses, a happy antithetical conduct of life, were acceptable enough as gifts of nature, he had regretfully to admit elsewhere that an Augustan façade of elegance and propriety was a flimsy protection against that "Fate," those rude and primitive forces in life which Reason could not tame. Yet the rational system which the culture of the eighteenth century had imposed upon life was so comforting to self-esteem and within limits so realisable, that it was long before these poets would admit its inadequacy. And in Pope, in the perfected cunning of his interlocked antitheses and the bland complacence of his philosophy, as defined in his *Essay on Man*, it found its apotheosis.

He who could arrange words to balance each other with an inspired cunning and an unfailing propriety found it easy to attribute to the Creator of the Universe a kindred aptitude. Pope could affirm the living order of the Universe so blandly because he viewed it quite externally. He fancied God making it as he made his own verses, with as orderly a precision and as polished a clarity.

> To Him no high, no low, no great, no small;
> He fills, He bounds, connects, and equals all.

It was this projection of his own accomplishment and decorum into the Universe itself that explains Pope's shallow serenity and that of so many of his contemporaries. For him the Deity was, like Viscount Bolingbroke, an admirable Augustan gentleman,

> From grave to gay, from lively to severe,
> Correct with spirit, eloquent with ease,
> Intent to reason, or polite to please.

But the more men obeyed his injunction

> Know then thyself, presume not God to scan,

the more they discovered in their nature cravings which the Universe had apparently little concern to satisfy, the more difficult they found it to assent that man was the measure of all God's creation.

The agreement between man and the Universe, the balance between reason and feeling, which Pope had achieved by imposing a strict economy and discipline on the latter, was disturbed. A new sensibility was trembling into life beneath the orderly surface of Augustan manners, a sense of the transcendent and also of the indifferent in Nature.

It was some time before cracks appeared on that glazed surface. Devotees of Nature and even Methodists reconciled at first with some success their transports with a decorous tradition. Yet the foundations of the structure so firmly and subtly adjusted had given way. The antithesis in all the most vital poets of the middle and later eighteenth century, with few exceptions, was abandoned. For the balance which it expressed was no longer a reality, and men were seeking uneasily for a new harmony in life and a new rhythm in poetry.

Those, then, who appreciate the real significance of the style of eighteenth-century poetry can hardly fail to discover how consistently it reveals an organic growth of sensibility, in which the domination, not of the heroic couplet, but of restrictive reason, was gradually sapped and softened by the emotions, and the ground prepared for an extension of both faculties fused together in a new apprehension of reality.

But even from a purely external standpoint the perpetuation of such catch-words as "the domination of the heroic couplet" is hard to explain. It is still, for example, a generally accepted dogma of criticism that Pope bestraddled his age like a crippled Colossus. Yet the briefest reference to the most vocal poets in each decade will disprove it. These, between 1700 and 1710, were Prior, Swift, and Addison, who, if definitely Augustan in temper, owed this quality to Dryden, but not to Pope. Between 1710 and 1720 Pope arrived; yet in the same decade we have Lady Winchilsea whose sprightly wit and elegance and delicately personal nuances owe nothing to Pope. Rather it was Pope, as has been suggested, who combined in his famous line,

Die of a rose in aromatic pain

two exquisitely evocative phrases borrowed from Lady Winchilsea's The Spleen, and cheapened what he borrowed. In the same decade we have Gay, also, who was not prevented by literary refinement from entering intimately, in The Shepherd's Week, into the humours of village life. And if in Parnell there are occasional hints of Pope's influence—for

the two men were intimately associated—the whole temper
of his mind was alien to Pope's. And the fact is proved not
only by the sentiment, but also by the diction and the rhythm
of his verse, which, though it be the verse of a scholar, has,
when most characteristic, an easy sweetness and a yielding
grace which are the very antithesis of Pope's hard brilliance.
Pope, in fact, owed far more to Parnell's scholarship in his
translation of the *Iliad* than Parnell to Pope's heroic couplet.

Between 1720 and 1740 Pope admittedly achieved and
preserved a wide popularity. Yet how little his influence
affected the really individual poets of the period is obvious
to any one who reads the verse of Dyer, Allan Ramsay,
Thomson, and Shenstone. The interests and emotional
attachments of these men were not urban, but rural. Their
country feeling, compared with Wordsworth's, may seem too
often clogged with conventional classicisms, but so far as they
were indebted, it was to the pastoral tradition of the past,
to old English poets, the study of whom was being revived,
and to the balladry which Ramsay was among the first to
renew in his *The Gentle Shepherd*. And in the following decade,
1740 to 1750, there is an emphatic rise in the tide of romantic
feeling. We need only mention Blair's *Grave*, Young's
Night Thoughts, Akenside's *Pleasures of Imagination*, Thomson's *Castle of Indolence*, Gray's *Elegy*, and Collins's *Ode to
Evening*. The personal feeling of these poets was still pent
within classical conventions, which it often failed completely
to inform and animate. But the convention was not Pope's,
and from the middle of the century there is hardly a poet of
standing, if we except the satirical Churchill, in whom we can
trace, in any real sense, Pope's influence. And if the age is
still seeking to conform to standards of prose and reason, its
poetry has passed into the hands of men who, if they do not
become enthusiasts with the Methodists, are captivated by
the dreamy forgeries of Macpherson or haunted by the melancholy of suppressed instincts and the madness of unsatisfied
romantic yearnings.

The prevalent conception then of eighteenth-century poetry
as typified in the work of Pope, will not bear examination.
It is, in fact, even more misleading than the similar assumption
that the Victorian age is a single, undifferentiated stretch of
time, revealing an unchanging attitude to life. And just as
Victorianism does in a sense extend from 1837 to 1902, while
revealing, as Mr. Michael Sadleir has shown, three distinct

and changing epochs, so the eighteenth century reveals a
certain constant temper throughout, while beneath its surface
and even more agitatingly perhaps than in the Victorian age,
the crust of its cool rationality is being shaken and dissolved
by generating fires. Pope, in fact, represented rather a last
refinement of the age of Dryden than the fertile forces of
his own age. His influence on the mere versifiers of the
century was potent, as the influence of Tennyson was on the
versifiers of his day and century. But even on the poets
who were his immediate contemporaries it has been greatly
exaggerated; on those who succeeded him it was inconsider-
able; and where, as in Crabbe, his heroic couplet recurs forty
years after his death, it is put to a purpose which defiantly
denies an affinity.

He occupies, therefore, a significant place in his century,
not by virtue of an all-pervading influence or by imposing a
certain kind of line and diction on his contemporaries and
successors, but because his line, or rather couplet, embodied,
in a deeper sense perhaps than even Mr. Lytton Strachey will
allow, a criticism of life, and a criticism which was typical,
not of the century as a whole, but only of its youth.

In Pope the intellect preserves an unruffled and self-
delighting mastery over the senses and the feelings and
impoverishes them and itself in the process. But the impulse
behind most of the poetry of the eighteenth century is a
protest, often doubtless sub-conscious, generally timid and
tentative, but growing in intensity and volume, against such
impoverishment.

II

The poets whom we have selected for this volume personify
in their different ways this quickening of the emotional pulse
of their century. Lady Winchilsea was born in 1661 and
died in 1720. She is, therefore, chronologically a transitional
poet, but it was not until 1701 that her verse first appeared
in Gildon's *Miscellany*, and not until 1713 that she published
a volume of selections from her poems, while many of them
were written in the early years of the new century. In 1713
Pope was already widely known through his *Pastorals*, *Essay
on Criticism*, and *Rape of the Lock*, and "Ardelia" sufficiently
coveted his favourable criticism to ask him to dinner. Her
advances were successful, although in later years Pope stooped

to satirise her as a female wit. There was in fact little in common between Lady Winchilsea's cool and graceful temper and Pope's hard mental incandescence, between her delicate simplicity of heart and his sophisticated head. She was typical of an "age of prose and reason" in this, that for her

> all pleasures left behind
> Contemplations of the mind.

Her feelings were for her the source of ideas rather than images, and she sat down "to describe," not to express, her heart. To order feeling elegantly, to point it with wit, to realise a temperate harmony, that "soft peace" which is

> The greatest blessing heav'n does give,
> Or can on earth be found,

was her ideal. The rash pursuit of ecstasy was not in her nature, which in its dislike of extremes approved the happy mean at times, we may think, to excess, choosing by preference to take the pleasures of the fields with her Daphnis

> When such a day blessed the Arcadian plain,
> Warm without sun, and shady without rain,

and commending a harmony

> Something less than joy, yet more than dull content.

Yet if she ranged herself with the nymphs who feared "disordered beauty," she had at her best an exquisite gift for evoking the indefinite out of the definite, for distilling a faint fragrance and drawing a silvery music out of things distinctly seen, heard, or felt. The enchanting quality in her memorable lines,

> Nor will in fading silks compose
> Faintly the inimitable rose,

or in these, which at once describe and evoke a sigh,

> Softest note of whisper'd anguish
> Harmony's refindest part
> Striking whilst thou seem'st to languish
> Full upon the list'ners heart,

owes nothing, as the magic of a Coleridge or a Poe does, to fever in the blood. It is the music, not of the dreaming or the drugged senses, but of a mind which floats above the sensible world with a soft awareness. Admittedly her mind was only in rare moments thus entranced. Generally it was too consciously engaged in imposing a graceful symmetry upon experience, and in ensuring that every object should produce

> Thoughts of pleasure and of use.

Yet on this lower level her achievement is a constant source of delight, because we feel in it a native grace of being, as well as a cultivated elegance,

> A pleasing and a sweet address,
> Beyond what affectation can express.

In her tributes to the dead, for example, or in such charming complimentary verses as she addressed to her hosts at Long-leate, elegance and sentiment are admirably blended. She could, too, as in *Ardelia's Answer to Ephelia*, indulge very entertainingly a gentle but sprightly malice, while the poems addressed to her husband prove that far from marriage being necessarily fatal to the Muse, a happy marriage may blossom into verses in which wit and tenderness, the intimacies and the courtesies of love are at once playfully and affectingly entwined. But it is perhaps in her attitude to Nature that we recognise best the early signs of a craving which, in spite of Pope, was to grow more and more imperative as the century advanced, until it became a dominating impulse in the Romantic movement.

Nature crept into the Augustan consciousness, loosening the tight cords of its sober and self-respecting moderation, by way of the garden and the country-seat. While later poets went credulously to Nature in search of a lost Eden of innocent anarchy, or to dissolve themselves in her elements, these poets at first sought her with the conscious aim of soothing their nerves and enhancing in "lowly dale," by river side, or on woody hill, that correct art of life which was still their chief concern.

Their garden-craft and their terror of anything approaching the elemental in Nature prove how jealously they guarded their sense of order against unruly forces. And by thus imposing their correctness upon her elementalism they could select from all she had to offer her sedative influences, could feel with Thomson that

> Men, woods and fields, all breathe untroubled life,
> Then keep each passion down, however dear.

They felt indeed the climate of the time to be too cultivated, but they valued their culture. They only wished to freshen it by a cleaner air, to forget the intrigues and agitations of society in quiet garden-paths and studious glades, to ease the tension without destroying the effectiveness of their self-sufficiency, which, in spite of an external complacence, they felt inwardly to dull and stereotype their response to life.

And so even at the beginning of the century we find Lady Winchilsea writing,

> Give me, O indulgent Fate!
> Give me, yet, before I die,
> A sweet, but absolute retreat,
> 'Mongst paths so lost, and trees so high,
> That the world may ne'er invade,
> Through such windings and such shade
> My unshaken liberty.

There was nothing self-abandoned in the liberty which she sought. It was a liberty to relax while preserving her self-awareness intact, to feel without endangering her powers of exact observance or comely bearing. "And falling waters," she writes, "we *distinctly* hear," and although "silent musings" may urge her mind to seek

> Something too high for syllables to speak,

she restrains the impulse which would shatter the approved mood of inward equilibrium

> When a sedate content the spirit feels,
> And no fierce light disturbs, whilst it reveals.

Yet in the contrast which she, like so many of these poets, draws between the country and the town, there is a moral implication. "Oh!" she wrote,

> for my groves, my country walks, and bow'rs,
> Trees blast not trees, nor flow'rs envenom flow'rs.

And we are reminded of Whitman thinking that he could turn and live with animals, because they are not dissatisfied or demented with the mania of owning things. But while Lady Winchilsea could read a moral lesson in the vegetable kingdom, she would never have read one in the animal. And her attitude to Nature differed essentially from Whitman's in that she viewed her with detachment. Nature was not only "the inferior world," but a world which had no concern with human desires or perplexities. "But oh! in vain," she wrote

> things void of sense we call,
> In vain implore the murmuring sound
> Of hollow groans from underneath the ground,
> Or court the loud lament of some steep water's fall;

> On things inanimate we would force
> Some share of our divided grief,
> Whilst Nature (unconcern'd for our relief)
> Pursues her settled path, her fixt and steady course.

And it was because she and her contemporaries were thus divided from Nature that they experienced a "divided grief." In her, because perhaps she was a woman, the malady of a divided being never became serious. She succeeded in combining a detached rationality, with a sense of "this soft endearing life," although in the process life often became in her verses a little pallid and insipid. But in perhaps her best known poem, *The Spleen*, she recorded a condition to which the poets of this century were increasingly to testify. Each of the poets in this volume confesses himself a victim of it, and Matthew Green devotes a long poem to describing its symptoms and prescribing for its cure. The characteristic disease, indeed, of the eighteenth century was the spleen. And the fact has a spiritual as well as a pathological significance. It shows that the inner conflict between reason and instinct and man and nature, which the Romantics strove to resolve and which has disintegrated the modern world, began to be consciously felt in the eighteenth century. For them it was rather a medical than a spiritual problem, although for such an orthodox poet as Lady Winchilsea it had a religious aspect, and was to be traced to the fall of man. Yet behind even her "inquiry after peace" there was a sense of disunity and imperfect adjustment to the primitive forces of nature. And by submitting her jaded nerves to the comfortable, the gently reanimating, quiet of the country, she was combating the typical disease of her age, the disease of prescribed conventions and mental exclusiveness.

The same tendency is found in Parnell, who was born in Dublin in 1679, ordained by the Bishop of Derry in 1700, began to frequent London in 1706, where he quickly became the intimate of Pope, Arbuthnot, Swift, Gay, Lord Oxford, Atterbury, and Congreve, and died in 1718. Less spirited and individual than Lady Winchilsea, his hand less often than hers

> delights to trace unusual things,
> And deviates from the known and common way.

But with more solemnity than her he woos a

> Lovely, lasting peace of mind
> Sweet delight of human-kind,

in which the fresh breezes and healthy activities of the

countryside may blend with the scholar's reading, and Eden
be regained but with the addition of a moral precept,

> Go rule thy will,
> Bid thy wild passions all be still.

It was this conscious intrusion of a negative and repressive
morality which cut these poets off so generally from the
"great source of Nature," in Whose honour they claimed to
sing. Yet in Parnell's *A Night-Piece on Death*, or *A Hymn
to Contentment*, there is an easy sweetness of diction, which, if
it owes something to Milton and never quite transcends the
bounds of a melodious propriety, has a creative buoyancy
and a blush of tender feeling. And the same qualities are
found in the many moral tales which he sang "to make the
Moderns wise." Unlike Lady Winchilsea, whose pen ran
somewhat too fluently in the channel of the fable, Parnell
when, like Æsop, he instructed

> his moral pen to draw
> A scene that obvious in the field he saw,

or to garnish with edification an incident borrowed from
classical or other sources, leavened his moral with more
humour than wit. There was in him something of the laughing
philosopher which inclined him primarily to amuse and only
as an after-thought to instruct. And it is only when the
moralist overpowers the humorist in the grimmer allegorical
parts of *The Hermit*, for example, or in his pietistic verses,
that his "tuneful mind" goes sadly flat or puts Pope's manner,

> Where couplets jingling on their accent run,

to the service of a conventional religiosity.

John Dyer, who was born in 1700, and died in 1758, was also
given to intermixing moral reflection with the description
of nature. But his were lay morals, and the Nature of which
he sung, if devoid of mystery, was uncircumscribed by classical
conventions. In him, too, we find the contrast stressed
between country health and the cities

> where, poets tell,
> The cries of sorrow sadden all the streets,
> And the diseases of intemperate wealth.

Yet Nature was only the background of *The Fleece*, and far
from foreseeing that the town would soon become a scar of
smoke and steam and sweated humanity in the countryside,
drawing away, too, much of its virtue and native strength,
Dyer saw it as but the beneficent crown of the pastoral
industry, which he described in such detail. He hung, in

fact, with innocent admiration over the cradle of modern industrialism,

> So appear
> The increasing walls of busy Manchester,
> Sheffield, and Birmingham, whose reddening fields
> Rise and enlarge their suburbs.   Lo, in throngs,
> For every realm, the careful factors meet,
> Whispering each other.   In long ranks the bales,
> Like war's bright files, beyond the sight extend.
> . . . Pursue,
> Ye sons of Albion, with unyielding heart,
> Your hardy labours: let the sounding loom
> Mix with the melody of every vale.

Thirty years later Cowper was to write very differently of merchants' morals; but so long as men could cherish a belief in the consonnance of "the sounding loom" and "the melody of every vale," so long could they try to blend a rational urban consciousness with that feeling for nature which could not be denied.

Nevertheless in Dyer that feeling has a far more realistic basis than in either Lady Winchilsea or Parnell, while the country which he describes with such loving, if somewhat pedestrian, fidelity is no enclosed rural retreat.   He is at his best when he is treating of sheep-farming in "Siluria's flowery vales" rather than recording variations in the craft or marking "the ways of traffic" in far continents.   Yet there is a satisfying substance in all of *The Fleece*, which earns it a secure place in that line of rural records which extends from Virgil's *Georgics* to Miss Sackville-West's *The Land*.   And in *Grongar Hill* and *The Country Walk* Dyer proved even more clearly that nearer approach to Nature which we have claimed as the underlying impulse of the century.   The characteristic desire for a life harmonised within and without recurs once again,

> O may I with myself agree,
> And never covet what I see:
> Content me with an humble shade,
> My passions tamed, my wishes laid.

But less than Lady Winchilsea, and far less than Parnell, does Dyer detach himself from the "woody valleys" and "the windy summit" which he views.   He is intimately receptive, and not only Nature's aspect, sensitively observed, but her flowing rhythm passes into his being and modulates his verse.

Matthew Green, who was born in London in 1696, of Quaker parents, and died in 1737, possessed a wit to which Dyer could never lay claim.   And it is a more original, if less elegant, wit than Lady Winchilsea's. On this ground alone *The Spleen* is full of excellent, almost epigrammatic entertainment. But in it too we feel a renewal of instinctive life. Green sketches in it a very similar scheme of life to that which John Pomfret outlined in *The Choice* forty years earlier. But how different, how much richer in vital sap is his verse!

> And may my humble dwelling stand
> Upon some chosen spot of land:
> A pond before full to the brim,
> Where cows may cool, and geese may swim;
> Behind, a green like velvet neat,
> Soft to the eye, and to the feet. . . .

Green's aim is still self-regarding, but it does not prevent him from entering into the green, liquescent world about him. His senses have thawed and the genial warmth of the sun-steeped earth has passed through him to his mind and melted its chilly decorum.

In Collins, however, the state of imperfect adjustment to life, which Green could discuss from an external and comparatively superficial standpoint in *The Spleen*, had become an acute disease. Like Smart, Chatterton, Cowper, and Gray, he possessed a sensibility which could not come to terms with an age of "prose and reason," which hungered for a reality beyond the actual. The eventual result of this was that he went melancholy-mad. But an earlier result was that he transcended the limited sanity of his age in a poetry which is pure of contemporary alloy, which is charged with that dateless and indefinable essence that only great poetry distills. This is not to say that he broke with the classical conventions of his age or that he always transcended them. He is, in fact, in point of style the most austerely classical poet represented in this volume. Mr. Mackail's assertion that "when Collins wrote in the style of his own age he transmuted it into something individual" calls, in our opinion, for qualification. And in his most magical poems, *The Ode to Evening*, for example, or *A Song from Shakespeare's "Cymbeline,"* he transmuted a style which he derived from classical models into something which was more than individual, which was impalpable. Yet the enchantment is closely woven into the verbal texture of the poems, sense and sound being reconciled in a form which is at once scrupulously ordered and rhythmically organic.

The exquisite music which Collins, at his best, made of English words reveals a temperament in which tenderness has dissolved the fetters of good sense, but which accepts, to transform, a classical idiom. In his purest poetry the new romantic faith that feeling is all and the old Augustan regard for self-respecting rationality achieved a tremulous harmony, in which the defects of each are transcended.

But, in fact, the underlying interest of the eighteenth century is to be found in this growing tenderness of mind, a tenderness for animals and green places, for the poor and unfortunate, or for an evening sky. This tenderness was not, as has been too often suggested, a discovery of Bowles, whose plaintive self-pity lacked just the masculine quality that is the virtue of this age.

It appears in Augustan poetry at first like wayward patches of faint green in the sober livery of a well-tilled field, and as the century advances the patches extend and their colour deepens. Or, to vary the metaphor, it is like the "smile of spring," coming and going with all spring's enchanting caprice across the winter of Augustan discontent, defying the best endeavours to "revive the just designs of Greece" or mimic the odes of Horace.

The verdict, therefore, of our century upon these poets is likely to differ from that of its predecessors in point of emphasis. Hitherto the emphasis has lain on the arbitrary and exclusive balance which Pope perfected, and on the finely organised but conventionalised diction which reflected it. That balance was for some time the dominating condition of eighteenth-century experience, but it was a balance achieved by excluding too much that is essential to a warm and vivid, a fully realised humanity.

And the majority of the poets of the century were too human to sustain it. Their significance lies in the various and progressive degrees to which they revolted against it. Our emphasis, therefore, is likely to lie increasingly on the forces of instinct and feeling which disturbed, strained to breaking point, and at last destroyed this balance. We shall see the eighteenth century, in short, not as the schoolroom of a prescribed classicism or of an accomplished sobriety, but as the nursery of our modern sensibility; not as an "age of prose and reason," but as one in which human consciousness was drawn from a provincial security towards the hazards of the imaginative life.

HUGH I'A. FAUSSET.

December, 1929.

CONTENTS

	PAGE
INTRODUCTION	vii

LADY WINCHILSEA:

The Introduction	3
The Apology	4
Fragment	5
On Myself	6
Ardelia to Melancholy	6
Invocation to Sleep	7
The Loss	8
The Consolation	9
A Song of Grief: set by Mr. Estwick	9
On Affliction	10
A Letter to Daphnis: April 2nd, 1685 . . .	10
To Mr. F., now Earl of W., who going abroad had desired Ardelia to write some verses upon whatever subject she thought fit, against his return in the evening	11
A Letter to the Same Person	14
An Invitation to Daphnis to leave his study and usual employments—mathematics, painting, etc.—and to take the pleasures of the fields with Ardelia . . .	15
Upon My Lord Winchilsea's Converting the Mount in his Garden to a Terrace	17
A Song. For my Brother Leslie Finch. Upon a punch bowl .	19
The Bargain: a song in dialogue between Bacchus and Cupid .	19
To my Sister Ogle: December 31, 1688 . . .	20
Ardelia's Answer to Ephelia, who had invited her to come to her in Town—reflecting on the coquetteries and detracting humour of the age	21
Glass	27
The Bird and the Arras	27
To the Honourable the Lady Worsley at Longleate, who had most obligingly desired my corresponding with her by letters	28
Lines occasioned by the Marriage of Edward Herbert, Esq. and Mrs. Elizabeth Herbert	31
On the Death of the Honourable Mr. James Thynne, younger son to the Right Honourable the Lord Viscount Weymouth	31
To the Right Honourable the Countess of Hertford with her volume of poems	34
Upon the Death of Sir William Twisden . . .	34
Inquiry after Peace: a Fragment	39
The Petition for an Absolute Retreat. Inscribed to the Right Honourable Catherine Countess of Thanet, mentioned in the poem under the name of Arminda . . .	41
The Change	48
The Circuit of Apollo	49
An Epilogue to the Tragedy of Jane Shore. To be spoken by Mrs. Oldfield the night before the poet's day . . .	51
To Mr. Prior, from a Lady unknown . . .	53
The Answer to Pope's Impromptu. . . .	53

LADY WINCHILSEA—*continued*:   PAGE

To a Fellow Scribbler 54
To a Friend in Praise of the Invention of Writing Letters . 55
Clarinda's Indifference at Parting with her Beauty . . 56
Some pieces out of the First Act of the Aminta of Tasso:
    Daphne's answer to Sylvia declaring she would esteem all
    as enemies who should talk to her of love . . 57
Melinda on an Insipid Beauty: in imitation of a Fragment of
    Sappho's 59
A Song for a Play: Alcander to Melinda 59
A Song: Melinda to Alcander 59
A Song 60
A Song 60
A Song 60
Jealousy: a Song 61
A Song 61
A Song 62
A Song 62
A Song 63
Moral Song 63
Honour: a Song 63
Timely Advice to Dorinda 64
The Phœnix: a Song 65
Hope 65
Life's Progress 65
A Sigh 67
Fragment at Tunbridge Wells 67
The Prodigy 68
The Cautious Lovers 69
Adam Posed 71
Ralph's Reflections upon the Anniversary of his Wedding . 71
The Unequal Fetters 72
Love, Death, and Reputation 73
There's no To-morrow: a Fable imitated from Sir Roger l'Estrange 74
Jupiter and the Farmer 75
For the Better: imitated from Sir Roger l'Estrange . . 76
The Atheist and the Acorn 77
The Shepherd Piping to the Fishes 78
The Owl Describing her Young Ones 79
The Hog, The Sheep, and The Goat Carrying to a Fair . 81
The Shepherd and the Calm 82
The Lord and the Bramble 84
The Young Rat and his Dam, the Cock and the Cat . . 85
A Tale of the Miser and the Poet 87
The Tradesman and the Scholar 89
Man's Injustice Towards Providence 91
The Dog and his Master 93
Fanscomb Barn (in imitation of Milton) 94
A Pastoral Between Menalcus and Damon on the Appearance of
    the Angels to the Shepherds on Our Saviour's Birthday . 97
Jealousy is the Rage of Man 101
The Spleen: a Pindaric Poem 101
A Pindaric Poem upon the Hurricane in November 1703 . 105
To the Echo in a Clear Night upon Astrop Walks . . 113
The Bird 113
The Tree 114
To the Nightingale 115
A Nocturnal Reverie 116
To Death 117

CONTENTS

LADY WINCHILSEA—*continued*:   PAGE

    Prologue to "Aristomenes": to my Lord Winchilsea upon the
        First Reading the Play to him at Eastwell in Kent . . . 118
    A Song designed to have been brought into the part between
        Climander and Herminia 119

THOMAS PARNELL:

    Hesiod; or, The Rise of Woman 123
    Song 129
    A Song 130
    Song 131
    Anacreonetic 132
    Anacreonetic 133
    A Fairy Tale in the Ancient English Style . . . 135
    To Mr. Pope 140
    Health: an Eclogue 143
    The Flies: an Eclogue 145
    An Elegy to an Old Beauty 147
    The Book-Worm 148
    An Allegory on Man 151
    An Imitation of some French Verses 154
    A Night-Piece on Death 155
    A Hymn to Contentment 157
    The Hermet 159
    Piety; or, The Vision 166
    Bacchus; or, The Drunken Metamorphosis . . . 169
    On Bishop Burnet's being Set on Fire in his Closet . . 171
    On Mrs. Arabella Fermor Leaving London . . . 172
    Chloris Appearing in a Looking-Glass 173
    Elysium 173
    The Judgment of Paris 177
    To a Young Lady on her Translation of the Story of Phœbus
        and Daphne from Ovid 179
    The Horse and the Olive 179
    On the Death of Mr. Viner 181
    Epigram 182
    Love in Disguise 183
    On a Lady with Foul Breath 184
    On the Number Three 184
    Essay on the Different Styles of Poetry: To Henry Lord Viscount
        Bolingbroke 185
    A Hymn for Morning 197
    A Hymn for Noon 198
    A Hymn for Evening 199
    The Gift of Poetry 200
    On Happiness in this Life 202
    Ecstasy 203
    On Divine Love: By Meditating on the Wounds of Christ . 206

MATTHEW GREEN:

    The Spleen: An Epistle to Mr. Cuthbert Jackson . . 209
    An Epigram on the Reverend Mr. Lawrence Echard's and
        Bishop Gilbert Burnet's Histories 230
    The Sparrow and Diamond: a Song 230
    The Seeker 232
    On Barclay's Apology for the Quakers . . . 233
    The Grotto: written under the name of Peter Drake, a fisherman
        of Brentford 236

JOHN DYER: PAGE

The Fleece: a Poem in Four Books 245
Grongar Hill 311
The Ruins of Rome: a Poem 315
The Country Walk 329
The Inquiry 332
Epistles:
To a Famous Painter 334
To Aaron Hill, Esq., on his poem called "Gideon" . . 336
To Mr. Savage, Son of the late Earl Rivers . . 337
To a Friend in Town 338

WILLIAM COLLINS:

Preface 343
Sonnet 344
Eclogue the First: Selim; or, The Shepherd's Moral . . 345
Eclogue the Second: Hassan; or, The Camel Driver . . 347
Eclogue the Third: Abra; or, The Georgian Sultana . . 349
Eclogue the Fourth: Agib and Secander; or, The Fugitives . 351
To Sir Thomas Hanmer 354
Ode to Pity 358
Ode to Fear 359
Ode to Simplicity 361
Ode to the Poetical Character 363
Ode (written in the beginning of the year 1746) . . 365
Ode to Mercy (written in 1746) 366
Ode to Liberty 367
Ode to a Lady on the Death of Colonel Ross in the Action of
    Fontenoy (written in May 1745, and addressed to Miss
    Elizabeth Goddard of Harting in Sussex) . . . 371
Ode to Evening 373
Ode to Peace 374
The Manners: an Ode (possibly written about the time that
    Collins left Oxford, 1744) 375
The Passions: an Ode for Music 377
To George Lyttleton, Esq.: Ode on the Death of Mr. Thomson . 380
A Song from Shakespear's Cymbeline, sung by Guiderus and
    Arviragus over Fidele, suppos'd to be dead . . 382
An Ode on the Popular Superstitions of the Highlanders of
    Scotland: Considered as the Subject of Poetry . 383
Written on a Paper which Contained a Piece of Bride Cake,
    given to the Author by a Lady 389
Song: the sentiments borrowed from Shakespeare . . 390

LADY WINCHILSEA

ANNE FINCH, COUNTESS OF WINCHILSEA (*d.* 1720)

The Spleen, published in Gildon's Miscellany, 1701.
Miscellany Poems written by a Lady, 1713.
Criticism: Cibber's *Lives of the Poets*. Monograph by J. Middleton
    Murry.

    The text used in this edition is based partly on the original
edition of 1713, and partly on the MSS. now in the possession of
the Earl of Winchilsea and Mr. Philip Gosse, whose kind permissions
have made this possible. In preparing the present text, while care
has been taken to preserve the original character of the poems,
with their somewhat irregular system of elision adopted from
Dryden, modernisation extends to spelling, use of capitals, and
to minor orthographical points generally, with an eye less to
historical accuracy than to convenience.

THE INTRODUCTION

Did I my lines intend for public view,
How many censures would their faults pursue.
Some would, because such words they do affect,
Cry they're insipid, empty, incorrect:
And many have attained, dull and untaught,
The name of wit only by finding fault.
True judges might condemn their want of wit,
And all might say they're by a woman writ.
Alas! a woman that attempts the pen
Such an intruder on the rights of men,   10
Such a presumptuous creature is esteemed
The fault can by no virtue be redeem'd.
They tell us we mistake our sex and way:
Good breeding, fashion, dancing, dressing, play,
Are the accomplishments we should desire:
To write, or read, or think, or to enquire
Would cloud our beauty and exhaust our time,
And interrupt the conquests of our prime;
Whilst the dull manage of a servile house
Is held by some our outmost art and use.   20

Sure 'twas not ever thus, nor are we told
Fables of women who excelled of old,
To whom, by the diffusive hand of heaven,
Some share of wit and poetry was given.
On that glad day on which the ark returned,
The holy pledge for which the land had mourned,
The joyful tribes attend it on the way,
The Levites do the sacred charge convey,
Whilst various instruments before it play.
Here holy virgins in the concert join   30
The louder notes to soften and refine,
And with alternate verse, complete the hymn divine.
Lo! the young poet, after God's own heart,
By Him inspired and taught the Muses' art,
Returned from conquest, a bright chorus meets
That sings his slain ten thousand in the streets.

3

In such loud numbers they his acts declare,
Proclaim the wonders of his early war,
That Saul upon the vast applause does frown,
And feels its mighty thunder shake the crown.　　　　40
What can the threatened judgment now prolong?
Half of the kingdom is already gone;
The fairest half whose influence guides the rest
Have David's empire o'er their hearts confessed.

　　A woman here, leads fainting Israel on;
She fights, she wins, she triumphs with a song;
Devout, majestic, for the subject fit,
And far above her arms exalts her wit:
Then, to the peaceful, shady palm withdraws,
And rules the rescu'd nation with her laws.　　　　50
How are we fal'n, fal'n by mistaken rules?
And education's more than nature's fools.
Debarred from all improvements of the mind,
And to be dull, expected and designed.
And if some one would soar above the rest,
With warmer fancy and ambition press't,
So strong the opposing faction still appears.
The hopes to thrive can ne'er outweigh the fears,
Be cautioned then, my Muse, and still retired;
Nor be despised, aiming to be admired.　　　　60
Conscious of wants, still with contracted wing,
To some few friends and to thy sorrows sing:
To groves of laurel thou wert never meant,
Be dark enough thy shades, and be thou there content,

THE APOLOGY

'Tis true I write, and tell me by what rule
I am alone forbid to play the fool,
To follow through the groves a wand'ring Muse,
And fain'd ideas for my pleasures choose?
Why should it in my pen be held a fault,
Whilst Mira paints her face, to paint a thought?
Whilst Lamia to the manly bumper flies,
And borrowed spirits sparkle in her eyes,

Why should it be in me a thing so vain
To heat with poetry my colder brain? 10
But I write ill, and therefore should forbear.
Does Flavia cease, now at her fortieth year,
In ev'ry place to let that face be seen
Which all the town rejected at fifteen?
Each woman has her weakness: mine indeed
Is still to write, tho' hopeless to succeed.
Nor to the men is this so easy found,
Even in most works with which the wits abound,
So weak are all since our first breach with heav'n,
There's less to be applauded than forgiven. 20

FRAGMENT

So here confin'd, and but to female clay,
Ardelia's soul mistook the rightful way:
Whilst the soft breeze of pleasure's tempting air
Made her believe felicity was there;
And basking in the warmth of early time,
To vain amusements dedicate her prime.
Ambition next allured her tow'ring eye,
For paradise, she heard, was placed on high;
Then thought the court, with all its glorious show,
Was sure above the rest, and paradise below. 10
There placed, too soon the flaming sword appear'd,
Remov'd those powers whom justly she revered,
Adher'd too in their wreck and in their ruin shared.
Now by the wheel's inevitable round,
With them thrown prostrate on the humble ground,
No more she takes (instructed by that fall)
For fix'd or worth her thought this rolling ball:
Towards a more certain station she aspires,
Unshaken by revolts, and owns no less desires.
But all in vain are prayers, ecstatic thoughts, 20
Recover'd moments and retracted faults,
Retirement, which the world moroseness calls,
Abandon'd pleasures in monastic walls.
These, but at distance, towards that purpose tend:
The lowly means to an exalted end,

Which He must perfect who allots her stay,
And that accomplish'd, will direct the way,
Pity her restless cares and weary strife,
And point some issue to escaping life,
Which so dismissed, no pen or human speech   30
Th' ineffable recess can ever teach.
Th' expanse, the light, the harmony, the throng,
The bride's attendance, and the bridal song,
The numerous mansions, and th' immortal tree,
No eye, unpurg'd by death, must ever see,
Or waves which through that wondrous city roll.
Rest then content, my too impatient soul:
Observe but here the easy precepts given,
Then wait with cheerful hope till heaven be known in heaven.

ON MYSELF

Good heav'n, I thank thee, since it was designed
I should be framed but of the weaker kind,
That yet my soul is rescu'd from the love
Of all those trifles which their passions move.
Pleasures, and praise, and plenty have with me
But their just value.   If allowed they be,
Freely and thankfully as much I taste
As will not reason or religion waste
If they're denied, I on myself can live,
And slight those aids unequal chance does give: 10
When in the sun, my wings can be displayed,
And in retirement, I can bless the shade.

ARDELIA TO MELANCHOLY

At last, my old inveterate foe,
No opposition shalt thou know.
Since I by struggling, can obtain
Nothing but increase of pain,
I will at last no more do so.
Tho' I confess I have applied
Sweet mirth and music, and have tried
A thousand other arts beside
To charm thee from my darken'd breast,
Thou who hast banish'd all my rest.   10

But, though sometimes a short reprieve they gave,
Unable they, and far too weak, to save:
All arts to quell did but augment thy force,
As rivers check'd break with a wilder course.

Friendship I to my heart have laid,
Friendship, th' applauded sov'reign aid,
And thought that charm so strong would prove
As to compel thee to remove.
And, to myself, I boasting said,
Now I a conqu'ror sure shall be,   20
The end of all my troubles see,
And noble triumph wait on me:
My dusky, sullen foe will sure
Ne'er this united charge endure.
But leaning on this reed, ev'n whilst I spoke,
It pierc'd my hand, and into pieces broke.
Still, some new object or new interest came
And loos'd the bonds and quite dissolv'd the claim.

These failing, I invok'd a Muse,
And poetry would often use   30
To guard me from thy tyrant pow'r;
And, to oppose thee every hour,
New troops of fancies did I choose.
Alas! in vain, for all agree
To yield me captive up to thee,
And heaven alone can set me free.
Thou, through my life, wilt with me go,
And make the passage sad and slow.
All, that could thy ill-got rule invade,
Their useless arms before thy feet have laid: 40
The fort is thine, now ruined all within,
Whilst by decays without thy conquest too is seen.

INVOCATION TO SLEEP

How shall I woo thee, gentle rest,
To a sad mind with cares oppress'd?
By what soft means shall I invite
Thy powers into my soul to-night?

Yet, gentle sleep, if thou wilt come,
Such darkness shall prepare the room
As thy own palace overspreads,
(Thy palace stor'd with peaceful beds)
And silence too shall on thee wait,
Deep, as in the Turkish state: 10
Whilst still as death, I will be found,
My arms by one another bound.
And my dull lids so closed shall be
As if already sealed by thee.
Thus I'll dispose the outward part,
Would I could quiet too my heart!
But, in its overburthened stead,
Behold, I offer thee my head:
My head I better can command,
And that I bow beneath thy hand.   20
Nor do I think that heretofore
Our first great father gave thee more,
When on a flow'ry bank he lay
And did thy strictest laws obey.
For to compose his lovely bride
He yielded not alone his side;
But, if we judge by the event,
Half of his heart too with it went;
Which, waken'd, drew him soon away
To Eve's fair bosom, where it lay,   30
Pleased to admit his rightful claim,
And tending, still, tow'rds whence it came.
Then, gentle sleep, expect from me
No more than I have proffer'd thee:
For if thou wilt not hear my prayers
Till I have vanquish'd all my cares,
Thou'lt stay till kinder death supplies thy place,
The surer friend, tho' with the harsher face.

THE LOSS

She sigh'd: but soon it mix'd with common air,
Too fleet a witness for her deep despair.
She wept: but tears no lasting grief can show,
For tears will fail and ebb, as well as flow.
She would her tongue to the sad subject force:

But all great passions are above discourse.
Thy heart alone, Ardelia, with it trust.
There grave it deep, alas! 'twill fall to dust.
Urania is no more, to me no more:
All these combin'd can ne'er that loss deplore.   10

THE CONSOLATION

SEE Phœbus breaking from the willing skies,
See how the soaring lark does with him rise,
And through the air is such a journey borne
As if she never thought of a return.
Now to his noon behold him proudly go,
And look with scorn on all that 's great below:
A monarch he, and ruler of the day,
A fav'rite she that in his beams does play.
Glorious and high! but shall they ever be
Glorious and high and fixt where now we see?   10
No: both must fall, nor can their stations keep,
She to the earth, and he below the deep.
At night both fall, but the swift hand of time
Renews the morning, and again they climb.
Then let no cloudy change create my sorrow:
I'll think 'tis night, and I may rise to-morrow.

A SONG OF GRIEF

SET BY MR. ESTWICK

OH grief! why hast thou so much pow'r?
    Why do the ruling fates decree
No state should e'er without thee be?
    Why dost thou joys and hopes devour,
And clothe ev'n love himself in thy dark livery?

Thou, and cold fear, thy close ally,
    Do not alone on life attend,
But following mortals to their end,
    Do wrack the wretches whilst they die,
And to eternal shades too often with them fly.   10

To thee, great monarch, I submit,
    Thy sables and thy cypress bring,
I own thy power, I own thee king,
    Thy title in my heart is writ,
And till that breaks, I ne'er shall freedom get.

Forc'd smiles thy rigour will allow,
    And whilst thy seat is in the soul,
And there all mirth thou dost control,
    Thou canst admit to outward show
The smooth appearance and dissembled brow.   2c

ON AFFLICTION

Welcome, what e'er my tender flesh may say,
    Welcome affliction to my reason still;
Though hard and rugged on that rock I lay,
    A sure foundation, which if rais'd with skill,
    Shall compass Babel's aim and reach th' Almighty's hill.

Welcome the rod, that does adoption show,
    The cup, whose wholesome dregs are giv'n me here:
There is a day behind, if God be true,
    When all these clouds shall pass and heav'n be clear,
    When those whom most they shade shall shine most gloriou
      here.   1c

Affliction is the line which every saint
    Is measured by, his stature taken right:
So much it shrinks as they repine or faint,
    But if their faith and courage stand upright,
    By that is made the crown and the full robe of light.

A LETTER TO DAPHNIS: APRIL 2ND, 1685

This to the crown and blessing of my life,
The much lov'd husband of a happy wife.
To him whose constant passion found the art
To win a stubborn and ungrateful heart:
And to the world by tenderest proof discovers
They err who say that husbands can't be lovers.

With such return of passion as is due,
Daphnis I love, Daphnis my thoughts pursue,
Daphnis, my hopes, my joys are bounded all in you.
Even I, for Daphnis, and my promise sake,   10
What I in woman censure, undertake.
But this from love, not vanity proceeds:
You know who writes, and I who 'tis that reads.
Many love well, though they express it ill,
And I your censure could with pleasure bear,
Would you but soon return and speak it here.

TO MR. F., NOW EARL OF W.

WHO GOING ABROAD, HAD DESIRED ARDELIA TO WRITE SOME
VERSES UPON WHATEVER SUBJECT SHE THOUGHT FIT,
AGAINST HIS RETURN IN THE EVENING

WRITTEN IN THE YEAR 1689

No sooner, Flavio, were you gone,
But your injunction thought upon,
    Ardelia took the pen;
Designing to perform the task
Her Flavio did so kindly ask,
    Ere he returned agen.

Unto Parnassus straight she sent,
And bid the messenger, that went
    Unto the Muses' court,
Assure them she their aid did need,   10
And begg'd they'd use their utmost speed,
    Because the time was short.

The hasty summons was allow'd:
And being well-bred they rose and bow'd,
    And said they'd post away:
That well they did Ardelia know,
And that no female's voice below
    They sooner would obey.

That many of that rhyming train
On like occasions sought in vain   20

Their industry t' excite:
But for Ardelia all they'd leave.
Thus flatt'ring can the Muse deceive
    And wheedle us to write.

Yet since there was such haste requir'd,
To know the subject 'twas desired
    On which they must infuse,
That they might temper words and rules,
And with their counsel carry tools
    As country doctors use.   30

Wherefore to cut off all delays,
'Twas soon replied, a husband's praise
    (Tho' in these looser times)
Ardelia gladly would rehearse
A husband's who indulged her verse,
    And now requir'd her rhymes.

A husband! echo'd all around:
And to Parnassus sure that sound
    Had never yet been sent.
Amazement in each face was read,   40
In haste th' affrighted sisters fled,
    And into council went.

Erato cried, since Grizel's days,
Since Troy-town pleas'd, and Chevy Chase,
    No such design was known;
And 'twas their business to take care
It reach'd not to the public ear,
    Or got about the town,

Nor came where evening beaux were met,
O'er billet-doux and chocolate,   50
    Lest it destroyed the house:
For in that place who could dispense
(That wore his clothes with common sense)
    With mention of a spouse?

'Twas put unto the vote at last,
And in the negative it past,

None to her aid should move;
Yet since Ardelia was a friend,
Excuses 'twas agreed to send
   Which plausible might prove: 60

That Pegasus of late had been
So often rid thro' thick and thin
   With neither fear nor wit,
In panegyric been so spurr'd,
He could not from the stall be stirr'd,
   Nor would endure a bit.

Melpomene had given a bond
By the new house alone to stand
   And write alone of war and strife;
Thalia, she had taken fees   70
And stipends from the patentees,
   And durst not for her life.

Urania only liked the choice;
Yet not to thwart the public voice,
   She whispering did impart:
They need no foreign aid invoke,
No help to draw a moving stroke,
   Who dictate from the heart.

Enough! the pleas'd Ardelia cried:
And slighting ev'ry Muse beside,   80
   Consulting now her breast.
Perceived that ev'ry tender thought
Which from abroad she vainly sought
   Did there in silence rest:

And should unmov'd that post maintain,
Till in his quick return again,
   Met in some neighb'ring grove,
(Where vice nor vanity appear)
Her Flavio them alone might hear
   In all the sounds of love.   90

For since the world does so despise
Hymen's endearments and its ties,

They should mysterious be:
Till we that pleasure too possess
(Which makes their fancied happiness)
    Of stolen secrecy.

A LETTER TO THE SAME PERSON

Sure of success, to you I boldly write,
Whilst love does ev'ry tender line endite;
Love, who is justly president of verse,
Which all his servants write, or else rehearse.
Phœbus (howe'er mistaken poets dream)
Ne'er used a verse till love became his theme.
To his stray'd son, still as his passion rose,
He rais'd his hasty voice in clam'rous prose:
But when in Daphne he would love inspire,
He woo'd in verse, set to his silver lyre.   10

The Trojan prince did pow'rful numbers join
To sing of war: but love was the design:
And sleeping Troy in flames again was drest
To light the fires in pitying Dido's breast.

Love without poetry's refining aid
Is a dull bargain, and but coarsely made;
Nor e'er could poetry successful prove,
Or touch the soul, but when the sense was love.

Oh! could they both in absence now impart
Skill to my hand, but to describe my heart: 20
Then should you see, impatient of your stay,
Soft hopes contend with fears of sad delay;
Love in a thousand fond endearments there,
And lively images of you appear.
But since the thoughts of a poetic mind
Will never be to syllables confined;
And whilst to fix what is conceived we try,
The purer parts evaporate and die:
You must perform what they want force to do,
And think what your Ardelia thinks of you.   30

21 October, 1690.

AN INVITATION TO DAPHNIS

TO LEAVE HIS STUDY AND USUAL EMPLOYMENTS—MATHEMATICS,
PAINTINGS, ETC.—AND TO TAKE THE PLEASURES OF THE
FIELDS WITH ARDELIA

When such a day blessed the Arcadian plain,
Warm without sun, and shady without rain,
Fanned by an air that scarcely bent the flowers,
Or wav'd the woodbines on the summer bowers,
The nymphs disordered beauty could not fear,
Nor ruffling winds uncurl the shepherd's hair,
On the fresh grass they trod their measures light,
And a long evening made from noon to night.
Come then, my Daphnis, from those cares descend
Which better may the winter season spend.   10
    Come, and the pleasures of the fields survey,
    And thro' the groves with your Ardelia stray.

Reading the softest poetry, refuse,
To view the subjects of each rural Muse;
Nor let the busy compasses go round
When faery circles better mark the ground.
Rich colours on the vellum cease to lay
When ev'ry lawn much nobler can display,
When on the dazzling poppy may be seen
A glowing red exceeding your carmine;   20
And for the blue that o'er the sea is born,
A brighter rises in our standing corn.
    Come then, my Daphnis, and the fields survey,
    And thro' the groves with your Ardelia stray.

Come, and let Sanson's World no more engage,
Altho' he gives a kingdom in a page;
O'er all the universe his lines may go,
And not a clime like temp'rate Britain show.
    Come then, my Daphnis, and her fields survey,
    And thro' the groves with your Ardelia stray.   30

Nor plead that you're immured and cannot yield,
That mighty bastions keep you from the field;
Think not tho' lodg'd in Mons, or in Namur,
You're from my dangerous attacks secure.

No! Louis shall his falling conquests fear
When by succeeding couriers he shall hear
Apollo and the Muses are drawn down
To storm each fort and take in ev'ry town.
Vauban, the Orphean lyre to mind shall call
That drew the stones to the old Theban wall,   40
And make no doubt, if it against him play,
They, from his works, will fly as fast away,
Which to prevent, he shall to peace persuade,
Of strong, confederate syllables afraid.
  Come then, my Daphnis, and the fields survey,
  And thro' the groves with your Ardelia stray.

Come, and attend how as we walk along
Each cheerful bird shall treat us with a song,
Not such as fops compose, where wit, nor art,
Nor plainer nature ever bear a part.   50
The crystal springs shall murmur as we pass,
But not like courtiers sinking to disgrace;
Nor shall the louder rivers in their fall
Like unpaid sailors, or hoarse pleaders brawl;
But all shall form a concert to delight,
And all to peace, and all to love invite.
  Come then, my Daphnis, and the fields survey,
  And thro' the groves with your Ardelia stray.

As Baucis and Philemon spent their lives,
Of husbands he the happiest, she of wives,   60
When thro' the painted meads their way they sought,
Harmless in act, and unperplext in thought,
Let us, my Daphnis, rural joys pursue,
And courts, or camps, not ev'n in fancy view.
  So let us thro' the groves, my Daphnis, stray,
  And so the pleasures of the fields survey.

UPON MY LORD WINCHILSEA'S CONVERTING THE MOUNT IN HIS GARDEN TO A TERRACE

AND OTHER ALTERATIONS AND IMPROVEMENTS IN HIS HOUSE, PARK, AND GARDENS

IF we those gen'rous sons deserv'dly praise
Who o'er their predecessors marble raise,
And by inscriptions, on their deeds and name,
To late posterity convey their fame,
What with more admiration shall we write
Of him who takes their errors from our sight?
And lest their judgments be in question brought,
Removes a mountain to remove a fault?
Which long had stood (though threaten'd oft in vain),
Concealing all the beauties of the plain.   10
Heedless when young, cautious in their decline,
None gone before pursued the vast design,
Till ripen'd judgment, join'd with youthful flame,
At last but came, and saw, and overcame.
And as old Rome refin'd what ere was rude,
And civilis'd as fast as she subdued,
So lies this hill, hewn from its rugged height,
Now levell'd to a scene of smooth delight,
Where on a terrace of its spoils we walk,
And of the task and the performer talk: 20
From whose unwearied genius men expect
All that can further polish and protect;
To see a shelt'ring grove the prospect bound,
Just rising from the same prolific ground,
Where late it stood, the glory of the seat,
Repell'd the winter blasts, and screen'd the summer's heat,
So prais'd, so lov'd that when untimely fate
Sadly prescrib'd it a too early date,
The heavy tidings cause a gen'ral grief,
And all combine to bring a swift relief.   30
Some plead, some pray, some counsel, some dispute,
Alas in vain where power is absolute.
Those whom paternal awe forbid to speak,
Their sorrows in their secret whispers break,
Sigh as they pass beneath the sentenc'd trees,
Which seem to answer in a mournful breeze.
The very clowns (hir'd by his daily pay)

Refuse to strike, nor will their lord obey,
Till to his speech he adds a leading stroke,
And by example does their rage provoke.   40
Then in a moment, ev'ry arm is rear'd,
And the robb'd palace sees what most she fear'd,
Her lofty grove, her ornamental shield,
Turn'd to a desert and forsaken field.
So fell Persepolis, bewail'd of all
But him whose rash resolve procur'd her fall.
No longer now we such destructions fear,
No longer the resounding axe we hear,
But in exchange behold the fabric stand,
Built and adorn'd by a supporting hand;   50
Complete in all its late unequal frame,
No loam and lath does now the building shame,
But graceful symmetry without is seen,
And use with beauty are improv'd within.
And though our ancestors did gravely plot,
As if one element they valued not,
Nor yet the pleasure of the noblest sense,
'Gainst light and air to raise a strong defence,
Their wiser offspring does those gifts renew,
And now we breathe and now the eager view   60
Through the enlarged windows takes her way,
Does beauteous fields and scatter'd woods survey,
Flies o'er th' extended land, and sinks but in the sea.
Or when contented with an easier flight,
The new wrought gardens give a new delight,
Where ev'ry fault that in the old was found
Is mended in the well disposed ground.
Such are th' effects when wine, nor loose delights
Devour the day, nor waste the thoughtless nights,
But gen'rous arts the studious hours engage   70
To bless the present and succeeding age.
Oh! may Eastwell still with their aid increase,
Plenty surround her, and within be peace.
Still may her temp'rate air his health maintain
From whom she does such strength and beauty gain.
Flourish her trees, and may the verdant grass
Again prevail where late the plough did pass:
Still may she boast a kind and fruitful soil,
And still new pleasures give to crown his toil.
And may some one, with admiration fill'd,   80

In just applauses, and in numbers skill'd,
Not with more zeal, but more poetic heat,
Throughly adorn what barely we relate,
Then should the theme to ev'ry verse afford,
Until the Muse, when to advantage soar'd,
Should take a nobler aim and dare describe her lord.

A SONG

FOR MY BROTHER LESLIE FINCH.   UPON A PUNCH BOWL

FROM the park and the play,
And Whitehall come away,
To the punch-bowl, by far more inviting.
To the fops and the beaux,
Leave those dull empty shows,
And see here what is truly delighting.

The half globe 'tis in figure,
(And would it were bigger)
Yet here's the whole universe floating;
Here's titles and places,   10
Rich lands and fair faces,
And all that is worthy our doting.

'Twas a world like to this
The hot Grecian did miss,
Of whom histories keep such a pother,
To the bottom he sunk,
And when one he had drunk,
Grew maudlin and wept for another.

THE BARGAIN

[A Song in dialogue between Bacchus and Cupid.]

CUPID

BACCHUS, to thee that turn'st the brain,
And dost o'er mighty punch bowls reign,
Enthron'd upon thy lusty barrel,
I drink to drown the ancient quarrel:
And mortals shall no more dispute
Which of us two is absolute.

BACCHUS

I pledge thee, Archer, nor disdain
Thou over hearts dost reign,
But tears thou drink'st drawn from low courage,
And cooled with sighs instead of borage: 10
Were that error once amended,
All might in champagne be ended.

CUPID

I am content, so we may join,
To mix my waters with thy wine.
Then henceforth farewell all defying,
And thus we'll still be found complying:
He that's in love shall fly to thee,
And he that's drunk shall reel to me.

TO MY SISTER OGLE, DECEMBER 31, 1688

WHEN, dear Teresa, shall I be
By heav'n again restor'd to you?
Thus, if once more your face I see,
Thus our lost pleasures we'll renew.

Our yesterday, when kindly past,
Shall teach how this should be enjoy'd,
And urge to-morrow's eager haste
As longing to be thus employ'd.

Time shall pay back the years and hours
That in our absence posted by;   10
Time shall submit to friendship's pow'rs,
And as we please, shall rest, or fly.

The sun, that stood to look on war,
And lengthen'd out that fatal day,
For kindness, more engaging far,
Will longer sure his fall delay.

At last, when fate the word shall give
That we no longer here below
This soft, endearing life shall live,
In triumph we'll together go,   20

New arts to find, new joys to try,
The height of friendship to improve:
'Tis worth our pains and fears to die,
To learn new mysteries of love.

ARDELIA'S ANSWER TO EPHELIA

WHO HAD INVITED HER TO COME TO HER IN TOWN—REFLECTING
ON THE COQUETTERIE AND DETRACTING HUMOUR OF THE AGE

I

ME, dear Ephelia, me in vain you court
With all your pow'rful influence, to resort
To that great town, where friendship can but have
The few spare hours which meaner pleasures leave.
No! Let some shade, or your large palace be
Our place of meeting, love and liberty,
To thoughts and words, and all endearments free.
But to those walls excuse my slow repair,
Who have no business, no diversion there;
No dazzling beauty to attract the gaze   10
Of wond'ring crowds to my applauded face;
Nor to my little wit the ill-nature join'd
To pass a general censure on mankind;
To call the young, and unaffected, fools;
Dull all the grave, that live by moral rules;
To say the soldier brags who, ask'd, declares
The nice escapes and dangers of his wars,
The poet's vain that knows his unmatch'd worth,
And dares maintain what the best Muse brings forth.
Yet this the humour of the age is grown,   20
And only conversation of the town:
In satire vers'd and sharp detraction be,
And you're accomplish'd for all company.

II

When my last visit I to London made,
Me to Almeria wretched chance betrayed:
The fair Almeria, in this art so known
That she discerns all feelings but her own.
With a loud welcome and a strict embrace,
Kisses on kisses in a public place,

Sh' extorts a promise that next day I dine   30
With her who for my sight did hourly pine,
And wonders how so far I can remove
From the beau monde, and the dull country love;
Yet vows, if but an afternoon 'twould cost,
To see me there, she could resolve almost
To quit the town, and for that time, be lost.

My word I keep, we dine, then rising late,
Take coach, which long had waited at the gate.
About the streets a tedious ramble go,
To see this monster, or that waxwork show,   40
Or anything that may the time bestow.
When by a church we pass, I ask to stay,
Go in and my devotions humbly pay
To that great Pow'r whom all the wise obey:
Whilst the gay thing, light as her feather'd dress,
Flies round the coach and does each cushion press,
Through ev'ry glass her sev'ral graces shows,
This does her face, and that, her shape expose
To envying beauties and admiring beaux.
One stops, and, as expected, all extols,   50
Clings to the door and on his elbow lolls,
Thrusts in his head, at once to view the fair
And keep his curls from discomposing air,
Then thus proceeds—
                    My wonder it is grown
To find Almeria here, and here alone,
Where are the nymphs that round you us'd to crowd,
Learning from you how to erect their hair,
And in perfection all their habit wear,
To place a patch in some peculiar way   60
That may an unmark'd smile to sight betray,
And the vast genius of the sex display?

Pity me then (she cries) and learn the fate
That makes me porter to a temple gate:
Ardelia came to town some weeks ago
Who does on books her rural hours bestow,
And is so rustic in her clothes and mien,
'Tis with her ungenteel to be seen,
Did not a long acquaintance plead excuse.
Besides, she likes no wit that's now in use,   70

Despises courtly vice, and plainly says
That sense and nature should be found in plays,
And therefore none will e'er be brought to see
But those of Dryden, Etherege, or Lee,
And some few authors old and dull to me.
To her I did engage my coach and day,
And here must wait while she within does pray.
Ere twelve was struck she calls me from my bed,
Nor once observes how well my toilette's spread;
Then, drinks the fragrant tea contented up   80
Without a compliment upon the cup,
Tho' to the ships, for the first choice I steer'd,
Through such a storm as the stout bargemen fear'd,
Lest that a praise, which I have long engross'd,
Of the best china equipage be lost.
Of fashions now, and colours I discours'd,
Detected shops that would expose the worst,
What silks, what lace, what rubans she must have,
And by my own, an ample pattern gave:
To which she, cold and unconcern'd, replied,   90
I deal with one that does all these provide,
Having of others cares enough beside,
And in a cheap, or an ill-chosen gown
Can value blood that's nobler than my own,
And therefore hope myself not to be weighed
By gold, or silver, on my garments laid,
Or that my wit or judgment should be read
In an uncommon colour on my head.

Stupid and dull! the shrugging zany cries.
When, service ended, me he moving spies,   100
Hastes to conduct me out, and in my ear
Drops some vile praise, too low for her to hear,
Which to avoid, more than the begging throng,
I reach the coach that swiftly rolls along
Lest to Hyde Park we should too late be brought,
And lose, ere night, an hour of finding fault.
Arriv'd, she cries—
                    That awkward creature see,
A fortune born, and would a beauty be
Could others but believe as fast as she.   110
Round me I look, some monster to descry,
Whose wealthy acres must a title buy,

Support my lord, and be, since his have fail'd,
With the high shoulder on his race entail'd,
When to my sight a lovely face appears,
Perfect in ev'rything, but growing years.
This I defend, to do my judgment right,
Can you dispraise a skin so smooth, so white,
That blush which o'er such well turn'd cheeks does rise,
That look of youth, and those enliven'd eyes?   120
Soon she replies—

           That skin, which you admire,
Is shrunk, and sickly, could you view it nigher.
The crimson lining and uncertain light
Reflects that blush and paints her to the sight.
Trust me, that look which you commend, betrays
A want of sense, more than the want of days,
And those wild eyes that round the circle stray,
Seem, as her wits, had but mistook the way—
As I did mine, I to myself repeat,   130
When by this envious side I took my seat.
Oh! for my groves, my country walks, and bow'rs,
Trees blast not trees, nor flow'rs envenom flow'rs,
As beauty here all beauty's praise devours.
But noble Piso passes—

           He's a wit,
As some (she says) would have it, tho' as yet
No line he in a lady's fan has writ,
Ne'er on their dress, in verse, soft things would say,
Or with loud clamour over-power'd a play,   140
And right or wrong, prevented the third day;
To read in public places is not known,
Or in his chariot, here appears alone;
Bestows no hasty praise on all that's new.
When first this coach came out to public view,
Met in a visit, he presents his hand
And takes me out, I make a wilful stand,
Expecting, sure, this would applause invite,
And often turn'd that way, to guide his sight,
Till finding him wrapp'd in a silent thought,   150
I ask'd if that the painter well had wrought,
Who then replied, he has in the fable erred,
Cov'ring Adonis with a monstrous beard;
Made Hercules (who by his club is shown)
A gentler fop than any of the town,

Whilst Venus from a bog is rising seen,
And eyes a-squint are given to beauty's queen.—
I had no patience longer to attend,
And know 'tis want of wit to discommend.

Must Piso, then, be judg'd by such as these,   160
Piso who from the Latin Virgil frees,
Who loos'd the bands, which old Silenus bound,
And made our Albion's rocks repeat the mystic sound,
"Whilst all he sung was present to our eyes,
And as he rais'd his verse, the poplars seem'd to rise"?
Scarce could I in my breast my thoughts contain,
Or for this folly hide my just disdain.
When see, she says, observe my best of friends,
And through the window half her length extends,
Exalts her voice that all the ring may hear   170
How fullsomely she oft repeats my dear,
Lets fall some doubtful words that we may know
There still a secret is, betwixt them two,
And makes a sign, the small white hand to show.
When, fate be prais'd, the coachman slacks the reins,
And o'er my lap no longer now she leans,
But how her choice I like does soon inquire.

Can I dislike, I cry, what all admire?
Discreet, and witty, civil and refin'd,
Nor in her person fairer than her mind   180
Is young Alinda, if report be just—
For half the character my eyes I trust.
What! changed Almeria, on a sudden cold,
As if I of your friend some tale had told?
No, she replies, but when I hear her praise
A secret failing does my pity raise:
Damon she loves, and 'tis my daily care
To keep the passion from the public ear.
I ask amazed, if this she has revealed?
No, but 'tis true, she cries, though much concealed.   190
I have observ'd it long, nor would betray
But to yourself, what now with grief I say,
Who this, to none but confidents must break,
Nor they to others but in whispers speak:
I am her friend and must consult her fame.
More was she saying when fresh objects came.

Now what's that thing? she cries, Ardelia guess!
A woman sure—
                    Ay and a poetess.
They say she writes, and 'tis a common jest,   200
Then sure she has publicly the skill professt,
I soon reply, or makes that gift her pride,
And all the world but scribblers does deride;
Sets out lampoons where only spite is seen,
Not fill'd with female wit, but female spleen;
Her flourish'd name does o'er a song expose,
Which through all ranks down to the carmen goes.
Or poetry is on her picture found,
In which she sits with painted laurel crown'd.
If no such flies, no vanity defile   210
The Heliconian balm, the sacred oil,
Why should we from that pleasing art be tied,
Or like state prisoners, pen and ink denied?
But see, the sun his chariot home has driven
From the vast shining ring of spacious heav'n,
Nor after him celestial beauties stay,
But crowd with sparkling wheels the milky way.
Shall we not then, the great example take,
And ours below, with equal speed forsake?
When to your favours adding this one more,   220
You'll stop and leave me thankful at my door.
How! ere you've in the drawing room appeared,
And all the follies there beheld and heard?
Since you've been absent such intrigues have grown,
Such new coquettes and fops are to be shown:
Without their sight you must not leave the town.
Excuse me, I replied, my eyes ne'er feast
Upon a fool, tho' ne'er so nicely dresst.
Nor is it music to my burthen'd ear
The unripe pratings of our sex to hear: 230
A noisy girl who's at fifteen talked more
Than grandmother, or mother here before,
In all the cautious, prudent years they bore.
Statesmen there are (she cried) whom I can show,
That bear the kingdom's cares on a bent brow;
Who take the weight of politics by grains,
And to the least, know what each skull contains,
Whose to be coach'd, whom talked to when abroad,
Who but the smile must have, and who the nod:

And when this is the utmost of their skill,   240
'Tis not much wonder if affairs go ill.
Then for the churchmen—
                              Hold! my lodging's here.
Nor can I longer a reproof forbear
When sacred things nor persons she would spare.

    We parted thus, the night in peace I spent,
And the next day, with haste and pleasure went
To the best seat of fam'd and fertile Kent.
Where let me live from all distraction free,
Till thus the world is criticised by me: 250
Till friend and foe I treat with such despite,
May I no scorn, the worst of ills, excite.

GLASS

O MAN! what inspiration was thy guide,
Who taught thee light and air thus to divide:
To let in all the useful beams of day,
Yet force as subtle winds without thy sash to stay;
T' extract from embers by a strange device,
Then polish fair these flakes of solid ice,
Which, silver'd o'er, redouble all in place,
And give thee back thy well or ill-complexion'd face;
To vessels blown, exceed the gloomy bowl
Which did the wine's full excellence control;   10
These show the body, whilst you taste the soul,
Its colour, sparkles, motion lets thee see,
Tho' yet th' excess the preacher warns to flee,
Lest men at length as clearly spy through thee.

THE BIRD AND THE ARRAS

By near resemblance see that bird betray'd
Who takes the well-wrought arras for a shade;
There hopes to perch and with a cheerful tune
O'er-pass the scorchings of the sultry noon.
But soon repulsed by the obdurate scene,
How swift she turns, but turns, alas, in vain!
That piece a grove, this shows an ambient sky
Where imitated fowl their pinions ply,

Seeming to mount in flight and aiming still more high.
All she outstrips, and with a moment's pride   1
Their under-station silent does deride,
Till the dash'd ceiling strikes her to the ground,
Nor intercepting shrub to break the fall is found.
Recovering breath, the window next she gains,
Nor fears a stop from the transparent panes.

    .   .   .   .   .

But we digress, and leave th' imprisoned wretch,
Now sinking low, now on a loftier stretch,
Flutt'ring in endless circles of dismay,
Till some kind hand directs the certain way,
Which through the casement an escape affords,   2
And leads to ample space, the only heav'n of birds.

TO THE HONOURABLE THE LADY WORSLEY
AT LONGLEATE

WHO HAD MOST OBLIGINGLY DESIRED MY CORRESPONDING
WITH HER BY LETTERS

If from some lonely and obscure recess,
The shunn'd retreat of solitary peace,
Lost to the world, and like Ardelia's seat
Fit only for the wretch oppress'd by fate,
A melancholy summons had been sent
To deal in woe and mingle discontent,
By sympathising lines t' attempt relief,
And load each post with sad exchange of grief,
No wonder had that common act express'd,
For still distress would herd with the distress'd,   1
And to our cares it seemed a short allay
To fold them close and from ourselves convey.

    But that Utresia seeks to correspond
With such a dull and disproportion'd hand,
Empty replies endeavours to obtain
From secret cells and from a clouded brain,
Is something so unusual (tho' so kind)
That scarce th' exalted motions of her mind,

Or charms in her's beyond each other tongue
(Had we not heard him speak from whom she sprung), 20
Could more amaze us than this friendly part
That she whom all aspire but to divert
Makes it of all her choice to soothe a sinking heart.
Utresia in her fresh and smiling bloom,
With joys encompass'd and new joys to come,
Who like the sun in meridian shows,
Surrounded with the lustre she bestows,
Herself dispensing, by her longed-for sight,
To every place she visits full delight:
For beauty this prerogative maintains, 30
And over both the sexes thus far reigns,
To cheer all hearts and to suspend our pains,
Who, when such eyes, so soft and bright, we view,
Soften our cares and grow enlighten'd too:
In sweet conformity to things so fine,
No motions feel but such as in them shine.
Could but the wit that on her paper flows
Affect my verse and tune it to her prose,
Through ev'ry line a kindly warmth inspire,
And raise my art equal to my desire, 40
Then should my hand snatch from the Muses' store
Transporting figures ne'er exposed before,
Something to please, so moving and so new
As not our Denham or our Cowley knew.
Or show (the harder labour to complete)
The real splendours of our fam'd Longleate,
Which above metaphor its structures rears,
Tho' all enchantment to our sight appears:
Magnificently great the eye to fill,
Minutely finish'd for our nicest skill, 50
Longleate that justly has all praise engross'd!
The stranger's wonder and our nation's boast
Paint her cascades that spread their sheets so wide
And emulate th' Italian waters pride,
Her fountains which so high their streams extend,
Th' amazed clouds now feel the rains ascend,
Whilst Phœbus, as they tow'rds his mansion flow,
Graces th' attempts and marks them with his bow.
Then should my pen (smooth as their turf) convey
Swift thought o'er terraces that lead the way 60
To flow'ry groves where evening odours stray

To lab'rinths into which, who fondly comes,
Attracted still and 'wildered with perfumes,
Till by acquaintance he their stations knows—
Here twists a woodbine, there a jasmin grows,
Next springs th' Hesperian broom and last th' Assyrian
     rose—
Shall endless rove, nor tread the way he went,
No thread to guide his steps, no clue but ravish'd scent.
But oh alas! could we this prospect give,
And make it in true lights and shadows live,   70
There 's yet a task at which 'twere vain to strive.
His genius who th' original improved
To this degree that has our wonder moved,
Too great appears and awes the trembling hand
Which can no colours for that draught command;
No syllables, the most sublimely wrought,
Can reach the loftier image of his thought,
Whose judgment plac'd in a superior height,
All things surveys with comprehensive sight:
Then, pitying us below, stoops to inform us right   80
In words that such convincing reasons bear
We silent wish that they engraven were,
And grudge those sounds to the dispersing air.
Protect him heaven, and long may he appear
The leading star to his great offspring here,
Their treasury of council and support,
Who, when at last he shall attend your court,
To all his future race the mark shall be
To stem the waves of life's tempestuous sea,
Who from abroad shall no examples need   90
Or men recorded, or who then exceed
To urge their virtue and exalt their fame,
Whilst their own Weymouth stands their noblest aim.
But we presume, and ne'er must hope to trace
His worth profound, his daughter's matchless grace,
Or draw paternal wit deriv'd into her face,
Though from his presence and her charms did grow
The joys Ardelia at Longleate did know.
So paradise did wondrous things enclose,
Yet surely not from them its name arose,   100
Not from the fruits in such profusion found,
Or early beauties of th' enamelled ground,
Not from the trees in their first leaves arrayed,

Or birds uncursed that warble in their shade,
Not from the streams that in new channels roll'd
O'er radiant beds of uncorrupted gold:
These might surprise, but 'twas th' accomplished pair
That gave the title and that made it fair.
All lesser thoughts imagination balk,
'Twas paradise in some expanded walk   110
To see her motions and attend his talk.

THE FOLLOWING LINES

OCCASIONED BY THE MARRIAGE OF EDWARD HERBERT, ESQ.
AND MRS. ELIZABETH HERBERT

CUPID one day ask'd his mother
    When she meant that he should wed.
You're too young, my boy, she said,
    Nor has nature made another
    Fit to match with Cupid's bed.

Cupid then her sight directed
    To a lately wedded pair,
Where himself the match effected,
    They as youthful, they as fair;

Having by example carried   10
    This first point in the dispute,
Worsley next he said 's not married:
    Hers with Cupid's charms may suit.

ON THE DEATH OF THE HONOURABLE
MR. JAMES THYNNE

YOUNGER SON TO THE RT. HONOURABLE
THE LORD VISCOUNT WEYMOUTH

FAREWELL, loved youth! since 'twas the will of heaven
So soon to take what had so late been given,
And thus our expectations to destroy,
Raising a grief where we had formed a joy;
Who once believed it was the fate's design
In him to double an illustrious line,

And in a second channel spread that race
Where ev'ry virtue shines, with ev'ry grace.
But we mistook, and 'twas not here below
That this engrafted scion was to grow: 10
The seats above required him, that each sphere
Might soon the offspring of such parents share.
Resign him, then, to the supreme intent,
You who but flesh to that blest spirit lent.
Again disrob'd, let him to bliss retire
And only bear from you, amidst that choir,
What precept or example did inspire:
A title to rewards from that rich store
Of pious works which you have sent before.
Then lay the fading relics which remain   20
In the still vault, excluding further pain,
Where kings and councillors their progress close,
And his renowned ancestors repose:
Where Coventry withdrew all but in name,
Leaving the world his benefits and fame:
Where his paternal predecessor lies,
Once large of thought and rank'd among the wise,
Whose genius in Longleate we may behold
(A pile as noble as if he'd been told
By Weymouth it should be in time possess'd,   30
And strove to suit the mansion to the guest).
Nor favour'd, nor disgraced, there Essex sleeps,
Nor Somerset his master's sorrows weeps,
Who to the shelter of th' unenvied grave
Conveyed the monarch whom he could not save,
Though, Roman-like, his own less valued head
He proffer'd in that injured martyr's stead.
Nor let that matchless female 'scape my pen
Who their whole duty taught to weaker men,
And of each sex the two best gifts enjoy'd—   40
The skill to write, the modesty to hide:
Whilst none should that performance disbelieve
Who led the life, might the directions give.
With such as these, whence he deriv'd his blood,
Great on record or eminently good,
Let him be laid, till death's long night shall cease
And breaking glory interrupt the peace.
Meanwhile, ye living parents, ease your grief
By tears, allowed as nature's due relief.

For when we offer to the Pow'rs above,   50
Like you, the dearest objects of our love;
When with that patient saint in holy writ
We've learned at once to grieve and to submit;
When contrite sighs, like hallowed incense, rise
Bearing our anguish to th' appeased skies,
Then may those show'rs, which take from sorrow birth,
And still are tending tow'rd this baleful earth,
O'er all our deep and parching cares diffuse
Like Eden's springs or Hermon's soft'ning dews.
But lend your succours, ye almighty pow'rs,   60
For as the wound, the balsam too is yours.
In vain are numbers or persuasive speech,
What poets write, or what the pastors preach,
Till you, who make, again repair the breach.
For when to shades of death our joys are fled,
When for a loss like this our tears are shed,
None can revive the heart but who can raise the dead.
But yet, my Muse, if thou had'st softer verse
Than e'er bewailed the melancholy hearse;
If thou had'st pow'r to dissipate the gloom   70
Inherent in the solitary tomb;
To rescue thence the memory and air
Of what we lately saw so fresh, so fair;
Then should this noble youth thy art engage
To show the beauties of his blooming age,
The pleasing light that from his eyes was cast,
Like hasty beams, too vigorous to last,
Where the warm soul, as on the confines, lay,
Ready for flight and for eternal day.
Gently dispos'd his nature should be shown,   80
And all the mother's sweetness made his own.
The father's likeness was but faintly seen,
As ripen'd fruits are figur'd by the green.
Nor could we hope, had he fulfilled his days,
He should have reach'd Weymouth's unequal'd praise.
Still one distinguished plant each lineage shows,
And all the rest beneath its stature grows:
Of Tully's race but he possess'd the tongue,
And none like Julius from the Cæsars sprung.
Next in his harmless sports he should be drawn,   90
Urging his courser o'er the flow'ry lawn,
Sprightly himself as th' enlivened game,

Bold in the chase and full of gen'rous flame;
Yet in the palace tractable and mild,
Perfect in all the duties of a child,
Which fond reflection pleases, whilst it pains,
Like penetrating notes of sad harmonious strains.
Selected friendships timely he began,
And seized in youth that best delight of man,
Leaving a growing race to mourn his end,   100
Their earliest and their age's promised friend.
But far away alas! that prospect moves,
Lost in the clouds, like distant hills and groves,
Whilst with increasing steps we all pursue
What time alone can bring to nearer view:
That future state, which darkness yet involves,
Known but by death which ev'ry doubt resolves.

TO THE RT. HONOURABLE THE COUNTESS OF HARTFORD

WITH HER VOLUME OF POEMS

Of sleepless nights and days with cares o'ercast,
Accept the fruits, tho' far beneath your taste;
Yet look with favour on Ardelia's Muse,
And what your father cherished, still excuse.
Whenever style or fancy in them shines,
Conclude his praise gave spirit to those lines:
So deep his judgment, so acute his wit,
No critic lived but did to him submit.
From him your gentle nature does proceed;
Then partial be, like him, while here you read,   10
Who could forgive the errors of a friend,
But knew no bounds when prompted to commend.

UPON THE DEATH OF SIR WILLIAM TWISDEN

I

Could rivers weep (as sometimes poets dream),
Could neigh'bring hills our sorrows know,
And thoughtless flocks, and fading flowers
Droop o'er the pastures and beneath the showers

To sympathise with man and answer to his woe,
Now should the Medway's fruitful stream
In broken drops dissolve away,
And pay in tears her tribute to the sea;
Now should the flocks forget to thrive,
Nor would th' ensuing blasted spring   10
One purple violet revive,
One fragrant odour bring;
Now by those echoes which returned his name,
When by the loud prevailing voice
Called to the senate by his country's choice,
Twisden amongst their rocks and deep recesses came;
Now should by them th' unwelcome news be spread
O'er all th' extended, mournful land,
O'er all the coasts, o'er all the Kentish strand,
That Twisden is no more, their matchless patriot's dead. 20

II

But oh! in vain, things void of sense we call,
In vain implore the murmuring sound
Of hollow groans from underneath the ground,
Or court the loud lament of some steep water's fall;
On things inanimate we would force
Some share of our divided grief,
Whilst Nature (unconcern'd for our relief)
Pursues her settled path, her fixt and steady course,
Leaving those ills which Providence allows
To check our pleasures and contract our brows,   30
Freely to act their uncontrolled part
Within the centre of the human breast,
There every lighter folly to molest,
And fill with anxious thoughts the sad, awaken'd heart,
From whence alone proceed those gathering clouds
Which every outward beauty shrouds;
From whence alone those sad complaints ascend
Which pitying echoes seem to lend;
And when through weeping eyes this world we view,
The ancient flood we to ourselves renew;   40
Then hasty ruin seizes all around,
All things to desolation tend,
All seems to die with a departed friend,
The earth unpeopled seems, and all again is drown'd.

III

Such were our thoughts, so with each mind it fared,
When first th' unhappy news we heard,
When told alas! that Twisden was expired,
Whom all lament, whom living, all admired.
For in his breast were such perfections sown,
Such numerous excellencies placed,   50
That every man with different talents graced,
Found something that improv'd or answer'd to his own.
He whose lov'd country was his chiefest care,
Might find her very archives there,
Her ancient statutes in their first design,
Prerogative and privilege to join,
The perfect draught of all-preserving law,
(Which, whilst unbiassed hands could round us draw,
Rebel, nor tyrant could encroach,
Nor that aspire, nor this extend too much;   60
None could beyond his happy limit go,
Not man depraved, nor demon from below
Could leap the hallow'd bound, or pass the magic line.)
Well did we in our far-applauded Kent,
Whilst pious, wise, heroic, and refin'd,
Whilst these strong rays of our old virtue shin'd,
Make him our choice, the whole to represent,
The worthiest pattern of the public mind,
Who, when alas! we more fanatic grew,
A heavier image of our country drew   70
(Like to a fault, in every altered part)
A rough, ill-wrought design, a work of Flemish art.

IV

Those whom a curious search had led
Where the fam'd Tiber, from his plenteous bed,
Such frequent treasures does unfold
As down his streams since Cæsar's days have rolled
T' upbraid new Rome with wonders of the old,
With him their great ideas might renew.
Enlighten'd more, and more amaz'd
Than when at first, with unexperienced view,   80
On those stupendous works they, less assisted, gazed,
With him, who rested not alone
In arts that, more than did the fabl'd fire,

Give painting breath, and do with life inspire
The new created rock, the man of polish'd stone:
But justly weigh'd, in his capacious mind,
Through ev'ry age, her past and present state,
What raised those arts, what made Rome once so great,
And by what failing steps, now ruin'd and declin'd,
All useful knowledge thence he brought,   90
And, 'gainst her dull, mistaken maxims, taught
(Let the constrain'd, severe Italian see)
A man designed for wisdom's last degree
Might wear an open face with a behaviour free.

V

The soften'd courtier might in him discern
(What to himself had cost much pains to learn,
And was at last but with dissembling worn)
A pleasing and a sweet address,
Beyond what affectation can express,
Good breeding, less acquir'd than with his temper born.
So was he vers'd in that allusive art   101
Which dying Israel did the first impart—
When he the royal lion did bestow
On him, from whom all sovereign rule should flow,
Rightly dispos'd the wolf, and loosen'd hind,
And blazon'd every coat, he to each tribe assigned—
That unto him all families were known:
Their distant branches, and their wide extent,
Their ancient rise, or more renown'd descent,
Modestly silent only of his own: 110
But silence could not that extraction wrong
Which all besides confess'd, which Kent has borne so long.

VI

With him we the traditions loose
Of great and of illustrious men,
Which his discourse reviv'd to us again:
Their unrecorded graces did disclose,
Their moving gestures, their engaging looks,
Of life the ornamental parts,
The powerful spells that influence our hearts;
Their secret motives and their apt replies   120
Which ignorance, or brevity, denies

To be at large enroll'd, or register'd in books:
With him they fell, though many years before
The world might their departed breath deplore;
'Tis now they to oblivion are resigned,
Or some short page of history confin'd,
'Tis now they cease to live, and now they are no more
So nicely could he all retain,
Of such a memory possessed,
So undisturb'd might every subject rest,
Or range that ample store-house of his brain,
Where ancient learning early was conveyed,
The solid and the useful ground
Where all the modern was profusely found,
Where what our own or neighb'ring wits could write,
What his yet clearer thoughts could to themselves endi
Was in such beauteous order laid
As made the symmetry entire,
And did the whole harmoniously inspire,
Whilst all was in the properest terms expressed,   1
When to our pleas'd attention still made known
In chosen words that best adorned his own,
Or in the numerous tongues of various countries dresse

VII

How had we sued so great a life to save
From yet descending to th' unactive grave?
How had the loud united prayers
Of that best church, (the object of his cares,
The object of his still awakened thought,
For which so well he spoke, so well his father wrote)
Imploring at the Throne above   1
With unresisted force, for his continuance strove,
Had not wise Heaven, our clamours to prevent,
So secretly the fatal message sent,
Bid the light essence his swift wings display,
Nor his commission to survey,
Till past the bounds of all th' angelic host,
Distant alike from our benighted coast,
Till sail'd into the midst of the ethereal way,
Lest that if either world should know
What sadly was decreed for ours below,   16
In favour of the happier skies,
Some pious heat might grow,

THE PETITION FOR AN ABSOLUTE RETREAT

INSCRIBED TO THE RT. HONOURABLE CATHERINE, COUNTESS OF
THANET, MENTIONED IN THE POEM UNDER THE NAME
OF ARMINDA

GIVE me, Oh indulgent fate!
Give me yet, before I die,
A sweet, but absolute retreat,
'Mongst paths so lost, and trees so high,
That the world may ne'er invade
Through such windings and such shade
My unshaken liberty.

No intruders thither come,
Who visit but to be from home!
None who their vain moments pass   10
Only studious of their glass;
News, that charm to list'ning ears,
That false alarm to hopes and fears,
That common theme of every fop,
From the statesmen to the shop,
In those coverts ne'er be spread
Of who's deceased, or who's to wed;
Be no tidings thither brought
But silent as a midnight thought:
Where the world may ne'er invade   20
Be those windings and that shade.

Courteous fate! afford me there
A table spread, without my care,
With what the neighb'ring fields impart,
Whose cleanliness be all its art.
When of old the calf was dressed
(Tho' to make an angel's feast)
In the plain, unstudied sauce,
Nor truffle, nor morillia was;
Nor could the mighty patriarch's bôard   30
One far-fetch'd ortolane afford.
Courteous fate, then give me there
Only plain and wholesome fare.
Fruits indeed would Heaven bestow,
All that did in Eden grow,

All, but the Forbidden Tree,
Would be coveted by me:
Grapes with juice so crowded up,
As breaking thro' the native cup,
Figs, yet growing, candied o'er   40
By the sun's attracting power,
Cherries, with the downy peach
All within my easy reach,
While creeping near the humble ground,
Should the strawberry be found,
Springing wheresoe'er I strayed,
Thro' those windings and that shade.

For my garments, let them be
What may with the times agree;
Warm when Phœbus does retire,   50
And is ill-supplied by fire:
But when he renews the year,
And verdant all the fields appear,
Beauty everything resumes,
Birds have dropt their winter plumes,
When the lily, full display'd,
Stands in purer white arrayed
Than the vest which heretofore
The luxurious monarch wore,
When from Salem's gates he drove   60
To the soft retreat of love,
Lebanon's all burnish'd house,
And the dear Egyptian spouse.
Clothe me, fate, tho' not so gay,
Clothe me light and fresh as May:
In the fountains let me view
All my habit cheap and new,
Such as, when sweet zephyrs fly,
With their motions may comply,
Gently waving to express   70
Unaffected carelessness.
No perfumes have there a part
Borrow'd from the chemist's art,
But such as rise from flow'ry beds,
Or the falling jasmin sheds!
'Twas the odour of the field
Esau's rural coat did yield

That inspir'd his father's pray'r
For blessings of the earth and air:
Of gums and powders had it smelt,   80
The supplanter, then unfelt,
Easily had been descried
For one that did in tents abide,
For some beauteous handmaid's joy,
And his mother's darling boy.
Let me then no fragrance wear
But what the winds from gardens bear,
In such kind, surprising gales
As gather'd from Fidentia's vales
All the flowers that in them grew,   90
Which, intermixing as they flew,
In wreathen garlands dropt again
On Lucullus and his men,
Who, cheer'd by the victorious sight,
Trebl'd numbers put to flight.
Let me, when I must be fine,
In such natural colours shine,
Wove and painted by the sun,
Whose resplendent rays to shun,
When they do too fiercely beat,   100
Let me find some close retreat
Where they have no passage made
Thro' those windings and that shade.

Give me there (since heaven has shown
It was not good to be alone)
A partner suited to my mind,
Solitary, pleas'd, and kind;
Who, partially, may something see
Preferr'd to all the world in me,
Slighting, by my humble side,   110
Fame and splendour, wealth and pride.
When but two the earth possessed,
'Twas their happiest days and best:
They by bus'ness, nor by wars,
They by no domestic cares,
From each other e'er were drawn,
But in some grove, or flow'ry lawn
Spent the swiftly flying time,
Spent their own and nature's prime

In love—that only passion given 120
To perfect man, whilst friends with heaven.
Rage, and jealousy, and hate,
Transports of this sullen state
(When by Satan's wiles betray'd)
Fly those windings and that shade!

Thus from crowds and noise remov'd,
Let each moment be improv'd;
Every object still produce
Thoughts of pleasure and of use.
When some river slides away 130
To increase the boundless sea,
Think we then how time does haste
To grow eternity at last.
By the willows on the banks,
Gather'd into social ranks,
Playing with the gentle winds,
Straight the boughs and smooth the rinds,
Moist each fibre, and each top
Wearing a luxurious crop,
Let the time of youth be shown, 140
The time alas! too soon outgrown.
Whilst a lonely, stubborn oak,
Which no breezes can provoke,
No less gusts persuade to move
Than those which in a whirlwind drove,
Spoil'd the old fraternal feast,
And left alive but one poor guest,
Rivell'd the distorted trunk,
Sapless limbs all bent and shrunk,
Sadly does the time presage 150
Of our too near approaching age.
When a helpless vine is found
Unsupported on the ground,
Careless all the branches spread,
Subject to each haughty tread,
Bearing neither leaves nor fruit,
Living only in the root,
Back reflecting let me say
So the sad Ardelia lay:
Blasted by a storm of fate, 160
Felt thro' all the British state;

Fall'n, neglected, lost, forgot,
Dark oblivion all her lot;
Faded till Arminda's love
(Guided by the pow'rs above)
Warm'd anew her drooping heart,
And life diffus'd thro' every part,
Mixing words in wise discourse
Of such weight and wondrous force
As could all her sorrows charm,   170
And transitory ills disarm;
Cheering the delightful day,
When dispos'd to be more gay,
With wit, from an unmeasured store,
To woman ne'er allowed before.
What nature, or refining art,
All that fortune could impart,
Heaven did to Arminda send,
Then gave her for Ardelia's friend:
To her cares the cordial drop,   180
Which else had overflowed the cup.
So when once the son of Jess
Every anguish did oppress,
Hunted by all kinds of ills,
Like a partridge on the hills,
Trains were laid to catch his life,
Baited with a royal wife,
From his house and country torn,
Made a heathen prince's scorn,
Fate to answer all these harms   190
Threw a friend into his arms.
Friendship still has been designed
The support of humankind;
The safe delight, the useful bliss,
The next world's happiness, and this.
Give then O indulgent fate!
Give a friend to that retreat
(Tho' withdrawn from all the rest)
Still a clue to reach my breast.
Let a friend be still conveyed   200
Thro' those windings and that shade!

Where, may I remain secure,
Waste, in humble joys and pure,

A life that can no envy yield,
Want of affluence my shield.
Thus, had Crassus been content,
When from Marius' rage he went,
With the seat that fortune gave,
The commodious ample cave
Form'd in a divided rock   210
By some mighty earthquake's shock
Into rooms of every size,
Fair as art could e'er devise,
Leaving, in the marble roof
('Gainst all storms and tempests proof)
Only passage for the light
To refresh the cheerful sight,
Whilst three sharers of his fate
On th' escape with joy dilate,
Beds of moss their bodies bore,   220
Canopied with ivy o'er;
Rising springs that near them play'd
O'er the native pavement stray'd;
When the hour arrived to dine,
Various meats and sprightly wine
On some neighb'ring cliff they spied,
Every day a-new supplied
By a friend's entrusted care:
Had he still continu'd there,
Made that lonely wondrous cave   230
Both his palace and his grave,
Peace and rest he might have found,
(Peace and rest are under ground)
Nor have been in that retreat
Fam'd for a proverbial fate:
In pursuit of wealth been caught
And punish'd with a golden draught.
Nor had he, who crowds could blind,
Whisp'ring with a snowy hind,
Made 'em think that from above   240
(Like the great impostor's dove)
Tidings to his ears she brought,
Rules by which he march'd and fought,
After Spain he had o'er-run,
Cities sack'd and battles won,
Drove Rome's consuls from the field,

Made her darling Pompey yield,
At a fatal, treacherous feast
Felt a dagger in his breast;
Had he his once-pleasing thought   250
Of solitude to practise brought:
Had no wild ambition sway'd,
In those islands had he stay'd
Justly call'd the Seats of Rest,
Truly fortunate and blest,
By the ancient poets giv'n
As their best discover'd heav'n.
Let me then, indulgent fate!
Let me still in my retreat
From all roving thoughts be freed,   260
Or aims that may contention breed:
Nor be my endeavours led
By goods that perish with the dead!
Fitly might the life of man
Be indeed esteem'd a span,
If the present moment were
Of delight his only share:
If no other joys he knew
Than what round about him grew.
But as those who stars would trace   270
From a subterranean place,
Through some engine lift their eyes
To the outward, glorious skies:
So th' immortal spirit may,
When descended to our clay,
From a rightly govern'd frame
View the height from whence she came:
To her paradise be caught,
And things unutterable taught.
Give me then, in that retreat,   280
Give me, O indulgent fate!
For all pleasures left behind
Contemplations of the mind.
Let the fair, the gay, the vain
Courtship and applause obtain;
Let th' ambitious rule the earth;
Let the giddy fool have mirth;
Give the epicure his dish,
Ev'ry one their sev'ral wish,

Whilst my transports I employ   290
On that more extensive joy:
When all heaven shall be survey'd
From those windings and that shade.

THE CHANGE

Poor river, now thou'rt almost dry,
What nymph or swain will near thee lie?
Since brought, alas! to sad decay,
What flocks or herds will near thee stay?
The swans, that sought thee in thy pride,
Now on new streams forgetful ride:
And fish, that in thy bosom lay,
Choose in more prosp'rous floods to play.
All leave thee, now thy ebb appears,
To waste thy sad remains in tears,   10
Nor will thy mournful murmurs heed.
Fly, wretched stream, with all thy speed,
Amongst those solid rocks thy griefs bestow,
For friends like those, alas! thou ne'er did'st know.

And thou, poor sun! that sat'st on high,
But late the splendour of the sky,
What flow'r, tho' by thy influence born,
Now clouds prevail, will tow'rds thee turn?
Now darkness sits upon thy brow,
What Persian votary will bow?   20
What river will her smiles reflect,
Now that no beams thou can'st direct?
By wat'ry vapours overcast,
Who thinks upon thy glories past?
If present light, nor heat we get,
Unheeded thou may'st rise and set:
Not all the past can one adorer keep,
Fall, wretched sun, to the more faithful deep!

Nor do thou, lofty structure! boast,
Since undermin'd by time and frost;   30
Since thou canst no reception give,
In untrod meadows thou may'st live.
None from his ready road will turn,
With thee thy wretched change to mourn.

Not the soft nights or cheerful days
Thou hast bestow'd can give thee praise.
No lusty tree that near thee grows
(Tho' it beneath thy shelter rose)
Will to thy age a staff become.
Fall, wretched building, to thy tomb,   40
Thou and thy painted roofs in ruin mixt,
Fall to the earth, for that alone is fixt.

The same, poor man, the same must be
Thy fate now fortune frowns on thee.
Her favour ev'ry one pursues,
And losing her, thou all must lose.
No love, sown in thy prosp'rous days,
Can fruit in this cold season raise:
No benefit by thee conferr'd
Can in this time of storms be heard.   50
All from thy troubl'd waters run:
The stooping fabric all men shun.
All do thy clouded looks decline
As if thou ne'er did'st on them shine.
O wretched man! to other worlds repair,
For faith and gratitude are only there.

THE CIRCUIT OF APOLLO

APOLLO as lately a circuit he made
Thro' the lands of the Muses when Kent he survey'd,
And saw there that poets were not very common,
But most that pretended to verse were the women,
Resolv'd to encourage the few that he found,
And she that writ best with a wreath should be crown'd.
A summons sent out was obeyed but by four,
When Phœbus, afflicted, to meet with no more,
And standing where sadly he now might descry
From the banks of the Stour the desolate Wye,   10
He lamented for Behn o'er that place of her birth,
And said, amongst females, was not on the earth
Her superior in fancy, in language, or wit,
Yet own'd that a little too loosely she writ:
Since the art of the Muse is to stir up soft thoughts,
Yet to make all hearts beat without blushes or faults.

But now to proceed, and their merits to know:
Before he on any the bays would bestow,
He order'd them, each in their several way,
To show him their papers, to sing, or to say   20
Whate'er they thought best their pretensions might prove,
When Alinda began with a song upon love.
So easy the verse, yet compos'd with such art,
That not one expression fell short of the heart.
Apollo himself did their influence obey,
He catch'd up his lyre and a part he would play,
Declaring, no harmony else could be found
Fit to wait upon words of so moving a sound.
The wreath he reach'd out to have plac'd on her head,
If Laura not quickly a paper had read,   30
Wherein she Orinda has praised so high
He own'd it had reach'd him while yet in the sky,
That he thought with himself, when it first struck his ear,
Whoe'er could write that ought the laurel to wear.
Betwixt them he stood, in a musing suspense,
Till Valeria withdrew him a little from thence,
And told him, as soon as she'd got him aside,
Her works by no other but him should be tried:
Which so often he read, and with still new delight,
That judgment 'twas thought would not pass till 'twas
          night.   40
Yet at length, he restor'd them, but told her withal,
If she kept it still close he'd the talent recall.
Ardelia came last, as expecting least praise,
Who writ for her pleasure, and not for the bays,
But yet, as occasion, or fancy should sway,
Would sometimes endeavour to pass a dull day
In composing a song, or a scene of a play,
Not seeking for fame, which so little does last,
That ere we can taste it, the pleasure is past.
But Apollo replied, tho' so careless she seem'd,   50
Yet the bays, if her share, would be highly esteem'd.

And now he was going to make an oration,
Has thrown by one lock with a delicate fashion,
Upon the left foot most genteelly did stand,
Had drawn back the other, and wav'd his white hand:
When calling to mind how the prize, altho' giv'n
By Paris to her who was fairest in heaven,

Had pull'd on the rash inconsiderate boy,
The fall of his house with the ruin of Troy,
Since in wit or in beauty it never was heard   60
One female could yield t' have another preferr'd,
He changed his design and divided his praise,
And said that they all had a right to the bays,
And that 'twere injustice one brow to adorn
With a wreath which so fitly by each might be worn.
Then smil'd to himself, and applauded his art,
Who thus nicely had acted so subtle a part:
Four women to wheedle, but found 'em too many,
For who would please all can never please any.
In vain then he thought it there longer to stay,   70
But told them he now must go drive on the day,
Yet the case to Parnassus should soon be referr'd,
And there, in a council of Muses, be heard
Who of their own sex best the title might try,
Since no man upon earth, nor himself in the sky,
Would be so imprudent, so dull, or so blind
To lose three parts in four from amongst womankind.

AN EPILOGUE TO THE TRAGEDY OF JANE SHORE

TO BE SPOKEN BY MRS. OLDFIELD THE NIGHT BEFORE THE
POET'S DAY

THE audience seems to-night so very kind,
I fancy I may freely speak my mind,
And tell you when the author nam'd Jane Shore,
I all her glorious history run o'er,
And thought he would have shown her on the stage
In the first triumphs of her blooming age:
Edward in public at her feet a slave,
The jealous queen in private left to rave,
Yet Jane superior still in all the strife—
For sure that mistress leads a wretched life   10
Who can't insult the keeper and the wife!
This, I concluded, was his right design,
To make her lavish, careless, gay and fine:
Not bring her here to mortify and whine.
I hate such parts as we have played to-day,
Before I promis'd, had I read the play,

I would have stayed at home and drank my tea.
Then why the husband should at last be brought
To hear her own and aggravate her fault,
Puzzled as much my discontented thought: 20
For were I to transgress, for all the poet,
I swear no friend of mine should ever know it.
But you perhaps are pleas'd to see her mended,
And so should I, had all her charms been ended:
But whilst another lover might be had,
The woman or the poet must be mad.
There is a season, which too fast approaches,
And every list'ning beauty nearly touches,
When handsome ladies falling to decay,
Pass thro' new epithets to smooth the way: 30
From "fair" and "young" transportedly confess'd,
Dwindle to "fine," "well-fashioned," and "well-
    dressed."
Thence, as their fortitude's extremest proof,
To "well as yet," from "well" to "well enough":
Till, having on such weak foundations stood,
Deplorably at last, they shrink to "good."
Abandon'd then, 'tis time to be retired,
And seen no more when not alas! admired.
By men, indeed, a better fate is known:
The pretty fellow that has youth outgrown,   40
Who nothing knew but how his clothes did sit,
Transforms to a "free-thinker" and a "wit,"
At operas becomes a skilled musician,
Ends in a party man and politician,
Maintains some figure while he keeps his breath,
And is a fop of consequence till death.
And so would I have had our mistress Shore
To make a figure till she pleased no more.
But if you better like her present sorrow,
Pray let me see you here again to-morrow,   50
And should the house be thronged the poet's day,
Whate'er he makes us women do or say
You'll not believe, that he'll go fast and pray.

TO MR. PRIOR FROM A LADY UNKNOWN

THE nymph whose virgin heart thy charms have taught
To cherish love, with secret wishes fraught,
Reserv'd at first, endeavours to conceal
What she had rather die than not reveal:
No fears the love-sick maid can long restrain,
None read thy verse, or hear thee speak in vain.
Thy melting numbers and polite address,
In every fair raise passion to excess.
In either sex you never fail, we find,
To cultivate the heart, or charm the mind.   10
In raptures lost, I fear not your disdain,
But own I languish to possess your vein.
As a fond bird, pleas'd with the teacher's note,
Expends his life to raise his mimic throat,
His little art exerting all he can,
Charmed with the tune, to imitate the man:
Rudely he chants, yet labours not in vain,
By wild essays just so much song to gain
As tempts his master to renew the strain.
Such is my verse, with equal zeal I burn,   20
Too happy should I meet the same return.

THE ANSWER

TO POPE'S IMPROMPTU

DISARM'D with so genteel an air,
    The contest I give o'er.
Yet, Alexander, have a care,
    And shock the sex no more.
We rule the world our life's whole race,
    Men but assume that right:
First slaves to ev'ry tempting face,
    Then martyrs to our spite.
You of one Orpheus sure have read,
    Who would like you have writ   10
Had he in London town been bred,
    And polish'd too his wit;
But he, poor soul, thought all was well,
    And great should be his fame,
When he had left his wife in hell,
    And birds and beasts could tame.

Yet venturing then with scoffing rhymes
    The women to incense,
Resenting heroines of those times
    Soon punished his offence;   20
And as the Hebrus roll'd his skull,
    And harp besmear'd with blood,
They, clashing as the waves grew full,
    Still harmonis'd the flood.
But you our follies gently treat,
    And spin so fine the thread,
You need not fear his awkward fate,
    The lock won't cost the head.
Our admiration you command
    For all that 's gone before;   30
What next we look for at your hand
    Can only raise it more.
Yet sooth the ladies I advise
    (As me too pride has wrought)
We're born to wit, but to be wise
    By admonitions taught.

TO A FELLOW SCRIBBLER

PRITHEE, friend, that hedge behold:
When all we rhyming fools grow old,
That hedge our state will represent,
Who in vain flourish life have spent:
Amidst it stands a rivall'd tree
Now representing sixty-three,
And like it you and I shall be.
The bare vine round about it clings
With mischievous, entangling strings,
The night-shade with a dismal flow'r,   10
Curls o'er it, like a lady's tower;
Or honesty with feather'd down,
Like grizzled hair deforms its crown;
Luxuriant plants that o'er it spread,
Not med'cinal for heart or head,
Which serve but to amuse the sight,
Are like the nothings that we write.
Yet still 'tis thought that tree 's well plac'd,
With beauteous eglantine embrac'd:

But see how false appearance proves,   20
If he that honeysuckle loves;
His love the honeysuckle scorns,
Which climbs by him to reach the thorns;
The rival thorn his age derides,
And gnaws like jealousy his sides.
Then let us cease, my friend, to sing
When ever youth is on the wing,
Unless we solidly indite,
Some good infusing while we write;
Lest with our follies hung around,   30
We like that tree and hedge be found,
Grotesque and trivial, shunn'd by all,
And soon forgotten when we fall.

TO A FRIEND

IN PRAISE OF THE INVENTION OF WRITING LETTERS

BLEST be the man! his memory at least,
Who found the art thus to unfold his breast,
And taught succeeding times an easy way
Their secret thoughts by letters to convey;
To baffle absence and secure delight
Which, till that time, was limited to sight.
The parting farewell spoke, the last adieu,
The less'ning distance past, then loss of view:
The friend was gone which some kind moments gave,
And absence separated like the grave.   10
The wings of love were tender too, till then
No quill thence pull'd was shap'd into a pen,
To send in paper sheets, from town to town,
Words smooth as they, and softer than his down.
O'er such he reigned, whom neighbourhood had join'd.
And hopt from bough to bough supported by the wind.
When for a wife the youthful patriarch sent,
The camels, jewels, and the steward went,
A wealthy equipage, tho' grave and slow:
But not a line that might the lover show.   20
The rings and bracelets woo'd her hands and arms;
But had she known of melting words, the charms
That under secret seals in ambush lie
To catch the soul when drawn into the eye,

The fair Assyrian had not took this guide,
Nor her soft heart in chains of pearl been tied.
Had these conveyances been then in date,
Joseph had known his wretched father's state,
Before a famine, which his life pursues,
Had sent his other sons to tell the news.   3
Oh! might I live to see an art arise,
As this to thoughts, indulgent to the eyes,
That the dark pow'rs of distance could subdue
And make me *see* as well as *talk* to you:
That tedious miles, nor tracts of air might prove
Bars to my sight, and shadows to my love!
Yet were it granted, such unbounded things
Are wand'ring wishes, born on fancy's wings,
They'd stretch themselves beyond this happy case,
And ask an art to help us to embrace.   4

CLARINDA'S INDIFFERENCE AT PARTING
WITH HER BEAUTY

Now, age came on, and all the dismal train
That fright the vicious and afflict the vain.
Departing beauty now Clarinda spies,
Pale in her cheeks and dying in her eyes;
That youthful air that wanders o'er the face,
That undescrib'd, that unresisted grace,
Those morning beams that strongly warm and shine,
Which men that feel and see can ne'er define,
Now, on the wings of restless time, were fled,
And ev'ning shades began to rise and spread;   1
When thus resolv'd, and ready soon to part,
Slighting the short reprieves of proffer'd art,
She spake—
"And what, vain beauty, didst thou e'er achieve,
When at thy height, that I thy fall should grieve?
When didst thou e'er successfully pursue?
When didst thou e'er th' appointed foe subdue?
'Tis vain of numbers, or of strength to boast,
In an undisciplin'd, unguided host,
And love, that did thy mighty hopes deride,   2
Would pay no sacrifice, but to thy pride.

When didst thou e'er a pleasing rule obtain?
A glorious empire's but a glorious pain.
Thou art, indeed, but vanity's chief source;
But foil to wit, to want of wit a curse:
For often by thy gaudy sign's descried
A fool, which unobserv'd, had been untried;
And when thou dost such empty things adorn,
'Tis but to make them more the public scorn.
I know thee well, but weak thy reign would be   30
Did none adore or praise thee more than me.
I see, indeed, thy certain ruin near,
But can't afford one parting sigh or tear,
Nor rail at time, nor quarrel with my glass,
But unconcern'd, can let thy glories pass."

SOME PIECES OUT OF THE FIRST ACT OF THE
AMINTA OF TASSO

DAPHNE'S ANSWER TO SYLVIA, DECLARING SHE WOULD ESTEEM
ALL AS ENEMIES WHO SHOULD TALK TO HER OF LOVE

THEN, to the snowy ewe, in thy esteem,
The father of the flock a foe must seem!
The faithful turtles to their yielding mates!
The cheerful spring which love and joy creates,
That reconciles the world by soft desires,
And tender thoughts in ev'ry breast inspires,
To you a hateful season must appear,
Whilst love prevails, and all are lovers here.
Observe the gentle murmurs of that dove,
And see, how billing, she confirms her love!   10
For this, the nightingale displays her throat,
And *love, love, love* is all her ev'ning note.
The very tigers have their tender hours,
And prouder lions bow beneath love's pow'rs.
Thou, prouder yet than that imperious beast,
Alone deny'st him shelter in thy breast,
But why should I the creatures only name
That sense partake, as owners of this flame?
Love farther goes, nor stops his course at these:
The plants he moves, and gently bends the trees.   20
See how these willows mix their am'rous boughs,

And how that vine clasps her supporting spouse!
The silver fir dotes on the stately pine:
By love those elms, by love those beeches join.
But view that oak, behold his rugged side:
Yet that rough bark the melting flame does hide.
All, by their trembling leaves, in sighs declare
And tell their passions to the gath'ring air:
Which, had but love o'er thee the least command,
Thou, by their motions, too might'st understand.

      Tho' we of small proportion see
      And slight the armed golden bee,
      Yet if her sting behind she leaves,
      No ease th' envenom'd flesh receives.
      Love, less to sight that is this fly,
      In a soft curl conceal'd can lie;
      Under an eyelid's lovely shade,
      Can form a dreadful ambuscade;
      Can the most subtle sight beguile
      Hid in the dimples of a smile.
      But if from thence a dart he throw,
      How sure, how mortal is the blow!
      How helpless all the pow'r of art
      To bind or to restore the heart!

PART OF THE DESCRIPTION OF THE GOLDEN AGE

      Then, by some fountain's flow'ry side
      The Loves unarm'd did still abide.
      Then, the loos'd quiver careless hung,
      The torch extinct, the bow unstrung.
      Then, by the nymphs no charms were worn
      But such as with the nymphs were born.
      The shepherd could not, then, complain,
      Nor told his am'rous tale in vain.
      No veil the beauteous face did hide,
      Nor harmless freedom was denied.
      Then, innocence and virtue reign'd,
      Pure, unaffected, unconstrain'd.
      Love was their pleasure and their praise,
      The soft employment of their days.

MELINDA ON AN INSIPID BEAUTY

IN IMITATION OF A FRAGMENT OF SAPPHO'S

You, when your body life shall leave,
Must drop entire into the grave;
Unheeded, unregarded lie,
And all of you together die:
Must hide that fleeting charm, that face in dust,
Or to some painted cloth the slighted image trust;
Whilst my fam'd works shall thro' all times surprise,
My polish'd thoughts, my bright ideas rise,
And to new men be known, still talking to their eyes.

A SONG FOR A PLAY

ALCANDER TO MELINDA

More than a sea of tears can show,
   Or thousand sighs can prove,
Than falt'ring speech can let you know,
   I fair Melinda love.

You then, must to yourself express
   The strength of my desire,
Who brings the fuel best may guess
   How great must be the fire.

Think on the pow'r that arms your eyes,
   The charms that in them shine,
Think on their aptness to surprise,
   And of the love in mine.

Then to my wishing looks afford
   The heart for which they sue,
And take a longing lover's word
   That some men can be true.

10

A SONG

MELINDA TO ALCANDER

Wit as free and unconfin'd
   As the universal air,
Was not allotted to mankind,
   Leaving us without our share:
No, we possess alike that fire,
And all you boast of we inspire.

Fancy does from beauty rise,
   Beauty teaches you to write,
Your flames are borrow'd from our eyes,
   You but speak what they indite.   10
Then cease to boast alone that fame.
Wit and love we give and claim.

A SONG

By love pursu'd, in vain I fly
To shades as lost and wild as I;
Cold earth my hopes, sharp thorns my cares,
Here lively paint and urge my tears:
Fancy makes all things bear a part,
And shows a rock for Sylvia's heart.

In vain I from the object go,
Since my own thoughts can wound me so:
I'll back again and ruin'd be
By hate, by scorn, or jealousy.   10
Such real ills attend us all,
Lovers by fancy need not fall.

A SONG

MIRANDA hides her from the sun,
   Beneath those shady beeches nigh,
Whilst I, by her bright rays undone,
   Can nowhere for refreshment fly.

In that fair grove, at height of noon,
   His fiercest glories she defies;
I have alas! such shelter none,
   No safe umbrella, 'gainst her eyes.

Thus, does th' unequal hand of fate
   Refuse its favours to divide,   10
Giving to her, a safe retreat,
   And all offensive arms beside.

A SONG

PERSUADE me not, there is a grace
   Proceeds from Sylvia's voice or lute
Against Miranda's charming face
   To make her hold the least dispute.

Music, which tunes the soul for love,
  And stirs up all our soft desires,
Does but the glowing flame improve
  Which pow'rful beauty first inspires.

Thus, whilst with art she plays and sings,
  I to Miranda, standing by,   10
Impute the music of the strings,
  And all the melting words apply.

JEALOUSY

A SONG

Vain love, why dost thou boast of wings
  That cannot help thee to retire!
When such quick flames suspicion brings
  As do the heart about thee fire.

Still swift to come, but when to go
Thou should'st be more—alas! how slow.
Lord of the world must surely be
  But thy bare title at the most,
Since jealousy is lord of thee,
  And makes such havoc on thy coast,   10

As does thy pleasant land deface,
Yet binds thee faster to the place.

A SONG

Love, thou art best of human joys,
  Our chiefest happiness below;
All other pleasures are but toys,
Music without thee is but noise,
  And beauty but an empty show.

Heav'n, who knew best what man would move,
  And raise his thoughts above the brute,
Said, Let him be, and let him love:
That must alone his soul improve,
  Howe'er philosophers dispute.   10

A SONG

'Tis strange, this heart within my breast,
    Reason opposing, and her pow'rs,
Cannot one gentle moment rest
    Unless it knows what's done in yours.

In vain I ask it of your eyes,
    Which subtly would my fears control:
For art has taught them to disguise
    Which nature made t' explain the soul.

In vain that sound your voice affords,
    Flatters sometimes my easy mind;
But of too vast extent are words
    In them the jewel truth to find.

Then let my fond inquiries cease,
    And so let all my troubles end:
For sure, that heart shall ne'er know peace
    Which on another's does depend.

A SONG

If for a woman I would die,
    It should for Gloriana be:
But lovers, you that talk so high,
Inform, whilst in the grave I lie,
    What reward can reach to me?

If I my freedom would resign,
    That freedom she alone should have:
But tell me, you that can define,
If I, by marriage, make her mine,
    Which may be call'd the greater slave?

Then Gloriana, since 'tis plain
    Love, with these two, can ne'er agree,
Since death and marriage are his bane,
Those melancholy thoughts we'll flee,
    And cheerful lovers always be.

A SONG

Let the fool still be true,
And one object pursue,
And for ever be jealous or dying,
Whilst he that better knows,
Will in love no time lose,
For that god still, that god still, that god still is flying.

Let the heart that wants heat,
But with one motion beat,
Lest that flame should decay which they sever;
But we, that boast of more,   10
Can each beauty adore,
And love all, and love all, and love all, for ever.

MORAL SONG

Would we attain the happiest state
    That is design'd us here,
No joy a rapture must create,
    No grief beget despair.
No injury fierce anger raise,
    No honour tempt to pride;
No vain desires empty praise
    Must in the soul abide.
No charms of youth or beauty move
    The constant, settl'd breast: 10
Who leaves a passage free for love
    Shall let in all the rest.
In such a heart soft peace will live,
    Where none of these abound:
The greatest blessing heav'n does give,
    Or can on earth be found.

HONOUR

A SONG

How dear is reputation bought!
    When we the purchase pay.
We set the sweets of life at nought,
    And make our joys away.

One most belov'd we often lose
   To pacify the crowd,
And even complaisance refuse
   Not to be chaste, but proud.

Though honour, which the world does awe,
   And makes our sex so nice,   10
Its self no pedigree can draw
   But what's derived from vice.

Thus tyrants who, usurping, rise
   To fix them in that wrong,
Do sharpest punishment devise
   For crimes from whence they sprung.

TIMELY ADVICE TO DORINDA

DORINDA, since you must decay,
   Your lover now resign,
As Charles that empire gave away
   He saw would soon decline.

'Tis better in the height of power
   Thus with your sway to part,
Than stay till that more fatal hour
   Of his revolted heart.

For wit but faintly will inspire
   Unless with beauty join'd,   1
And when our eyes have lost their fire
   'Tis useless in the mind.

Be then advis'd and now remove
   All further thoughts about it,
Since youth we find too short for love,
   Though life's too long without it.

THE PHŒNIX

A SONG

A FEMALE friend advis'd a swain
  (Whose heart she wish'd at ease),
Make love thy pleasure, not thy pain,
  Nor let it deeply seize.

Beauty, when vanities abound
  No serious passion claims:
Then 'till a phœnix can be found,
  Do not admit the flames.

But griev'd, she finds that his replies
  (Since prepossess'd when young)
Take all her hints from Sylvia's eyes,
  None from Ardelia's tongue.

Thus, Cupid, of our aim we miss,
  Who would unbend thy bow;
And each slight nymph a phœnix is
  When love will have it so.

HOPE

THE tree of knowledge we in Eden prov'd;
The tree of life was thence to heav'n remov'd:
Hope is the growth of earth, the only plant
Which either heav'n or paradise could want.

Hell knows it not, to us alone confin'd,
And cordial only to the human mind.
Receive it then, t' expel these mortal cares,
Nor waive a med'cine which thy God prepares.

LIFE'S PROGRESS

How gaily is at first begun
  Our life's uncertain race!
Whilst that sprightly morning sun,
With which we just set out to run,
  Enlightens all the place.

How smiling the world's prospect lies,
　　How tempting to go through!
Not Canaan to the prophet's eyes,
From Pisgah with a sweet surprise,
　　Did more inviting show.　　　　　　　10

How promising 's the book of fate,
　　Till thoroughly understood!
Whilst partial hopes such lots create
As may the youthful fancy treat
　　With all that 's great and good.

How soft the first ideas prove,
　　Which wander through our minds!
How full of joys, how free the love
Which does that early season move,
　　As flow'rs the western winds.　　　　20

Our sighs are then but vernal air,
　　But April-drops our tears,
Which swiftly passing, all grows fair,
Whilst beauty compensates our care,
　　And youth each vapour clears.

But oh! too soon we climb.
　　Scarce feeling we ascend
The gently rising hill of time,
From whence with grief we see that prime,
　　And all its sweetness end.　　　　　30

The die now cast, our station known,
　　Fond expectation past;
The thorns, which former days had sown,
To crops of late repentance grown,
　　Thro' which we toil at last.

Whilst ev'ry care 's a driving harm
　　That helps to bear us down,
Which faded smiles no more can charm,
But ev'ry tear 's a winter-storm,
　　And ev'ry look 's a frown.

Till with succeeding ills opprest,
   For joys we hop'd to find;
By age too rumpl'd and undrest,
We gladly sinking down to rest,
   Leave following crowds behind.

A SIGH

Gentlest air, thou breath of lovers
   Vapour from a secret fire,
Which by thee itself discovers
   Ere yet daring to aspire.

Softest note of whisper'd anguish,
   Harmony's refin'dest part,
Striking, whilst thou seem'st to languish,
   Full upon the listener's heart.

Safest messenger of passion
   Stealing through a crowd of spies,
Which constrain the outward fashion,
   Close the lips and guard the eyes:

Shapeless sigh, we ne'er can show thee,
   Formed but to assault the ear,
Yet ere to their cost they know thee
   Ev'ry nymph may read thee here.

FRAGMENT AT TUNBRIDGE WELLS

For he that made, must new create us,
Ere Seneca or Epictetus,
With all their serious admonitions,
Can, for the spleen, prove good physicians.
The heart's unruly palpitation
Will not be laid by a quotation:
Nor will the spirits move the lighter
For the most celebrated writer.
Sweats, swoonings, and convulsive motions
Will not be cur'd by words and notions.
Then live, old Brown! with thy chalybeats
Which keep us from becoming idiots.

At Tunbridge let us still be drinking,
Though 'tis th' Antipodes to thinking:
Such hurry, whilst the spirit 's flying,
Such stupefaction when 'tis dying:
Yet these, and not sententious papers,
Must brighten life, and cure the vapours. . . .

THE PRODIGY

[A poem written at Tunbridge Wells, anno 1706, on the admiration that
many expressed at a gentleman's being in love, and their endeavours to
dissuade him from it, with some advice to the young ladies how to maintain
their natural prerogative.]

PROTECT the State, and let old England thrive,
Keep all crown'd heads this wondrous year alive;
Preserve their palaces from wind and flame,
Safe be our fleets, and be the Scotchmen tame:
Avert, kind fate; whate'er th' event might prove,
For here's a prodigy, a man in love!
Wasted and pale, he languishes in sight,
And spends in am'rous verse the sleepless night;
While happier youths, with colder spirits born,
View the distress with pity, or with scorn,   10
And maids, so long unus'd to be ador'd,
Think it portends the pestilence or sword.

How chang'd is Britain to the blooming fair,
Whom now the men no longer make their care;
But of indifference arrogantly boast,
And scarce the wine gets down some famous toast!
Not so (as still declare their works) it prov'd
When Spencer, Sidney, and when Waller lov'd,
Who with soft numbers wing'd successful darts,
Nor thought the passion less'ning to their parts.   20
Then let such patterns countenance his fire,
Whom love and verse do now afresh inspire,
'Gainst all who blame or at the fate admire;
And learn the nymphs how to regain their sway,
And make the stubborn sex once more obey;
Call back the fugitives by modest pride,
And let them fear sometimes to be denied;
Stay till their courtship may deserve that name,
And take not ev'ry look for love and flame;

To mercenary ends no charms employ,　　　　30
Nor stake their smiles against some raffled toy:
For every fop lay not th' insnaring train,
Nor lose the worthy to allure the vain.
Keep at due distance all attempts at bliss,
Nor let too near a whisper seem a kiss;
Be not the constant partner of a swain,
Except his long address that favour gain;
Nor be transported when some trifle's view
Directs his giddy choice to fix on you.
Amend whatever may your charms disgrace,　　　40
And trust not wholly to a conquering face;
Nor be your motions rude, coquet or wild,
Shuffling or lame, as if in nursing spoil'd:
Slight not th' advantage of a graceful mien,
Tho' Paris gave the prize to beauty's queen,
When Juno mov'd, Venus could scarce be seen.
And if to fashion past you can't submit,
Pretend at least to some degree of wit;
The men who fear now with it to accost,
Still love the name, tho' you've the habit lost.　　50
Assert your pow'r in early days begun;
Born to undo, be not yourselves undone,
Condemn'd, and cheap, as easy to be won.
If thus, like sov'reigns you maintain your ground,
The rebels at your feet will soon be found:
And when with wise authority you move,
No new surprise, no prodigy will prove,
To see a man, or the whole race in love.

THE CAUTIOUS LOVERS

Sylvia, let's from the crowd retire:
　　For what to you and me,
(Who but each other do desire)
　　Is all that here we see?

Apart we'll live, tho' not alone:
　　For who *alone* can call
Those who in deserts live with one,
　　If in that one they've all?

The world a vast meander is,
  Where hearts confus'dly stray;
Where few do hit, whilst thousands miss,
  The happy mutual way;   10

Where hands are by stern parents tied,
  Who oft, in Cupid's scorn,
Do for the widow'd state provide,
  Before that love is born:

Where some too soon themselves misplace,
  Then in another find
The only temper, wit, or face   20
  That could affect their mind.

Others (but oh! avert that fate!)
  A well-chose object change.
Fly, Sylvia, fly ere 'tis too late,
  Fall'n nature's prone to range.

And, tho' in heat of love we swear
  More than perform we can,
No goddess you, but woman are,
  And I no more than man.

Th' impatient Sylvia heard thus long,
  Then with a smile replied: 30
These bands could ne'er be very strong
  Which accidents divide.

Who e'er was mov'd yet to go down
  By such o'er-cautious fear,
Or for one lover left the town,
  Who might have numbers here?

Your heart, 'tis true, is worth them all,
  And still preferr'd the first;
But since confess'd so apt to fall,   4
  'Tis good to fear the worst.

In ancient history we meet
  A flying nymph betray'd,
Who, had she kept in fruitful Crete,
  New conquest might have made.

And sure, as on the beach she stood
    To view the parting sails,
She curs'd herself more than the flood,
    Or the conspiring gales.

False Theseus, since thy vows are broke,
    May following nymphs beware: 50
Methinks I hear how thus he spoke,
    And will not trust too far.

In love, in play, in war,
    They best themselves acquit,
Who, tho' their int'rests shipwreckt are,
    Keep unreprov'd their wit.

ADAM POSED

COULD our first father, at his toilsome plough,
Thorns in his path and labour on his brow,
Cloth'd only in a rude, unpolish'd skin,
Could he a vain fantastic nymph have seen,
In all her airs, in all her antic graces,
Her various fashions, and more various faces,
How had it pos'd that skill, which late assign'd
Just appellations to each several kind,
A right idea of the sight to frame!
T' have guessed from what new element she came,   10
To have hit the wav'ring form, or giv'n this thing a
    name!

RALPH'S REFLECTIONS

UPON THE ANNIVERSARY OF HIS WEDDING

THIS day, says Ralpho, I was free,
    'Till one unlucky hour
And some few mutter'd words by me
    Put freedom past my pow'r.

Th' expressions I remember well,
    For better or for worse,
Till death us part, I take thee Nell,
    (That is, I take a purse.)

'Tis gold must make that pill go down,
   The priest without his fee,
Nor simple clerk, but for half-crown
   Would execution see.

Rubands, and gloves, the standers by
   To patience must incline,
Besides the hopes of a supply
   Of biscuits and of wine.

The friends that wait us to our beds
   (Who could no longer cross it)
But throw our stockings at our heads,
   Or drown us with a posset.

Oh! happy state of human life,
   If marriage be thy best!
Poor Ralpho cried, yet kiss'd his wife,
   And no remorse confess'd.

THE UNEQUAL FETTERS

COULD we stop the time that 's flying,
   Or recall it when 'tis past,
Put far off the day of dying,
   Or make youth for ever last,
To love would then be worth our cost.

But since we must lose those graces
   Which at first your hearts have won,
And you seek for in new faces
   When our spring of life is done,
It would but urge our ruin on.

Free as nature's first intention
   Was to make us, I'll be found,
Nor by subtle man's invention
   Yield to be in fetters bound
By one that walks a freer round.

Marriage does but slightly tie men,
  Whilst close pris'ners we remain:
They the larger slaves of Hymen,
  Still are begging love again
At the full length of all their chain.   20

LOVE, DEATH, AND REPUTATION

Reputation, love, and death,
(The last all bones, the first all breath,
The midst compos'd of restless fire)
From each other would retire;
Thro' the world resolv'd to stray,
Every one a several way,
Exercising as they went
Each such power as fate had lent:
Which, if it united were,
Wretched mortals could not bear: 10
But as parting friends do show
To what place they mean to go,
Correspondence to engage,
Nominate their utmost stage,
Death declar'd he would be found
Near the fatal trumpet's sound,
Or where pestilences reign,
And quacks the greater plagues maintain,
Shaking still his sandy glass
And mowing human flesh like grass.   20
Love, as next his leave he took,
Cast on both so sweet a look
As their tempers near disarm'd,
One relax'd, and t'other warmed.
Shades for his retreat he chose,
Rural plains and soft repose;
Where no dowry e'er was paid,
Where no jointure e'er was made;
No ill tongue the nymph perplex'd,
Where no forms the shepherd vex'd;   30
Where himself should be the care
Of the fond and of the fair:
Where that was they soon should know,
Au revoir ! then turn'd to go.

Reputation made a pause,
Suiting her severer laws:
Second thoughts, and third she us'd,
Weighing consequences, mus'd,
When at length to both she cried:
You two safely may divide,
To the Antipodes may fall,
And re-ascend th' encompast ball,
Certain still to meet again
In the breasts of tortur'd men,
Who by one (too far) betray'd,
Call in t'other to their aid:
Whilst I, tender, coy, and nice,
Either fix with those I grace,
Or abandoning the place,
No return my nature bears;
From green youth, or hoary hairs,
If thro' guilt or chance I sever,
I once parting, part for ever.

THERE 'S NO TO-MORROW

A FABLE IMITATED FROM SIR ROGER L'ESTRANGE

Two long had lov'd, and now the nymph desir'd
The cloak of wedlock, as the case requir'd;
Urg'd that the day he wrought her to this sorrow,
He vow'd that he would marry her to-morrow.
Again he swears, to shun the present storm,
That he to-morrow will that vow perform.
The morrows in their due successions came;
Impatient still on each, the pregnant dame
Urg'd him to keep his word, and still he swore
    same.
When tir'd at length, and meaning no redress,
But yet the lie not caring to confess,
He for his oath this salvo chose to borrow,
That he was free, since there was no to-morrow:
For when it comes in place to be employed,
'Tis then to-day: to-morrow 's ne'er enjoy'd!
The tale's a jest, the moral is a truth:
To-morrow and to-morrow cheat our youth.

In riper age, to-morrow still we cry,
Not thinking that the present day we die,
Unpractis'd all the good we had design'd: 20
There 's no to-morrow to a willing mind.

JUPITER AND THE FARMER

WHEN poets gave their god in Crete a birth,
Then Jupiter held traffic with the earth,
And had a farm to let.   The fine was high,
For much the treas'ry wanted a supply,
By Danaë's wealthy show'r exhausted quite, and dry.
But Merc'ry, who as steward kept the court,
So rack'd the rent that all who made resort
Unsatisfy'd returned, nor could agree
To use the lands, or pay his secret fee:
Till one poor clown (thought subtler than the rest   10
Thro' various projects rolling in his breast)
Consents to take it, if at his desire
All weathers tow'rds his harvest may conspire:
The frost to kill the worm, the brooding snow,
The filling rains may come, and Phœbus glow.
The terms accepted, sign'd and seal'd the lease,
His neighbour's grounds afford their due increase,
The care of heav'n; the owner's cares may cease;
Whilst the new tenant, anxious in his mind,
Now asks a show'r, now craves a rustling wind   20
To raise what that had lodged, that he the sheaves may
          bind.
The sun, th' o'er-shadowing clouds, the moist'ning dews,
He with such contrariety does choose:
So often and so oddly shifts the scene,
Whilst others load, he scarce has what to glean.

O Jupiter! with famine pinch'd he cries,
No more will I direct th' unerring skies;
No more my substance on a project lay,
No more a sullen doubt I will betray:
Let me but live to reap, do thou appoint the way.   30

FOR THE BETTER

IMITATED FROM SIR ROGER L'ESTRANGE

A QUACK, to no true skill in physic bred,
With frequent visits cursed his patient's bed,
Inquiring how he did his broths digest,
How chim'd his pulse, and how he took his rest;
If shudd'ring cold by burnings was pursu'd,
And at what time the aguish fit renew'd.
The whining wretch, each day become more faint,
In like proportion doubles his complaint;
Now swooning sweats he begs him to allay,
Now give his lungs more liberty to play,　　　　　1
And take from emptied veins these scorching heat
　　　away:
Or, if he saw the danger did increase,
To warn him fair, and let him part in peace.
My life for yours, no hazard in your case,
The quack replies.　Your voice, your pulse, your face
Good signs afford and what you seem to feel
Proceeds from vapours—Your belov'd disease!
Your ignorance's screen, your what-you-please,
With which you cheat poor females of their lives,
Whilst men dispute not, so it rid their wives.　　　2
For me, I'll speak free as I've paid my fees:
My flesh consumes, I perish by degrees,
And as thro' weary nights I count my pains,
No rest is left me, and no strength remains.
All for the better, sir! the quack rejoins:
Exceeding promising are all these signs.
Falling away, your nurses can confirm,
Was ne'er in sickness thought a mark of harm:
The want of strength is for the better still,
Since men of vigour soonest fevers kill.　　　　　3
Ev'n with this gust of passion I am pleased,
For they're most patient who the most are seiz'd.
But let me see! here's that which all repels!
Then shakes, as he some formal story tells,
The treacle-water mixt with powder'd shells.
My stomach's gone (what do you infer from thence?)
Nor will with the least sustenance dispense.

The better; for, where appetite endures,
Meats intermingle and no med'cine cures.
The stomach, you must know, sir, is a part—   40
But sure, I feel death's pangs about my heart.
Nay then, farewell! I need no more attend,
The quack replies.   A sad approaching friend
Questions the sick, why he retires so fast,
Who says, because of fees I've paid the last:
And whilst all symptoms tow'rd my cure agree,
Am, for the better, dying as you see.

THE ATHEIST AND THE ACORN

METHINKS this world is oddly made,
    And ev'ry thing 's amiss,
A dull presuming atheist said,
As stretch'd, he lay beneath a shade,
    And instanced in this:

Behold, quoth he, that mighty thing,
    A pumpkin, large and round,
Is held but by a little string,
Which upwards cannot make it spring,
    Or bear it from the ground.   10

Whilst on this oak a fruit so small,
    So disproportion'd, grows,
That, who with sense surveys this All,
This universal, casual ball,
    Its ill contrivance knows.

My better judgment would have hung
    That weight upon a tree,
And left this mast, thus slightly strung,
'Mongst things which on the surface sprung,
    And small and feeble be.   20

No more the caviller could say,
    Nor further faults descry,
For as he upward, gazing lay,
An acorn, loosen'd from the stay,
    Fell down upon his eye.

Th' offended part with tears ran o'er,
　　As punish'd for the sin.
Fool! had that bough a pumpkin bore,
Thy whimsies must have work'd no more,
　　Nor skull had kept them in.   30

THE SHEPHERD PIPING TO THE FISHES

A SHEPHERD seeking with his lass,
　　To shun the heat of day,
Was seated on the shadow'd grass,
Near which a flowing stream did pass,
　　And fish within it play.

To Phillis he an angle gave,
　　And bid her toss the line.
For sure, quoth he, each fish must have,
Who does not seek to be thy slave,
　　A harder heart than mine.   10

Assemble here you wat'ry race,
　　Transportedly he cries,
And if, when you behold her face,
You e'er desire to quit the place,
　　You see not with my eyes.

But you, perhaps, are by the ear
　　More easy to be caught,
If so I have my bagpipe here,
The only music that's not dear,
　　Nor in great cities bought.   20

So sprightly was the tune he chose,
　　And often did repeat,
That Phillis, tho' not up she rose,
Kept time with every thrilling close,
　　And jigg'd upon her seat.

But not a fish would nearer draw,
　　No harmony or charms
Their frozen blood, it seems, could thaw;
Nor all they heard, nor all they saw,
　　Could woo them to such terms.   3

The angry shepherd in a pet,
  Gives o'er his wheedling arts,
And from his shoulder throws the net,
Resolv'd he would a supper get
  By force if not by parts.

Thus stated laws are always best
  To rule the vulgar throng,
Who grow more stubborn when caressed,
Or with soft rhetoric addressed,
  If taking measures wrong.   40

THE OWL DESCRIBING HER YOUNG ONES

Why was that baleful creature made,
Which seeks our quiet to invade,
And screams ill omens through the shade?

'Twas, sure, for every mortal good,
When, by wrong painting of her brood
She doom'd them for the eagle's food:

Who proffer'd safety to her tribe,
Would she but show them or describe,
And serving him, his favour bribe.

When thus she did his highness tell;   10
In looks my young do all excel,
Nor nightingales can sing so well.

You'd joy to see the pretty souls,
With waddling steps and frowzy polls,
Come creeping from their secret holes.

But I ne'er let them take the air,
The fortune-hunters do so stare,
And heiresses indeed they are.

This ancient yew three hundred years,
Has been possess'd by lineal heirs: 20
The males extinct, now all is theirs.

I hope I've done their beauties right,
Whose eyes outshine the stars by night,
Their muffs and tippets are so white.

The king of cedars waiv'd his power,
And swore he'd fast ev'n from that hour,
Ere he'd such lady birds devour.

Th' agreement seal'd, on either part,
The owl now promis'd, from her heart,
All his night dangers to divert;   30

As sentinel to stand and whoop,
If single fowl, or shoal, or troop,
Should at his palace aim or stoop.

But home one evening without meat
The eagle comes, and takes his seat,
Where they did these conditions treat.

The mother owl was prowl'd away,
To seek abroad for needful prey,
And forth the misses came to play.

What's here! the hungry monarch cried,   40
When near him living flesh he spied,
With which he hoped to be supplied.

But recollecting 'twas the place
Where he'd so lately promis'd grace,
To an enchanting, beauteous race,

He paus'd a while, and kept his maw,
With sober temperance, in awe,
Till all their lineaments he saw.

What are these things, and of what sex,
At length he cried, with vulture's becks,   50
And shoulders higher than their necks?

These wear no palatines, nor muffs,
Italian silks, nor Doyley stuffs,
But motley calicoes and ruffs.

Nor brightness in their eyes is seen,
But through the film a dusky green,
And like old Margery is their mien.

Then for my supper they're designed,
Nor can be of that lovely kind,
To whom my pity was inclin'd.   60

No more delays: as soon as spoke,
The plumes are stript, the grisles broke,
And near the feeder was to choke.

When now return'd the grisly dame
(Whose family was out of frame)
Against league-breakers does exclaim.

How! quoth the lord of soaring fowls,
(Whilst horribly she wails and howls)
Were then your progeny but owls?

I thought some phœnix was their sire,   70
Who did those charming looks inspire,
That you prepar'd me to admire.

Upon yourself the blame be laid,
My talons you've to blood betray'd,
And lied in every word you said.

Faces or books, beyond their worth extoll'd,
Are censured most, and thus to pieces pull'd.

THE HOG, THE SHEEP, AND GOAT, CARRYING
TO A FAIR

Who does not wish ever to judge aright,
    And in the course of life's affairs,
To have a quick and far-extended sight,
    Tho' it too often multiplies his cares?
And who has greater sense, but greater sorrow shares?

Thus felt th' swine, now carrying to the knife,
    And whilst the lamb and silent goat
In the same fatal cart lay void of strife,
    He widely stretches his foreboding throat,
Deaf'ning the easy crew with his outrageous note.   10

The angry driver chides th' unruly beast,
   And bids him all his noise forbear;
Nor be more loud, nor clamorous than the rest,
   Who with him travelled to the neighb'ring fair,
And quickly should arrive and be unfetter'd there.

This, quoth the swine, I do believe is true,
   And see we're very near the town;
Whilst these poor fools, of short and bounded view,
   Think 'twill be well when you have set them down,
And eas'd one of her milk, the other of her gown.   2

But all the dreadful butchers in a row,
   To my far-searching thoughts appear,
Who know indeed, we to the shambles go,
   Whilst I, whom none but Beelzebub would shear,
Nor but his dam would milk, must for my carcase fear.

But tell me then, will it prevent thy fate?
   The rude, unpitying farmer cries;
If not, the wretch who tastes his suff'rings late,
   Not he, who thro' th' unhappy future pries,
Must of the two be held most fortunate and wise?   3

THE SHEPHERD AND THE CALM

SOOTHING his passions with a warbling sound,
A shepherd-swain lay stretch'd upon the ground;
Whilst all were moved, who their attention lent,
Or with the harmony in chorus went
To something less than joy, yet more than dull content
(Between which two extremes true pleasure lies,
O'errun by fools, unreach'd at by the wise.)
But yet, a fatal prospect to the sea
Would often draw his greedy sight away.
He saw the barques unlading on the shore,
And guessed their wealth, then scorn'd his little store:
Then would that little lose, or else would make it more
To merchandise converted is the fold,
The bag, the bottle, and the hurdles sold;
The dog was chang'd away, the pretty skell

Whom he had fed, and taught, and lov'd so well.
In vain the Phillis wept, which heretofore
Receiv'd his presents, and his garlands wore.
False and upbraided, he forsakes the downs,
Nor courts her smiles, nor fears the ocean's frowns.   20
For smooth it lay, as if one single wave
Made all the sea, nor winds that sea could heave;
Which blew no more than might his sails supply:
Clear was the air below, and Phœbus laugh'd on high.
With this advent'rer everything combines,
And gold to gold his happy voyage joins.
But not so prosp'rous was the next essay,
For rugged blasts, encounter'd on the way,
Scarce could the men escape, the deep had all their prey.
Our broken merchant in the wreck was thrown   30
Upon those lands which once had been his own;
Where other flocks now pastur'd on the grass,
And other Corydons had woo'd his lass.
A servant, for small profits, there he turns,
Yet thrives again, and less and less he mourns;
Re-purchases again the abandon'd sheep,
Which sad experience taught him now to keep.
When from that very bank, one halcyon day,
On which he lean'd when tempted to the sea,
He notes a calm: the winds and waves were still,   40
And promis'd what nor winds nor waves fulfil,
A settl'd quiet, and conveyance sure,
To him that wealth by traffic would procure.
But the rough part the shepherd now performs,
Reviles the cheat, and at the flatt'ry storms.
Ev'n thus (quoth he) you seem'd all rest and ease,
You sleeping tempests, you untroubl'd seas,
That ne'er to be forgot, that luckless hour,
In which I put my fortunes in your pow'r;
Quitting my slender, but secure estate,   50
My undisturb'd repose, my sweet retreat,
For treasures which you ravish'd in a day,
But swept my folly with my goods away.
Then smile no more, nor these false shows employ,
Thou momentary calm, thou fleeting joy;
No more on me shall these fair signs prevail,
Some other novice may be won to sail,
Give me a certain fate in th' obscurest vale.

THE LORD AND THE BRAMBLE

To view his stately walks and groves,
    A man of pow'r and place
Was hast'ning on; but as he roves,
His foe the slighted bramble proves,
    And stops his eager pace.

That shrub was qualified to bite,
    And now there went a tale,
That this injurious partial wight
Had bid his gard'ner rid it quite,
    And throw it o'er the pale.   10

Often the briar had wish'd to speak,
    That this might not be done;
But from the abject and the weak,
Who no important figure make,
    What statesman does not run?

But clinging now about his waist,
    Ere he had time to fly,
My lord (quoth he) for all your haste,
I'll know why I must be displac'd,
    And 'mongst the rubbish lie.   20

Must none but buffle-headed trees,
    Within your ground be seen?
Or tap'ring yews court here the breeze,
That, like some beaux whom time does freeze,
    At once look old and green?

I snarl, 'tis true, and sometimes scratch
    A tender-footed squire,
Who does a rugged tartar catch,
When me he thinks to over-match,
    And jeers at my attire.   30

As to yourself, who 'gainst me fret,
    E'en give this project o'er:
For know, where'er my root is set,
These rambling twigs will passage get,
    And vex you more and more.

No wants, no threat'nings, nor the jail
  Will curb an angry wit:
Then think not to chastise or rail:
Appease the man, if you'd prevail,
  Who some sharp satire writ.   40

THE YOUNG RAT AND HIS DAM, THE COCK
AND THE CAT

No cautions of a matron, old and sage,
Young Rattlehead to prudence could engage;
But forth the offspring of her bed would go,
Nor reason gave, but that he *would* do so.
Much counsel was, at parting, thrown away,
Ev'n all the mother rat to son could say;
Who followed him with utmost reach of sight,
Then, lost in tears, and in abandon'd plight,
Turn'd to her mournful cell, and bid the world good-night.
But Fortune, kinder than her boding thought,   10
In little time the vagrant homeward brought,
Rais'd in his mind, and mended in his dress,
Who the *bel-air* did every way confess,
Had learnt to flour his wig, nor brush'd away
The falling meal, that on his shoulders lay:
And from a nut-shell, wimbl'd by a worm,
Took snuff, and could the Government reform.
The mother, weeping from maternal love,
To see him thus prodigiously improve,
Expected mighty changes too, within,   20
And wisdom to avoid the cat, and gin.
Whom did you chiefly note, sweetheart, quoth she,
Of all the strangers you abroad did see?
Who grac'd you most, or did your fancy take?
The younger rat then curs'd a noisy rake
That barr'd the best acquaintance he could make,
And fear'd him so, he trembl'd ev'ry part,
Nor to describe him scarce could have the heart.
High on his feet (quoth he) himself he bore,
And terribly, in his own language, swore;   30
A feather'd arm came out from either side,
Which loud he clapp'd, and combatants defied,
And to each leg a bayonet was tied:

And certainly his head with wounds was sore,
For that, and both his cheeks, a sanguine colour wore.
Near him there lay the creature I admir'd,
And for a friend by sympathy desir'd:
His make like ours as far as tail and feet,
With coat of fur in parallel did meet,
Yet seeming of a more exalted race,   40
Tho' humble meekness beautified his face:
A purring sound compos'd his gentle mind,
Whilst frequent slumbers did his eyelids bind,
Whose soft, contracted paw lay calmly still,
As if unused to prejudice, or kill.
I paus'd a while to meditate a speech,
And now was stepping just within his reach,
When that rude clown began his hectoring cry,
And made me for my life, and from th' attempt to fly.
Indeed 'twas time, the shiv'ring beldam said,   50
To scour the plain and be of life afraid.
Thou base, degen'rate seed of injur'd rats,
Thou veriest fool (she cried) of all my brats!
Would'st thou have shaken hands with hostile cats,
And dost thou not thine own and country's foe
At this expense of time and travel know?
Alas! that swearing, staring, bullying thing,
That tore his throat and bluster'd with his wing,
Was but some paltry, dunghill, craven cock,
Who serves the early household for a clock,   60
And we his oats and barley often steal,
Nor fear he should revenge his pilfer'd meal:
Whilst that demure, and seeming harmless puss
Herself and mewing chits regales with us.
If then, of useful sense thou gain'st no more
Than ere thou'dst past the threshold of my door,
Be here, my son, content to dress and dine,
Steeping the list of beauties in thy wine,
And neighb'ring vermin with false gloss outshine.
    Amongst mankind a thousand fops we see   70
Who in their rambles learn no more than thee:
Cross o'er the Alps, and make the tour of France
To learn a paltry song or antic dance;
Bringing their noddles and valises pack'd
With mysteries from shops and tailors rack'd:
But what may prejudice their native land,

Whose troops are raising, or whose fleet is mann'd,
Ne'er moves their thoughts, nor do they understand.
Thou, my dear Rattlehead, and such as these
Might keep at home and brood on sloth and ease,   80
Whilst others, more adapted to the age,
May vig'rously in warlike feats engage,
And live on foreign spoils, or dying thin the stage.

A TALE OF THE MISER AND THE POET

[Written about the year 1709.]

A WIT, transported with enditing,
Unpay'd, unprais'd, yet ever writing,
Who, for all fights and fav'rite friends,
Had poems at his finger ends;
For new events was still providing,
Yet now desirous to be riding,
He pack'd up ev'ry ode and ditty
And in vacation left the city.
So rapt with figures and allusions,
With secret passions, sweet confusions;   10
With sentences from plays well-known,
A thousand couplets of his own,
That ev'n the chalky road looked gay,
And seem'd to him the Milky Way.
But Fortune, who the ball is tossing,
And poets ever will be crossing,
Misled the steed, which ill he guided,
Where several gloomy paths divided.
The steepest in descent he follow'd,
Enclos'd by rocks which time had hollow'd,   20
Till he believed, alive and booted,
He'd reach'd the shades by Homer quoted.
But all that he could there discover
Was in a pit, with thorns grown over,
Old Mammon digging, straining, sweating,
As bags of gold he thence was getting;
Who, when reproved for such dejections
By him who lived on high reflections,
Replied: Brave sir, your time is ended,
And poetry no more befriended.   30

I hid this coin when Charles was swaying,
When all was riot, masking, playing;
When witty beggars were in fashion,
And learning had o'errun the nation:
But since mankind is so much wiser,
And none is valued like the miser,
I thence it draw, and now these sums
In proper soil grow up to plums,
Which gather'd once, in that rich minute,
We rule the world and all that's in it.   40

But, quoth the poet, can you raise
As well as plum-trees groves of bays?
Where you, which I would choose much rather,
May fruits of reputation gather?
Will men of quality and spirit
Regard you for intrinsic merit?
And seek you out, before your betters,
For conversation, wit, and letters?

Fool, quoth the churl, who knew no breeding,
Have these been times for such proceeding?   50
Instead of honour'd and rewarded,
Are you not slighted or discarded?
What have you met with, but disgraces?
Your Prior could not keep in places,
And your Van Burgh had found no quarter
But for his dabbling in the mortar.
Rowe no advantages could hit on,
Till verse he left, to write *North Briton*.
Philips, who's by the *Shilling* known,
Ne'er saw a shilling of his own.   60
Meets Philomela, in the town
Her due proportion of renown?
What pref'rence has Ardelia seen,
T' expel, tho' she could write the *Spleen*?
Of coach, or tables can you brag,
Or better clothes than poet Rag?
Do wealthy kindred, when they meet you,
With kindness or distinction greet you?
Or have your lately flatter'd heroes
Enrich'd you like the Roman Maroes?   70

No—quoth the man of broken slumbers.
Yet we have patrons for our numbers:
There are Mecænas's among them.

Quoth Mammon, pray sir, do not wrong 'em.
But in your censures use a conscience,
Nor charge great men with thriftless nonsense:
Since they, as your own poets sing,
Now grant no worth in anything
But so much money as 'twill bring.
Then, never more from your endeavours   80
Expect preferment, or less favours.
But if you'll 'scape contempt, or worse,
Be sure put money in your purse:
Money! which only can relieve you
When fame and friendship will deceive you.

Sir (quoth the poet humbly bowing,
And all that he had said allowing)
Behold me and my airy fancies
Subdu'd like giants in romances.
I here submit to your discourses,   90
Which, since experience too enforces,
I, in that solitary pit,
Your gold withdrawn, will hide my wit:
Till time, which hastily advances,
And gives to all new turns and chances,
Again may bring it into use;
Roscommons may again produce,
New Augustean days revive,
When wit shall please and poets thrive.
Till when, let those converse in private   100
Who taste what others don't arrive at:
Yielding that Mammonists surpass us,
And let the Bank out-swell Parnassus.

THE TRADESMAN AND THE SCHOLAR

A CITIZEN of mighty pelf,
But much a blockhead in himself,
Disdain'd a man of shining parts,
Master of sciences and arts,

Who left his book scarce once a day
For sober coffee, smoke, or tea;
Nor spent more money in the town
Than bought, when need requir'd, a gown;
Which way of living much offends
The alderman, who gets and spends,   10
And grudges him the vital air,
Who drives no trade and takes no care.
Why bookworm! to him once he cried,
Why, setting thus the world aside,
Dost thou thy useless time consume
Enclos'd within a lonely room,
And poring damnify thy wit
Till not for men or manners fit?
Hop'st thou, with urging of thy vein,
To spin a fortune from thy brain?   20
Or gain a patron that shall raise
Thy solid state, for empty praise?
No! trust not to your soothings vile,
Receiv'd per me 's the only style.
Your book 's but frown'd on by my lord,
If mine's uncross'd, I reach his board.
In slighting yours he shuts his hand,
Protracting mine, devolves the land.
Then let advantage be the test
Which of us two ev'n writes the best.   30
Besides, I often scarlet wear,
And strut to church just next the Mayor;
Whilst rusty black, with inch of band,
Is all the dress you understand;
Who in the pulpit thresh to please,
While I below can snore at ease.
Yet, if you prove me there a sinner,
I let you go without a dinner.
This prate was so beneath the sense
Of one who wisdom could dispense,   40
Unheard, or unreturn'd, it past.
But war now laid the city waste,
And plunder'd goods profusely fell
By length of pike, not length of ell.
Abroad th' inhabitants are forc'd,
From shops, and trade, and wealth divorc'd.
The student, leaving but his book,

The tumult of the place forsook.
In foreign parts, one tells his tale,
How rich he'd been, how quick his sale,   50
Which does for scanty alms prevail:
The chance of war whilst he deplores,
And dines at charitable doors,
The man of letters, known by fame,
Was welcom'd wheresoe'er he came,
Still, potentates entreat his stay,
Whose coaches meet him on the way,
And universities contest
Which shall exceed or use him best.
Amaz'd the burgomaster sees,   60
On foot and scorn'd, such turns as these,
And sighing, now deplores too late
His cumb'rous trash and shallow pate:
Since, loaded but with double chest
Of learned head, and honest breast,
The scholar moves from place to place,
And finds in every climate grace.

Wit and the arts, on that foundation rais'd,
(Howe'er the vulgar are with shows amaz'd)
Is all that recommends or can be justly prais'd.   70

MAN'S INJUSTICE TOWARDS PROVIDENCE

A THRIVING merchant who no loss sustained,
In little time a mighty fortune gained.
No pirate seized his still returning freight,
Nor found'ring vessel sunk with its own weight,
No ruin enter'd through dissever'd planks,
No wreck at sea, nor in the public banks.
Aloft he sails, above the reach of chance,
And does in pride, as fast as wealth, advance.
His wife, too, had her town and country seat,
And rich in purse, concludes her person great.   10
A duchess wears not so much gold and lace;
Then 'tis with her an undisputed case,
The finest petticoat must take the place.
Her rooms, anew at ev'ry christ'ning drest,

Put down the court, and vex the city guest:
Grinning mulattos in true ermine stare;
The best Japan, and clearest China ware
Are but as common Delft and English lacquer there;
No luxury's by either unenjoy'd,
Or cost withheld, tho' awkwardly employ'd.   20
How comes this wealth? a country friend demands,
Who scarce could live on product of his lands,
How is it that when trading is so bad
That some are broke, and some with fears run mad,
You can in better state yourself maintain,
And your effects still unimpair'd remain?
My industry, he cried, is all the cause:
Sometimes I interlope and slight the laws:
I wiser measures than my neighbours take,
And better speed, who wiser bargains make.   30
I knew the Smyrna Fleet would fall a prey,
And therefore sent no vessel out that way;
My busy factors prudently I choose,
And in strait bonds their friends and kindred noose.
At home I to the public funds advance,
Whilst, under-hand in fee with hostile France,
I care not for your Tourvilles and Du Barts
No more than for the rocks and shelves in charts:
My own sufficiency creates my gain,
Rais'd and secur'd by this unfailing brain.   40
This idle vaunt had scarcely past his lips,
When tidings came his ill-provided ships,
Some thro' the want of skill, and some of care,
Were lost or back return'd without their fare.
From bad to worse, each day his state declin'd,
Till leaving town, and wife, and debts behind,
To his acquaintance at a rural seat
He skulks and humbly sues for a retreat.
Whence comes this change?   Has wisdom left that head
(His friend demands) where such right schemes were
          bred?   50
What frenzy, what delirium mars the skull
Which fill'd the chests, and was itself so full?
Here interrupting, sadly he replied,
In me's no change, but fate must all things guide.
To Providence I attribute my loss.

Vain-glorious man does thus the praise engross
When prosp'rous days around him spread their beams:
But, if revolv'd to opposite extremes,
Still his own sense he fondly will prefer,
And Providence, not he, in his affairs must err!   60

THE DOG AND HIS MASTER

No better dog e'er kept his master's door
Than honest Snarl, who spar'd not rich nor poor,
But gave the alarm when anyone drew nigh,
Not let pretended friends pass fearless by:
For which reprov'd, as better fed than taught,
He rightly thus expostulates the fault.

To keep the house from rascals was my charge:
The task was great, and the commission large.
Nor did your worship e'er declare your mind
That to the begging crew it was confin'd,   10
Who shrink an arm, or prop an able knee,
Or turn up eyes till they're not seen, nor see;
To thieves who know the penalty of stealth
And fairly stake their necks against your wealth;
These are the known delinquents of the times,
And whips and Tyburn testify their crimes:
But since to me there was by nature lent
An exquisite discerning by the scent,
I trace a flatt'rer when he fawns and leers,
A rallying wit when he commends and jeers;   20
The greedy parasite I grudging note,
Who praises the good bits that oil his throat.
I mark the lady you so fondly toast,
Who plays your gold, when all her own is lost;
The knave who fences your estate by law,
Yet still reserves an undermining flaw.
These and a thousand more, which I could tell,
Provoke my growling and offend my smell.

FANSCOMB BARN

[In imitation of Milton.]

In Fanscomb Barn (who knows not Fanscomb Barn?)
Seated between the sides of rising hills,
Whose airy tops o'erlook the Gallic seas,
Whilst, gentle Stour, thy waters near them flow,
To beautify the seats that crown their banks;
     In this retreat
Through ages past consign'd for harbour meet,
And place of sweet repose to wand'rers poor,
The weary Strolepedon felt that ease
Which many a dangerous borough had denied   10
To him, and his Budgeta, lov'd compeer.
Nor food was wanting to that happy pair,
Who with meek aspect, and precarious tone,
Well suited to their hunger and degree,
Had mov'd the hearts of hospitable dames
To furnish such repast as nature crav'd.
Whilst more to please, the swarthy bowl appears,
Replete with liquor, globulous to sight,
And threat'ning inundation o'er the brim.
Yet ere it to the longing lips was rais'd   20
Of him who held it at its true desert,
And more than all entreated bounty priz'd,
Into the strong profundity he throws
The floating healths of females, blithe and young,
Who there had rendezvous'd in past delight,
And to stol'n plenty added clamorous mirth,
With song and dance and every jovial prank
Befitting buxom crew untied by forms:
Whilst kind Budgeta nam'd such sturdy youths
As next into her tender thoughts revolv'd,   30
And now were straggling east, and west, and south,
Hoof-beating and at large as chance directs,
Still shifting paths, lest men (tho' styl'd of peace)
Should urge their calmer thoughts to iron war,
Or force them to promote coercive laws,
Beating that hemp which oft entraps their lives,
Or into cordage pleated and amass'd,
Deprives unruly flesh of tempting skin.
Thus kind remembrance brought the absent near,

And hasten'd the return of either's pledge.   40
Brown were the toasts, but not unsav'ry found
To fancies clear'd by exercise and air,
Which the spirituous nectar still improves,
And gliding now thro' ev'ry cherish'd vein,
New warmth diffused, new cogitations bred,
With self-conceit of person, and of parts.
When Strolepedon (late distorted wight,
Limb-wanting to the view, and all mis-shap'd)
Permits a pinion'd arm to fill the sleeve,
Erst pendant, void, and waving with the wind,   50
The timber leg obsequiously withdraws,
And gives to that of bone precedence due.
Thus undisguis'd that form again he wears
Which damsel fond had drawn from household toils,
And strict behest of parents, old and scorn'd;
Whilst farther yet his intellects confess
The boozy spell dilated and enhanc'd,
Ripe for description and set turns of speech,
Which to congenial spouse were thus address'd:
My wife (acknowledged such thro' maunding tribes,   60
As long as mutual love, the only law,
Of hedge or barn, can bind our easy faiths),
Be thou observant of thy husband's voice,
Sole auditor of flights and figures bold:
Know that the valley which we hence descry
Richly adorn'd, is Fanscomb Bottom call'd:
But whether from these walls it takes the name,
Or they from that, let antiquaries tell,
And men well-read in stories obsolete,
Whilst such denomination either claims,   70
As speaks affinity contiguous—
Thence let thy scatter'd sight, and oft-griev'd smell,
Engulf the sweets and colours free dispos'd
To flowers promiscuous and redundant plants.
And (if the drowsy vapour will admit,
Which from the bowl soon triumphs o'er thy lids,
And thee the weaker vessel still denotes)
With looks erect observe the verdant slope
Of graceful hills, fertile in bush and brake,
Whose height attain'd, th' expatiated downs   80
Shall wider scenes display of rural glee,
Where banner'd lords and fair escutcheon'd knights,

With gentle squires, and the staff-griping clown,
Pursue the trembling prey impetuous;
Which yet escaping, when the night returns,
And downy beds enfold their careless limbs,
More wakeful Trundle (knapsack-bearing cur)
Follows the scent untrac'd by nobler hounds,
And brings to us the fruit of all their toil.

    Thus sung the bard, whom potent liquor rais'd,   9ϵ
Nor so contented, wish'd sublimer aid.
Ye wits! (he cried) ye poets! (loiterers vain,
Who like to us, in idleness and want,
Consume fantastic hours) hither repair,
And tell to list'ning mendicants the cause
Of wonders, here observ'd but not discuss'd:
Where the White Sparrow never soil'd her plumes,
Nor the dull russet clothes the Snowy Mouse.
To Helicon you might the spring compare
That flows near Pickersdane, renowned stream,   10ᴄ
Which, for disport and play, the youths frequent,
Who, train'd in learned school of ancient Wye,
First at this fount suck in the Muses' lore,
When, mixt with product of the Indian cane,
They drink delicious draughts, and part inspir'd,
Fit for the banks of Isis, or of Cam,
(For Cam and Isis to the bard were known,
A servitor when young in college hall,
Tho' vagrant liberty he early chose,
Who yet, when drunk, retain'd poetic phrase).   11ᴄ
Nor should (quoth he) that well, o'erhung with shade,
Amidst those neighb'ring trees of dateless growth,
Be left unfathom'd by your nicer skill,
Who thence could extricate a thousand charms,
Or to oblivious Lethe might convert
The stagnant waters of the sleepy pool.
But most unhappy was that Morphean sound
For lull'd Budgeta, who had long desir'd
Dismission from fair tales, not throughly scann'd,
Thinking her love a sympathy confest,   12ᴄ
When the word sleepy parted from his lips,
Sunk affable and easy to that rest
Which straw affords to mind unvex'd with cares.

A PASTORAL

BETWEEN MENALCUS AND DAMON ON THE APPEARANCE OF THE
ANGELS TO THE SHEPHERDS ON OUR SAVIOUR'S BIRTHDAY

MENALCUS.

DAMON, whilst thus we nightly watches keep,
Breaking the gentle bands of downy sleep,
Lest to the greedy wolves, that hungry stray,
Our wand'ring flocks become an easy prey,
Do thou, for song renown'd, some one recite,
To charm the season and deceive the night.
　　Whether thou Sampson's nervous strength wilt choose
And in bold numbers exercise thy Muse?
Or if to tender subjects more inclin'd,
That move soft pity and dissolve the mind,　　　　　　10
Thou Joseph's story rather wilt rehearse,
And weep o'er Benjamin in melting verse,
Begin, whilst list'ning to thy voice, we lie,
Nor mind the whist'ling winds that o'er us fly.
So! Jesse's son, upon these plains, when young,
Watch'd o'er his flocks, and so the shepherd sung.

DAMON.

So rais'd indeed, that youth his voice divine,
Fir'd with the promis'd glories of his line,
As if on heaven's high mount himself had trod,
And seen his seed ascend the seat of God.　　　　　　20
　　Oh! had he lately on our pastures been,
And heard the tidings, and the vision seen,
When heav'nly spirits, cloth'd in robes of light,
Broke the thick shadows, and expell'd the night,
Proclaiming peace below, and praise above,
And op'ning all the mysteries of love,
How had he then, above all other skill'd,
In raptures sung of prophesies fulfill'd?
Our gath'ring flocks upon the splendour gaz'd—
The weary slept not, nor the hungry graz'd,　　　　　30
Their leaders, by them stood, delighted and amaz'd.
A pleasing wonder, tho' allayed with fear,
Fill'd every breast and opened every ear,
When thus begun the messengers of heaven:

To you a Child is born, to you a Son is giv'n,
Praises they gave, and titles did increase:
Wonderful! Counsellor! and Prince of Peace!
Long since Emanuel, by the prophet styl'd,
Now God with us! they call'd the glorious child.

But hold, a shepherd while his flock does feed,   40
Must choose a subject suited to his reed,
Nor with mistaken strength attempt the sky,
But o'er the plains with easy motion fly.
Enough by us, Menalcus, may be said
Of the first shepherds and that lovely maid
Whose eyes could seven years servitude ally,
And make them doubl'd seem but as a day.

Now, to the silver streams their flock they led,
Now, where the friendly beech his arms had spread
Wide open to invite 'em to his shade,   50
Behold the happy pair, securely laid.
Oh Israel! how did heav'n thy joys approve,
Who plac'd thy profit where it plac'd thy love?
This be my subject while with reverend awe
My words, from what they cannot reach, withdraw.
Begin my Muse, begin the tender song,
The season shan't be cold, nor shall the night be long.

MENALCUS.

As much this song (at other times approv'd)
Would grate thy hearers with those wonders mov'd,
As if wild gourds were offer'd to the taste,   60
When the full vine with purple fruit was grac'd,
    As if Dametas should to sing incline,
And raise his voice when we expected thine.
    But let thy Muse attempt that nobler song,
The season shan't be cold, nor shall the night be long.

DAMON.

Then be it so, tho' much I fear to try
The lofty measures of a flight so high:
The fallen moon had now her beams withdrawn,
And left the skies, ere morning light could dawn.
The swains were silent, and the flocks were still,   70
The rapid stream that flows from yonder hill,
Did by its winding banks so softly stray
As if it meant, unseen, to steal away.

A general darkness o'er the world was spread,
And not one star would show his trembling head,
Conscious, no doubt (their dwelling being so nigh)
Of greater glory breaking from the sky.
   And lo! it came.   Th' Eternal Princes came,
Gently reclin'd on hills of harmless flame,
Upon the wind's officious wings they flew,   80
And fairer seem'd still as they nearer drew.
Mysterious wreaths upon their heads they wore,
And in their hands the smiling olive bore,
Emblems, no doubt, of what they came to move,
For all their words were peace, and all their looks were
    love.
But ne'er by me, the vision be expressed:
By the sun's rising from the radiant east!
But ne'er by me their voices be compar'd
To Pan's own notes when on the mountains heard.
But ne'er by me be that transcendent show   90
Liken'd to aught we glorious call below.
Night, in her sable mantle wrapt her head,
And with unusual haste, to lower worlds she fled.
   Fear, that at distance, had our hearts possessed,
To softer passions yielded ev'ry breast,
When thus began the messengers of heav'n,
To you a Child is born, to you a Son is giv'n.
   Such joy as ends the harvest's happy toil,
Such joy as when the victors part the spoil,
Upon your ransom'd heads shall ever smile.   100
   When to full stature and perfection grown,
Possess'd of holy David's sacred throne,
He shall, th' immortal and triumphant Boy,
Th' infernal powers and all their rule destroy:
The cursed serpent's head his weight shall feel,
And threaten'd vengeance for his bruised heel.
The flaming cherub shall his charge remit,
And Paradise again be open set.
Angels and God shall dwell with men below,
And men releas'd, to God and angels go.   110
Peace, to the troubl'd world he shall restore,
And bloody discord shall prevail no more.
The lamb his side by the tam'd wolf shall lay,
And o'er the aspic's den the child shall play.
Contending elements his pow'r shall own,

The winds shall at his word their rage lay down,
And the chaf'd billows shall forbear to frown.
Th' untun'd creation (by the fall of man)
Shall move harmoniously as it began.
The fruitful autumn, and the gaudy spring   120
Shall sure returns of sweets and plenty bring;
And thorough every grove the holy swains shall sing
Of weighty truths preserv'd in sacred rhymes,
T' instruct the pastors of succeeding times
In the soft rules of charity and love,
Goodwill to men and praise to heaven above.
And thou, poor Bethlehem, enclos'd with shade,
Shalt thro' all ages be illustrious made,
Since in thy bosom the Redeemer laid:
Thousands in Judea did thy state despise,   130
Thousands in Judea now thy lot shall prize.
Now Beor's son, the star by thee foretold,
Newly adorn'd in pointed rays of gold,
Calls from thy learned east th' adoring kings,
And ev'ry one a several tribute brings;
Sabean odours and Arabian ore
Shall now be offer'd from their choicest store.
Go with them, shepherds, go, and with like faith adore.
    But see! whilst in these pleasing paths I stray,
Night has resign'd her rule to rising day: 140
Behind those eastern hills the sun appears,
And the gay horizon about him cheers.
Our joyful flocks the cheerful morning view,
And from their fleeces shake the orient dew.
No more, Menalcus, we no more must sing,
But now our sheep to the fresh pastures bring.

MENALCUS.

Oh! happy shepherd, favour'd with that sight,
That can when but repeated, thus delight.
    Not flow'ry garlands in the pride of May,
Nor rural presents can thy merits pay.   150
Not our first lambs or choicest fruits that grow
Enough, alas! our gratitude can show!
There shall a bowl of antique date be thine,
And Joseph's 'twas by which he did divine;
Upon the sides is carv'd in works of gold,
The mystic sense of what thou dost unfold.

Clusters of grapes about its borders twine,
That seem, when fill'd, to have produc'd the wine.
To me, by long inheritance, it came,
Now thy reward and witness to thy fame.   160
   When night returns, repeat again thy song,
The season sha'nt be cold, nor shall it then be long.

JEALOUSY IS THE RAGE OF MAN

WHILST with his falling wings, the courtly dove
Sweeps the low earth and singles out his love,
Now murmurs soft, then with a rolling note
Extends his crop, and fills his am'rous throat,
On ev'ry side accosts the charming fair,
Turns round and bows with an enticing air:
She, carelessly neglecting all his pain,
Or shifts her ground, or pecks the scatter'd grain.
But if he cease, and through the flight would range,
(For though renown'd for truth, ev'n doves will change) 10
The mildness of her nature laid aside,
The seeming coldness, and the careless pride,
On the next rival in a rage she flies:
Smooth ev'ry clinging plume with anger lies,
Employs in feeble fight her tender beck,
And shakes the fav'rite's parti-colour'd neck.
Thus, jealousy through ev'ry species moves,
And if so furious, in the gall-less doves,
No wonder that th' experienc'd Hebrew sage
Of man pronounc'd it the extremest rage.   20

THE SPLEEN

A PINDARIC POEM

WHAT art thou, Spleen, which ev'ry thing dost ape?
   Thou Proteus to abus'd mankind,
   Who never yet thy real cause could find,
Or fix thee to remain in one continued shape.
   Still varying thy perplexing form,
   Now a Dead Sea thou'lt represent,
   A calm of stupid discontent,

Then, dashing on the rocks, wilt rage into a storm.
   Trembling sometimes thou dost appear,
   Dissolved into a panic fear;   1
   On sleep intruding dost thy shadows spread,
   Thy gloomy terrors round the silent bed,
And crowd with boding dreams the melancholy head;
   Or, when the midnight hour is told,
   And drooping lids thou still dost waking hold,
   Thy fond delusions cheat the eyes:
   Before them antic spectres dance,
Unusual fires their pointed heads advance,
   And airy phantoms rise.
   Such was the monstrous vision seen   2
When Brutus (now beneath his cares opprest,
And all Rome's fortunes rolling on his breast,
   Before Philippi's latest field,
Before his fate did to Octavius lead)
   Was vanquish'd by the spleen.

   Falsely the mortal part we blame
   Of our depressed and pond'rous frame,
   Which, till the first degrading sin
   Let thee, its dull attendant, in,
   Still with the other did comply,   3
Nor clogg'd the active soul, dispos'd to fly,
And range the mansions of its native sky.
   Nor, whilst in his own heaven he dwelt,
   Whilst man his Paradise posses'd,
His fertile garden in the fragrant east,
   And all united odours smelt,
   No armed sweets, until thy reign,
   Could shock the sense, or in the face
   A flush't unhandsome colour place.
Now the jonquil o'ercomes the feeble brain;   4
We faint beneath the aromatic pain,
Till some offensive scent thy pow'rs appease,
And pleasure we resign for short and nauseous ease.

   In ev'ryone thou dost possess
   New are thy motions and thy dress:
   Now in some grove a list'ning friend
   Thy false suggestions must attend,

Thy whisper'd griefs, thy fancied sorrows hear,
Breath'd in a sigh, and witness'd by a tear;
    Whilst in the light and vulgar crowd,   50
    Thy slaves, more clamorous and loud,
By laughters unprovok'd thy influence too confess.
In the imperious wife thou vapours art,
    Which from o'er-heated passions rise
    In clouds to the attractive brain,
    Until descending thence again
    Thro' the o'er-cast and show'ring eyes,
    Upon her husband's soften'd heart,
    He the disputed point must yield,
Something resign of the contested field: 60
Till lordly man, born to imperial sway,
Compounds for peace, to make that right away,
And woman, arm'd with spleen, does servilely obey.

    The fool, to imitate the wits,
    Complains of thy pretended fits,
    And dullness, born with him, would lay
    Upon thy accidental sway;
    Because, sometimes, thou dost presume
    Into the ablest heads to come,
    That, often, men of thoughts refin'd,   70
    Impatient of unequal sense,
Such slow returns where they so much dispense,
Retiring from the crowd, are to thy shades inclin'd.
    O'er me alas! thou dost too much prevail:
    I feel thy force whilst I against thee rail:
I feel my verse decay, and my crampt numbers fail.
Thro' thy black jaundice, I all objects see,
    As dark and terrible as thee,
My lines decried, and my employment thought
An useless folly, or presumptuous fault: 80
    Whilst in the Muses' paths I stray,
Whilst in their groves and by their secret springs
My hand delights to trace unusual things,
And deviates from the known and common way;
    Nor will in fading silks compose
    Faintly th' inimitable rose,
Fill up an ill-drawn bird, or paint on glass
The sov'reign's blurr'd and undistinguished face,
The threat'ning angel, and the speaking ass.

Patron thou art to ev'ry gross abuse,   9
    The sullen husband's feign'd excuse,
When the ill humour with his wife he spends,
And bears recruited wit and spirits to his friends.
    The son of Bacchus pleads thy pow'r,
    As to the glass he still repairs,
    Pretends but to remove his cares,
Snatch from thy shades one gay and smiling hour,
And drown thy kingdom in a purple show'r.
When the coquette, whom ev'ry fool admires,
    Would in variety be fair,   10
    And, changing hastily the scene
    From light, impertinent and vain,
Assumes a soft and melancholy air,
And of her eyes rebates the wand'ring fires,
The careless posture, and the head reclin'd,
    The thoughtful and composed face,
Proclaiming the withdrawn, the absent mind,
Allows the fop more liberty to gaze,
Who gently for the tender cause enquires:
The cause indeed is a defect in sense,   11
Yet is the spleen alleg'd, and still the dull pretence.
    But these are thy fantastic harms,
    The tricks of thy pernicious stage,
    Which do the weaker sex engage:
Worse are the dire effects of thy more pow'rful charms.
    By thee religion, all we know,
    That should enlighten here below,
    Is veil'd in darkness and perplext
    With anxious doubts, with endless scruples vext,
And some restraint implied from each perverted text.   12
    Whilst touch-not, taste-not what is freely giv'n
Is but thy niggard voice, disgracing bounteous heav'n.
    From speech restrain'd, by thy deceits abus'd,
    To deserts banish'd, or in cells reclus'd,
    Mistaken vot'ries to the Powers Divine,
    Whilst they a purer sacrifice design,
Do but the spleen obey, and worship at thy shrine.
    In vain to chase thee ev'ry art we try,
    In vain all remedies apply,
    In vain the Indian leaf infuse,   1.
    Or the parch'd eastern berry bruise;
Some pass, in vain, those bounds and nobler liquors use.

Now harmony, in vain, we bring,
Inspire the flute and touch the string.
From harmony no help is had:
Music but soothes thee, if too sweetly sad,
And if too light, but turns thee gaily mad.
Tho' the physician's greatest gains,
Altho' his growing wealth he sees
Daily increas'd by ladies' fees,   140
Yet dost thou baffle all his studious pains.
Not skilful Lower thy source could find,
Or thro' the well-dissected body trace
The secret, the mysterious ways
By which thou dost surprise, and prey upon the mind.
Tho' in the search, too deep for human thought,
With unsuccessful toil he wrought,
Till thinking thee t' have catch'd, himself by thee
        was caught,
Retained thy prisoner, thy acknowledg'd slave,
And sank beneath thy chain to a lamented grave. 150

A PINDARIC POEM

UPON THE HURRICANE IN NOVEMBER 1703, REFERRING TO
THIS TEXT IN PSALM 148, VERSE 8: "WINDS AND STORMS
FULFILLING HIS WORD"

You have obey'd, you winds, that must fulfil
    The Great Disposer's righteous will;
Throughout the land unlimited you flew,
Nor sought, as heretofore, with friendly aid
    Only, new motion to bestow
Upon the sluggish vapours, bred below,
Condensing into mists and melancholy shade.
    No more such gentle methods you pursue,
    But marching now in terrible array,
        Undistinguish'd was your prey: 10
In vain the shrubs, with lowly bent,
Sought their destruction to prevent;
The beech in vain, with out-stretch'd arms,
Deprecates th' approaching harms;
In vain the oak (so often storm'd)

Relied upon that native force
By which already was perform'd
So much of his appointed course,
As made him, fearless of decay,
    Wait but the accomplish'd time   2
Of his long-wish'd and useful prime,
To be remov'd with honour to the sea.
    The straight and ornamental pine
    Did in the like ambition join,
    And thought his fame should ever last
When in some royal ship he stood the planted mast;
    And should again his length of timber rear,
    And new-engrafted branches wear
    Of fibrous cordage and impending shrouds,
Still trimm'd with human care, and water'd by the clouds
But oh, you trees! who solitary stood;   3
    Or you, whose numbers form'd a wood;
    You who on mountains chose to rise,
    And drew them nearer to the skies;
    Or you whom valleys late did hold
    In flexible and lighter mould;
You num'rous breth'ren of the leafy kind,
    To whatsoever use design'd,
    Now vain you found it to contend
With not, alas! one element your friend.   4
Your mother earth, thro' long preceeding rains
    (Which undermining sink below)
No more her wonted strength retains;
Nor you so fix'd within her bosom grow,
That for your sakes she can resolve to bear
    These furious shocks of hurrying air;
But finding all your ruin did conspire,
She soon her beauteous progeny resigned
To this destructive, this imperious wind,
That check'd your nobler aims and gives you to the fire. 5

    Thus! have thy cedars, Libanus, been struck
        As the lithe osiers twisted round;
    Thus! Cadez, has thy wilderness been shook,
    When the appalling and tremendous sound
        Of rattl'ing tempests o'er you broke,
        And made your stubborn glories bow,
    When in such whirlwinds the Almighty spoke,

Warning Judea then as our Britannia now.
    Yet these were the remoter harms,
 Foreign the care, and distant the alarms: 60
    Whilst but shelt'ring trees alone,
    Master'd soon, and soon o'erthrown,
    Felt these gusts which since prevail,
    And loftier palaces assail;
    Whose shaken turrets now give way,
With vain inscriptions which the frieze has borne
Through ages past, t' extol and to adorn,
    And to our latter times convey
    Who did the structure's deep foundations lay,
    Forcing his praise upon the gazing crowd,   70
    And, whilst he moulders in a scanty shroud,
Telling both earth and skies he when alive was proud.
    Now down at once comes the superfluous lead,
       The costly fret-work with it yields,
    Whose imitated fruits and flow'rs are strew'd
Like those of real growth o'er the autumnal fields.
       The present owner lifts his eyes,
    And the swift change with sad affrightment spies
    The ceiling gone, that late the roof conceal'd,
    The roof until'd, thro' which the heav'ns reveal'd, 80
Exposes now his head when all defence has fail'd.

       What alas, is to be done!
    Those, who in cities would from dangers run,
       Do but increasing dangers meet,
And death in various shapes attending in the street;
       While some, too tardy in their flight,
       O'ertaken by a worse mischance,
       Their upward parts do scarce advance,
When on their following limbs th' extending ruins light.
    One half 's interr'd, the other yet survives,   90
    And for release with fainting vigour strives;
    Implores the aid of absent friends in vain;
    With falt'ring speech and dying wishes calls
    Those whom perhaps their own domestic walls
By parallel distress, or swifter death, retain.

       O Wells! thy bishop's mansion we lament,
So tragical the fall, so dire th' event!
    But let no daring thought presume
To point a cause for that oppressive doom.

Yet, strictly pious Ken! had'st thou been there,   10
This fate, we think, had not become thy share;
   Nor had that awful fabric bow'd,
   Sliding from its loosen'd bands;
   Nor yielding timbers been allow'd
   To crush thy ever-lifted hands,
     Or interrupt thy prayer.
  Those orisons that nightly watches keep,
Had call'd thee from thy bed, or there secur'd thy sleep.
  Whilst you, bold winds and storms! his word obey'd
  Whilst you his scourge the great Jehovah made,   11
And into ruin'd heaps our edifices laid.
  You south and west, the tragedy began,
As with disorder'd haste, you o'er the surface ran,
   Forgetting that you were design'd
   (Chiefly thou Zephyrus, thou softest wind!)
Only our heats, when sultry, to allay.
And chase th' od'rous gums by your dispersing play.
   Now, by new orders and decrees,
   For our chastisement issu'd forth,
  You on his confines the alarmed north   12
    With equal fury sees,
  And summons swiftly to his aid
    Eurus, his confederate made,
  His eager second in th' opposing fight,
  That even the winds may keep their balance right,
Nor yield increase of sway to arbitrary might.
   Meeting now, they all contend,
   Those assail, while these defend;
   Fierce and turbulent the war,
   And in the loud tumultuous jar   13
  Winds their own fifes and clarions are.
Each cavity which art or nature leaves,
Their inspiration hastily receives;
  Whence, from their various forms and size,
  As various symphonies arise,
  Their trumpet ev'ry hollow tube is made,
  And, when more solid bodies they invade,
   Enrag'd they can no further come,
  The beaten flat, whilst it repels the noise,
  Resembles but with more outrageous voice   14
   The soldiers threat'ning drum:
And when they compass thus our world around,

When they our rocks and mountains rend,
When they our sacred piles to their foundations send,
  No wonder if our echoing caves rebound,
  No wonder if our list'ning sense they wound,
When arm'd with so much force, and usher'd with such
    sound.

  Nor scarce, amidst the terrors of that night,
  When you, fierce winds, such desolation wrought,
When you from out his stores the Great Commander
    brought,   150
    Could the most righteous stand upright;
    Scarcely the holiest man performs
    The service that becomes it best,
By ardent vows and solemn prayers address'd,
Nor finds the calm, so usual in his breast,
    Full proof against such storms.
  How should the guilty then be found,
  The men in wine, or looser pleasures drown'd,
To fix a steadfast hope, or to maintain their ground!
  When at his glass the late companion feels,   160
That giddy like himself the tott'ring mansion reels!
    The miser, who with many a chest
    His gloomy tenement oppress'd,
    Now fears the over-burthen'd floor,
And trembles for his life, but for his treasure more.
  What shall he do, or to what pow'rs apply?
  To those which threaten from on high,
  By him ne'er call'd upon before,
Who also will suggest, th' impossible restore?
  No, Mammon, to thy laws he will be true,   170
And rather than his wealth, will bid the world adieu.
    The rafters sink, and buried with his coin
    That fate does with his living thoughts combine,
For still his heart's enclos'd within a golden mine.

    Contention with its angry brawls
    By storms o'er-clamour'd, shrinks and falls;
Nor Whig nor Tory now the rash contender calls.
    Those who but vanity allow'd,
    Nor thought it reach'd the name of sin
    To be of their perfections proud,   180
Too much adorn'd without, or too much rais'd within,

Now find that even the lightest things,
   As the minuter parts of air,
When number to their weight addition brings,
   Can like the small, but numerous insects' stings,
Can like th' assembled winds, urge ruin and despair.

Thus you've obey'd, you winds, that must fulfil
   The Great Disposer's righteous will:
Thus did your breath a strict enquiry make,
Thus did you our most secret sins awake,   190
   And thus chastis'd their ill.

Whilst vainly those of a rapacious mind
   Fields to other fields had laid,
By force, or by injurious bargains join'd,
With fences for their guard impenetrable made:
    Thus juster tempest mocks the wrong,
    And sweeps, in its directed flight,
    Th' inclosures of another's right,
Driving at once the bound and licens'd herds along.
    Then earth again one general scene appears;   200
    No regular distinction now,
    Betwixt the grounds for pasture or the plough,
    The face of Nature wears.

Free as the men, who wild confusion love,
    And lawless liberty approve,
    Their fellow brutes pursue their way,
To their own loss and disadvantage stray,
As wretched in their choice, as unadvis'd as they.
    The tim'rous deer, whilst he forsakes the park,
    And wanders on in the misguiding dark,   210
    Believes a foe from ev'ry unknown bush
    Will on his trembling body rush,
    Taking the winds, that vary in their notes,
For hot pursuing hounds with deeply bellowing throats.
    Th' awaken'd birds, shook from their nightly seats,
    Their unavailing pinions ply,
    Repuls'd as they attempt to fly
In hopes they might attain to more secure retreats.
    But where, ye wilder'd fowls, would you repair?
    When this your happy portion given,   22

Your upward lot, your firmament of heaven,
Your unentail'd, your undivided air,
Where no proprietor was ever known,
Where no litigious suits have ever grown,
Whilst none from star to star could call the space his
  own;
When this no more your middle flights can bear,
But some rough blast too far above conveys,
Or to unquitted earth confines your weak essays.
Nor you, nor wiser man could find repose,
Nor could our industry produce   230
Expedients of the smallest use,
To ward our greater cares, or mitigate your woes.
Ye clouds! that pitied our distress,
And by your pacifying showers
(The soft and usual methods of success)
Kindly essay'd to make this tempest less;
Vainly your aid was now alas! employ'd,
In vain you wept o'er those destructive hours
In which the winds full tyranny enjoy'd,
Nor would allow you to prevail,   240
But drove your scorn'd and scatter'd tears to wail
The land that lay destroy'd.

Whilst you obey'd, you winds! that must fulfil
The Just Disposer's righteous will;
Whilst not the earth alone you disarray,
But to more ruin'd seas wing'd your impetuous way.
Which to foreshow, the still portentous sun,
Beamless and pale of late, his race begun,
Quenching the rays he had no joy to keep
In the obscure and sadly threaten'd deep.   250
Further than we, that eye of heaven discerns,
And near plac'd to our malignant stars,
Our brooding tempests and approaching wars
Anticipating learns.
When now, too soon the dark event
Shows what that faded planet meant;
Whilst more the liquid empire undergoes,
More she resigns of her entrusted stores,
The wealth, the strength, the pride of diff'rent
  shores
In one devoted, one recorded night,   260

Than years had been destroy'd by generous fight,
    Or privateering foes.
All rules of conduct laid aside,
No more the baffl'd pilot steers,
Or knows an art, when it each moment veers,
To vary with th' winds or stem th' unusual tide.
    Dispers'd and loose, the shatter'd vessels stray,
      Some perish within sight of shore,
    Some, happier thought, obtain a wider sea,
But never to return, or cast an anchor more!   270
      Some on the northern coasts are thrown,
And by congealing surges compass'd round,
    To fixt and certain ruin bound,
      Immovable are grown:
The fatal Goodwin swallows all that come
Within the limits of that dangerous sand,
Amphibious in its kind, nor sea nor land;
Yet kin to both, a false and faithless strand,
Known only to our cost for a devouring tomb.
      Nor seemed the hurricane content,   280
    Whilst only ships were wreckt and tackle rent:
      The sailors too must fall a prey,
    Those that command, with those that did obey;
    The best supporters of thy pompous style,
    Thou far renown'd, thou pow'rful British Isle!
Foremost in naval strength and sov'reign of the sea!
  These from thy aid that wrathful night divides,
  Plung'd in those waves o'er which this title rides,
  What art thou, envied greatness, at the best,
    In thy deluding splendours drest?   290
  What are thy glorious titles and thy forms?
  Which cannot give security and rest
  To favour'd men or kingdoms that contest
With popular assaults, or providential storms!
  Whilst on th' Omnipotent our fate depends,
And they are only safe whom He alone defends.
  Then let to heaven our general praise be sent,
Which did our farther loss, our total wreck prevent.
  And as our aspirations do ascend,
  Let every thing be summon'd to attend;   300
  And let the poet *after God's own heart*
  Direct our skill in that sublimer part,
    And our weak numbers mend!

TO THE ECHO

IN A CLEAR NIGHT UPON ASTROP WALKS

SAY lovely nymph, where dost thou dwell?
Where is that secret sylvan seat,
That melancholy, sweet retreat
From whence thou dost these notes repel?
And moving syllables repeat?
Oh lovely nymph, our joys to swell,
Thy hollow leafy mansion tell;
Or if thou only charm'st the ear
And never wilt to sight appear,
But dost alone in voice excel,   10
Still with it fix us here,
Where Cynthia lends her gentle light,
Whilst the appeas'd, expanded air
A passage for thee dost prepare,
And Strephon's tuneful voice invite
Thine a soft part with him to bear.
Oh pleasure! when thou'dst take a flight
Beyond thy common, mortal height,
When to thy sphere above thou'dst press,
And men like angels thou would'st bless,   20
Thy season be like this fair night,
And harmony thy dress.

THE BIRD

KIND bird, thy praises I design,
Thy praises, like thy plumes, should shine;
Thy praises should thy life out-live,
Could I the fame I wish thee give.
Thou my domestic music art,
And dearest trifle of my heart.
Soft in thy notes and in thy dress,
Softer than numbers can express,
Softer than love, softer than light
When just escaping from the night,   10
When first she rises, unarray'd,
And steals a passage through the shade;

Softer than air, or flying clouds
Which Phoebus' glory thinly shrouds,
Gay as the spring, gay as the flowers
When lightly strew'd with pearly showers.
Ne'er to the woods shalt thou return,
Nor thy wild freedom shalt thou mourn,
Thou to my bosom shalt repair,
And find a safer shelter there;   20
There shalt thou watch, and should I sleep,
My heart, thy charge, securely keep.
Love, who a stranger is to me,
Must by thy wings be kin to thee:
So painted o'er, so seeming fair,
So soft his first addresses are,
Thy guard he ne'er can pass unseen.
Thou, surely, thou hast often been,
Whilst yet a wand'rer in the grove,
A false accomplice with this love: 30
In the same shade hast thou not sate,
And seen him work some wretch's fate?
Hast thou not sooth'd him in the wrong,
And grac'd his mischief with a song,
Tuning thy loud conspiring voice
O'er falling lovers to rejoice?
If so, thy wicked faults redeem
In league with me, no truce with him
Do thou admit, but warn my heart,
And all his sly designs impart,   40
Lest to that breast by craft he get
Which has defied and brav'd him yet.

THE TREE

FAIR tree! for thy delightful shade
'Tis just that some return be made;
Sure, some return is due from me
To thy cool shadows and to thee.
When thou to birds dost shelter give,
Thou music dost from them receive;
If travellers beneath thee stay,
Till storms have worn themselves away,

That time in praising thee they spend,
And thy protecting pow'r commend;   10
The shepherd, here from scorching freed,
Tunes to thy dancing leaves his reed;
Whilst his lov'd nymph, in thanks, bestows
Her flow'ry chaplets on thy boughs.
Shall I then only silent be,
And no return be made by me?
No: let this wish upon thee wait,
And still to flourish be thy fate;
To future ages may'st thou stand,
Untouch'd by the rash workman's hand,   20
Till that large stock of sap is spent
Which gives thy summer's ornament;
Till the fierce winds that vainly strive
To shock thy greatness whilst alive,
Shall on thy lifeless hour attend,
Prevent the axe, and grace thy end:
Their scatter'd strength together call,
And to the clouds proclaim thy fall,
Who then their ev'ning dews may spare,
When thou no longer art their care,   30
But shalt, like ancient heroes, burn,
And some bright hearth be made thy urn.

TO THE NIGHTINGALE

EXERT thy voice, sweet harbinger of spring!
    This moment is thy time to sing,
    This moment I attend thy praise,
And set my numbers to thy lays.
    Free as thine shall be the song,
    As thy music, short or long.
Poets, wild as thou, were born,
    Pleasing best when unconfin'd,
    When to please is least design'd,
Soothing but their cares to rest.   10
    Cares do still their thoughts molest,
    And still th' unhappy poet's breast,
Like thine, when best he sings, is plac'd against a thorn.

She begins. Let all be still!
    Muse, thy promise now fulfil!
Sweet, oh sweet! still sweeter yet!
Can thy words such accents fit,
Canst thou syllables refine,
Melt a sense that shall retain
Still some spirit of the brain,   20
Till with sounds like these it join?
    'Twill not be! then change thy note,
    Let division shake thy throat.
Hark! division now she tries,
Yet as far the Muse outflies.
    Cease then, prithee, cease thy tune:
    Trifler, wilt thou sing till June?
Till thy bus'ness all lies waste,
And the time of building 's past!
    Thus we poets that have speech,   30
Unlike what thy forests teach,
    If a fluent vein be shown
    That 's transcendent to our own,
Criticise, reform, or preach,
Or censure what we cannot teach.

A NOCTURNAL REVERIE

In such a night when every louder wind
Is to its distant cavern safe confin'd;
And only gentle Zephyr fans its wings,
And lonely Philomel, still waking, sings;
Or from some tree, fam'd for the owl's delight,
She, hollowing clear, directs the wand'rer right;
In such a night, when passing clouds give place,
Or thinly veil the heaven's mysterious face;
When in some river overhung with green,
The waving moon and trembling leaves are seen;   10
When fresh'ned grass now bears itself upright,
And makes cool banks to pleasing rest invite,
Whence springs the woodbine and the bramble-rose,
And where the sleepy cowslip shelter'd grows;
Whilst now a paler hue the foxglove takes,
Yet chequers still with red the dusky brakes,

When scatter'd glow-worms, but in twilight fine,
Show trivial beauties watch their hour to shine;
Whilst Salisbury stands the test of every light,
In perfect charm and perfect virtue bright;   20
When odours, which declin'd repelling day,
Thro' temp'rate air uninterrupted stray;
When darken'd groves their softest shadows wear,
And falling waters we distinctly hear;
When thro' the gloom more venerable shows
Some ancient fabric, awful in repose,
While sunburnt hills their swarthy looks conceal,
And swelling haycocks thicken up the vale;
When the loos'd horse now, as his pasture leads,
Comes slowly grazing thro' th' adjoining meads,   30
Whose stealing pace, and lengthen'd shade we fear,
Till torn up forage in his teeth we hear:
When nibbling sheep at large pursue their food,
And unmolested kine rechew the cud;
When curlews cry beneath the village walls,
And to her straggling brood the partridge calls;
Their short-lived jubilee the creatures keep,
Which but endures whilst tyrant man does sleep;
When a sedate content the spirit feels,
And no fierce light disturbs, whilst it reveals,   40
But silent musings urge the mind to seek
Something too high for syllables to speak;
Till the free soul to a compos'dness charm'd,
Finding the elements of rage disarm'd,
O'er all below, a solemn quiet grown,
Joys in th' inferior world and thinks it like her own:
In such a night let me abroad remain,
Till morning breaks, and all's confus'd again:
Our cares, our toils, our clamours are renew'd,
Or pleasures, seldom reach'd, again pursued.   50

TO DEATH

O KING of terrors, whose unbounded sway
All that have life must certainly obey;
The king, the priest, the prophet all are thine,
Nor would ev'n God (in flesh) thy stroke decline.

My name is on thy roll, and sure I must
Increase thy gloomy kingdom in the dust.
My soul at this no apprehension feels,
But trembles at thy swords, thy racks, thy wheels;
Thy scorching fevers, which distract the sense,
And snatch us raving, unprepar'd, from hence;   10
At thy contagious darts that wound the heads
Of weeping friends who wait at dying beds.
Spare these, and let thy time be when it will:
My bus'ness is to die, and thine to kill.
Gently thy fatal sceptre on me lay,
And take to thy cold arms, insensibly, thy prey.

PROLOGUE TO "ARISTOMENES"

TO MY LORD WINCHILSEA, UPON THE FIRST READING THE PLAY
TO HIM AT EASTWELL IN KENT

WHEN first upon the stage a play appears
'Tis not the multitude a poet fears,
Who, from example, praise or damn by rote,
And give their censure as some members vote.
But if in the expecting box or pit
The wretch discerns one true, substantial wit,
Tow'rds him his doubtful sight he'll still direct,
Whose very looks can all his faults detect.
So, though no crowd is gather'd here to-day,
And you my lord, alone, must judge this play,   10
Much more the ignorant author is concern'd
Than if whole troops of vulgar critics swarm'd;
Since Horace, by your mouth, must all condemn,
And 'tis her loss that you're so great with him.
But, when good plays scarce please our Charles's
          court,
(So nice himself, and the refin'der sort)
A droll would at Newmarket make them sport
Where rusty copper deck'd the strolling vermin,
And flannel dash'd with ink made princely ermine.
Then let not this poor poem quite despair,   20
The country asks but plain and homely fare;

And if this please, by a good winter fire,
More than a visit from a neigh'bring squire,
Or tedious sheet or doubtful news from Dyer,
The writer 's too well paid for all her pain,
Who'll now begin in King Cambyses' strain,
Heroics, such as Falstaff heretofore
Repeated when a cushion crown he wore.
Yet those the Hostess mov'd her eyes to wet;
These lines she fears no passions will beget,   30
But 'twill appear, in spite of all enditing,
A woman's way to charm is not by writing.

A SONG

ESIGNED TO HAVE BEEN BROUGHT INTO THE PART BETWEEN
CLIMANDER AND HERMINIA

WRETCHED Amintor with a flame
    Too strong to be subdu'd,
A nymph above his rank and name
    Still eagerly pursu'd.

To gain her ev'ry art he tried,
    But no return procur'd,
Mistook her prudence for her pride,
    Nor guess'd what she endur'd.

Till prostrate at her feet one day
    Urging in deep despair,   10
Thus softly was she heard to say,
    Or sigh'd it to the air:

Witness ye secret cares I prove,
    Which is the greater trial,
To sue for unrewarded love,
    Or die by self-denial.

THOMAS PARNELL

THOMAS PARNELL (1679–1718)

Contributions to *Spectator* and *Guardian*, 1712–13.
Essay on the Different Styles of Poetry, 1713.
Poem on Queen Anne's Peace, 1713.
Contributions to Steele's Poetical Miscellanies, 1713.
Essay on the Life, Writings and Learning of Homer, for
    Pope's *Iliad*, 1715.
Homer's Battle of the Frogs and Mice, 1717.
Poems, 1721.
Posthumous Works of Thomas Parnell, 1758.
Criticism: Johnson's *Lives of the Poets*.

HESIOD; OR, THE RISE OF WOMAN

WHAT ancient times, those times we fancy wise,
Have left on long record of woman's rise,
What morals teach it, and what fables hide,
What author wrote it, how that author died,
All these I sing.   In Greece they fram'd the tale;
In Greece, 'twas thought a woman might be frail,
Ye modern beauties! where the poet drew
His softest pencil, think he dreamt of you;
And warn'd by him, ye wanton pens, beware
How heaven's concern'd to vindicate the fair.   10
The case was Hesiod's; he the fable writ;
Some think with meaning, some with idle wit:
Perhaps 'tis either, as the ladies please;
I waive the contest, and commence the lays.

In days of yore, no matter where or when,
'Twas ere the low creation swarm'd with men,
That one Prometheus, sprung of heavenly birth
Our author's song can witness, liv'd on earth.
He carv'd the turf to mould a manly frame,
And stole from Jove his animating flame.   20
The sly contrivance o'er Olympus ran,
When thus the monarch of the stars began.

O vers'd in arts! whose daring thoughts aspire
To kindle clay with never-dying fire!
Enjoy thy glory past, that gift was thine;
The next thy creature meets, be fairly mine:
And such a gift, a vengeance so design'd,
As suits the counsel of a God to find;
A pleasing bosom-cheat, a specious ill,
Which felt they curse, yet covet still to feel.   30

He said, and Vulcan straight the sire commands,
To temper mortar with ethereal hands;
In such a shape to mould a rising fair,
As virgin-goddesses are proud to wear;

To make her eyes with diamond-water shine,
And form her organs for a voice divine.
'Twas thus the sire ordain'd; the power obeyed;
And work'd, and wonder'd at the work he made;
The fairest, softest, sweetest frame beneath,   3
Now made to seem, now more than seem, to breathe.

As Vulcan ends, the cheerful queen of charms
Clasp'd the new-panting creature in her arms;
From that embrace a fine complexion spread,
Where mingled whiteness glow'd with softer red.
Then in a kiss she breath'd her various arts,
Of trifling prettily with wounded hearts;
A mind for love, but still a changing mind;
The lisp affected, and the glance design'd;
The sweet confusing blush, the secret wink,

The gentle-swimming walk, the courteous sink,   5
The stare for strangeness fit, for scorn the frown,
For decent yielding looks declining down,
The practis'd languish, where well-feign'd desire
Would own its melting in a mutual fire;
Gay smiles to comfort; April showers to move;
And all the nature, all the art, of love.

Gold-sceptred Juno next exalts the fair;
Her touch endows her with imperious air,
Self-valuing fancy, highly-crested pride,
Strong sovereign will, and some desire to chide: 6
For which, an eloquence, that aims to vex,
With native tropes of anger, arms the sex.

Minerva, skilful goddess, train'd the maid
To twirl the spindle by the twisting thread,
To fix the loom, instruct the reeds to part,
Cross the long weft, and close the web with art,
A useful gift; but what profuse expense,
What world of fashions, took its rise from hence!

Young Hermes next, a close-contriving god,
Her brows encircled with his serpent rod: 7
Then plots and fair excuses fill'd her brain,
The views of breaking amorous vows for gain,

The price of favours, the designing arts
That aim at riches in contempt of hearts;
And for a comfort in a marriage life,
The little, pilfering temper of a wife.

Full on the fair his beams Apollo flung,
And fond persuasion tipp'd her easy tongue;
He gave her words, where oily flattery lays
The pleasing colours of the art of praise;   80
And wit, to scandal exquisitely prone,
Which frets another's spleen to cure its own.

Those sacred Virgins whom the bards revere,
Tun'd all her voice, and shed a sweetness there,
To make her sense with double charms abound,
Or make her lively nonsense please by sound.

To dress the maid, the decent Graces brought
A robe in all the dyes of beauty wrought,
And plac'd their boxes o'er a rich brocade
Where pictur'd loves on every cover play'd;   90
Then spread those implements that Vulcan's art
Had fram'd to merit Cytherea's heart;
The wire to curl, the close-indented comb
To call the locks, that lightly wander, home;
And chief, the mirror, where the ravish'd maid
Beholds and loves her own reflected shade.

Fair Flora lent her stores, the purpled Hours
Confin'd her tresses with a wreath of flowers;
Within the wreath arose a radiant crown;
A veil pellucid hung depending down;   100
Back roll'd her azure veil with serpent fold,
The purfled border deck'd the floor with gold.

Her robe (which closely by the girdle brac't
Reveal'd the beauties of a slender waist)
Flow'd to the feet; to copy Venus' air,
When Venus' statues have a robe to wear.

The new-sprung creature finish'd thus for harms,
Adjusts her habit, practises her charms,

With blushes glows, or shines with lively smiles,
Confirms her will, or recollects her wiles: 11
Then conscious of her worth, with easy pace
Glides by the glass, and turning views her face.

A finer flax than what they wrought before,
Through time's deep cave the sister Fates explore,
Then fix the loom, their fingers nimbly weave,
And thus their toil prophetic songs deceive.

Flow from the rock, my flax! and swiftly flow,
Pursue thy thread; the spindle runs below.
A creature fond and changing, fair and vain,
The creature woman, rises now to reign.   12
New beauty blooms, a beauty form'd to fly;
New love begins, a love produc'd to die;
New parts distress the troubled scenes of life,
The fondling mistress, and the ruling wife.

Men, born to labour, all with pains provide;
Women have time, to sacrifice to pride:
They want the care of man, their want they know,
And dress to please with heart-alluring show,
The show prevailing, for the sway contend,
And make a servant where they meet a friend.   13

Thus in a thousand wax-erected forts
A loitering race the painful bee supports;
From sun to sun, from bank to bank he flies,
With honey loads his bag, with wax his thighs;
Fly where he will, at home the race remain,
Prune the silk dress, and murmuring eat the gain.

Yet here and there we grant a gentle bride,
Whose temper betters by the father's side;
Unlike the rest that double human care,
Fond to relieve, or resolute to share: 14
Happy the man whom thus his stars advance!
The curse is general, but the blessing chance.

Thus sung the Sisters, while the gods admire
Their beauteous creature, made for man in ire;
The young Pandora she, whom all contend
To make too perfect not to gain her end:

Then bid the winds that fly to breathe the spring,
Return to bear her on a gentle wing;
With wafting airs the winds obsequious blow,
And land the shining vengeance safe below.   150
A golden coffer in her hand she bore,
(The present treacherous, but the bearer more)
'Twas fraught with pangs; for Jove ordain'd above,
That gold should aid, and pangs attend on love.

Her gay descent the man perceiv'd afar
Wondering he run to catch the falling star;
But so surpris'd, as none but he can tell,
Who lov'd so quickly, and who lov'd so well.
O'er all his veins the wandering passion burns,
He calls her nymph, and every nymph by turns.   160
Her form to lovely Venus he prefers,
Or swears that Venus' must be such as hers.
She, proud to rule, yet strangely fram'd to tease,
Neglects his offers while her airs she plays,
Shoots scornful glances from the bended frown,
In brisk disorder trips it up and down,
Then hums a careless tune to lay the storm,
And sits, and blushes, smiles, and yields, in form.

"Now take what Jove design'd," she softly cried,
"This box thy portion, and myself thy bride":   170
Fir'd with the prospect of the double charms,
He snatch'd the box, and bride, with eager arms.

Unhappy man! to whom so bright she shone:
The fatal gift, her tempting self, unknown!
The winds were silent, all the waves asleep,
And heaven was trac'd upon the flattering deep;
But whilst he looks unmindful of a storm,
And thinks the water wears a stable form,
What dreadful din around his ears shall rise!
What frowns confuse his picture of the skies!   180

At first the creature man was fram'd alone,
Lord of himself, and all the world his own.
For him the Nymphs in green forsook the woods,
For him the Nymphs in blue forsook the floods;
In vain the Satyrs rage, the Tritons rave;

They bore him heroes in the secret cave.
No care destroy'd, no sick disorder prey'd,
No bending age his sprightly form decay'd,
No wars were known, no females heard to rage,
And poets tell us, 'twas a golden age.   190

When woman came, those ills the box confin'd
Burst furious out, and poison'd all the wind,
From point to point, from pole to pole they flew,
Spread as they went, and in the progress grew:
The Nymphs regretting left the mortal race,
And altering nature wore a sickly face;
New terms of folly rose, new states of care;
New plagues to suffer, and to please, the fair!
The days of whining, and of wild intrigues,
Commenc'd, or finish'd, with the breach of leagues:
The mean designs of well-dissembled love;   201
The sordid matches never join'd above;
Abroad, the labour, and at home the noise,
(Man's double sufferings for domestic joys);
The curse of jealousy; expense, and strife;
Divorce, the public brand of shameful life;
The rival's sword; the qualm that takes the fair;
Disdain for passion, passion in despair—
These, and a thousand, yet unnam'd, we find;
Ah fear the thousand, yet unnam'd, behind!   210

Thus on Parnassus tuneful Hesiod sung:
The mountain echoed, and the valley rung;
The sacred groves a fix'd attention show;
The crystal Helicon forbore to flow;
The sky grew bright; and (if his verse be true)
The Muses came to give the laurel too.
But what avail'd the verdant prize of wit,
If love swore vengeance for the tales he writ?
Ye fair offended, hear your friend relate
What heavy judgment prov'd the writer's fate,   220
Though when it happen'd, no relation clears,
'Tis thought in five, or five and twenty years.

Where, dark and silent, with a twisted shade
The neighb'ring woods a native arbour made,
There oft a tender pair for amorous play
Retiring, toy'd the ravish'd hours away;

A Locrian youth, the gentle Troilus he,
A fair Milesian, kind Evanthe she:
But swelling nature in a fatal hour
Betray'd the secrets of the conscious bower;   230
The dire disgrace her brothers count their own,
And track her steps, to make its author known.

It chanc'd one evening, ('twas the lover's day)
Conceal'd in brakes the jealous kindred lay;
When Hesiod wandering, mus'd along the plain,
And fix'd his seat where love had fix'd the scene:
A strong suspicion straight possess'd their mind,
(For poets ever were a gentle kind.)
But when Evanthe near the passage stood,
Flung back a doubtful look, and shot the wood,   240
"Now take," at once they cry, "thy due reward,"
And urg'd with erring rage, assault the bard.
His corpse the sea received.   The dolphins bore
('Twas all the gods would do) the corpse to shore.

Methinks, I view the dead with pitying eyes,
And see the dreams of ancient wisdom rise;
I see the Muses round the body cry,
But hear a Cupid loudly laughing by;
He wheels his arrow with insulting hand,
And thus inscribes the moral on the sand.   250
"Here Hesiod lies: ye future bards, beware
How far your moral tales incense the fair:
Unlov'd, unloving, 'twas his fate to bleed;
Without his quiver Cupid caus'd the deed:
He judg'd this turn of malice justly due,
And Hesiod died for joys he never knew."

SONG

When thy beauty appears,
    In its graces and airs,
All bright as an angel new dropt from the sky;
    At distance I gaze, and am aw'd by my fears
    So strangely you dazzle my eye!

But when without art,
Your kind thoughts you impart,
When your love runs in blushes through every vein;
When it darts from your eyes, when it pants in your
    heart,
Then I know you're a woman again.   10

There's a passion and pride
In our sex, she replied,
And thus (might I gratify both) I would do;
Still an angel appear to each lover beside,
But still be a woman to you.

A SONG

Thirsis, a young and amorous swain
Saw two, the beauties of the plain,
    Who both his heart subdue:
Gay Cælia's eyes were dazzling fair,
Sabina's easy shape and air
    With softer magic drew.

He haunts the stream, he haunts the grove,
Lives in a fond romance of love,
    And seems for each to die;
Till each a little spiteful grown,   10
Sabina Cælia's shape ran down,
    And she Sabina's eye.

Their envy made the shepherd find
Those eyes, which love could only blind;
    So set the lover free:
No more he haunts the grove or stream,
Or with a true-love knot and name
    Engraves a wounded tree.

Ah Cælia! sly Sabina cried,
Though neither love, we're both denied;   20
Now to support the sex's pride,
    Let either fix the dart.

Poor girl! says Cælia, say no more;
For should the swain but one adore,
That spite which broke his chains before,
    Would break the other's heart.

SONG

My days have been so wondrous free
    The little birds that fly
With careless ease from tree to tree,
    Were but as bless'd as I.

Ask gliding waters, if a tear
    Of mine increas'd their stream?
Or ask the flying gales, if e'er
    I lent one sigh to them?

But now my former days retire,
    And I'm by beauty caught,
The tender chains of sweet desire
    Are fix'd upon my thought.

Ye nightingales, ye twisting pines!
    Ye swains that haunt the grove!
Ye gentle echoes, breezy winds!
    Ye close retreats of love!

With all of nature, all of art,
    Assist the dear design;
O teach a young, unpractis'd heart,
    To make my Nancy mine!

The very thought of change I hate,
    As much as of despair;
Nor ever covet to be great,
    Unless it be for her.

'Tis true, the passion in my mind
    Is mix'd with soft distress;
Yet while the fair I love is kind,
    I cannot wish it less.

ANACREONTIC

WHEN spring came on with fresh delight,
To cheer the soul, and charm the sight,
While easy breezes, softer rain,
And warmer suns salute the plain;
'Twas then, in yonder piny grove,
That Nature went to meet with Love.

Green was her robe, and green her wreath,
Where'er she trod, 'twas green beneath;
Where'er she turn'd, the pulses beat
With new recruits of genial heat;   10
And in her train the birds appear,
To match for all the coming year.

Rais'd on a bank where daisies grew,
And violets intermix'd a blue,
She finds the boy she went to find;
A thousand pleasures wait behind,
Aside, a thousand arrows lie,
But all unfeather'd wait to fly.

When they met, the dame and boy,
Dancing Graces, idle Joy,   20
Wanton Smiles, and airy Play,
Conspir'd to make the scene be gay;
Love pair'd the birds through all the grove,
And Nature bid them sing to Love,
Sitting, hopping, fluttering, sing,
And pay their tribute from the wing,
To fledge the shafts that idly lie,
And yet unfeather'd wait to fly.

'Tis thus, when spring renews the blood,
They meet in every trembling wood,   30
And thrice they make the plumes agree,
And every dart they mount with three,
And every dart can boast a kind,
Which suits each proper turn of mind.

From the towering eagle's plume
The generous hearts accept their doom:
Shot by the peacock's painted eye,

The vain and airy lovers die:
For careful dames and frugal men,
The shafts are speckled by the hen: 40
The pies and parrots deck the darts,
When prattling wins the panting hearts:
When from the voice the passions spring
The warbling finch affords a wing:
Together, by the sparrow stung,
Down fall the wanton and the young:
And fledg'd by geese the weapons fly,
When others love they know not why.

All this, as late I chanced to rove,
I learn'd in yonder waving grove.   50
And see, says Love, who called me near,
How much I deal with Nature here,
How both support a proper part,
She gives the feather, I the dart.
Then cease for souls averse to sigh,
If Nature cross ye, so do I;
My weapon there unfeather'd flies,
And shakes and shuffles through the skies:
But if the mutual charms I find
By which she links you, mind to mind,   60
They wing my shafts, I poise the darts,
And strike from both, through both your hearts.

ANACREONTIC

GAY Bacchus liking Estcourt's wine,
    A noble meal bespoke us;
And for the guests that were to dine,
    Brought Comus, Love, and Jocus.

The god near Cupid drew his chair,
    Near Comus, Jocus plac'd:
For wine makes Love forget its care,
    And Mirth exalts a feast.

The more to please the sprightly god,
    Each sweet engaging Grace   10
Put on some clothes to come abroad,
    And took a waiter's place.

Then Cupid nam'd at every glass
  A lady of the sky;
While Bacchus swore he'd drink the lass,
  And had it bumper-high.

Fat Comus toss'd his brimmers o'er,
  And always got the most;
Jocus took care to fill him more,
  Whene'er he miss'd the toast.   20

They call'd, and drank at every touch;
  He fill'd, and drank again;
And if the gods can take too much,
  'Tis said, they did so then.

Gay Bacchus little Cupid stung,
  By reckoning his deceits;
And Cupid mock'd his stammering tongue
  With all his staggering gaits:

And Jocus droll'd on Comus' ways,
  And tales without a jest;   30
While Comus call'd his witty plays
  But waggeries at best.

Such talk soon set them all at odds;
  And, had I Homer's pen,
I'd sing ye, how they drank like gods,
  And how they fought like men.

To part the fray, the Graces fly,
  Who make 'em soon agree;
Nay, had the Furies' selves been nigh,
  They still were three to three.   40

Bacchus appeas'd, rais'd Cupid up,
  And gave him back his bow;
But kept some darts to stir the cup
  Where sack and sugar flow.

Jocus took Comus' rosy crown,
  And gaily wore the prize,
And thrice in mirth he push'd him down,
  As thrice he strove to rise.

Then Cupid sought the myrtle grove,
  Where Venus did recline;
And Venus close embracing Love,   50
  They join'd to rail at wine.

And Comus loudly cursing wit,
  Roll'd off to some retreat,
Where boon companions gravely sit
  In fat unwieldy state.

Bacchus and Jocus, still behind,
  For one fresh glass prepare;
They kiss, and are exceeding kind,
  And vow to be sincere.   60

But part in time, whoever hear
  This our instructive song;
For though such friendships may be dear,
  They can't continue long.

A FAIRY TALE

IN THE ANCIENT ENGLISH STYLE

IN Britain's isle and Arthur's days,
When midnight faeries daunc'd the maze,
  Liv'd Edwin of the green;
Edwin, I wis, a gentle youth,
Endow'd with courage, sense, and truth,
  Though badly shap'd he been.

His mountain back mote well be said
To measure heighth against his head,
  And lift itself above:
Yet spite of all that nature did   10
To make his uncouth form forbid,
  This creature dar'd to love.

He felt the charms of Edith's eyes,
Nor wanted hope to gain the prize,
  Could ladies look within;
But one Sir Topaz dress'd with art,
And, if a shape could win a heart,
  He had a shape to win.

Edwin, if right I read my song,
With slighted passion pac'd along,
    All in the moony light:
'Twas near an old enchaunted court,
Where sportive faeries made resort
    To revel out the night.

His heart was drear, his hope was cross'd,
'Twas late, 'twas farr, the path was lost
    That reach'd the neighbour-town;
With weary steps he quits the shades,
Resolv'd the darkling dome he treads,
    And drops his limbs adown.

But scant he lays him on the floor,
When hollow winds remove the door,
    A trembling rocks the ground:
And, well I ween to count aright,
At once an hundred tapers light
    On all the walls around.

Now sounding tongues assail his ear,
Now sounding feet approachen near,
    And now the sounds encrease;
And from the corner where he lay
He sees a train profusely gay
    Come pranckling o'er the place.

But, trust me, gentles, never yet
Was dight a masquing half so neat,
    Or half so rich before;
The country lent the sweet perfumes,
The sea the pearl, the sky the plumes,
    The town its silken store.

Now whilst he gaz'd, a gallant drest
In flaunting robes above the rest,
    With awfull accent cried,
What mortal of a wretched mind,
Whose sighs infect the balmy wind,
    Has here presumed to hide?

At this the swain, whose venturous soul
No fears of magic art controul,

Advanc'd in open sight;
"Nor have I cause of dreed," he said,
"Who view, by no presumption led,
    Your revels of the night.   60

"'Twas grief for scorn of faithful love,
Which made my steps unweeting rove
    Amid the nightly dew."
'Tis well, the gallant cries again,
We faeries never injure men
    Who dare to tell us true.

Exalt thy love-dejected heart,
Be mine the task, or ere we part,
    To make thee grief resign;
Now take the pleasure of thy chaunce;   70
Whilst I with Mab my partner daunce,
    Be little Mable thine.

He spoke, and all a sudden there
Light musick floats in wanton air;
    The monarch leads the queen;
The rest their faerie partners found,
And Mable trimly tript the ground
    With Edwin of the green.

The dauncing past, the board was laid,
And siker such a feast was made   80
    As heart and lip desire;
Withouten hands the dishes fly,
The glasses with a wish come nigh,
    And with a wish retire.

But now to please the faerie king,
Full every deal they laugh and sing,
    And antick feats devise;
Some wind and tumble like an ape,
And other-some transmute their shape
    In Edwin's wondering eyes.   90

Till one at last that Robin hight,
Renown'd for pinching maids by night,
    Has hent him up aloof;

And full against the beam he flung,
Where by the back the youth he hung
   To spraul unneath the roof.

From thence, "Reverse my charm," he cries,
"And let it fairly now suffice
   The gambol has been shown."
But Oberon answers with a smile,   100
Content thee, Edwin, for a while,
   The vantage is thine own.

Here ended all the phantome play;
They smelt the fresh approach of day,
   And heard a cock to crow;
The whirling wind that bore the crowd
Has clapp'd the door, and whistled loud,
   To warn them all to go.

Then screaming all at once they fly,
And all at once the tapers die;   11
   Poor Edwin falls to floor;
Forlorn his state, and dark the place,
Was never wight in sike a case
   Through all the land before.

But soon as Dan Apollo rose,
Full jolly creature home he goes,
   He feels his back the less;
His honest tongue and steady mind
Han rid him of the lump behind
   Which made him want success.   12

With lusty livelyhed he talks
He seems a dauncing as he walks;
   His story soon took wind;
And beauteous Edith sees the youth,
Endow'd with courage, sense and truth,
   Without a bunch behind.

The story told, Sir Topaz mov'd,
The youth of Edith erst approv'd,
   To see the revel scene:
At close of eve he leaves his home,   1
And wends to find the ruin'd dome
   All on the gloomy plain.

As there he bides, it so befell,
The wind came rustling down a dell,
    A shaking seiz'd the wall:
Up spring the tapers as before,
The faeries bragly foot the floor,
    And musick fills the hall.

But certes sorely sunk with woe
Sir Topaz sees the elfin show,   140
    His spirits in him die:
When Oberon cries, "A man is near,
A mortall passion, cleeped fear,
    Hangs flagging in the sky."

With that Sir Topaz, hapless youth!
In accents faultering ay for ruth
    Intreats them pity graunt;
For als he been a mister wight,
Betray'd by wandering in the night
    To tread the circled haunt.   150

"Ah losell vile!" at once they roar,
"And little skill'd of faerie lore,
    Thy cause to come we know:
Now has thy kestrell courage fell;
And faeries, since a lie you tell,
    Are free to work thee woe."

Then Will, who bears the wispy fire
To trail the swains among the mire,
    The caitive upward flung;
There like a tortoise in a shop   160
He dangled from the chamber-top,
    Where whilome Edwin hung.

The revel now proceeds apace,
Deffly they frisk it o'er the place,
    They sit, they drink, and eat;
The time with frolick mirth beguile,
And poor Sir Topaz hangs the while
    Till all the rout retreat.

By this the starrs began to wink,
They shriek, they fly, the tapers sink,   170
    And down ydrops the knight:
For never spell by faerie laid
With strong enchantment bound a glade
    Beyond the length of night.

Chill, dark, alone, adreed, he lay,
Till up the welkin rose the day,
    Then deem'd the dole was o'er:
But wot ye well his harder lot?
His seely back the bunch has got   180
    Which Edwin lost afore.

This tale a Sybil-nurse ared;
She softly strok'd my youngling head,
    And when the tale was done,
"Thus some are born, my son," she cries,
"With base impediments to rise,
    And some are born with none.

"But virtue can itself advance
To what the favourite fools of chance
    By fortune seem'd design'd;
Virtue can gain the odds of fate,   190
And from itself shake off the weight
    Upon th' unworthy mind."

TO MR. POPE

To praise, yet still with due respect to praise,
A bard triumphant in immortal bays,
The learn'd to show, the sensible commend,
Yet still preserve the province of the friend,
What life, what vigour, must the lines require!
What music tune them! what affection fire!

O might thy genius in my bosom shine!
Thou shouldst not fail of numbers worthy thine,
The brightest ancients might at once agree
To sing within my lays, and sing of thee.   10

Horace himself would own thou dost excel
In candid arts to play the critic well.

Ovid himself might wish to sing the dame
Whom Windsor forest sees a gliding stream;
On silver feet, with annual osier crown'd,
She runs for ever through poetic ground.

How flame the glories of Belinda's hair,
Made by thy Muse the envy of the fair!
Less shone the tresses Egypt's princess wore,
Which sweet Callimachus so sung before.   20
Here courtly trifles set the world at odds,
Belles war with beaux, and whims descend for gods.
The new machines in names of ridicule,
Mock the grave phrenzy of the chymic fool:
But know, ye fair, a point conceal'd with art,
The Sylphs and Gnomes are but a woman's heart:
The Graces stand in sight; a Satyr train
Peep o'er their heads, and laugh behind the scene.

In Fame's fair temple, o'er the boldest wits
Inshrin'd on high the sacred Virgil sits,   30
And sits in measures, such as Virgil's Muse
To place thee near him might be fond to choose.
How might he tune th' alternate reed with thee,
Perhaps a Strephon thou, a Daphnis he,
While some old Damon o'er the vulgar wise,
Thinks he deserves, and thou deserv'st the prize!
Rapt with the thought my fancy seeks the plains,
And turns me shepherd while I hear the strains.
Indulgent nurse of every tender gale,
Parent of flowerets, old Arcadia, hail!   40
Here in the cool my limbs at ease I spread,
Here let thy poplars whisper o'er my head;
Still slide thy waters soft among the trees,
Thy aspens quiver in a breathing breeze;
Smile all thy valleys in eternal spring,
Be hush'd, ye winds! while Pope and Virgil sing.

In English lays, and all sublimely great,
Thy Homer warms with all his ancient heat;
He shines in council, thunders in the fight,
And flames with every sense of great delight.   50

Long has that poet reign'd, and long unknown,
Like monarchs sparkling on a distant throne;
In all the majesty of Greek retir'd,
Himself unknown, his mighty name admir'd;
His language failing, wrapp'd him round with night,
Thine, rais'd by thee, recalls the work to light.
So wealthy mines, that ages long before
Fed the large realms around with golden ore,
When chok'd by sinking banks, no more appear,
And shepherds only say, the mines were here!   60
Should some rich youth, if nature warm his heart,
And all his projects stand inform'd with art,
Here clear the caves, there ope the leading vein;
The mines detected flame with gold again.

How vast, how copious are thy new designs!
How every music varies in thy lines!
Still as I read, I feel my bosom beat,
And rise in raptures by another's heat.
Thus in the wood, when summer dress'd the days
When Windsor lent us tuneful hours of ease,   70
Our ears the lark, the thrush, the turtle blest,
And Philomela, sweetest o'er the rest:
The shades resound with song—O softly tread!
While a whole season warbles round my head.

This to my friend—and when a friend inspires,
My silent harp its master's hand requires,
Shakes off the dust, and makes these rocks resound,
For Fortune plac'd me in unfertile ground;
Far from the joys that with my soul agree,
From wit, from learning,—far, O far from thee!   80
Here moss-grown trees expand the smallest leaf,
Here half an acre's corn is half a sheaf;
Here hills with naked heads the tempest meet,
Rocks at their side, and torrents at their feet;
Or lazy lakes, unconscious of a flood,
Whose dull brown Naiads ever sleep in mud.

Yet here content can dwell, and learned ease,
A friend delight me, and an author please;
Even here I sing, while Pope supplies the theme,
Show my own love, though not increase his fame.   90

HEALTH: AN ECLOGUE

Now early shepherds o'er the meadow pass,
And print long footsteps in the glittering grass;
The cows neglectful of their pasture stand,
By turns obsequious to the milker's hand.

When Damon softly trod the shaven lawn,
Damon, a youth from city cares withdrawn;
Long was the pleasing walk he wander'd through,
A cover'd arbour clos'd the distant view;
There rests the youth, and, while the feather'd throng
Raise their wild music, thus contrives a song.   10

Here, wafted o'er by mild Etesian air,
Thou country goddess, beauteous Health, repair!
Here let my breast through quivering trees inhale
Thy rosy blessings with the morning gale.
What are the fields, or flowers, or all I see?
Ah! tasteless all, if not enjoy'd with thee.

Joy to my soul! I feel the Goddess nigh,
The face of nature cheers as well as I;
O'er the flat green refreshing breezes run,
The smiling daisies blow beneath the sun,   20
The brooks run purling down with silver waves,
The planted lanes rejoice with dancing leaves,
The chirping birds from all the compass rove
To tempt the tuneful echoes of the grove:
High sunny summits, deeply shaded dales,
Thick mossy banks, and flowery winding vales,
With various prospect gratify the sight,
And scatter fix'd attention in delight.

Come, country Goddess, come! nor thou suffice,
But bring thy mountain-sister, Exercise.   30
Call'd by thy lively voice, she turns her pace,
Her winding horn proclaims the finish'd chace;
She mounts the rocks, she skims the level plain,
Dogs, hawks, and horses, crowd her early train;
Her hardy face repels the tanning wind,
And lines and meshes loosely float behind.
All these as means of toil the feeble see,
But these are helps to pleasure join'd with thee.

Let Sloth lie softening till high noon in down,
Or lolling fan her in the sultry town,   40
Unnerv'd with rest; and turn her own disease,
Or foster others in luxurious ease:
I mount the courser, call the deep-mouth'd hounds
The fox unkennell'd flies to covert grounds;
I lead where stags through tangled thickets tread,
And shake the saplings with their branching head;
I make the falcons wing their airy way,
And soar to seize, or stooping strike their prey;
To snare the fish I fix the luring bait;
To wound the fowl I load the gun with fate.   50
'Tis thus through change of exercise I range,
And strength and pleasure rise from every change.
   Here, beauteous Health, for all the year remain;
   When the next comes, I'll charm thee thus again.

O come, thou Goddess of my rural song,
And bring thy daughter, calm Content, along!
Dame of the ruddy cheek and laughing eye,
From whose bright presence clouds of sorrow fly:
For her I mow my walks, I plat my bowers,
Clip my low hedges, and support my flowers;   60
To welcome her, this summer seat I drest,
And here I court her when she comes to rest;
When she from exercise to learned ease
Shall change again, and teach the change to please.

Now friends conversing my soft hours refine,
And Tully's Tusculum revives in mine:
Now to grave books I bid the mind retreat,
And such as make me rather good than great;
Or o'er the works of easy fancy rove,
Where flutes and innocence amuse the grove;   70
The native bard that on Sicilian plains
First sung the lowly manners of the swains,
Or Maro's Muse, that in the fairest light
Paints rural prospects and the charms of sight:
These soft amusements bring content along,
And fancy, void of sorrow, turns to song.
   Here, beauteous Health, for all the year remain;
   When the next comes, I'll charm thee thus again.

THE FLIES: AN ECLOGUE

WHEN in the river cows for coolness stand,
And sheep for breezes seek the lofty land,
A youth, whom Æsop taught that every tree,
Each bird and insect, spoke as well as he,
Walk'd calmly musing in a shaded way,
Where flowering hawthorn broke the sunny ray,
And thus instructs his moral pen to draw
A scene that obvious in the field he saw.

Near a low ditch, where shallow waters meet,
Which never learnt to glide with liquid feet,   10
Whose Naiads never prattle as they play,
But screen'd with hedges slumber out the day,
There stands a slender fern's aspiring shade,
Whose answering branches regularly laid
Put forth their answering boughs, and proudly rise
Three stories upward, in the nether skies.

For shelter here, to shun the noonday heat,
An airy nation of the flies retreat;
Some in soft air their silken pinions ply,
And some from bough to bough delighted fly,   20
Some rise, and circling light to perch again;
A pleasing murmur hums along the plain.
So, when a stage invites to pageant shows,
If great and small are like, appear the beaux;
In boxes some with spruce pretension sit,
Some change from seat to seat within the pit,
Some roam the scenes, or turning cease to roam;
Preluding music fills the lofty dome.

When thus a fly (if what a fly can say
Deserves attention) rais'd the rural lay.   30

Where late Amintor made a nymph a bride,
Joyful I flew by young Favonia's side,
Who, mindless of the feasting, went to sip
The balmy pleasure of the shepherd's lip.
I saw the wanton, where I stoop'd to sup,
And half resolv'd to drown me in the cup;
Till, brush'd by careless hands, she soar'd above:

Cease, beauty, cease to vex a tender love.
Thus ends the youth, the buzzing meadow rung,
And thus the rival of his music sung.   40

When suns by thousands shone in orbs of dew,
I wafted soft with Zephyretta flew;
Saw the clean pail, and sought the milky cheer,
While little Daphne seiz'd my roving dear.
Wretch that I was! I might have warn'd the dame,
Yet sat indulging as the danger came.
But the kind huntress left her free to soar:
Ah! guard, ye lovers, guard a mistress more.

Thus from the fern, whose high-projecting arms,
The fleeting nation bent with dusky swarms,   50
The swains their love in easy music breathe,
When tongues and tumult stun the field beneath.
Black ants in teams come darkening all the road,
Some call to march, and some to lift the load;
They strain, they labour with incessant pains,
Press'd by the cumbrous weight of single grains.
The flies struck silent gaze with wonder down:
The busy burghers reach their earthy town,
Where lay the burthens of a wintry store,
And thence unwearied part in search of more.   60
Yet one grave sage a moment's space attends,
And the small city's loftiest point ascends,
Wipes the salt dew that trickles down his face,
And thus harangues them with the gravest grace.

Ye foolish nurslings of the summer air,
These gentle tunes and whining songs forbear;
Your trees and whispering breeze, your grove and
        love,
Your Cupid's quiver, and his mother's dove.
Let bards to business bend their vigorous wing,
And sing but seldom, if they love to sing: 70
Else, when the flowerets of the season fail,
And this your ferny shade forsakes the vale,
Though one would save ye, not one grain of wheat
Should pay such songsters idling at my gate.

He ceas'd: the flies, incorrigibly vain,
Heard the mayor's speech, and fell to sing again.

AN ELEGY, TO AN OLD BEAUTY

In vain, poor nymph, to please our youthful sight
You sleep in cream and frontlets all the night,
Your face with patches soil, with paint repair,
Dress with gay gowns, and shade with foreign hair.
If truth, in spite of manners, must be told,
Why really fifty-five is something old.

Once you were young; or one, whose life's so long
She might have borne my mother, tells me wrong:
And once, since envy's dead before you die,
The women own, you play'd a sparkling eye,   10
Taught the light foot a modish little trip,
And pouted with the prettiest purple lip.

To some new charmer are the roses fled,
Which blew, to damask all thy cheek with red;
Youth calls the Graces there to fix their reign,
And airs by thousands fill their easy train.
So parting summer bids her flowery prime
Attend the sun to dress some foreign clime,
While withering seasons in succession, here,
Strip the gay gardens, and deform the year.   20

But thou, since nature bids, the world resign;
'Tis now thy daughter's daughter's time to shine.
With more address, or such as pleases more,
She runs her female exercises o'er,
Unfurls or closes, raps or turns the fan,
And smiles, or blushes at the creature man.
With quicker life, as gilded coaches pass,
In sideling courtesy she drops the glass.
With better strength, on visit-days, she bears
To mount her fifty flights of ample stairs.   30
Her mien, her shape, her temper, eyes, and tongue,
Are sure to conquer,—for the rogue is young;
And all that's madly wild, or oddly gay,
We call it only pretty Fanny's way.

Let time, that makes you homely, make you sage;
The sphere of wisdom is the sphere of age.
'Tis true, when beauty dawns with early fire,
And hears the flattering tongues of soft desire,

If not from virtue, from its gravest ways
The soul with pleasing avocation strays: 40
But beauty gone, 'tis easier to be wise;
As harpers better, by the loss of eyes.

Henceforth retire, reduce your roving airs,
Haunt less the plays, and more the public prayers,
Reject the Mechlin head, and gold brocade,
Go pray, in sober Norwich crape array'd.
Thy pendant diamonds let thy Fanny take,
(Their trembling lustre shows how much you shake;)
Or bid her wear thy necklace row'd with pearl,
You'll find your Fanny an obedient girl.   50
So for the rest, with less incumbrance hung,
You walk through life, unmingled with the young;
And view the shade and substance, as you pass,
With joint endeavour trifling at the glass,
Or Folly drest, and rambling all her days,
To meet her counterpart, and grow by praise:
Yet still sedate yourself, and gravely plain,
You neither fret, nor envy at the vain.

'Twas thus, if man with woman we compare,
The wise Athenian cross'd a glittering fair.   60
Unmov'd by tongues and sights, he walk'd the place,
Through tape, toys, tinsel, gimp, perfume, and lace;
Then bends from Mars's hill his awful eyes,
And—"What a world I never want!" he cries;
But cries unheard; for Folly will be free.
So parts the buzzing gaudy crowd, and he:
As careless he for them, as they for him;
He wrapt in wisdom, and they whirl'd by whim.

THE BOOK-WORM

Come hither, boy, we'll hunt to-day
The book-worm, ravening beast of prey,
Produc'd by parent Earth, at odds,
As fame reports it, with the gods.
Him frantic hunger wildly drives
Against a thousand authors' lives:
Through all the fields of wit he flies;

Dreadful his head with clustering eyes,
With horns without, and tusks within,
And scales to serve him for a skin.   10
Observe him nearly, lest he climb
To wound the bards of ancient time,
Or down the vale of fancy go
To tear some modern wretch below.
On every corner fix thine eye,
Or ten to one he slips thee by.

See where his teeth a passage eat:
We'll rouse him from the deep retreat.
But who the shelter's forc'd to give?
'Tis sacred Virgil, as I live!   20
From leaf to leaf, from song to song,
He draws the tadpole form along,
He mounts the gilded edge before,
He's up, he scuds the cover o'er,
He turns, he doubles, there he past,
And here we have him, caught at last.

Insatiate brute, whose teeth abuse
The sweetest servants of the Muse—
Nay, never offer to deny,
I took thee in the fact to fly.   30
His roses nipt in every page,
My poor Anacreon mourns thy rage;
By thee my Ovid wounded lies;
By thee my Lesbia's Sparrow dies;
Thy rabid teeth have half destroy'd
The work of love in Biddy Floyd;
They rent Belinda's locks away,
And spoil'd the Blouzelind of Gay.
For all, for every single deed,
Relentless justice bids thee bleed: 40
Then fall a victim to the Nine,
Myself the priest, my desk the shrine.

Bring Homer, Virgil, Tasso near,
To pile a sacred altar here:
Hold, boy, thy hand out-runs thy wit,
You reach'd the plays that Dennis writ;
You reach'd me Philips' rustic strain;
Pray take your mortal bards again.

Come, bind the victim,—there he lies,
And here between his numerous eyes   50
This venerable dust I lay,
From manuscripts just swept away.

The goblet in my hand I take,
For the libation's yet to make:
A health to poets! all their days,
May they have bread, as well as praise;
Sense may they seek, and less engage
In papers fill'd with party rage.
But if their riches spoil their vein,
Ye Muses, make them poor again.   60

Now bring the weapon, yonder blade,
With which my tuneful pens are made.
I strike the scales that arm thee round,
And twice and thrice I print the wound;
The sacred altar floats with red,
And now he dies, and now he's dead.

How like the son of Jove I stand,
This Hydra stretch'd beneath my hand!
Lay bare the monster's entrails here,
To see what dangers threat the year: 70
Ye gods! what sonnets on a wench!
What lean translations out of French!
'Tis plain, this lobe is so unsound,
S—— prints, before the months go round.

But hold, before I close the scene.
The sacred altar should be clean.
O had I Shadwell's second bays,
Or, Tate, thy pert and humble lays!
(Ye pair, forgive me, when I vow
I never miss'd your works till now,)   80
I'd tear the leaves to wipe the shrine,
That only way you please the Nine:
But since I chance to want these two,
I'll make the songs of Durfey do.

Rent from the corpse, on yonder pin,
I hang the scales that brac'd it in;
I hang my studious morning gown,
And write my own inscription down.

"This trophy from the Python won,
This robe, in which the deed was done,   90
These, Parnell, glorying in the feat,
Hung on these shelves, the Muses' seat.
Here Ignorance and Hunger found
Large realms of wit to ravage round;
Here Ignorance and Hunger fell;
Two foes in one I sent to hell.
Ye poets, who my labours see,
Come share the triumph all with me!
Ye critics, born to vex the Muse,
Go mourn the grand ally you lose!"   100

AN ALLEGORY ON MAN

A THOUGHTFUL being, long and spare,
Our race of mortals call him Care,
(Were Homer living, well he knew
What name the gods have call'd him too,)
With fine mechanic genius wrought,
And lov'd to work, though no one bought.

This being, by a model bred
In Jove's eternal sable head,
Contriv'd a shape impower'd to breathe,
And be the worldling here beneath.   10

The man rose staring, like a stake;
Wondering to see himself awake!
Then look'd so wise, before he knew
The business he was made to do;
That, pleas'd to see with what a grace
He gravely show'd his forward face,
Jove talk'd of breeding him on high,
An under-something of the sky.

But ere he gave the mighty nod,
Which ever binds a poet's god: 20
(For which his curls ambrosial shake,
And mother Earth's oblig'd to quake,)
He saw old mother Earth arise,
She stood confess'd before his eyes;

But not with what we read she wore,
A castle for a crown before,
Nor with long streets and longer roads
Dangling behind her, like commodes;
As yet with wreaths alone she drest,
And trail'd a landskip-painted vest.   30
Then thrice she rais'd, as Ovid said,
And thrice she bow'd her weighty head.

Her honours made, great Jove, she cried,
This thing was fashion'd from my side;
His hands, his heart, his head, are mine;
Then what hast thou to call him thine?

Nay rather ask, the monarch said,
What boots his hand, his heart, his head,
Were what I gave remov'd away?
Thy part's an idle shape of clay.   40

Halves, more than halves! cried honest Care,
Your pleas would make your titles fair,
You claim the body, you the soul,
But I who join'd them, claim the whole.

Thus with the gods debate began,
On such a trivial cause, as man.
And can celestial tempers rage?
Quoth Virgil in a later age.

As thus they wrangled, Time came by;
(There's none that paint him such as I,   50
For what the fabling ancients sung
Makes Saturn old, when Time was young.)
As yet his winters had not shed
Their silver honours on his head;
He just had got his pinions free
From his old sire Eternity.
A serpent girdled round he wore,
The tail within the mouth, before;
By which our almanacks are clear
That learned Egypt meant the year.   60
A staff he carried, where on high
A glass was fix'd to measure by,

As amber boxes made a show
For heads of canes an age ago.
His vest, for day, and night, was py'd;
A bending sickle arm'd his side;
And spring's new months his train adorn;
The other seasons were unborn.

Known by the gods, as near he draws,
They make him umpire of the cause. 70
O'er a low trunk his arm he laid,
Where since his hours a dial made;
Then leaning heard the nice debate,
And thus pronounc'd the words of fate.

Since body from the parent Earth,
And soul from Jove receiv'd a birth,
Return they where they first began;
But since their union makes the man,
Till Jove and Earth shall part these two,
To Care, who join'd them, man is due. 80

He said, and sprung with swift career
To trace a circle for the year;
Where ever since the seasons wheel,
And tread on one another's heel.

'Tis well, said Jove; and for consent
Thundering he shook the firmament:
Our umpire Time shall have his way,
With Care I let the creature stay.
Let business vex him, avarice blind,
Let doubt and knowledge rack his mind, 90
Let error act, opinion speak,
And want afflict, and sickness break,
And anger burn, dejection chill,
And joy distract, and sorrow kill:
Till, arm'd by Care, and taught to mow,
Time draws the long destructive blow;
And wasted man, whose quick decay
Comes hurrying on before his day,
Shall only find by this decree,
The soul flies sooner back to me. 100

AN IMITATION OF SOME FRENCH VERSES

RELENTLESS Time! destroying power,
　　Whom stone and brass obey,
Who giv'st to every flying hour
　　To work some new decay;
Unheard, unheeded, and unseen,
　　Thy secret saps prevail,
And ruin man, a nice machine,
　　By nature form'd to fail.
My change arrives; the change I meet,
　　Before I thought it nigh:　　　　　　　　10
My spring, my years of pleasure fleet,
　　And all their beauties die.
In age I search, and only find
　　A poor unfruitful gain,
Grave Wisdom stalking slow behind,
　　Oppress'd with loads of pain.
My ignorance could once beguile,
　　And fancied joys inspire;
My errors cherish'd Hope to smile
　　On newly-born Desire.　　　　　　　　20
But now experience shews the bliss
　　For which I fondly sought,
Not worth the long impatient wish,
　　And ardour of the thought.
My youth met Fortune fair array'd,
　　(In all her pomp she shone,)
And might, perhaps, have well essay'd
　　To make her gifts my own:
But when I saw the blessings shower
　　On some unworthy mind,　　　　　　　30
I left the chase, and own'd the power
　　Was justly painted blind.
I pass'd the glories which adorn
　　The splendid courts of kings,
And while the persons mov'd my scorn,
　　I rose to scorn the things.
My manhood felt a vigorous fire,
　　By love increas'd the more;
But years with coming years conspire
　　To break the chains I wore.　　　　　　40

In weakness safe, the sex I see
   With idle lustre shine;
For what are all their joys to me,
   Which cannot now be mine?
But hold—I feel my gout decrease,
   My troubles laid to rest,
And truths, which would disturb my peace,
   Are painful truths at best.
Vainly the time I have to roll
   In sad reflection flies;   50
Ye fondling passions of my soul!
   Ye sweet deceits! arise.
I wisely change the scene within,
   To things that us'd to please;
In pain, philosophy is spleen,
   In health, 'tis only ease.

A NIGHT-PIECE ON DEATH

By the blue taper's trembling light,
No more I waste the wakeful night,
Intent with endless view to pore
The schoolmen and the sages o'er:
Their books from wisdom widely stray,
Or point at best the longest way.
I'll seek a readier path, and go
Where wisdom's surely taught below.

How deep yon azure dyes the sky,
Where orbs of gold unnumber'd lie,   10
While through their ranks in silver pride
The nether crescent seems to glide!
The slumbering breeze forgets to breathe,
The lake is smooth and clear beneath,
Where once again the spangled show
Descends to meet our eyes below.
The grounds which on the right aspire,
In dimness from the view retire:
The left presents a place of graves,
Whose wall the silent water laves.   20
That steeple guides thy doubtful sight

Among the livid gleams of night.
There pass, with melancholy state,
By all the solemn heaps of fate,
And think, as softly-sad you tread
Above the venerable dead,
"Time was, like thee they life possest,
And time shall be, that thou shalt rest."

Those graves, with bending osier bound,
That nameless heave the crumbled ground,   30
Quick to the glancing thought disclose,
Where toil and poverty repose.

The flat smooth stones that bear a name,
The chisel's slender help to fame,
(Which ere our set of friends decay
Their frequent steps may wear away,)
A middle race of mortals own,
Men, half ambitious, all unknown.

The marble tombs that rise on high,
Whose dead in vaulted arches lie,   40
Whose pillars swell with sculptur'd stones,
Arms, angels, epitaphs, and bones,
These, all the poor remains of state,
Adorn the rich, or praise the great;
Who while on earth in fame they live,
Are senseless of the fame they give.

Hah! while I gaze, pale Cynthia fades,
The bursting earth unveils the shades!
All slow, and wan, and wrapp'd with shrouds,
They rise in visionary crowds,   50
And all with sober accent cry,
"Think, mortal, what it is to die."

Now from yon black and funeral yew,
That bathes the charnel-house with dew,
Methinks I hear a voice begin;
(Ye ravens, cease your croaking din,
Ye tolling clocks, no time resound
O'er the long lake and midnight ground!)
It sends a peal of hollow groans,
Thus speaking from among the bones.   60

"When men my scythe and darts supply,
How great a king of fears am I!
They view me like the last of things:
They make, and then they dread, my stings.
Fools! if you less provok'd your fears,
No more my spectre form appears.
Death's but a path that must be trod,
If man would ever pass to God;
A port of calms, a state of ease
From the rough rage of swelling seas.   70

"Why then thy flowing sable stoles,
Deep pendant cypress, mourning poles,
Loose scarfs to fall athwart thy weeds,
Long palls, drawn hearses, cover'd steeds,
And plumes of black, that, as they tread,
Nod o'er the scutcheons of the dead?
Nor can the parted body know,
Nor wants the soul, these forms of woe.
As men who long in prison dwell,
With lamps that glimmer round the cell,   80
Whene'er their suffering years are run,
Spring forth to greet the glittering sun:
Such joy, though far transcending sense,
Have pious souls at parting hence.
On earth, and in the body plac'd,
A few, and evil, years they waste;
But when their chains are cast aside,
See the glad scene unfolding wide,
Clap the glad wing, and tower away,
And mingle with the blaze of day."   90

A HYMN TO CONTENTMENT

LOVELY, lasting peace of mind!
Sweet delight of human-kind!
Heavenly-born, and bred on high,
To crown the favourites of the sky
With more of happiness below,
Than victors in a triumph know!
Whither, O whither art thou fled,
To lay thy meek, contented head;

What happy region dost thou please
To make the seat of calms and ease!   10

Ambition searches all its sphere
Of pomp and state, to meet thee there,
Increasing Avarice would find
Thy presence in its gold enshrin'd.
The bold adventurer ploughs his way
Through rocks amidst the foaming sea,
To gain thy love; and then perceives
Thou wert not in the rocks and waves.
The silent heart, which grief assails,
Treads soft and lonesome o'er the vales,   20
Sees daisies open, rivers run,
And seeks, as I have vainly done,
Amusing thought; but learns to know
That solitude's the nurse of woe.
No real happiness is found
In trailing purple o'er the ground:
Or in a soul exalted high,
To range the circuit of the sky,
Converse with stars above, and know
All nature in its forms below;   30
The rest it seeks, in seeking dies,
And doubts at last, for knowledge, rise.

Lovely, lasting peace, appear!
This world itself, if thou art here,
Is once again with Eden blest,
And man contains it in his breast.

'Twas thus, as under shade I stood,
I sung my wishes to the wood,
And lost in thought, no more perceiv'd
The branches whisper as they wav'd: 40
It seem'd, as all the quiet place
Confess'd the presence of the Grace.
When thus she spoke—"Go rule thy will,
Bid thy wild passions all be still,
Know God—and bring thy heart to know
The joys which from religion flow:
Then every Grace shall prove its guest,
And I'll be there to crown the rest."

Oh! by yonder mossy seat,
In my hours of sweet retreat, 50
Might I thus my soul employ,
With sense of gratitude and joy!
Rais'd as ancient prophets were,
In heavenly vision, praise, and prayer;
Pleasing all men, hurting none,
Pleas'd and bless'd with God alone:
Then while the gardens take my sight,
With all the colours of delight;
While silver waters glide along,
To please my ear, and court my song; 60
I'll lift my voice, and tune my string,
And thee, great source of nature, sing.

The sun that walks his airy way,
To light the world, and give the day;
The moon that shines with borrow'd light;
The stars that gild the gloomy night;
The seas that roll unnumber'd waves;
The wood that spreads its shady leaves;
The field whose ears conceal the grain,
The yellow treasure of the plain; 70
All of these, and all I see,
Should be sung, and sung by me:
They speak their maker as they can,
But want and ask the tongue of man.

Go search among your idle dreams,
Your busy or your vain extremes;
And find a life of equal bliss,
Or own the next begun in this.

THE HERMIT

FAR in a wild, unknown to public view,
From youth to age a reverend hermit grew;
The moss his bed, the cave his humble cell,
His food the fruits, his drink the crystal well:
Remote from man, with God he pass'd the days
Prayer all his business, all his pleasure praise.

A life so sacred, such serene repose,
Seem'd heaven itself, till one suggestion rose;
That vice should triumph, virtue vice obey,
This sprung some doubt of Providence's sway: 10
His hopes no more a certain prospect boast,
And all the tenour of his soul is lost.
So when a smooth expanse receives imprest
Calm nature's image on its watery breast,
Down bend the banks, the trees depending grow,
And skies beneath with answering colours glow:
But if a stone the gentle scene divide,
Swift ruffling circles curl on every side,
And glimmering fragments of a broken sun,
Banks, trees, and skies, in thick disorder run.   20

To clear this doubt, to know the world by sight,
To find if books, or swains, report it right,
(For yet by swains alone the world he knew,
Whose feet came wandering o'er the nightly dew,)
He quits his cell; the pilgrim-staff he bore,
And fix'd the scallop in his hat before;
Then with the sun a rising journey went,
Sedate to think, and watching each event.

The morn was wasted in the pathless grass,
And long and lonesome was the wild to pass;   30
But when the southern sun had warm'd the day,
A youth came posting o'er a crossing way;
His raiment decent, his complexion fair,
And soft in graceful ringlets wav'd his hair.
Then near approaching, "Father, hail!" he cried;
"And hail, my son," the reverend sire replied;
Words follow'd words, from question answer flow'd,
And talk of various kind deceiv'd the road;
Till each with other pleas'd, and loth to part,
While in their age they differ, join in heart: 40
Thus stands an aged elm in ivy bound,
Thus youthful ivy clasps an elm around.

Now sunk the sun; the closing hour of day
Came onward, mantled o'er with sober gray;
Nature in silence bid the world repose;
When near the road a stately palace rose:

There by the moon through ranks of trees they pass,
Whose verdure crown'd their sloping sides of grass.
It chanc'd the noble master of the dome
Still made his house the wandering stranger's home: 50
Yet still the kindness, from a thirst of praise,
Prov'd the vain flourish of expensive ease.
The pair arrive: the liveried servants wait;
Their lord receives them at the pompous gate.
The table groans with costly piles of food,
And all is more than hospitably good.
Then led to rest, the day's long toil they drown,
Deep sunk in sleep, and silk, and heaps of down.

At length 'tis morn, and at the dawn of day,
Along the wide canals the zephyrs play; 60
Fresh o'er the gay parterres the breezes creep,
And shake the neighbouring wood to banish sleep.
Up rise the guests, obedient to the call:
An early banquet deck'd the splendid hall;
Rich luscious wine a golden goblet grac'd,
Which the kind master forc'd the guests to taste.
Then, pleas'd and thankful, from the porch they go;
And, but the landlord, none had cause of woe;
His cup was vanish'd; for in secret guise
The younger guest purloin'd the glittering prize. 70

As one who spies a serpent in his way,
Glistening and basking in the summer ray,
Disorder'd stops to shun the danger near,
Then walks with faintness on, and looks with fear;
So seem'd the sire; when far upon the road,
The shining spoil his wily partner show'd.
He stopp'd with silence, walk'd with trembling heart,
And much he wish'd, but durst not ask to part:
Murmuring he lifts his eyes, and thinks it hard,
That generous actions meet a base reward. 80

While thus they pass, the sun his glory shrouds,
The changing skies hang out their sable clouds;
A sound in air presag'd approaching rain,
And beasts to covert scud across the plain.
Warn'd by the signs, the wandering pair retreat,
To seek for shelter at a neighbouring seat.

'Twas built with turrets, on a rising ground,
And strong, and large, and unimprov'd around;
Its owner's temper, timorous and severe,
Unkind and griping, caus'd a desert there.   90

As near the miser's heavy doors they drew,
Fierce rising gusts with sudden fury blew;
The nimble lightning mix'd with showers began,
And o'er their heads loud rolling thunder ran.
Here long they knock, but knock or call in vain,
Driven by the wind, and batter'd by the rain.
At length some pity warm'd the master's breast,
('Twas then, his threshold first receiv'd a guest,)
Slow creaking turns the door with jealous care,
And half he welcomes in the shivering pair;   100
One frugal faggot lights the naked walls,
And nature's fervour through their limbs recalls:
Bread of the coarsest sort, with eager wine,
Each hardly granted, serv'd them both to dine;
And when the tempest first appear'd to cease,
A ready warning bid them part in peace.

With still remark the pondering hermit view'd
In one so rich, a life so poor and rude;
And why should such, within himself he cried,
Lock the lost wealth a thousand want beside?   110
But what new marks of wonder soon took place
In every settling feature of his face,
When from his vest the young companion bore
That cup, the generous landlord own'd before,
And paid profusely with the precious bowl
The stinted kindness of this churlish soul!

But now the clouds in airy tumult fly;
The sun emerging opes an azure sky;
A fresher green the smelling leaves display,
And, glittering as they tremble, cheer the day: 120
The weather courts them from the poor retreat,
And the glad master bolts the wary gate.

While hence they walk, the pilgrim's bosom wrought
With all the travel of uncertain thought;
His partner's acts without their cause appear,
'Twas there a vice, and seem'd a madness here:

Detesting that, and pitying this, he goes,
Lost and confounded with the various shows.

Now night's dim shades again involve the sky,
Again the wanderers want a place to lie,   130
Again they search, and find a lodging nigh:
The soil improv'd around, the mansion neat,
And neither poorly low, nor idly great:
It seem'd to speak its master's turn of mind,
Content, and not for praise, but virtue kind.

Hither the walkers turn with weary feet,
Then bless the mansion, and the master greet:
Their greeting fair bestow'd, with modest guise,
The courteous master hears, and thus replies:

"Without a vain, without a grudging heart,   140
To him who gives us all, I yield a part;
From him you come, for him accept it here,
A frank and sober, more than costly cheer."
He spoke, and bid the welcome table spread,
Then talk'd of virtue till the time of bed,
When the grave household round his hall repair,
Warn'd by a bell, and close the hours with prayer.

At length the world, renew'd by calm repose,
Was strong for toil, the dappled morn arose.
Before the pilgrims part, the younger crept   150
Near the clos'd cradle where an infant slept,
And writh'd his neck: the landlord's little pride,
O strange return! grew black, and gasp'd, and died.
Horror of horrors! what! his only son!
How look'd our hermit when the fact was done?
Not hell, though hell's black jaws in sunder part,
And breathe blue fire, could more assault his heart.

Confus'd, and struck with silence at the deed,
He flies, but, trembling, fails to fly with speed.
His steps the youth pursues: the country lay   160
Perplex'd with roads, a servant show'd the way:
A river cross'd the path; the passage o'er
Was nice to find; the servant trod before:
Long arms of oaks an open bridge supplied,
And deep the waves beneath the bending glide.

The youth, who seem'd to watch a time to sin,
Approach'd the careless guide, and thrust him in;
Plunging he falls, and rising lifts his head,
Then flashing turns, and sinks among the dead.

Wild, sparkling rage inflames the father's eyes,   170
He bursts the bands of fear, and madly cries,
"Detested wretch!"—but scarce his speech began,
When the strange partner seem'd no longer man:
His youthful face grew more serenely sweet;
His robe turn'd white, and flow'd upon his feet;
Fair rounds of radiant points invest his hair;
Celestial odours breathe through purpled air;
And wings, whose colours glitter'd on the day,
Wide at his back their gradual plumes display.
The form ethereal bursts upon his sight,   180
And moves in all the majesty of light.

Though loud at first the pilgrim's passion grew,
Sudden he gaz'd, and wist not what to do;
Surprise in secret chains his words suspends,
And in a calm his settling temper ends.
But silence here the beauteous angel broke,
The voice of music ravish'd as he spoke.

"Thy prayer, thy praise, thy life to vice unknown,
In sweet memorial rise before the throne:
These charms, success in our bright region find,   190
And force an angel down, to calm thy mind;
For this, commission'd, I forsook the sky,
Nay, cease to kneel—thy fellow-servant I.

"Then know the truth of government divine,
And let these scruples be no longer thine.

"The Maker justly claims that world he made,
In this the right of Providence is laid;
Its sacred majesty through all depends
On using second means to work his ends:
'Tis thus, withdrawn in state from human eye,   200
The power exerts his attributes on high,
Your actions uses, nor controls your will,
And bids the doubting sons of men be still.

"What strange events can strike with more surprise,
Than those which lately struck thy wondering eyes?
Yet taught by these, confess th' Almighty just,
And where you can't unriddle, learn to trust!

"The great, vain man, who far'd on costly food,
Whose life was too luxurious to be good;
Who made his ivory stands with goblets shine,   210
And forc'd his guests to morning draughts of wine,
Has, with the cup, the graceless custom lost,
And still he welcomes, but with less of cost.

"The mean, suspicious wretch, whose bolted door
Ne'er mov'd in duty to the wandering poor;
With him I left the cup, to teach his mind
That heaven can bless, if mortals will be kind.
Conscious of wanting worth, he views the bowl,
And feels compassion touch his grateful soul.
Thus artists melt the sullen ore of lead,   220
With heaping coals of fire upon its head;
In the kind warmth the metal learns to glow,
And loose from dross, the silver runs below.

"Long had our pious friend in virtue trod,
But now the child half-wean'd his heart from God;
Child of his age, for him he liv'd in pain,
And measur'd back his steps to earth again.
To what excesses had this dotage run!
But God, to save the father, took the son.
To all but thee, in fits he seem'd to go,   230
And 'twas my ministry to deal the blow.
The poor fond parent, humbled in the dust,
Now owns in tears the punishment was just.

"But how had all his fortune felt a wrack,
Had that false servant sped in safety back!
This night his treasur'd heaps he meant to steal,
And what a fund of charity would fail!

"Thus Heaven instructs thy mind: this trial o'er,
Depart in peace, resign, and sin no more."

On sounding pinions here the youth withdrew,   240
The sage stood wondering as the seraph flew.

Thus look'd Elisha, when, to mount on high,
His master took the chariot of the sky;
The fiery pomp ascending left the view;
The prophet gaz'd, and wish'd to follow too.

The bending hermit here a prayer begun,
"Lord! as in heaven, on earth thy will be done!"
Then gladly turning, sought his ancient place,
And pass'd a life of piety and peace.

PIETY; OR, THE VISION

'TWAS when the night in silent sable fled,
When cheerful morning sprung with rising red,
When dreams and vapours leave to crowd the brain,
And best the vision draws its heavenly scene;
'Twas then, as slumbering on my couch I lay,
A sudden splendour seem'd to kindle day,
A breeze came breathing in, a sweet perfume,
Blown from eternal gardens, fill'd the room;
And in a void of blue, that clouds invest,
Appear'd a daughter of the realms of rest;   10
Her head a ring of golden glory wore,
Her honour'd hand the sacred volume bore,
Her raiment glittering seem'd a silver white,
And all her sweet companions sons of light.

Straight as I gaz'd, my fear and wonder grew,
Fear barr'd my voice, and wonder fix'd my view;
When lo! a cherub of the shining crowd
That sail'd as guardian in her azure cloud,
Fann'd the soft air, and downwards seem'd to glide,
And to my lips a living coal applied.   20
Then while the warmth o'er all my pulses ran
Diffusing comfort, thus the maid began:

"Where glorious mansions are prepar'd above,
The seats of music, and the seats of love,
Thence I descend, and Piety my name,
To warm thy bosom with celestial flame,
To teach thee praises mix'd with humble prayers,
And tune thy soul to sing seraphic airs.

Be thou my bard."   A vial here she caught,
(An angel's hand the crystal vial brought,)   30
And as with awful sound the word was said,
She pour'd a sacred unction on my head;
Then thus proceeded: "Be thy Muse thy zeal,
Dare to be good, and all my joys reveal.
While other pencils flattering forms create,
And paint the gaudy plumes that deck the great;
While other pens exalt the vain delight,
Whose wasteful revel wakes the depth of night;
Or others softly sing in idle lines
How Damon courts, or Amaryllis shines;   40
More wisely thou select a theme divine,
Fame is their recompense, 'tis heaven is thine.
Despise the raptures of discorded fire,
Where wine, or passion, or applause inspire
Low restless life, and ravings born of earth,
Whose meaner subjects speak their humble birth,
Like working seas, that, when loud winters blow,
Not made for rising, only rage below.
Mine is a warm and yet a lambent heat,
More lasting still, as more intensely great,   50
Produc'd where prayer, and praise, and pleasure breathe
And ever mounting whence it shot beneath.
Unpaint the love, that, hovering over beds,
From glittering pinions guilty pleasure sheds;
Restore the colour to the golden mines
With which behind the feather'd idol shines;
To flowering greens give back their native care,
The rose and lily, never his to wear;
To sweet Arabia send the balmy breath;
Strip the fair flesh, and call the phantom Death;   60
His bow be sabled o'er, his shafts the same,
And fork and point them with eternal flame.

"But urge thy powers, thine utmost voice advance,
Make the loud strings against thy fingers dance;
'Tis love that angels praise and men adore,
'Tis love divine that asks it all and more.
Fling back the gates of ever-blazing day,
Pour floods of liquid light to gild the way;
And all in glory wrapt, through paths untrod,
Pursue the great unseen descent of God;   70

Hail the meek virgin, bid the child appear,
The child is God, and call him Jesus here.
He comes, but where to rest?   A manger 's nigh,
Make the great Being in a manger lie;
Fill the wide sky with angels on the wing,
Make thousands gaze, and make ten thousand sing;
Let men afflict him, men he came to save,
And still afflict him till he reach the grave;
Make him resign'd, his loads of sorrow meet,
And me, like Mary, weep beneath his feet;   80
I'll bathe my tresses there, my prayers rehearse,
And glide in flames of love along thy verse.

"Ah! while I speak, I feel my bosom swell,
My raptures smother what I long to tell.
'Tis God! a present God! through cleaving air
I see the throne, and see the Jesus there
Plac'd on the right.   He shows the wounds he bore,
(My fervours oft have won him thus before);
How pleas'd he looks! my words have reach'd his ear;
He bids the gates unbar; and calls me near."   90

She ceas'd.   The cloud on which she seem'd to tread
Its curls unfolded, and around her spread;
Bright angels waft their wings to raise the cloud,
And sweep their ivory lutes, and sing aloud;
The scene moves off, while all its ambient sky
Is turn'd to wondrous music as they fly;
And soft the swelling sounds of music grow,
And faint their softness, till they fail below.

My downy sleep the warmth of Phœbus broke,
And while my thoughts were settling, thus I spoke.   100
"Thou beauteous vision! on the soul impress'd,
When most my reason would appear to rest,
'Twas sure with pencils dipt in various lights
Some curious angel limn'd thy sacred sights;
From blazing suns his radiant gold he drew,
While moons the silver gave, and air the blue.
I'll mount the roving wind's expanded wing,
And seek the sacred hill, and light to sing;
('Tis known in Jewry well) I'll make my lays,
Obedient to thy summons, sound with praise."   110

But still I fear, unwarm'd with holy flame,
I take for truth the flatteries of a dream;
And barely wish the wondrous gift I boast,
And faintly practise what deserves it most.

Indulgent Lord! whose gracious love displays
Joy in the light, and fills the dark with ease!
Be this, to bless my days, no dream of bliss;
Or be, to bless the nights, my dreams like this.

BACCHUS; OR, THE DRUNKEN METAMORPHOSIS

As Bacchus, ranging at his leisure,
(Jolly Bacchus, king of pleasure!)
Charm'd the wide world with drink and dances
And all his thousand airy fancies,
Alas! he quite forgot the while
His favourite vines in Lesbos isle.

The god, returning ere they died,
"Ah! see my jolly Fauns," he cried,
"The leaves but hardly born are red,
And the bare arms for pity spread: 10
The beasts afford a rich manure;
Fly, my boys, to bring the cure;
Up the mountains, o'er the vales,
Through the woods, and down the dales;
For this, if full the clusters grow,
Your bowls shall doubly overflow."

So cheer'd, with more officious haste
They bring the dung of every beast;
The loads they wheel, the roots they bare,
They lay the rich manure with care;   20
While oft he calls to labour hard,
And names as oft the red reward.
The plants refresh'd, new leaves appear,
The thickening clusters load the year;
The season swiftly purple grew,
The grapes hung dangling deep with blue.

A vineyard ripe, a day serene
Now calls them all to work again.
The Fauns through every furrow shoot
To load their flaskets with the fruit;   30
And now the vintage early trod,
The wines invite the jovial god.

Strow the roses, raise the song,
See the master comes along;
Lusty Revel join'd with Laughter,
Whim and Frolic follow after:
The Fauns aside the vats remain,
To show the work, and reap the gain.
All around, and all around,
They sit to riot on the ground;   40
A vessel stands amidst the ring,
And here they laugh, and there they sing
Or rise a jolly jolly band,
And dance about it hand in hand;
Dance about, and shout amain,
Then sit to laugh and sing again.
Thus they drink, and thus they play
The sun and all their wits away.

But, as an ancient author sung,
The vine manur'd with every dung,   50
From every creature strangely drew
A twang of brutal nature too;
'Twas hence in drinking on the lawns
New turns of humour seiz'd the Fauns.

Here one was crying out, "By Jove!"
Another, "Fight me in the grove";
This wounds a friend, and that the trees;
The lion's temper reign'd in these.

Another grins, and leaps about,
And keeps a merry world of rout,   60
And talks impertinently free,
And twenty talk the same as he;
Chattering, idle, airy, kind;
These take the monkey's turn of mind.

Here one, that saw the Nymphs which stood
To peep upon them from the wood,
Skulks off to try if any maid
Be lagging late beneath the shade;
While loose discourse another raises
In naked nature's plainest phrases,   70
And every glass he drinks enjoys,
With change of nonsense, lust, and noise,
Mad and careless, hot and vain;
Such as these the goat retain.

Another drinks and casts it up,
And drinks, and wants another cup;
Solemn, silent, and sedate,
Ever long, and ever late,
Full of meats, and full of wine;
This takes his temper from the swine.   80

Here some who hardly seem to breathe,
Drink, and hang the jaw beneath.
Gaping, tender, apt to weep;
Their nature's alter'd by the sheep.

'Twas thus one autumn all the crew,
(If what the poets say be true)
While Bacchus made the merry feast,
Inclin'd to one or other beast;
And since, 'tis said, for many a mile
He spread the vines of Lesbos isle.   90

ON BISHOP BURNET'S BEING SET ON FIRE IN HIS CLOSET

FROM that dire era, bane to Sarum's pride,
Which broke his schemes, and laid his friends aside,
He talks and writes that popery will return,
And we, and he, and all his works will burn.
What touch'd himself was almost fairly prov'd:
Oh, far from Britain be the rest remov'd!
For, as of late he meant to bless the age,
With flagrant prefaces of party-rage,

O'er-wrought with passion, and the subject's weight,
Lolling, he nodded in his elbow seat;   1c
Down fell the candle; grease and zeal conspire,
Heat meets with heat, and pamphlets burn their sire.
Here crawls a preface on its half-burn'd maggots,
And there an introduction brings its faggots:
Then roars the prophet of the northern nation,
Scorch'd by a flaming speech on moderation.

Unwarn'd by this, go on, the realm to fright,
Thou Briton vaunting in thy second-sight!
In such a ministry you safely tell,
How much you'd suffer, if religion fell.   2c

ON MRS. ARABELLA FERMOR LEAVING LONDON

From town fair Arabella flies;
    The beaux unpowder'd grieve:
The rivers play before her eyes;
The breezes, softly breathing, rise;
    The Spring begins to live.

Her lovers swore, they must expire,
    Yet quickly find their ease;
For, as she goes, their flames retire;
Love thrives before a nearer fire,
    Esteem by distant rays.   1c

Yet soon the fair one will return,
    When Summer quits the plain:
Ye rivers, pour the weeping urn;
Ye breezes, sadly sighing, mourn;
    Ye lovers, burn again!

'Tis constancy enough in love
    That nature's fairly shown:
To search for more, will fruitless prove;
Romances, and the turtle-dove,
    The virtue boast alone.   2c

CHLORIS APPEARING IN A LOOKING-GLASS

OFT have I seen a piece of art,
  Of light and shade the mixture fine,
Speak all the passions of the heart,
  And show true life in every line.

But what is this before my eyes,
  With every feature, every grace,
That strikes with love, and with surprise,
  And gives me all the vital face?

It is not Chloris: for, behold,
  The shifting phantom comes and goes;   10
And when 'tis here, 'tis pale and cold,
  Nor any female softness knows.

But 'tis her image, for I feel
  The very pains that Chloris gives;
Her charms are there, I know them well,
  I see what in my bosom lives.

Oh, could I but the picture save!
  'Tis drawn by her own matchless skill;
Nature the lively colours gave,
  And she need only look to kill.   20

Ah! fair one, will it not suffice,
  That I should once your victim lie;
Unless you multiply your eyes,
  And strive to make me doubly die?

ELYSIUM

IN airy fields, the fields of bliss below,
Where woods of myrtle, set by Maro, grow,
Where grass beneath, and shade diffus'd above,
Refresh the fevers of distracted love;
There at a solemn tide the beauties, slain
By tender passion, act their fates again;
Thro' gloomy light, that just betrays the grove,
In orgies all disconsolately rove;

They range the reeds, and o'er the poppies sweep,
That nodding bend beneath their load of sleep,   10
By lakes subsiding with a gentle face,
And rivers gliding with a silent pace;
Where kings and swains, by ancient authors sung,
Now chang'd to flow'rets o'er the margin hung;
The self-admirer, white Narcissus, so
Fades at the brink, his picture fades below:
In bells of azure hyacinth arose,
In crimson painted young Adonis glows,
The fragrant crocus shone with golden flame,
And leaves inscrib'd with Ajax' haughty name.   20
A sad remembrance brings their lives to view,
And with their passion makes their tears renew,
Unwinds the years, and lays the former scene,
Where after death they live for deaths again.

Lost by the glories of her lover's state,
Deluded Semele bewails her fate,
And runs, and seems to burn, the flames arise
And fan with idle fury as she flies.

The lovely Cænis, whose transforming shape
Secur'd her honour from a second rape,   30
Now moans the first, with ruffled dress appears,
Feels her whole sex return, and bathes with tears.

The jealous Procris wipes a seeming wound,
Whose trickling crimson dyes the bushy ground,
Knows the sad shaft, and calls before she go,
To kiss the favourite hand that gave the blow.
Where ocean feigns a rage, the Sestian fair
Holds a dim taper from a tower of air;
A noiseless wind assaults the wavering light,
The beauty tumbling mingles with the night.   40

Where curling shades for rough Leucate rose,
With love distracted tuneful Sappho goes,
Sings to mock clifts a melancholy lay,
And with a lover's leap affrights the sea.

The sad Eryphile retreats to moan,
What wrought her husband's death and caus'd her own;
Surveys the glittering veil, the bribe of Fate,
And tears the shadow, but she tears too late.

In thin design and airy picture fleet
The tales that stain the royal house of Crete: 50
To court a lovely bull Pasiphaë flies,

The snowy phantom feeds before her eyes.
Lost Ariadne raves; the thread she bore
Trails on unwinding as she walks the shore;
And Phædra, desperate, seeks the lonely groves,
To read her guilty letter while she roves:
Red shame confounds the first, the second wears
A starry crown, the third a halter bears.
Fair Laodamia mourns her nuptial night,
Of love defrauded by the thirst of fight;   60
Yet for another as delusive cries,
And dauntless sees her Hero's ghost arise.

    Here Thisbe, Canace, and Dido, stand,
All arm'd with swords, a fair, but angry band:
This sword a lover own'd; a father gave
The next; a stranger chanc'd the last to leave.

    And there ev'n she, the goddess of the grove,
Join'd with the phantom-fairs, affects to rove;
As once for Latmos she forsook the plain,
To steal the kisses of a slumbering swain;   70
Around her head a starry fillet twines,
And at the front a silver crescent shines.

    These, and a thousand and a thousand more,
With sacred rage recall the pangs they bore,
Strike the deep dart afresh, and ask relief,
Or soothe the wound with softening words of grief.
At such a tide unheedful Love invades
The dark recesses of the madding shades;
Thro' long descent he fans the fogs around,
His purple feathers as he flies resound: 80
The nimble beauties, crowding all to gaze,
Perceive the common troubler of their ease;
Though dulling mists and dubious day destroy
The fine appearance of the fluttering boy,
Though all the pomp that glitters at his side
The golden belt, the clasp and quiver, hide;
And though the torch appear a gleam of white
That faintly spots and moves in hazy night,
Yet still they know the god, the general foe,
And threatening lift their airy hands below.   90

    From hence they lead him where a myrtle stood,
The saddest myrtle in the mournful wood,
Devote to vex the gods; 'twas here before
Hell's awful empress soft Adonis bore,

When the young hunter scorn'd her graver air,
And only Venus warm'd his shadow there.

 Fix'd to the trunk the tender boy they bind,
They cord his feet beneath, his hands behind;
He mourns, but vainly mourns, his angry fate,
For beauty, still relentless, acts in hate.   100
Though no offence be done, no judge be nigh,
Love must be guilty by the common cry;
For all are pleas'd, by partial passion led,
To shift their follies on another's head.

 Now sharp reproaches ring their shrill alarms,
And all the heroines brandish all their arms,
And every heroine makes it her decree
That Cupid suffer just the same as she.
To fix the desperate halter one assay'd,
One seeks to wound him with an empty blade; 110
Some headlong hang the nodding rocks of air,
They fall in fancy, and he feels despair;
Some toss the hollow seas around his head
(The seas that want a wave afford a dread),
Or shake the torch; the sparkling fury flies,
And flames that never burn'd afflict his eyes.

 The mournful Myrrha bursts her rended womb,
And drowns his visage in a moist perfume;
While others, seeming mild, advise to wound
With humorous pains, by sly Derision found, 120
That prickling bodkins teach the blood to flow,
From whence the roses first begin to glow,
Or in their flames to singe the boy prepare,
That all should choose by wanton fancy where.

 The lovely Venus, with a bleeding breast,
She too securely thro' the circle prest,
Forgot the parent, urg'd his hasty fate,
And spurr'd the female rage beyond debate;
O'er all her scenes of frailty swiftly runs,
Absolves herself, and makes the crime her son's, 130
That, clasp'd in chains, with Mars she chanc'd to lie,
A noted fable of the laughing sky;
That from her love's intemperate heat began
Sicanian Eryx, born a savage man,
The loose Priapus, and the monster wight
In whom the sexes shamefully unite.

 Nor words suffice the goddess of the fair,

She snaps the rosy wreath that binds her hair,
Then on the god, who fear'd a fiercer woe,
Her hands unpitying dealt the frequent blow; 140
From all his tender skin a purple dew
The dreadful scourges of the chaplet drew,
From whence the rose, by Cupid ting'd before,
Now, doubly tinging, flames with lustre more.

Here ends their wrath; the parent seems severe,
The strokes unfit for little Love to bear;
To save their foe the melting beauties fly,
And, "Cruel Mother! spare thy child," they cry.
To Love's account they plac'd their death of late,
And now transfer the sad account to Fate: 150
The mother pleas'd, beheld the storm asswage,
Thank'd the calm mourners, and dismiss'd her rage.

Thus Fancy, once in dusky shade exprest,
With empty terrors work'd the time of rest,
Where wretched Love endur'd a world of woe
For all a winter's length of night below;
Then soar'd, as sleep dissolv'd, unchain'd away,
And thro' the port of ivory reach'd the day,
As mindless of their rage, he slowly sails
On pinions cumber'd in the misty vales 160
(Ah, fool to light!) the Nymphs no more obey,
Nor was this region ever his to sway:
Cast in a deepen'd ring they close the plain,
And seize the god reluctant all in vain.

THE JUDGMENT OF PARIS

WHERE waving pines the brows of Ida shade,
The swain, young Paris, half supinely laid,
Saw the loose flocks thro' shrubs unnumber'd rove,
And piping call'd them to the gladded grove:
'Twas there he met the message of the skies,
That he, the judge of beauty, deal the prize.

The message known, one Love with anxious mind,
To make his mother guard the time assign'd,
Drew forth her proud white swans, and trac'd the pair
That wheel her chariot in the purple air: 10
A golden bow behind his shoulder bends,
A golden quiver at his side depends;

Pointing to these he nods with fearless state,
And bids her safely meet the grand debate.
Another Love proceeds with anxious care,
To make his ivory sleek the shining hair,
Moves the loose curls, and bids the forehead show
In full expansion all its native snow.
A third enclasps the many-colour'd cest,
And, rul'd by Fancy, sets the silver vest,   20
When to her sons, with intermingled sighs,
The goddess of the rosy lips applies.

"'Tis now, my darling Boys! a time to show
The love you feel, the filial aids you owe;
Yet would we think that any dar'd to strive
For charms, when Venus and her Loves alive?
Or, should the prize of beauty be deny'd,
Has beauty's Empress aught to boast beside?
And ting'd with poison, pleasing while it harms,
My darts I trusted to your infant arms;   30
If when your hands have arch'd the golden bow,
The world's great Ruler bending owns the blow,
Let no contending form invade my due,
Tall Juno's mien, nor Pallas' eyes of blue;
But grac'd with triumph, to the Paphian shore
Your Venus bears the palms of conquest o'er,
And joyful see my hundred altars there
With costly gums perfume the wanton air."

While thus the Cupids hear the Cyprian dame,
The groves resounded where a goddess came;   40
The warlike Pallas march'd with mighty stride,
Her shield forgot, her helmet laid aside;
Her hair unbound, in curls and order flow'd,
And peace, or something like, her visage show'd;
So with her eyes serene, and hopeful haste,
The long-stretch'd alleys of the wood she trac'd;
But where the woods a second entrance found,
With sceptred pomp and golden glory crown'd,
The stately Juno stalk'd to reach the seat,
And hear the sentence in the last debate;   50
And long, severely long, resent the grove,
In this what boots it she's the wife of Jove.

Arm'd with a grace at length, secure to win,
The lovely Venus smiling enters in;
All sweet and shining near the youth she drew,

Her rosy neck ambrosial odours threw;
The sacred scents diffus'd among the leaves,
Ran down the woods, and fill'd their hoary caves;
The charms, so amorous all, and each so great,
The conquer'd Judge no longer keeps his seat;   60
Oppress'd with light, he drops his weary'd eyes,
And fears he should be thought to doubt the prize.

TO A YOUNG LADY

ON HER TRANSLATION OF THE STORY OF PHŒBUS AND DAPHNE,
FROM OVID

In Phœbus Wit (as Ovid said)
Enchanting Beauty woo'd;
In Daphne Beauty coyly fled,
While vainly Wit pursu'd.

But when you trace what Ovid writ,
A different turn we view;
Beauty no longer flies from Wit,
Since both are join'd in you.

Your lines the wondrous change impart
From whence our laurels spring,   10
In numbers fram'd to please the heart,
And merit what they sing.

Methinks thy Poet's gentle shade
Its wreath presents to thee;
What Daphne owes you as a maid,
She pays you as a tree.

THE HORSE AND THE OLIVE

With moral tale let ancient wisdom move,
Whilst thus I sing to make the Moderns wise;
Strong Neptune once with sage Minerva strove,
And rising Athens was the victor's prize.

By Neptune Plutus (guardian power of gain),
By great Minerva bright Apollo stood;
But Jove, superior, bade the side obtain
Which best contriv'd to do the nation good.

Then Neptune striking, from the parted ground
The warlike Horse came pawing on the plain,   10
And as it toss'd its mane, and pranc'd around,
"By this," he cries, "I'll make the people reign."

The goddess, smiling, gently bow'd her spear,
"And rather thus they shall be bless'd," she said:
Then upward shooting in the vernal air,
With loaded boughs the fruitful Olive spread.

Jove saw what gift the rural powers design'd,
And took th' impartial scales, resolv'd to show
If greater bliss in warlike pomp we find,
Or in the calm which peaceful times bestow.   20

On Neptune's part he plac'd victorious days,
Gay trophies won, and fame extending wide;
But Plenty, Safety, Science, Arts, and Ease,
Minerva's scale with greater weight supply'd.

Fierce War devours whom gentle Peace would save;
Sweet Peace restores what angry War destroys;
War made for Peace with that rewards the brave,
While Peace its pleasures from itself enjoys.

Hence vanquish'd Neptune to the sea withdrew,
Hence wise Minerva rul'd Athenian lands;   30
Her Athens hence in arts and honours grew,
And still her Olives deck pacific hands.

From fables thus disclos'd, a monarch's mind
May form just rules to choose the truly great,
And subjects, weary'd with distresses, find
Whose kind endeavours most befriend the state.

Ev'n Britain here may learn to place her love,
If cities won her kingdom's wealth have cost;
If Anna's thoughts the patriot souls approve,
Whose cares restore that wealth the wars had lost. 40

But if we ask, the moral to disclose,
Whom her best patroness Europa calls,
Great Anna's title no exception knows,
And, unapply'd in this, the fable falls.

With her nor Neptune or Minerva vies:
Whene'er she pleas'd her troops to conquest flew;
Whene'er she pleases peaceful times arise:
She gave the Horse, and gives the Olive too.

ON THE DEATH OF MR. VINER

Is Viner dead? and shall each Muse become
Silent as Death, and as his music dumb?
Shall he depart without a Poet's praise,
Who oft to harmony has tun'd their lays?
Shall he, who knew the elegance of sound,
Find no one voice to sing him to the ground?
Music and Poetry are sister-arts,
Shew a like genius, and consenting hearts:
My soul with his is secretly ally'd,
And I am forc'd to speak, since Viner dy'd.   10
    Oh, that my Muse, as once his notes, could swell!
That I might all his praises fully tell;
That I might say with how much skill he play'd,
How nimbly four extended strings survey'd;
How bow and fingers, with a noble strife,
Did raise the vocal fiddle into life;
How various sounds, in various order rang'd,
By unobserv'd degrees minutely chang'd,
Through a vast space could in divisions run,
Be all distinct, yet all agree in one: 20
And how the fleeter notes could swiftly pass,
And skip alternately from place to place;
The strings could with a sudden impulse bound,
Speak every touch, and tremble into sound.
    The liquid harmony, a tuneful tide,
Now seem'd to rage, anon would gently glide;
By turns would ebb and flow, would rise and fall,
Be loudly daring, or be softly small:
While all was blended in one common name,
Wave push'd on wave, and all compos'd a stream.   30
    The different tones melodiously combin'd,
Temper'd with art, in sweet confusion join'd;
The soft, the strong, the clear, the shrill, the deep,
Would sometimes soar aloft, and sometimes creep;

While every soul upon his motions hung,
As though it were in tuneful concert strung,
His touch did strike the fibres of the heart,
And a like trembling secretly impart;
Where various passions did by turns succeed,
He made it cheerful, and he made it bleed;   40
Could wind it up into a glowing fire,
Then shift the scene, and teach it to expire.

    Oft have I seen him, on a public stage,
Alone the gaping multitude engage;
The eyes and ears of each spectator draw,
Command their thoughts, and give their passions law
While other music, in oblivion drown'd,
Seem'd a dead pulse, or a neglected sound.

    Alas! he 's gone, our great Apollo's dead,
And all that's sweet and tuneful with him fled;   50
Hibernia, with one universal cry,
Laments the loss, and speaks his elegy.
Farewell, thou author of refin'd delight.
Too little known, too soon remov'd from sight;
Those fingers, which such pleasure did convey,
Must now become to stupid worms a prey:
Thy grateful fiddle will for ever stand
A silent mourner for its master's hand:
Thy art is only to be match'd above,
Where Music reigns, and in that Music Love: 60
Where thou wilt in the happy chorus join, ⎫
And quickly thy melodious soul refine   ⎬
To the exalted pitch of Harmony Divine. ⎭

EPIGRAM

Haud facile emergunt, quorum virtutibus obstat
   Res angusta domi—

THE greatest gifts that Nature does bestow,
Can't unassisted to perfection grow:
A scanty fortune clips the wings of Fame,
And checks the progress of a rising name:
Each dastard virtue drags a captive's chain,
And moves but slowly, for it moves with pain:
Domestic cares sit hard upon the mind,

And cramp those thoughts which should be unconfin'd:
The cries of Poverty alarm the soul,
Abate its vigour, its designs control: 10
The stings of Want inflict the wounds of Death,
And motion always ceases with the breath.
The love of friends is found a languid fire,
That glares but faintly, and will soon expire;
Weak is its force, nor can its warmth be great,
A feeble light begets a feeble heat.
Wealth is the fuel that must feed the flame,
It dies in rags, and scarce deserves a name.

LOVE IN DISGUISE

To stifle passion, is no easy thing;
A heart in love is always on the wing;
 The bold betrayer flutters still,
 And fans the breath prepar'd to tell:
It melts the tongue, and tunes the throat,
And moves the lips to form the note;
  And when the speech is lost,
  It then sends out its ghost,
   A little sigh,
   To say we die.   10
'Tis strange the air that cools, a flame should prove;
But wonder not, it is the air of love.

Yet, Chloris, I can make my love look well,
And cover bleeding wounds I can't conceal;
 My words such artful accents break,
 You think I rather act than speak:
My sighs, enliven'd through a smile,
Your unsuspecting thoughts beguile;
  My eyes are vary'd so,
  You can't their wishes know: 20
   And I'm so gay,
   You think I play.
Happy contrivance! such as can't be priz'd,
To live in love, and yet to live disguis'd!

ON A LADY WITH FOUL BREATH

ART thou alive?   It cannot be,
There's so much rottenness in thee,
Corruption only is in death;
And what's more putrid than thy breath?
Think not you live because you speak,
For graves such hollow sounds can make;
And respiration can't suffice,
For vapours do from caverns rise:
From thee such noisome stenches come,
Thy mouth betrays thy breast a tomb.   10
Thy body is a corpse that goes,
By magic rais'd from its repose:
A pestilence, that walks by day,
But falls at night to worms and clay.
But I will to my Chloris run,
Who will not let me be undone:
The sweets her virgin-breath contains
Are fitted to remove my pains;
There will I healing nectar sip,
And, to be sav'd, approach her lip   20
Though, if I touch the matchless dame,
I'm sure to burn with inward flame.
Thus, when I would one danger shun,
I'm straight upon another thrown:
I seek a cure, one sore to ease,
Yet in that cure's a new disease.
But Love, though fatal, still can bless,
And greater dangers hide the less;
I'll go where passion bids me fly,
And choose my death, since I must die;   30
As doves, pursued by birds of prey,
Venture with milder man to stay.

ON THE NUMBER THREE

BEAUTY rests not in one fix'd place,
But seems to reign in every face;
'Tis nothing sure but fancy then,
In various forms, bewitching men;

Or is its shape and colour fram'd,
Proportion just, and Woman nam'd?
If Fancy only rul'd in Love,
Why should it then so strongly move?
Or why should all that look agree
To own its mighty power in Three?   10
In Three it shows a different face,
Each shining with peculiar grace.
Kindred a native likeness gives,
Which pleases, as in all it lives;
And, where the features disagree,
We praise the dear variety.
Then Beauty surely ne'er was yet,
So much unlike itself, and so complete.

ESSAY ON THE DIFFERENT STYLES OF POETRY

TO HENRY LORD VISCOUNT BOLINGBROKE

—Vatibus addere calcar,
Ut studio majore petant Helicona virentem.
Hor., Ep. II. i.

I HATE the vulgar with untuneful mind;
Hearts uninspir'd, and senses unrefin'd.
Hence, ye prophane: I raise the sounding string,
And Bolingbroke descends to hear me sing.
  When Greece could Truth in mystic fable shroud,
And with delight instruct the listening crowd,
An ancient poet (Time has lost his name)
Deliver'd strains on verse to future fame.
Still, as he sung, he touch'd the trembling lyre,
And felt the notes a rising warmth inspire.   10
Ye sweetening Graces, in the music throng,
Assist my genius, and retrieve the song
From dark oblivion.   See, my genius goes
To call it forth.   'Twas thus the poem rose.
  "Wit is the Muses' horse, and bears on high
The daring rider to the Muses' sky:
Who, while his strength to mount aloft he tries,
By regions varying in their nature flies.
  At first, he riseth o'er a land of toil,
A barren, hard, and undeserving soil,   20

Where only weeds from heavy labour grow,
Which yet the nation prune, and keep for show.
Where couplets jingling on their accent run,
Whose point of epigram is sunk to pun;
Where wings by fancy never feather'd fly,
Where lines by measure form'd in hatchets lie;
Where altars stand, erected porches gape,
And sense is cramp'd while words are par'd to shape;
Where mean acrostics, labour'd in a frame
On scatter'd letters, raise a painful scheme;   30
And, by confinement in their work, control
The great enlargings of the boundless soul;
Where if a warrior's elevated fire
Would all the brightest strokes of verse require,
Then straight in anagram a wretched crew
Will pay their undeserving praises too;
While on the rack his poor disjointed name
Must tell its master's character to Fame.
And (if my fire and fears aright presage)
The labouring writers of a future age   40
Shall clear new ground, and grots and caves repair,
To civilise the babbling echoes there.
Then, while a lover treads a lonely walk,
His voice shall with its own reflection talk,
The closing sounds of all the vain device
Select by trouble frivolously nice,
Resound through verse, and with a false pretence
Support the dialogue, and pass for sense.
Can things like these to lasting praise pretend?
Can any Muse the worthless toil befriend?   50
Ye sacred Virgins, in my thoughts ador'd,
Ah, be for ever in my lines deplor'd,
If tricks on words acquire an endless name,
And trifles merit in the court of Fame!"
     At this the poet stood concern'd a while,
And view'd his objects with a scornful smile:
Then other images of different kind,
With different workings, enter'd on his mind;
At whose approach, he felt the former gone,
And shiver'd in conceit, and thus went on: 60
     "By a cold region next the rider goes,
Where all lies cover'd in eternal snows;
Where no bright genius drives the chariot high,

To glitter on the ground, and gild the sky.
Bleak level realm, where frigid styles abound,
Where never yet a daring thought was found,
But counted feet is poetry defin'd;
And starv'd conceits, that chill the reader's mind,
A little sense in many words imply,
And drag in loitering numbers slowly by.   70
Here dry sententious speeches, half asleep,
Prolong'd in lines, o'er many pages creep;
Nor ever show the passions well express'd,
Nor raise like passions in another's breast.
Here flat narrations fair exploits debase,
In measures void of every shining grace;
Which never arm their hero for the field,
Nor with prophetic story paint the shield,
Nor fix the crest, nor make the feathers wave,
Nor with their characters reward the brave;   80
Undeck'd they stand, and unadorn'd with praise,
And fail to profit while they fail to please.
Here forc'd description is so strangely wrought,
It never stamps its image on the thought;
The lifeless trees may stand for ever bare,
And rivers stop, for aught the readers care;
They see no branches trembling in the woods,
Nor hear the murmurs of increasing floods,
Which near the roots of ruffled waters flow,
And shake the shadows of the boughs below.   90
Ah, sacred Verse, replete with heavenly flame,
Such cold endeavours would invade thy name!
The writer fondly would in these survive,
Which, wanting spirit, never seem'd alive:
But, if applause or fame attend his pen,
Let breathless statues pass for breathing men."
    Here seem'd the singer touch'd at what he sung,
And grief a while delay'd his hand and tongue:
But soon he check'd his fingers, chose a strain,
And flourish'd shrill, and thus arose again: 100
    "Pass the next region which appears to show:
'Tis very open, unimprov'd, and low;
No noble flights of elevated thought,
No nervous strength of sense maturely wrought,
Possess this realm; but common turns are there,
Which idly sportive move with childish air,

On callow wings, and like a plague of flies,
The little fancies in a poem rise,
The jaded reader everywhere to strike,
And move his passions everywhere alike.   110
There all the graceful nymphs are forc'd to play
Where any water bubbles in the way:
There shaggy satyrs are oblig'd to rove
In all the fields, and over all the grove:
There every star is summon'd from its sphere,
To dress one face, and make Clorinda fair:
There Cupids fling their darts in every song,
While Nature stands neglected all along:
Till the teas'd hearer, vex'd at last to find
One constant object still assault the mind,   120
Admires no more at what 's no longer new,
And hastes to shun the persecuting view.
There bright surprises of poetic rage
(Whose strength and beauty, more confirm'd in age
For having lasted, last the longer still)
By weak attempts are imitated ill,
Or carried on beyond their proper light,
Or with refinement flourish'd out of sight.
There metaphors on metaphors abound,
And sense by differing images confound: 130
Strange injudicious management of thought,
Not born to rage, nor into method brought.
Ah, sacred Muse! from such a realm retreat,
Nor idly waste the influence of thy heat
On shallow soils, where quick productions rise,
And wither as the warmth that rais'd them dies."
     Here o'er his breast a sort of pity roll'd,
Which something labouring in the mind control'd,
And made him touch the loud resounding strings,
While thus with music's stronger tones he sings: 140
     "Mount higher still, still keep thy faithful seat,
Mind the firm reins, and curb thy courser's heat;
Nor let him touch the realms that next appear,
Whose hanging turrets seem a fall to fear;
And strangely stand along the tracts of air,
Where thunder rolls, and bearded comets glare.
The thoughts that most extravagantly soar,
The words that sound as if they meant to roar;
For rant and noise are offer'd here to choice,

And stand elected by the public voice.   150
All schemes are slighted which attempt to shine
At once with strange and probable design;
'Tis here a mean conceit, a vulgar view,
That bears the least respect to seeming true;
While every trifling turn of things is seen
To move by gods descending in machine.
Here swelling lines with stalking strut proceed,
And in the clouds terrific rumblings breed;
Here single heroes deal grim deaths around,
And armies perish in tremendous sound;   160
Here fearful monsters are preserv'd to die,
In such a tumult as affrights the sky;
For which the golden sun shall hide with dread,
And Neptune lift his sedgy-matted head,
Admire the roar, and dive with dire dismay,
And seek his deepest chambers in the sea.
To raise their subject thus the lines devise,
And false extravagance would fain surprise;
Yet still, ye gods, ye live untouch'd by fear,
And undisturb'd at bellowing monsters here: 170
But with compassion guard the brain of men,
If thus they bellow through the poet's pen:
So will the reader's eyes discern aright
The rashest sally from the noblest flight,
And find that only boast and sound agree
To seem the life and voice of majesty,
When writers rampant on Apollo call,
And bid him enter and possess them all,
And make his flames afford a wild pretence
To keep them unrestrain'd by common sense.   180
Ah, sacred Verse! lest Reason quit thy seat,
Give none to such, or give a gentler heat."
　'Twas here the singer felt his temper wrought
By fairer prospects, which arose to thought;
And in himself a while collected sat,
And much admir'd at this, and much at that;
Till all the beauteous forms in order ran,
And then he took their track, and thus began:
　"Above the beauties, far above the show
In which weak Nature dresses here below,   190
Stands the great palace of the Bright and Fine,
Where fair ideas in full glory shine;

Eternal models of exalted parts,
The pride of minds, and conquerors of hearts.
    Upon the first arrival here, are seen
Rang'd walks of bay, the Muses' ever-green,
Each sweetly springing from some sacred bough,
Whose circling shade adorn'd a poet's brow,
While through the leaves, in unmolested skies,
The gentle breathing of applauses flies,   200
And flattering sounds are heard within the breeze,
And pleasing murmur runs among the trees,
And falls of water join the flattering sounds,
And murmur softening from the shore rebounds.
The warbled melody, the lovely sights,
The calms of solitude inspire delights,
The dazzled eyes, the ravish'd ears, are caught,
The panting heart unites to purer thought,
And grateful shiverings wander o'er the skin,
And wondrous ecstasies arise within,   210
Whence admiration overflows the mind,
And leaves the pleasure felt, but undefin'd.
Stay, daring rider, now no longer rove;
Now pass to find the palace through the grove:
Whate'er you see, whate'er you feel, display
The realm you sought for; daring rider, stay.
    Here various Fancy spreads a varied scene,
And Judgment likes the sight, and looks serene,
And can be pleas'd itself, and helps to please,
And joins the work, and regulates the lays.   220
Thus, on a plan design'd by double care,
The building rises in the glittering air,
With just agreement fram'd in every part,
And smoothly polish'd with the nicest art.
    Here laurel-boughs, which ancient heroes wore,
Now not so fading as they prov'd before,
Wreathe round the pillars which the poets rear,
And slope their points to make a foliage there.
Here chaplets, pull'd in gently-breathing wind,
And wrought by lovers innocently kind,   230
Hung o'er the porch, their fragrant odours give,
And fresh in lasting song for ever live.
The shades, for whom with such indulgent care
Fame wreathes the boughs, or hangs the chaplets there,
To deathless honours thus preserv'd above,

For ages conquer, or for ages love.
    Here bold Description paints the walls within,
Her pencil touches, and the world is seen:
The fields look beauteous in their flowery pride,
The mountains rear aloft, the vales subside;   240
The cities rise, the rivers seem to play,
And hanging rocks repel the foaming sea;
The foaming seas their angry billows show,
Curl'd white above, and darkly roll'd below,
Or cease their rage, and, as they calmly lie,
Return the pleasing pictures of the sky;
The skies, extended in an open view,
Appear a lofty distant arch of blue,
In which Description stains the painted bow,
Or thickens clouds, and feathers-out the snow,   250
Or mingles blushes in the morning ray,
Or gilds the noon, or turns an evening gray.
    Here, on the pedestals of War and Peace,
In different rows, and with a different grace,
Fine statues proudly ride, or nobly stand,
To which Narration with a pointing hand
Directs the sight, and makes examples please
By boldly venturing to dilate in praise;
While chosen beauties lengthen out the song,
Yet make her hearers never think it long.   260
Or if, with closer art, with sprightly mien,
Scarce like herself, and more like Action seen,
She bids their facts in images arise,
And seem to pass before the reader's eyes,
The words like charms enchanted motion give,
And all the statues of the palace live.
Then hosts embattled stretch their lines afar,
Their leaders' speeches animate the war,
The trumpets sound, the feather'd arrows fly,
The sword is drawn, the lance is toss'd on high,   270
The brave press on, the fainter forces yield,
And death in different shapes deforms the field.
Or, should the shepherds be dispos'd to play,
Amintor's jolly pipe beguiles the day,
And jocund echoes dally with the sound,
And nymphs in measures trip along the ground,
And, ere the dews have wet the grass below,
Turn homewards singing all the way they go.

Here, as on circumstance narrations dwell,
And tell what moves, and hardly seem to tell,   28o
The toil of heroes on the dusty plains,
Or on the green the merriment of swains,
Reflection speaks: then all the Forms that rose
In life's enchanted scene themselves compose;
Whilst the grave voice, controlling all the spells,
With solemn utterance, thus the Moral tells:
"So Public Worth its enemies destroys,
Or Private Innocence itself enjoys."
    Here all the Passions, for their greater sway,
In all the power of words themselves array;   29o
And hence the soft Pathetic gently charms,
And hence the bolder fills the breast with arms.
Sweet Love in numbers finds a world of darts,
And with Desirings wounds the tender hearts.
Fair Hope displays its pinions to the wind,
And flutters in the lines, and lifts the mind.
Brisk Joy with transport fills the rising strain,
Breaks in the notes, and bounds in every vein.
Stern Courage, glittering in the sparks of ire,
Inflames those lays that set the breast on fire.   30o
Aversion learns to fly with swifter will,
In numbers taught to represent an ill.
By frightful accents Fear produces fears;
By sad expression Sorrow melts to tears:
And dire amazement and despair are brought
By words of horror through the wilds of thought.
'Tis thus tumultuous Passions learn to roll;
Thus, arm'd with poetry, they win the soul.
    Pass further through the dome, another view
Would now the pleasures of thy mind renew,   31o
Where oft Description for the colours goes,
Which raise and animate its native shows;
Where oft Narration seeks a florid grace
To keep from sinking ere 'tis time to cease;
Where easy turns Reflection looks to find,
When Morals aim at dress to please the mind;
Where lively Figures are for use array'd,
And these an Action, those a Passion, aid.
There modest Metaphors in order sit,
With unaffected, undisguising Wit,   32
That leave their own, and seek another's place,

Not forc'd, but changing with an easy pace,
To deck a notion faintly seen before,
And Truth preserves her shape, and shines the more.
   By these the beauteous Similes reside,
In look more open, in design ally'd,
Who, fond of likeness, from another's face
Bring every feature's corresponding grace,
With near approaches in expression flow,
And take the turn their pattern loves to show;   330
As in a glass the shadows meet the fair,
And dress and practise with resembling air.
Thus Truth by pleasure doth her aim pursue,
Looks bright, and fixes on the doubled view.
   There Repetitions one another meet,
Expressly strong, or languishingly sweet,
And raise the sort of sentiment they please,
And urge the sort of sentiment they raise.
   There close in order are the Questions plac'd,
Which march with art conceal'd in shows of haste,   340
And work the reader till his mind be brought
To make its answers in the writer's thought.
For thus the moving Passions seem to throng,
And with their quickness force the soul along;
And thus the soul grows fond they should prevail,
When every Question seems a fair appeal;
And if by just degrees of strength they soar,
In steps as equal each affects the more.
   There strange Commotion, naturally shown,
Speaks on regardless that she speaks alone,   350
Nor minds if they to whom she talks be near,
Nor cares if that to which she talks can hear.
The warmth of Anger dares an absent foe;
The words of Pity speak to tears of woe;
The Love that hopes, on errands sends the breeze;
And Love despairing moans to naked trees.
   There stand the new creations of the Muse,
Poetic persons, whom the writers use
Whene'er a cause magnificently great
Would fix attention with peculiar weight.   360
'Tis hence that humble Provinces are seen
Transform'd to Matrons with neglected mien,
Who call their warriors in a mournful sound,
And show their crowns of turrets on the ground,

While over urns reclining rivers moan
They should enrich a nation not their own.
'Tis hence the virtues are no more confin'd
To be but rules of reason in the mind;
The heavenly Forms start forth, appear to breathe,
And in bright shapes converse with men beneath;   370
And, as a god in combat Valour leads,
In council Prudence as a goddess aids.

  There Exclamations all the voice employ
In sudden flushes of concern or joy:
Then seem the sluices, which the Passions bound,
To burst asunder with a speechless sound;
And then with tumult and surprise they roll,
And show the case important in the soul.

  There rising Sentences attempt to speak,
Which Wonder, Sorrow, Shame, or Anger break;   380
But so the Part directs to find the rest,
That what remains behind is more than guess'd.
Thus fill'd with ease, yet left unfinish'd too,
The sense looks large within the reader's view:
He freely gathers all the passion means,
And artful silence more than words explains.
Methinks a thousand Graces more I see,
And I could dwell—but when would thought be free?
Engaging Method ranges all the band,
And smooth Transition joins them hand in hand: 390
Around the music of my lays they throng,
Ah, too deserving objects of my song!
Live, wondrous palace, live secure of time,
To Senses harmony, to Souls sublime,
And just proportion all, and great design,
And lively colours, and an air divine.

  'Tis here that, guided by the Muses' fire,
And fill'd with sacred thought, her friends retire,
Unbent to care, and unconcern'd with noise,
To taste repose and elevated joys,   400
Which in a deep untroubled leisure meet,
Serenely ravishing, politely sweet.
From hence the Charms that most engage they choose,
And, as they please, the glittering objects use;
While to their genius, more than Art, they trust,
Yet Art acknowledges their labours just.
From hence they look, from this exalted show,

To choose their subject in the world below,
And where an hero well deserves a name,
They consecrate his acts in song to Fame;   410
Or, if a science unadorn'd they find,
They smooth its look to please and teach the mind;
And where a friendship's generously strong,
They celebrate the knot of souls in song;
Or, if the verses must inflame Desire,
The thoughts are melted, and the words on fire:
But, when the temples deck'd with glory stand,
And hymns of gratitude the gods demand,
Their bosoms kindle with celestial love,
And then alone they cast their eyes above.   420
    Hail, sacred Verse! ye sacred Muses, hail!
Could I your pleasures with your fire reveal,
The world might then be taught to know you right,
And court your rage, and envy my delight.
But, whilst I follow where your pointed beams
My course directing shoot in golden streams,
The bright appearance dazzles Fancy's eyes,
And weary'd-out the fix'd attention lies;
Enough, my Verses, have you work'd my breast,
I'll seek the sacred grove, and sink to rest."   430
    No longer now the ravish'd poet sung,
His voice in easy cadence left the tongue;
Nor o'er the music did his fingers fly,
The sounds ran tingling, and they seem'd to die.
    O, Bolingbroke! O favourite of the skies,
O born to gifts by which the noblest rise,
Improv'd in arts by which the brightest please,
Intent to business, and polite for ease;
Sublime in eloquence, where loud applause
Hath styl'd thee Patron of a nation's cause.   440
'Twas there the world perceiv'd and own'd thee great,
Thence Anna call'd thee to the reins of State;
"Go," said the greatest queen, "with Oxford go,
And still the tumults of the world below,
Exert thy powers, and prosper; he that knows
To move with Oxford, never should repose."
    She spake: the Patriot overspread thy mind,
And all thy days to public good resign'd.
Else might thy soul, so wonderfully wrought
For every depth and turn of curious thought,   450

To this the poet's sweet recess retreat,
And thence report the pleasures of the seat,
Describe the raptures which a writer knows,
When in his breast a vein of fancy glows,
Describe his business while he works the mine,
Describe his temper when he sees it shine,
Or say, when readers easy verse insnares,
How much the writer's mind can act on theirs:
Whence images, in charming numbers set,
A sort of likeness in the soul beget,   460
And what fair visions oft we fancy nigh
By fond delusions of the swimming eye,
Or further pierce through Nature's maze to find
How passions drawn give passions to the mind.

    Oh, what a sweet confusion! what surprise!
How quick the shifting views of pleasure rise!
While, lightly skimming, with a transient wing,
I touch the beauties which I wish to sing.
Is Verse a sovereign Regent of the soul,
And fitted all its motions to control?   470
Or are they sisters, tun'd at once above,
And shake like unisons if either move?
For, when the numbers sing an eager fight,
I've heard a soldier's voice express delight;
I've seen his eyes with crowding spirits shine,
And round his hilt his hand unthinking twine.
When from the shore the fickle Trojan flies,
And in sweet measures poor Eliza dies,
I've seen the book forsake the virgin's hand,
And in her eyes the tears but hardly stand.   480
I've known her blush at soft Corinna's name,
And in red characters confess a flame:
Or wish success had more adorn'd his arms,
Who gave the world for Cleopatra's charms.

    Ye Sons of Glory, be my first appeal,
If here the power of lines these lines reveal.
When some great youth has with impetuous thought
Read o'er achievements which another wrought,
And seen his courage and his honour go
Through crowding nations in triumphant show,   490
His soul, enchanted by the words he reads,
Shines all impregnated with sparkling seeds,
And courage here, and honour there, appears

In brave design that soars beyond his years,
And this a spear, and that a chariot lends,
And war and triumph he by turn attends;
Thus gallant pleasures are his waking dream,
Till some fair cause have call'd him forth to fame.
Then, form'd to life on what the poet made,
And breathing slaughter, and in arms array'd,   500
He marches forward on the daring foe,
And emulation acts in every blow.
Great Hector's shade in fancy stalks along,
From rank to rank amongst the martial throng;
While from his acts he learns a noble rage,
And shines like Hector in the present age.
Thus Verse will raise him to the victor's bays;
And Verse, that rais'd him, shall resound his praise.
   Ye tender Beauties, be my witness too,
If Song can charm, and if my song be true.   510
With sweet experience oft a Fair may find
Her passions mov'd by passions well design'd;
And then she longs to meet a gentle swain,
And longs to love, and to be lov'd again.
And if by chance an amorous youth appears,
With pants and blushes she the courtship hears;
And finds a tale that must with theirs agree,
And he's Septimius, and his Acme she:
Thus lost in thought her melted heart she gives,
And the rais'd lover by the poet lives.   520

A HYMN FOR MORNING

See, the star that leads the day,
Rising shoots a golden ray,
To make the shades of darkness go
From Heaven above and earth below,
And warn us early with the sight
To leave the beds of silent night,
From an heart sincere and sound,
From its very deepest ground,
Send devotion up on high,
Wing'd with heat, to reach the sky.   10
See the time for sleep has run,
Rise before or with the sun,

Lift thine hands, and humble pray
The Fountain of eternal day,
That as the light serenely fair
Illustrates all the tracts of air,
The sacred Spirit so may rest
With quickening beams upon thy breast,
And kindly clean it all within
From darker blemishes of sin,   20
And shine with grace, until we view
The realm it gilds with glory too.
See the day that dawns in air,
Brings along its toil and care,
From the lap of Night it springs
With heaps of business on its wings;
Prepare to meet them in a mind
That bows submissively resign'd,
That would to works appointed fall,
And knows that God has order'd all.   3
And whether with a small repast
We break the sober morning fast,
Or in our thoughts and houses lay
The future methods of the day,
Or early walk abroad to meet
Our business, with industrious feet,
Whate'er we think, whate'er we do,
His glory still be kept in view.
O Giver of eternal bliss!
Heavenly Father! grant me this,   4
Grant it all as well as me,
All whose hearts are fix'd on thee,
Who revere thy Son above,
Who thy sacred Spirit love.

A HYMN FOR NOON

THE sun is swiftly mounted high,
It glitters in the southern sky,
Its beams with force and glory beat,
And fruitful earth is fill'd with heat.
Father! also with thy fire
Warm the cold, the dead desire,
And make the sacred love of thee

Within my soul a sun to me:
Let it shine so fairly bright,
That nothing else be took for light, 10
That worldly charms be seen to fade,
And in its lustre find a shade:
Let it strongly shine within,
To scatter all the clouds of sin,
That drive when gusts of passion rise,
And intercept it from our eyes:
Let its glory more than vie
With the sun that lights the sky:
Let it swiftly mount in air,
Mount with that, and leave it there, 20
And soar with more aspiring flight
To realms of everlasting light.
Thus, while here I'm forc'd to be,
I daily wish to live with thee,
And feel that union which thy love
Will, after death, complete above.
From my soul I send my prayer,
Great Creator! bow thine ear;
Thou, for whose propitious sway
The world was taught to see the day, 30
Who spake the word, and earth begun,
And show'd its beauties in the sun,
With pleasure I thy creatures view,
And would with good affection too,
Good affection sweetly free,
Loose from them, and move to thee:
O teach me due returns to give,
And to thy glory let me live,
And then my days shall shine the more,
Or pass more blessed than before. 40

A HYMN FOR EVENING

THE beam-repelling mists arise,
And evening spreads obscurer skies:
The twilight will the night forerun,
And night itself be soon begun.
Upon thy knees devoutly bow,
And pray the Lord of glory now

To fill thy breast, or deadly sin
May cause a blinder night within.
And whether pleasing vapours rise,
Which gently dim the closing eyes,   10
Which makes the weary members blest
With sweet refreshment in their rest,
Or whether spirits in the brain
Dispel their soft embrace again,
And on my watchful bed I stay,
Forsook by sleep, and waiting day;
Be God for ever in my view,
And never he forsake me too;
But still as day concludes in night,
To break again with new-born light,   20
His wondrous bounty let me find
With still a more enlighten'd mind.
When grace and love in one agree,
Grace from God, and love from me,
Grace that will from Heaven inspire,
Love that seals it in desire,
Grace and love that mingle beams,
And fill me with increasing flames.
Thou that hast thy palace far
Above the moon and every star,   30
Thou that sittest on a throne
To which the night was never known,
Regard my voice, and make me blest
By kindly granting its request.
If thoughts on thee my soul employ,
My darkness will afford me joy,
Till thou shalt call and I shall soar,
And part with darkness evermore.

THE GIFT OF POETRY

FROM realms of never-interrupted peace,
From thy fair station near the throne of Grace,
From choirs of angels, joys in endless round,
And endless Harmony's enchanting sound,
Charm'd with a zeal the Maker's praise to show,
Bright Gift of Verse descend, and here below
My ravish'd heart with rais'd affection fill,

And warbling o'er the soul incline my will.
Among thy pomp let rich Expression wait,
Let ranging Numbers form thy train complete,   10
While at thy motions over all the sky
Sweet sounds, and echoes sweet, resounding fly;
And where thy feet with gliding beauty tread,
Let Fancy's flowery spring erect its head.

  It comes, it comes with unaccustom'd light!
The tracts of airy thought grow wondrous bright;
Its notions ancient Memory reviews,
And young Invention new designs pursues;
To some attempt my will and wishes press,
And pleasure, rais'd in hope, forebodes success.   20
My God! from whom proceed the gifts divine,
My God! I think I feel the gift is thine.
Be this no vain illusion which I find,
Nor Nature's impulse on the passive mind,
But Reason's act, produc'd by good desire,
By grace enliven'd with celestial fire;
While base conceits, like misty sons of Night,
Before such beams of glory take their flight,
And frail affections, born of earth, decay,
Like weeds that wither in the warmer ray.   30

  I thank thee, Father! with a grateful mind,
Man's undeserving, and thy mercy kind;
I now perceive I long to sing thy praise,
I now perceive I long to find my lays,
The sweet incentives of another's love,
And sure such longings have their rise above;
My resolution stands confirm'd within,
My lines aspiring eagerly begin;
Begin, my Lines! to such a subject due,
That aids our labours and rewards them too;   40
Begin, while Canaan opens to mine eyes,
Where souls and songs divinely form'd arise.

  As one whom o'er the sweetly-vary'd meads
Entire recess and lonely pleasure leads,
To verdur'd banks, to paths adorn'd with flowers,
To shady trees, to closely-waving bowers,
To bubbling fountains, and aside the stream
That softly gliding soothes a waking dream,
Or bears the thought inspir'd with heat along,
And with fair images improves a song;   50

Thro' sacred anthems so may Fancy range,
So still from beauty still to beauty change,
To feel delights in all the radiant way,
And with sweet numbers what it feels repay:
For this I call that ancient Time appear,
And bring his rolls to serve in method here;
His rolls, which acts that endless honour claim
Have rank'd in order for the voice of Fame.

My call is favour'd: Time, from first to last,
Unwinds his years; the present sees the past:
I view their circles as he turns them o'er,
And fix my footsteps where he went before.

The page unfolding would a top disclose,
Where sounds melodious in their birth arose;
Where first the morning stars together sung,
Where first their harps the sons of glory strung
With shouts of joy, while hallelujahs rise
To prove the chorus of eternal skies;
Rich sparkling strokes the letters doubly gild,
And all's with love and admiration fill'd.

ON HAPPINESS IN THIS LIFE

THE morning opens very freshly gay,
And life itself is in the month of May.
With green my fancy paints an arbour o'er,
And flowerets with a thousand colours more,
Then falls to weaving that, and spreading these,
And softly shakes them with an easy breeze;
With golden fruit adorns the bending shade,
Or trails a silver water o'er its bed.
Glide, gentle water! still more gently by,
While in this summer-bower of bliss I lie,
And sweetly sing of sense-delighting flames,
And nymphs' and shepherds' soft-invented names;
Or view the branches which around me twine,
And praise their fruit, diffusing sprightly wine;
Or find new pleasures in the world to praise,
And still with this return adorn my lays,
"Range round your gardens of eternal spring;
Go range, my Senses! while I sweetly sing."

In vain, in vain, alas! seduc'd by ill,
And acted wildly by the force of will,   20
I tell my soul it will be constant May,
And charm a season never made to stay;
My beauteous arbour will not stand a storm,
The world but promises, and can't perform:
Then fade, ye leaves! and wither, all ye flowers!
I'll dote no longer in enchanted bowers,
But sadly mourn, in melancholy song,
The vain conceits that held my soul so long,
The lusts that tempt us with delusive show,
And sin, brought forth for everlasting woe.   30
Thus shall the notes to sorrow's object rise,
While frequent rests procure a place for sighs;
And as I moan upon the naked plain,
Be this the burthen closing every strain:
"Return, my Senses! range no more abroad;
He'll only find his bliss who seeks for God."

ECSTASY

THE fleeting joys which all affords below
Work the fond heart with unperforming show;
The wish that makes our happier life complete,
Nor grasps the wealth nor honours of the great,
Nor loosely sails on Pleasure's easy stream,
Nor gathers wreaths from all the groves of Fame;
Weak Man! who charms to these alone confine,
Attend my prayer, and learn to make it thine.
    From thy rich throne, where circling trains of light
Make day that 's endless infinitely bright,   10
Thence, heavenly Father! thence with mercy dart
One beam of brightness to my longing heart:
Dawn thro' the mind, drive Error's clouds away,
And still the rage in Passion's troubled sea,
That the poor banish'd soul, serene, and free,
May rise from earth to visit Heaven and thee.
    Come, Peace divine! shed gently from above;
Inspire my willing bosom, wondrous Love!
Thy purpled pinions to my shoulders tie,
And point the passage where I want to fly.   20

But whither, whither now! what powerful fire
With this bless'd influence equals my desire?
I rise (or Love, the kind deluder, reigns
And acts in fancy such enchanted scenes),
Earth lessening flies, the parting skies retreat,
The fleecy clouds my waving feathers beat;
And now the sun, and now the stars, are gone;
Yet still, methinks, the spirit bears me on
Where tracts of ether purer blue display,
And edge the golden realm of native day.   30

   Oh! strange enjoyment of a bliss unseen!
Oh! ravishment! oh! sacred rage within!
Tumultuous pleasure, rais'd on peace of mind,
Sincere, excessive, from the world refin'd!
I see the light that veils the throne on high,
A light unpierc'd by man's impurer eye;
I hear the words that issuing thence proclaim,
"Let God's attendants praise his awful name!"
Then heads unnumber'd bend before the shrine,
Mysterious seat of Majesty divine!   40
And hands unnumber'd strike the silver string,
And tongues unnumber'd hallelujah sing.
See where the shining seraphim appear,
And sink their decent eyes with holy fear;
See flights of angels all their feathers raise,
And range the orbs, and as they range they praise:
Behold the great Apostles! sweetly met,
And high on pearls of azure ether set:
Behold the Prophets, full of heavenly fire,
With wandering finger wake the trembling lyre;   50
And hear the Martyrs tune, and all around
The Church triumphant makes the region sound.
With harps of gold, with bows of ever-green,
With robes of white, the pious throngs are seen,
Exalted anthems all their hours employ,
And all is music and excess of joy.

   Charm'd with the sight, I long to bear a part,
The pleasure flutters at my ravish'd heart.
Sweet saints and angels of the heavenly choir!
If love has warm'd you with celestial fire,   60
Assist my words, and as they move along,
With hallelujahs crown the burthen'd song.

   Father of all above and all below,

O Great! and far beyond expression so,
No bounds thy knowledge, none thy power, confine,
For power and knowledge in their source are thine;
Around thee Glory spreads her golden wing;
Sing, glittering Angels! hallelujah sing.

   Son of the Father, first begotten Son!
Ere the short measuring line of time begun,   70
The world has seen thy works, and joy'd to see
The bright effulgence manifest in thee.
The world must own thee Love's unfathom'd spring;
Sing, glittering Angels! hallelujah sing.

  Proceeding Spirit! equally divine,
In whom the Godhead's full perfections shine,
With various graces, comforts unexprest,
With holy transports you refine the breast,
And earth is heavenly where your gifts you bring;
Sing, glittering Angels! hallelujah sing.   80

   But where's my rapture, where my wondrous heat,
What interruption makes my bliss retreat?
This world's got in, the thoughts of t'other's crost,
And the gay picture's in my fancy lost.
With what an eager zeal the conscious soul
Would claim its seat, and soaring pass the pole!
But our attempts these chains of earth restrain,
Deride our toil, and drag us down again.
So from the ground aspiring meteors go,
And, rank'd with planets, light the world below;   90
But their own bodies sink them in the sky,
When the warmth's gone that taught them how to fly.

ON DIVINE LOVE

BY MEDITATING ON THE WOUNDS OF CHRIST

    HOLY Jesus! God of Love!
    Look with pity from above,
    Shed the precious purple tide
    From thine hands, thy feet, thy side;
    Let thy streams of comfort roll,
    Let them please and fill my soul:
    Let me thus for ever be
    Full of gladness, full of thee;

This for which my wishes pine
Is the cup of love divine.   10
Sweet affections flow from hence,
Sweet above the joys of sense;
Blessed philtre! how we find
Its sacred worships! how the mind
Of all the world, forgetful grown,
Can despise an earthly throne,
Raise its thoughts to realms above,
Think of God, and sing of love!
    Love celestial! wondrous heat!
O beyond expression great!   20
What resistless charms were thine
In thy good, thy best design!
When God was hated, Sin obey'd,
And man undone without thy aid,
From the seats of endless peace
They brought the Son, the Lord of grace,
They taught him to receive a birth,
To clothe in flesh, to live on earth,
And after lifted him on high,
And taught him on the cross to die.   30
    Love celestial! ardent fire!
O extreme of sweet desire!
Spread thy brightly raging flame
Thro' and over all my frame;
Let it warm me, let it burn,
Let my corpse to ashes turn;
And might thy flame thus act with me,
To set the soul from body free,
I next would use thy wings, and fly
To meet my Jesus in the sky.   40

MATTHEW GREEN

MATTHEW GREEN (1696–1737)

The Grotto, privately printed, 1732.
The Spleen, appeared posthumously in 1737.
Several poems in Dodsley's collections.
Poems, edited by Aikin, 1796.

THE SPLEEN

AN EPISTLE TO MR. CUTHBERT JACKSON

THIS motley piece to you I send,
Who always were a faithful friend;
Who, if disputes should happen hence,
Can best explain the author's sense;
And, anxious for the public weal,
Do what I sing so often feel.

The want of method pray excuse,
Allowing for a vapour'd Muse;
Nor to a narrow path confined,
Hedge in by rules a roving mind.   10

The child is genuine, you may trace
Throughout the sire's transmitted face.
Nothing is stolen: my Muse, though mean,
Draws from the spring she finds within;
Nor vainly buys what Gildon [1] sells,
Poetic buckets for dry wells.

School-helps I want, to climb on high,
Where all the ancient treasures lie,
And there unseen commit a theft
On wealth in Greek exchequers left.   20
Then where? from whom? what can I steal,
Who only with the moderns deal?
This were attempting to put on
Raiment from naked bodies won: [2]
They safely sing before a thief,
They cannot give who want relief;
Some few excepted, names well known,
And justly laurel'd with renown,

[1] Gildon's *Art of Poetry*.
[2] A painted vest Prince Vortiger had on,
Which from a naked Pict his grandsire won.
HOWARD'S *British Princes*.

Whose stamp of genius marks their ware,
And theft detects: of theft beware;
From More [1] so lashed, example fit,
Shun petty larceny in wit.

First know, my friend, I do not mean
To write a treatise on the Spleen;
Nor to prescribe when nerves convulse;
Nor mend the alarum watch, your pulse.
If I am right, your question lay,
What course I take to drive away
The day-mare Spleen, by whose false pleas
Men prove mere suicides in ease;
And how I do myself demean
In stormy world to live serene.

When by its magic lantern Spleen
With frightful figures spread life's scene,
And threatening prospects urged my fears,
A stranger to the luck of heirs;
Reason, some quiet to restore,
Showed part was substance, shadow more;
With Spleen's dead weight though heavy grown,
In life's rough tide I sunk not down,
But swam, 'till Fortune threw a rope,
Buoyant on bladders filled with hope.

I always choose the plainest food
To mend viscidity of blood.
Hail! water-gruel, healing power,
Of easy access to the poor;
Thy help love's confessors implore,
And doctors secretly adore;
To thee I fly, by thee dilute—
Through veins my blood doth quicker shoot,
And by swift current throws off clean
Prolific particles of Spleen.

I never sick by drinking grow,
Nor keep myself a cup too low,
And seldom Chloe's lodgings haunt,
Thirsty of spirits which I want.

[1] James More Smith, Esq. See Dunciad, B. ii. l. 50, and the notes, where the circumstances of the transaction here alluded to are very fully explained

Hunting I reckon very good
To brace the nerves, and stir the blood:
But after no field honours itch,
Achieved by leaping hedge and ditch.   70
While Spleen lies soft relaxed in bed,
Or o'er coal fire inclines the head,
Hygeia's sons with hound and horn,
And jovial cry awake the Morn.
These see her from the dusky plight,
Smeared by th' embraces of the Night,
With roral wash redeem her face,
And prove herself of Titan's race,
And, mounting in loose robes the skies,
Shed light and fragrance as she flies.   80
Then horse and hound fierce joy display,
Exulting at the hark-away,
And in pursuit o'er tainted ground
From lungs robust field-notes resound.
Then, as St. George the dragon slew,
Spleen pierced, trod down, and dying view;
While all their spirits are on wing;
And woods, and hills, and valleys ring.

To cure the mind's wrong bias, Spleen,
Some recommend the bowling green;   90
Some, hilly walks; all, exercise;
Fling but a stone, the giant dies.
Laugh and be well. Monkeys have been
Extreme good doctors for the Spleen;
And kitten, if the humour hit,
Has harlequin'd away the fit.

Since mirth is good in this behalf,
At some partic'lars let us laugh.
Witlings, brisk fools, cursed with half sense,
That stimulates their impotence;   100
Who buzz in rhyme, and, like blind flies,
Err with their wings for want of eyes.
Poor authors worshipping a calf,
Deep tragedies that make us laugh,
A strict dissenter saying grace,
A lecturer preaching for a place,
Folks, things prophetic to dispense,

Making the past the future tense,
The popish dubbing of a priest,
Fine epitaphs on knaves deceased,   110
Green-apron'd Pythonissa's rage,
Great Æsculapius on his stage,
A miser starving to be rich,
The prior of Newgate's dying speech,
A jointured widow's ritual state,
Two Jews disputing tête-à-tête,
New almanacs composed by seers,
Experiments on felons' ears,
Disdainful prudes, who ceaseless ply
The superb muscle of the eye,   120
A coquette's April-weather face,
A Queenb'rough mayor behind his mace,
And fops in military show,
Are sovereign for the case in view.

    If spleen-fogs rise at close of day,
I clear my evening with a play,
Or to some concert take my way.
The company, the shine of lights,
The scenes of humour, music's flights,
Adjust and set the soul to rights.   130

    Life's moving pictures, well-wrought plays,
To others' grief attention raise:
Here, while the tragic fictions glow,
We borrow joy by pitying woe;
There gaily comic scenes delight,
And hold true mirrors to our sight.
Virtue, in charming dress array'd,
Calling the passions to her aid,
When moral scenes just actions join,
Takes shape, and shows her face divine.   140

    Music has charms, we all may find,
Ingratiate deeply with the mind.
When art does sound's high power advance,
To music's pipe the passions dance;
Motions unwill'd its powers have shown,
Tarantulated by a tune.
Many have held the soul to be
Nearly allied to harmony.

Her have I known indulging grief,
And shunning company's relief,   150
Unveil her face, and looking round,
Own, by neglecting sorrow's wound,
The consanguinity of sound.

In rainy days keep double guard,
Or Spleen will surely be too hard;
Which, like those fish by sailors met,
Fly highest, while their wings are wet.
In such dull weather, so unfit
To enterprise a work of wit,
When clouds one yard of azure sky,   160
That's fit for simile, deny,
I dress my face with studious looks,
And shorten tedious hours with books.
But if dull fogs invade the head,
That memory minds not what is read,
I sit in window dry as ark,
And on the drowning world remark:
Or to some coffee-house I stray
For news, the manna of a day,
And from the hipp'd discourses gather,   170
That politics go by the weather:
Then seek good-humour'd tavern chums,
And play at cards, but for small sums;
Or with the merry fellows quaff,
And laugh aloud with them that laugh;
Or drink a joco-serious cup
With souls who've took their freedom up,
And let my mind, beguiled by talk,
In Epicurus' garden walk,
Who thought it heaven to be serene;   180
Pain, hell; and purgatory, spleen.

Sometimes I dress, with women sit,
And chat away the gloomy fit;
Quit the stiff garb of serious sense,
And wear a gay impertinence,
Nor think nor speak with any pains,
But lay on fancy's neck the reins:
Talk of unusual swell of waist
In maid of honour loosely laced,

And beauty borrowing Spanish red,   190
And loving pair with separate bed,
And jewels pawned for loss of game,
And then redeemed by loss of fame;
Of Kitty (aunt left in the lurch
By grave pretence to go to church)
Perceived in hack with lover fine,
Like Will. and Mary on the coin:
And thus in modish manner we,
In aid of sugar, sweeten tea.

    Permit, ye fair, your idol form,   200
Which e'en the coldest heart can warm,
May with its beauties grace my line,
While I bow down before its shrine,
And your throng'd altars with my lays
Perfume, and get by giving praise.
With speech so sweet, so sweet a mien
You excommunicate the Spleen,
Which, fiend-like, flies the magic ring
You form with sound, when pleased to sing;
Whate'er you say, howe'er you move,   210
We look, we listen, and approve.
Your touch, which gives to feeling bliss,
Our nerves officious throng to kiss;
By Celia's pat, on their report,
The grave-aired soul, inclined to sport,
Renounces wisdom's sullen pomp,
And loves the floral game, to romp.
But who can view the pointed rays,
That from black eyes scintillant blaze?
Love on his throne of glory seems   220
Encompass'd with satellite beams.
But when blue eyes, more softly bright,
Diffuse benignly humid light,
We gaze, and see the smiling loves,
And Cytherea's gentle doves,
And raptured fix in such a face
Love's mercy-seat and throne of grace.
Shine but on age, you melt its snow;
Again fires long-extinguished glow,
And, charmed by witchery of eyes,   230
Blood long congealèd liquefies!

True miracle, and fairly done
By heads which are adored while on.

But oh, what pity 'tis to find
Such beauties both of form and mind,
By modern breeding much debased,
In half the female world at least!
Hence I with care such lotteries shun,
Where, a prize missed, I'm quite undone;
And han't, by venturing on a wife,   240
Yet run the greatest risk in life.

Mothers, and guardian aunts, forbear
Your impious pains to form the fair,
Nor lay out so much cost and art,
But to deflower the virgin heart;
Of every folly-fostering bed
By quickening heat of custom bred.
Rather than by your culture spoiled,
Desist, and give us nature wild,
Delighted with a hoyden soul,   250
Which truth and innocence control.
Coquettes, leave off affected arts,
Gay fowlers at a flock of hearts;
Woodcocks to shun your snares have skill,
You show so plain you strive to kill.
In love the artless catch the game,
And they scarce miss who never aim.

The world's great Author did create
The sex to fit the nuptial state,
And meant a blessing in a wife   260
To solace the fatigues of life;
And old inspired times display,
How wives could love, and yet obey.
Then truth, and patience of control,
And housewife arts adorned the soul;
And charms, the gift of nature, shone;
And jealousy, a thing unknown;
Veils were the only masks they wore;
Novels (receipts to make a whore)
Nor ombre, nor quadrille they knew,   270
Nor Pam's puissance felt at loo.

Wise men did not, to be thought gay,
Then compliment their power away:
But lest, by frail desires misled,
The girls forbidden paths should tread,
Of ignorance raised the safe high wall;
We sink ha-has, that show them all.
Thus we at once solicit sense,
And charge them not to break the fence.

Now, if untired, consider, friend,   280
What I avoid to gain my end.

I never am at meeting seen,
Meeting, that region of the Spleen;
The broken heart, the busy fiend,
The inward call, on Spleen depend.

Law, licensed breaking of the peace,
To which vacation is disease;
A gipsy diction scarce known well
By the magi, who law-fortunes tell,
I shun; nor let it breed within   290
Anxiety, and that the Spleen;
Law, grown a forest, where perplex
The mazes, and the brambles vex;
Where its twelve verdurers every day
Are changing still the public way:
Yet if we miss our path and err,
We grievous penalties incur;
And wanderers tire, and tear their skin,
And then get out where they went in.

I never game, and rarely bet,   300
Am loth to lend, or run in debt.
No compter-writs me agitate;
Who moralising pass the gate,
And there mine eyes on spendthrifts turn,
Who vainly o'er their bondage mourn.
Wisdom, before beneath their care,
Pays her upbraiding visits there,
And forces folly through the grate
Her panegyric to repeat.
This view, profusely when inclined,   310
Enters a caveat in the mind:

Experience joined with common sense,
To mortals is a providence.

Passion, as frequently is seen,
Subsiding settles into Spleen.
Hence, as the plague of happy life,
I turn away from party-strife.
A prince's cause, a church's claim,
I've known to raise a mighty flame,
And priest, as stoker, very free   320
To throw in peace and charity.

That tribe, whose practicals decree
Small beer the deadliest heresy;
Who, fond of pedigree, derive
From the most noted whore alive;
Who own wine's old prophetic aid,
And love the mitre Bacchus made,
Forbid the faithful to depend
On half-pint drinkers for a friend,
And in whose gay red-lettered face   330
We read good living more than grace:
Nor they so pure, and so precise,
Immac'late as their white of eyes,
Who for the spirit hug the Spleen,
Phylacter'd throughout all their mien;
Who their ill-tasted home-brewed prayer
To the State's mellow forms prefer;
Who doctrines, as infectious, fear,
Which are not steeped in vinegar,
And samples of heart-chested grace   340
Expose in show-glass of the face,
Did never me as yet provoke
Either to honour band and cloak,[1]
Or deck my hat with leaves of oak.[2]

I rail not with mock-patriot grace
At folks, because they are in place;
Nor, hired to praise with stallion pen,
Serve the ear-lechery of men;
But to avoid religious jars
The laws are my expositors,   350

[1] Badge of Puritan.   [2] Of cavalier—from Royal Oak.

Which in my doubting mind create
Conformity to Church and State.
I go, pursuant to my plan,
To Mecca with the caravan;
And think it right in common sense
Both for diversion and defence.

Reforming schemes are none of mine;
To mend the world's a vast design:
Like theirs, who tug in little boat,
To pull to them the ship afloat,   360
While to defeat their laboured end,
At once both wind and stream contend:
Success herein is seldom seen,
And zeal, when baffled, turns to Spleen.

Happy the man, who, innocent,
Grieves not at ills he can't prevent;
His skiff does with the current glide,
Not puffing pulled against the tide.
He, paddling by the scuffling crowd,
Sees unconcerned life's wager rowed,   370
And when he can't prevent foul play,
Enjoys the folly of the fray.

By these reflections I repeal
Each hasty promise made in zeal.
When gospel propagators say,
We're bound our great light to display,
And Indian darkness drive away,
Yet none but drunken watchmen send
And scoundrel link-boys for that end;
When they cry up this holy war,   380
Which every Christian should be for,
Yet such as owe the law their ears,
We find employed as engineers;
This view my forward zeal so shocks,
In vain they hold the money-box.
At such a conduct, which intends
By vicious means such virtuous ends,
I laugh off Spleen, and keep my pence
From spoiling Indian innocence.

Yet philosophic love of ease 390
I suffer not to prove disease,
But rise up in the virtuous cause
Of a free press, and equal laws.
The press restrained! nefandous thought!
In vain our sires have nobly fought:
While free from force the press remains,
Virtue and Freedom cheer our plains,
And Learning largesses bestows,
And keeps uncensured open house.
We to the nation's public mart 400
Our works of wit, and schemes of art,
And philosophic goods this way,
Like water carriage, cheap convey.
This tree, which knowledge so affords,
Inquisitors with flaming swords
From lay-approach with zeal defend,
Lest their own paradise should end.
The press from her fecundous womb
Brought forth the arts of Greece and Rome;
Her offspring, skilled in logic war, 410
Truth's banner waved in open air;
The monster Superstition fled,
And hid in shades its Gorgon head;
And lawless power, the long-kept field,
By reason quelled, was forced to yield.
This nurse of arts, and freedom's fence
To chain, is treason against sense;
And, Liberty, thy thousand tongues
None silence, who design no wrongs;
For those who use the gag's restraint, 420
First rob, before they stop complaint.

Since disappointment galls within,
And subjugates the soul to Spleen,
Most schemes, as money-snares, I hate,
And bite not at projector's bait.
Sufficient wrecks appear each day,
And yet fresh fools are cast away.
Ere well the bubbled can turn round,
Their painted vessel runs aground;
Or in deep seas it oversets 430
By a fierce hurricane of debts;

Or helm-directors in one trip,
Freight first embezzled, sink the ship.
Such was of late a corporation,[1]
The brazen serpent of the nation,
Which when hard accidents distress'd,
The poor must look at to be bless'd,
And thence expect, with paper sealed
By fraud and usury, to be healed.

I in no soul-consumption wait   440
Whole years at levees of the great,
And hungry hopes regale the while
On the spare diet of a smile.
There you may see the idol stand
With mirror in his wanton hand;
Above, below, now here, now there
He throws about the sunny glare.
Crowds pant, and press to seize the prize,
The gay delusion of their eyes.

When Fancy tries her limning skill   450
To draw and colour at her will,
And raise and round the figures well,
And shew her talent to excel,
I guard my heart, lest it should woo
Unreal beauties Fancy drew,
And disappointed, feel despair
At loss of things that never were.

When I lean politicians mark
Grazing on ether in the Park;
Whoe'er on wing with open throats   460
Fly at debates, expresses, votes,
Just in the manner swallows use,
Catching their airy food of news;
Whose latrant stomachs oft molest
The deep-laid plans their dreams suggest;

[1] The Charitable Corporation, instituted for the relief of the industrious poor, by assisting them with small sums upon pledges at legal interest By the villainy of those who had the management of this scheme, the proprietors were defrauded of very considerable sums of money. In 1732 the conduct of the directors of this body became the subject of a parliamentary inquiry, and some of them, who were members of the House of Commons, were expelled for their concern in this iniquitous transaction.

Or see some poet pensive sit,
Fondly mistaking Spleen for wit:
Who, though short-winded, still will aim
To sound the epic trump of Fame;
Who still on Phœbus' smiles will doat, 470
Nor learn conviction from his coat;
I bless my stars, I never knew
Whimsies which, close pursued, undo,
And have from old experience been
Both parent and the child of Spleen.
These subjects of Apollo's state,
Who from false fire derive their fate,
With airy purchases undone
Of lands, which none lend money on,
Born dull, had followed thriving ways, 480
Nor lost one hour to gather bays.
Their fancies first delirious grew,
And scenes ideal took for true.
Fine to the sight Parnassus lies,
And with false prospects cheats their eyes;
The fabled gods the poets sing,
A season of perpetual spring,
Brooks, flowery fields, and groves of trees,
Affording sweets and similes,
Gay dreams inspired in myrtle bowers, 490
And wreaths of undecaying flowers,
Apollo's harp with airs divine,
The sacred music of the Nine,
Views of the temple raised to Fame,
And for a vacant niche proud aim,
Ravish their souls, and plainly shew
What Fancy's sketching power can do.
They will attempt the mountain steep,
Where on the top, like dreams in sleep,
The Muses revelations shew, 500
That find men cracked, or make them so.

You, friend, like me, the trade of rhyme
Avoid, elaborate waste of time,
Nor are content to be undone,
To pass for Phœbus' crazy son.
Poems, the hop-grounds of the brain,
Afford the most uncertain gain;

And lotteries never tempt the wise
With blanks so many to a prize.
I only transient visits pay,   510
Meeting the Muses in my way,
Scarce known to the fastidious dames,
Nor skilled to call them by their names.
Nor can their passports in these days,
Your profit warrant, or your praise.
On poems by their dictates writ,
Critics, as sworn appraisers, sit,
And mere upholsterers in a trice
On gems and painting set a price.
These tailoring artists for our lays   520
Invent cramp'd rules, and with strait stays
Striving free Nature's shape to hit,
Emaciate sense, before they fit.

A common place, and many friends,
Can serve the plagiary's ends,
Whose easy vamping talent lies,
First wit to pilfer, then disguise.
Thus some, devoid of art and skill
To search the mine on Pindus' hill,
Proud to aspire and workmen grow,   530
By genius doomed to stay below,
For their own digging shew the town
Wit's treasure brought by others down.
Some wanting, if they find a mine,
An artist's judgment to refine,
On fame precipitately fixed,
The ore with baser metals mixed
Melt down, impatient of delay,
And call the vicious mass a play.
All these engage to serve their ends,   540
A band select of trusty friends,
Who, lesson'd right, extol the thing,
As Psapho [1] taught his birds to sing;
Then to the ladies they submit,
Returning officers on wit:

[1] Psapho was a Libyan, who, desiring to be accounted a god, effected it by this invention: he took young birds and taught them to sing, "Psapho is a great god." When they were perfect in their lesson, he let them fly; and other birds learning the same ditty, repeated it in the woods; on which his countrymen offered sacrifice to him, and considered him as a deity.

A crowded house their presence draws,
And on the beaux imposes laws,
A judgment in its favour ends,
When all the pannel are its friends:
Their natures merciful and mild   550
Have from mere pity saved the child;
In bulrush ark the bantling found
Helpless, and ready to be drowned,
They have preserved by kind support,
And brought the baby-muse to court.

But there's a youth [1] that you can name,
Who needs no leading strings to fame,
Whose quick maturity of brain
The birth of Pallas may explain:
Dreaming of whose depending fate,   560
I heard Melpomene debate,
"This, this is he, that was foretold
Should emulate our Greeks of old.
Inspired by me with sacred art,
He sings, and rules the varied heart;
If Jove's dread anger he rehearse,
We hear the thunder in his verse;
If he describes love turned to rage,
The furies riot in his page.
If he fair liberty and law   570
By ruffian power expiring draw,
The keener passions then engage
Aright, and sanctify their rage;
If he attempt disastrous love,
We hear those plaints that wound the grove.
Within the kinder passions glow,
And tears distilled from pity flow."

From the bright vision I descend,
And my deserted theme attend.

Me never did ambition seize,   580
Strange fever most inflamed by ease!
The active lunacy of pride,
That courts jilt Fortune for a bride,
This par'dise tree, so fair and high,
I view with no aspiring eye:

[1] Mr. Glover, the excellent author of *Leonidas*, *Boadicea*, *Medea*, etc.

Like aspen shake the restless leaves,
And Sodom-fruit our pains deceives,
Whence frequent falls give no surprise,
But fits of Spleen, called *growing wise*.
Greatness in glittering forms displayed   590
Affects weak eyes much used to shade,
And by its falsely envied scene
Gives self-debasing fits of Spleen.
We should be pleased that things are so,
Who do for nothing see the show,
And, middle-sized, can pass between
Life's hubbub safe, because unseen,
And 'midst the glare of greatness trace
A watery sunshine in the face,
And pleasures fled to, to redress   600
The sad fatigue of idleness.

     Contentment, parent of delight,
So much a stranger to our sight,
Say, goddess, in what happy place
Mortals behold thy blooming face;
Thy gracious auspices impart,
And for thy temple choose my heart.
They, whom thou deignest to inspire,
Thy science learn, to bound desire;
By happy alchymy of mind   610
They turn to pleasure all they find;
They both disdain in outward mien
The grave and solemn garb of Spleen,
And meretricious arts of dress,
To feign a joy, and hide distress;
Unmoved when the rude tempest blows,
Without an opiate they repose;
And covered by your shield, defy
The whizzing shafts that round them fly:
Nor, meddling with the gods' affairs,   620
Concern themselves with distant cares;
But place their bliss in mental rest,
And feast upon the good possess'd.

     Forced by soft violence of prayer,
The blithesome goddess soothes my care,
I feel the deity inspire,

And thus she models my desire.
Two hundred pounds half-yearly paid,
Annuity securely made,
A farm some twenty miles from town,   630
Small, tight, salubrious, and my own;
Two maids, that never saw the town,
A serving-man not quite a clown,
A boy to help to tread the mow,
And drive, while t'other holds the plough;
A chief, of temper formed to please,
Fit to converse, and keep the keys;
And better to preserve the peace,
Commission'd by the name of niece;
With understandings of a size   640
To think their master very wise.
May heaven (it 's all I wish for) send
One genial room to treat a friend,
Where decent cupboard, little plate,
Display benevolence, not state.
And may my humble dwelling stand
Upon some chosen spot of land:
A pond before full to the brim,
Where cows may cool, and geese may swim;
Behind, a green like velvet neat,   650
Soft to the eye, and to the feet;
Where odorous plants in evening fair
Breathe all around ambrosial air;
From Eurus, foe to kitchen ground,
Fenced by a slope with bushes crowned,
Fit dwelling for the feathered throng,
Who pay their quit-rents with a song;
With opening views of hill and dale,
Which sense and fancy too regale,
Where the half-cirque, which vision bounds,   660
Like amphitheatre surrounds:
And woods impervious to the breeze,
Thick phalanx of embodied trees,
From hills through plains in dusk array
Extended far, repel the day.
Here stillness, height, and solemn shade
Invite, and contemplation aid:
Here nymphs from hollow oaks relate
The dark decrees and will of fate,

And dreams beneath the spreading beech   670
Inspire, and docile fancy teach;
While soft as breezy breath of wind,
Impulses rustle through the mind:
Here Dryads, scorning Phœbus' ray,
While Pan melodious pipes away,
In measured motions frisk about,
'Till old Silenus puts them out.
There see the clover, pea, and bean,
Vie in variety of green;
Fresh pastures speckled o'er with sheep,   680
Brown fields their fallow sabbaths keep,
Plump Ceres golden tresses wear,
And poppy top-knots deck her hair,
And silver streams through meadows stray,
And Naiads on the margin play,
And lesser nymphs on side of hills
From plaything urns pour down the rills.

     Thus sheltered, free from care and strife,
May I enjoy a calm through life;
See faction, safe in low degree,   690
As men at land see storms at sea,
And laugh at miserable elves,
Not kind, so much as to themselves,
Cursed with such souls of base alloy,
As can possess, but not enjoy;
Debarred the pleasure to impart
By avarice, sphincter of the heart;
Who wealth, hard earned by guilty cares,
Bequeath untouched to thankless heirs.
May I, with look ungloom'd by guile,   700
And wearing Virtue's livery-smile,
Prone the distressèd to relieve,
And little trespasses forgive,
With income not in Fortune's power,
And skill to make a busy hour,
With trips to town life to amuse,
To purchase books, and hear the news,
To see old friends, brush off the clown,
And quicken taste at coming down,
Unhurt by sickness' blasting rage,   710
And slowly mellowing in age,

When Fate extends its gathering gripe,
Fall off like fruit grown fully ripe,
Quit a worn being without pain,
Perhaps to blossom soon again.

   But now more serious see me grow,
And what I think, my Memmius, know.

   The enthusiast's hope, and raptures wild,
Have never yet my reason foiled.
His springy soul dilates like air,   720
When free from weight of ambient care,
And, hushed in meditation deep,
Slides into dreams, as when asleep;
Then, fond of new discoveries grown,
Proves a Columbus of her own,
Disdains the narrow bounds of place,
And through the wilds of endless space,
Borne up on metaphysic wings,
Chases light forms and shadowy things
And, in the vague excursion caught,   730
Brings home some rare exotic thought.
The melancholy man such dreams,
As brightest evidence, esteems;
Fain would he see some distant scene
Suggested by his restless Spleen,
And Fancy's telescope applies
With tinctured glass to cheat his eyes.
Such thoughts as love the gloom of night,
I close examine by the light;
For who, though bribed by gain to lie,   740
Dare sunbeam-written truths deny,
And execute plain common sense
On faith's mere hearsay evidence?

   That superstition mayn't create,
And club its ills with those of fate,
I many a notion take to task,
Made dreadful by its visor-mask.
Thus scruple, spasm of the mind,
Is cured, and certainty I find;
Since optic reason shews me plain,   750
I dreaded spectres of the brain;

And legendary fears are gone,
Though in tenacious childhood sown.
Thus in opinions I commence
Freeholder in the proper sense,
And neither suit nor service do,
Nor homage to pretenders show,
Who boast themselves by spurious roll
Lords of the manor of the soul;
Preferring sense, from chin that 's bare,   760
To nonsense throned in whiskered hair.

 To thee, Creator uncreate,
O Entium Ens! divinely great!——
Hold, Muse, nor melting pinions try,
Nor near the blazing glory fly,
Nor straining break thy feeble bow,
Unfeathered arrows far to throw;
Through fields unknown nor madly stray,
Where no ideas mark the way.
With tender eyes, and colours faint,   770
And trembling hands forbear to paint.
Who, features veiled by light, can hit?
Where can, what has no outline, sit?
My soul, the vain attempt forego,
Thyself, the fitter subject, know.
He wisely shuns the bold extreme,
Who soon lays by the unequal theme,
Nor runs, with wisdom's Sirens caught,
On quicksands swallowing shipwrecked thought;
But, conscious of his distance, gives   780
Mute praise, and humble negatives.
In one, no object of our sight,
Immutable, and infinite,
Who can't be cruel, or unjust,
Calm and resigned, I fix my trust;
To him my past and present state
I owe, and must my future fate.
A stranger into life I'm come,
Dying may be our going home,
Transported here by angry Fate,   790
The convicts of a prior state.
Hence I no anxious thoughts bestow
On matters I can never know;

Through life's foul way, like vagrant, pass'd,
He'll grant a settlement at last;
And with sweet ease the wearied crown,
By leave to lay his being down.
If doomed to dance the eternal round
Of life no sooner lost but found,
And dissolution soon to come,   800
Like sponge, wipes out life's present sum,
But can't our state of power bereave
An endless series to receive;
Then, if hard dealt with here by fate,
We balance in another state,
And consciousness must go along,
And sign the acquittance for the wrong.
He for his creatures must decree
More happiness than misery,
Or be supposèd to create,   810
Curious to try, what 'tis to hate:
And do an act, which rage infers,
'Cause lameness halts, or blindness errs.
   Thus, thus I steer my bark, and sail
On even keel with gentle gale;
At helm I make my reason sit,
My crew of passions all submit.
If dark and blustering prove some nights,
Philosophy puts forth her lights;
Experience holds the cautious glass,   820
To shun the breakers, as I pass,
And frequent throws the wary lead,
To see what dangers may be hid:
And once in seven years I'm seen
At Bath or Tunbridge, to careen.
Though pleased to see the dolphins play,
I mind my compass and my way.
With store sufficient for relief,
And wisely still prepared to reef,
Nor wanting the dispersive bowl   830
Of cloudy weather in the soul,
I make (may heaven propitious send
Such wind and weather to the end)
Neither becalmed, nor over-blown,
Life's voyage to the world unknown.

AN EPIGRAM

ON THE REVEREND MR. LAURENCE ECHARD'S, AND BISHOP
GILBERT BURNET'S HISTORIES

GIL's history appears to me
Political anatomy,
A case of skeletons well done,
And malefactors every one.
His sharp and strong incision pen
Historically cuts up men,
And does with lucid skill impart
Their inward ails of head and heart.
Laurence proceeds another way,
And well-dressed figures doth display: 10
His characters are all in flesh,
Their hands are fair, their faces fresh;
And from his sweetening art derive
A better scent than when alive.
He wax-work made to please the sons,
Whose fathers were Gil's skeletons.

THE SPARROW AND DIAMOND

A SONG

1   I LATELY saw, what now I sing,
        Fair Lucia's hand displayed;
    This finger graced a diamond ring,
        On that a sparrow played.

2   The feathered play-thing she caressed,
        She stroked its head and wings;
    And while it nestled on her breast,
        She lisped the dearest things.

3   With chisel'd bill a spark ill-set
        He loosened from the rest,
    And swallowed down to grind his meat,   1
        The easier to digest.

4 She seized his bill with wild affright,
    Her diamond to descry:
'Twas gone! she sickened at the sight,
    Moaning her bird would die.

5 The tongue-tied knocker none might use,
    The curtains none undraw,
The footmen went without their shoes,
    The street was laid with straw.   20

6 The doctor used his oily art
    Of strong emetic kind,
The apothecary played his part,
    And engineered behind.

7 When physic ceased to spend its store,
    To bring away the stone,
Dicky, like people given o'er,
    Picks up, when let alone.

8 His eyes dispelled their sickly dews,
    He pecked behind his wing;   30
Lucia recovering at the news,
    Relapses for the ring.

9 Meanwhile within her beauteous breast
    Two different passions strove;
When avarice ended the contest,
    And triumphed over love.

10 Poor little, pretty, fluttering thing,
    Thy pains the sex display,
Who only to repair a ring,
    Could take thy life away.   40

11 Drive avarice from your breasts, ye fair,
    Monster of foulest mien:
Ye would not let it harbour there,
    Could but its form be seen.

12 It made a virgin put on guile,
    Truth's image break her word,
A Lucia's face forbear to smile,
    A Venus kill her bird.

THE SEEKER

1 When I first came to London, I rambled about
    From sermon to sermon, took a slice and went out.
    Then on me, in divinity bachelor, tried
    Many priests to obtrude a Levitical bride;
    And urging their various opinions, intended
    To make me wed systems, which they recommended.

2 Said a lech'rous old friar skulking near Lincoln's-Inn,
    (Whose trade 's to absolve, but whose pastime 's to sin;
    Who, spider-like, seizes weak Protestant flies,
    Which hung in his sophistry cobweb he spies;)   10
    "Ah! pity your soul, for without our church pale,
    If you happen to die, to be damn'd you can't fail;
    The Bible you boast, is a wild revelation:
    Hear a church that can't err if you hope for salvation."

3 Said a formal non-con, (whose rich stock of grace
    Lies forward exposed in shop-window of face,)
    "Ah! pity your soul: come, be of our sect:
    For then you are safe, and may plead you're elect.
    As it stands in the Acts, we can prove ourselves saints,
    Being Christ's little flock everywhere spoke against."   20

4 Said a jolly church parson, (devoted to ease,
    While penal law dragons guard his golden fleece,)
    "If you pity your soul, I pray listen to neither;
    The first is in error, the last a deceiver:
    That ours is the true church, the sense of our tribe is,
    And surely *in medio tutissimus ibis.*"

5 Said a yea and nay friend with a stiff hat and band,
    (Who while he talked gravely would hold forth his hand,)
    "Dominion and wealth are the aim of all three,
    Though about ways and means they may all disagree;   30
    Then pr'ythee be wise, go the quakers' by-way,
    'Tis plain, without turnpikes, so nothing to pay."

ON BARCLAY'S APOLOGY FOR THE QUAKERS

THESE sheets primeval doctrines yield,
Where revelation is revealed;
Soul-phlegm from literal feeding bred,
Systems lethargic to the head
They purge, and yield a diet thin,
That turns to gospel-chyle within.
Truth sublimate may here be seen
Extracted from the parts terrene.
In these is shown, how men obtain
What of Prometheus poets feign: 10
To scripture-plainness dress is brought,
And speech, apparel to the thought.
They hiss from instinct at red coats,
And war, whose work is cutting throats,
Forbid, and press the law of love:
Breathing the spirit of the dove.
Lucrative doctrines they detest,
As manufactured by the priest:
And throw down turnpikes, where we pay
For stuff, which never mends the way;   20
And tithes, a Jewish tax, reduce,
And frank the gospel for our use.
They sable standing armies break;
But the militia useful make:
Since all unhired may preach and pray,
Taught by these rules as well as they;
Rules, which, when truths themselves reveal,
Bid us to follow what we feel.

The world can't hear the small still voice,
Such is its bustle and its noise;   30
Reason the proclamation reads,
But not one riot passion heeds.
Wealth, honour, power the graces are,
Which here below our homage share:
They, if one votary they find
To mistress more divine inclined,
In truth's pursuit to cause delay
Throw golden apples in his way.

Place me, O Heaven, in some retreat,
There let the serious death-watch beat,   40

There let me self in silence shun,
To feel thy will, which should be done.

Then comes the Spirit to our hut,
When fast the senses' doors are shut;
For so divine and pure a guest
The emptiest rooms are furnished best.

O Contemplation! air serene,
From damps of sense, and fogs of spleen!
Pure mount of thought! thrice holy ground,
Where grace, when waited for, is found!   5〈

Here 'tis the soul feels sudden youth,
And meets exulting, virgin Truth;
Here, like a breeze of gentlest kind,
Impulses rustle through the mind;
Here shines that light with glowing face,
The fuse divine that kindles grace;
Which, if we trim our lamps, will last,
'Till darkness be by dying past,
And then goes out at end of night,
Extinguished by superior light.   6〈

Ah me! the heats and colds of life,
Pleasure's and pain's eternal strife,
Breed stormy passions, which confined,
Shake, like th' Æolian cave, the mind,
And raise despair my lamp can last,
Placed where they drive the furious blast.

False eloquence, big empty sound,
Like showers that rush upon the ground,
Little beneath the surface goes,
All streams along and muddy flows.   7〈
This sinks, and swells the buried grain,
And fructifies like southern rain.

His art, well hid in mild discourse,
Exerts persuasion's winning force,
And nervates [1] so the good design,
That King Agrippa's case is mine.

[1] Strengthens.

Well-natured, happy shade, forgive!
Like you I think, but cannot live.
Thy scheme requires the world's contempt,
That, from dependence life exempt;   80
And constitution framed so strong,
This world's worst climate cannot wrong.
Not such my lot, not Fortune's brat,
I live by pulling off the hat;
Compelled by station every hour
To bow to images of power;
And in life's busy scenes immers'd
See better things, and do the worst.

Eloquent Want, whose reasons sway,
And make ten thousand truths give way,   90
While I your scheme with pleasure trace,
Draws near, and stares me in the face.
Consider well your state, she cries,
Like others kneel, that you may rise;
Hold doctrines, by no scruples vexed,
To which preferment is annexed,
Nor madly prove, where all depends,
Idolatry upon your friends.
See, how you like my rueful face,
Such you must wear, if out of place.   100
Cracked is your brain to turn recluse
Without one farthing out at use.
They who have lands and safe bank-stock,
With faith so founded on a rock,
May give a rich invention ease,
And construe Scripture how they please.

The honoured prophet, that of old
Used Heaven's high counsels to unfold,
Did, more than courier angels, greet
The crows, that brought him bread and meat.

THE GROTTO [1]

WRITTEN UNDER THE NAME OF PETER DRAKE, A FISHERMAN OF
BRENTFORD

Scilicet hic possis curvo dignoscere rectum,
Atque inter silvas Academi quærere verum.

HOR.

Our wits Apollo's influence beg,
The Grotto makes them all with egg:
Finding this chalkstone in my nest,
I strain, and lay among the rest.

ADIEU awhile, forsaken flood,
To ramble in the Delian wood,
And pray the god my well-meant song
May not my subject's merit wrong.

Say, father Thames, whose gentle pace
Gives leave to view what beauties grace
Your flowery banks, if you have seen
The much sung Grotto of the queen.
Contemplative, forget awhile
Oxonian towers, and Windsor's pile,   10
And Wolsey's pride [2] (his greatest guilt)
And what great William since has built;
And flowing fast by Richmond scenes,
(Honour'd retreat of two great queens) [3]
From Sion-House, [4] whose proud survey
Brow-beats your flood, look 'cross the way,
And view, from highest swell of tide,
The milder scenes of Surrey side.

Though yet no palace grace the shore,
To lodge that pair you should adore;   20
Nor abbeys, great in ruin, rise,
Royal equivalents for vice;
Behold a Grot, in Delphic grove,

---

[1] A building in Richmond Gardens, erected by Queen Caroline, and committed to the custody of Stephen Duck. At the time this poem was written many other verses appeared on the same subject.

[2] Hampton Court, begun by Cardinal Wolsey, and improved by King William III.

[3] Queen Anne, consort of King Richard II and Queen Elizabeth, both died at Richmond.

[4] Sion-House is now a seat belonging to the Duke of Northumberland.

The Graces' and the Muses' love.
(O, might our Laureate study here,
How would he hail his new-born year!)
A temple from vain glories free,
Whose goddess is Philosophy,
Whose sides such licensed idols crown
As superstition would pull down;   30
The only pilgrimage I know,
That men of sense would choose to go:
Which sweet abode, her wisest choice,
Urania cheers with heavenly voice,
While all the Virtues gather round,
To see her consecrate the ground.
If thou, the god with wingèd feet,
In council talk of this retreat,
And jealous gods resentment show
At altars raised to men below;   40
Tell those proud lords of heaven, 'tis fit
Their house our heroes should admit;
While each exists, as poets sing,
A lazy lewd immortal thing,
They must (or grow in disrepute)
With earth's first commoners recruit.

    Needless it is in terms unskill'd
To praise whatever Boyle [1] shall build;
Needless it is the busts to name
Of men, monopolists of fame.   50
Four chiefs adorn the modest stone,[2]
For virtue as for learning known;
The thinking sculpture helps to raise
Deep thoughts, the genii of the place:
To the mind's ear, and inward sight,
Their silence speaks, and shade gives light:
While insects from the threshold preach,
And minds disposed to musing teach:
Proud of strong limbs and painted hues,
They perish by the slightest bruise;   60
Or maladies, begun within,

---

[1] Richard Boyle, Earl of Burlington, a nobleman remarkable for his
ine taste in architecture.

[2] The author should have said five; there being the busts of Newton,
Locke, Wollaston, Clarke, and Boyle.

Destroy more slow life's frail machine;
From maggot-youth through change of state
They feel like us the turns of Fate;
Some, born to creep, have lived to fly,
And change earth-cells for dwellings high;
And some that did their six wings keep,
Before they died been forced to creep.
They politics like ours profess,
The greater prey upon the less: 7c
Some strain on foot huge loads to bring;
Some toil incessant on the wing;
And in their different ways explore
Wise sense of want by future store;
Nor from their vigorous schemes desist
'Till death, and then are never miss'd.
Some frolic, toil, marry, increase,
Are sick and well, have war and peace,
And, broke with age, in half a day
Yield to successors, and away.   8c

  Let not profane this sacred place,
Hypocrisy with Janus' face;
Or Pomp, mixed state of pride and care;
Court kindness, Falsehood's polished ware;
Scandal disguised in Friendship's veil,
That tells, unasked, the injurious tale;
Or art politic, which allows
The Jesuit-remedy for vows;
Or priest perfuming crownèd head,
'Till in a swoon Truth lies for dead;   9c
Or tawdry critic, who perceives
No grace, which plain proportion gives,
And more than lineaments divine
Admires the gilding of the shrine;
Or that self-haunting spectre Spleen,
In thickest fog the clearest seen;
Or Prophecy, which dreams a lie,
That fools believe and knaves apply;
Or frolic Mirth, profanely loud,
And happy only in a crowd;   10c
Or Melancholy's pensive gloom,
Proxy in Contemplation's room.

O Delia, when I touch this string,
To thee my Muse directs her wing.
Unspotted fair, with downcast look
Mind not so much the murmuring brook;
Nor fixed in thought, with footsteps slow
Through cypress alleys cherish woe:
I see the soul in pensive fit,
And moping like sick linnet sit,   110
With dewy eye and moulting wing,
Unperched, averse to fly or sing;
I see the favourite curls begin
(Disused to toilet discipline,)
To quit their post, lose their smart air,
And grow again like common hair;
And tears, which frequent kerchiefs dry,
Raise a red circle round the eye;
And by this bur about the moon,
Conjecture more ill weather soon.   120
Love not so much the doleful knell,
And news the boding night-birds tell;
Nor watch the wainscot's hollow blow;
And hens portentous when they crow;
Nor sleepless mind the death-watch beat;
In taper find no winding sheet;
Nor in burnt coal a coffin see,
Though thrown at others, meant for thee;
Or when the coruscation gleams,
Find out not first the bloody streams;   130
Nor in impress'd remembrance keep
Grim tapestry figures wrought in sleep;
Nor rise to see in antique hall
The moonlight monsters on the wall,
And shadowy spectres darkly pass
Trailing their sables o'er the grass.
Let vice and guilt act how they please
In souls, their conquered provinces;
By Heaven's just charter it appears,
Virtue's exempt from quartering fears.   140
Shall then armed fancies fiercely dress'd
Live at discretion in your breast?
Be wise, and panic fright disdain,
As notions, meteors of the brain;
And sights performed, illusive scene!

By magic lantern of the spleen.
Come here, from baleful cares released,
With Virtue's ticket, to a feast,
Where decent mirth and wisdom joined
In stewardship, regale the mind.   150
Call back the Cupids to your eyes;
I see the godlings with surprise,
Not knowing home in such a plight,
Fly to and fro, afraid to light.—

    Far from my theme, from method far,
Conveyed in Venus' flying car,
I go compelled by feathered steeds,
That scorn the rein when Delia leads.

    No daub of elegiac strain
These holy wars shall ever stain;   160
As spiders Irish wainscot flee,
Falsehood with them shall disagree:
This floor let not the vulgar tread,
Who worship only what they dread:
Nor bigots who but one way see
Through blinkers of authority;
Nor they who its four saints defame
By making virtue but a name;
Nor abstract wit, (painful regale
To hunt the pig with slippery tail!)   170
Artists who richly chase their thought,
Gaudy without, but hollow wrought,
And beat too thin, and tool'd too much
To bear the proof and standard touch;
Nor fops to guard this sylvan ark
With necklace bells in treble bark;
Nor Cynics growl and fiercely paw,
The mastiffs of the moral law.
Come, Nymph, with rural honours dress'd,
Virtue's exterior form confess'd,   180
With charms untarnished, innocence
Display, and Eden shall commence:
When thus you come in sober fit,
And wisdom is preferred to wit;
And looks diviner graces tell,
Which don't with giggling muscles dwell;

And beauty like the ray-clipt sun,
With bolder eye we look upon;
Learning shall with obsequious mien
Tell all the wonders she has seen;   190
Reason her logic armour quit,
And proof to mild persuasion fit;
Religion with free thought dispense,
And cease crusading against sense;
Philosophy and she embrace,
And their first league again take place;
And morals pure, in duty bound,
Nymph-like the sisters' chief surround:
Nature shall smile, and round this cell
The turf to your light pressure swell,   200
And knowing beauty by her shoe,
Well air its carpet from the dew.
The Oak, while you his umbrage deck,
Lets fall his acorns in your neck:
Zephyr his civil kisses gives,
And plays with curls, instead of leaves:
Birds, seeing you, believe it spring,
And during their vacation sing;
And flowers lean forward from their seats
To traffic in exchange of sweets;   210
And angels bearing wreaths descend,
Preferred as vergers to attend
This fane, whose deity entreats
The fair to grace its upper seats.

O kindly view our lettered strife,
And guard us through polemic life;
From poison vehicled in praise,
For satire's shots but slightly graze;
We claim your zeal, and find within,
Philosophy and you are kin.   220

What Virtue is we judge by you;
For actions right are beauteous too;
By tracing the sole female mind,
We best what is true Nature find:
Your vapours bred from fumes declare,
How steams create tempestuous air,
'Till gushing tears and hasty rain

Make heaven and you serene again:
Our travels through the starry skies
Were first suggested by your eyes;   23o
We by the interposing fan,
Learn how eclipses first began;
The vast ellipse from Scarbro's home,
Describes how blazing comets roam;
The glowing colours of the cheek
Their origin from Phœbus speak;
Our watch how Luna strays above
Feels like the care of jealous love;
And all things we in science know
From your known love for riddles flow.   24o

Father! forgive, thus far I stray,
Drawn by attraction from my way.
Mark next with awe, the foundress well
Who on these banks delights to dwell;
You on the terrace see her plain,
Move like Diana with her train.
If you then fairly speak your mind,
In wedlock since with Isis joined,
You'll own, you never yet did see,
At least in such a high degree,   25o
Greatness delighted to undress;
Science a sceptred hand caress;
A queen the friends of freedom prize;
A woman wise men canonise.

JOHN DYER

JOHN DYER (1700?–1758)

Grongr Hill, 1727.
Ode, in volume of miscellaneous poems published by
    Savage, 1726.
Ruins of Rome, 1740.
The Fleece, 1757.
Shorter poems, collected, 1761.
Criticism: Scott of Amwell, Johnson, Drake.

THE FLEECE

A POEM. IN FOUR BOOKS

"Post majores quadrupedes ovilli pecoris secunda ratio est, quæ prima sit,
si ad utilitatis magnitudinem referas: nam id præcipue nos contra frigoris
violentiam protegit, corporibusque nostris liberaliora præbet velamina."—

COLUMELLA.

BOOK I

THE ARGUMENT

The subject proposed. Dedicatory address. Of pastures in general
fit for sheep: for fine-woolled sheep: for long-woolled sheep. Defects of
pastures, and their remedies. Of climates. The moisture of the English
climate vindicated. Particular beauties of England. Different kinds of
English sheep: the two common sorts of rams described. Different kinds
of foreign sheep. The several sorts of food. The distempers arising from
thence, and their remedies. Sheep led by instinct to their proper food
and physic. Of the shepherd's scrip, and its furniture. Care of sheep
in tupping time. Of the castration of lambs, and the folding of sheep.
Various precepts relative to changes of weather and seasons. Particular
care of new-fallen lambs. The advantages and security of the English
shepherd above those in hotter or colder climates; exemplified with
respect to Lapland, Italy, Greece, and Arabia. Of sheep-shearing. Song
on that occasion. Custom in Wales of sprinkling the rivers with flowers.
Sheep-shearing feast and merriments on the banks of the Severn.

THE care of sheep, the labours of the loom,
And arts of trade, I sing. Ye rural nymphs,
Ye swains, and princely merchants, aid the verse.
And ye, high-trusted guardians of our isle,
Whom public voice approves, or lot of birth
To the great charge assigns: ye good, of all
Degrees, all sects, be present to my song.
So may distress, and wretchedness, and want,
The wide felicities of labour learn:
So may the proud attempts of restless Gaul   10
From our strong borders, like a broken wave,
In empty foam retire. But chiefly thou,
The people's Shepherd,[1] eminently placed
Over the numerous swains of every vale,
With well-permitted power and watchful eye,
On each gay field to shed beneficence,

[1] The king, namely.

245

Celestial office! thou protect the song.
   On spacious airy downs, and gentle hills,
With grass and thyme o'erspread, and clover wild,
Where smiling Phœbus tempers every breeze,   20
The fairest flocks rejoice: they, nor of halt,
Hydropic tumours, nor of rot, complain;
Evils deformed and foul: nor with hoarse cough
Disturb the music of the pastoral pipe:
But, crowding to the note, with silence soft
The close woven carpet graze; where nature blends
Flowerets and herbage of minutest size,
Innoxious luxury.   Wide airy downs
Are health's gay walks to shepherd and to sheep.
   All arid soils, with sand, or chalky flint,   30
Or shells diluvian mingled; and the turf,
That mantles over rocks of brittle stone,
Be thy regard: and where low-tufted broom,
Or box, or berry'd juniper arise;
Or the tall growth of glossy-rinded beech;
And where the burrowing rabbit turns the dust;
And where the dappled deer delights to bound.
   Such are the downs of Banstead, edged with woods,
And towery villas; such Dorcestrian fields,
Whose flocks innumerous whiten all the land: 40
Such those slow-climbing wilds, that lead the step
Insensibly to Dover's windy cliff,
Tremendous height! and such the clover'd lawns
And sunny mounts of beauteous Normanton,[1]
Health's cheerful haunt, and the selected walk
Of Heathcote's leisure: such the spacious plain
Of Sarum, spread like Ocean's boundless round,
Where solitary Stonehenge, gray with moss,
Ruin of ages, nods: such too the leas
And ruddy tilth, which spiry Ross beholds,   50
From a green hillock, o'er her lofty elms;
And Lemster's brooky tract, and airy Croft[2];
And such Harleian Eyewood's[3] swelling turf,
Waved as the billows of a rolling sea:
And Shobden,[4] for its lofty terrace famed,
Which from a mountain's ridge, elate o'er woods

---

[1] A seat of Sir John Heathcote in Rutlandshire.
[2] A seat of Sir Archer Croft.
[3] Of the Earl of Oxford.   [4] Of Lord Bateman.

And girt with all Siluria,[1] sees around
Regions on regions blended in the clouds.
Pleasant Siluria, land of various views,
Hills, rivers, woods, and lawns, and purple groves   60
Pomaceous,[2] mingled with the curling growth
Of tendril hops, that flaunt upon their poles,
More airy wild than vines along the sides
Of treacherous Falernum[3]; or that hill
Vesuvius, where the bowers of Bacchus rose,
And Herculanean and Pompeian domes.
    But if thy prudent care would cultivate
Leicestrian fleeces, what the sinewy arm
Combs through the spiky steel in lengthened flakes;
Rich saponaceous loam, that slowly drinks   70
The black'ning shower, and fattens with the draught,
Or marl with clay deep-mixed, be then thy choice,
Of one consistence, one complexion, spread
Through all thy glebe; where no deceitful veins
Of envious gravel lurk beneath the turf,
To loose the creeping waters from their springs,
Tainting the pasturage: and let thy fields
In slopes descend and mount, that chilling rains
May trickle off, and hasten to the brooks.
    Yet some defect in all on earth appears;   80
All seek for help, all press for social aid.
Too cold the grassy mantle of the marl,
In stormy winter's long and dreary nights,
For cumbent sheep; from broken slumber oft
They rise benumbed, and vainly shift the couch;
Their wasted sides their evil plight declare.
Hence tender in his care, the shepherd swain
Seeks each contrivance. Here it would avail,
At a meet distance from the upland ridge,
To sink a trench, and on the hedge-long bank   90
Sow frequent sand, with lime and dark manure;
Which to the liquid element will yield
A porous way, a passage to the foe.
Plough not such pastures: deep in spongy grass

---

[1] The part of England which lies west of the Severn, viz., Herefordshire, Monmouthshire, etc.
[2] Fruit-bearing.
[3] Because part of the hills of Falernum was many years ago overturned ~~by~~ an eruption of fire, and is now a high and barren mount of cinders, called Monte Novo.

The oldest carpet is the warmest lair,
And soundest; in new herbage coughs are heard.
    Nor love too frequent shelter: such as decks
The vale of Severn, nature's garden wide,
By the blue steeps of distant Malvern [1] walled,
Solemnly vast.   The trees of various shade,   100
Scene behind scene, with fair delusive pomp
Enrich the prospect, but they rob the lawns.
Nor prickly brambles, white with woolly theft,
Should tuft thy fields.   Applaud not the remiss
Dimetians,[2] who along their mossy dales
Consume, like grasshoppers, the summer hour;
While round them stubborn thorns and furze increase,
And creeping briars.   I knew a careful swain,
Who gave them to the crackling flames, and spread
Their dust saline upon the deepening grass: 110
And oft with labour-strengthen'd arm he delved
The draining trench across his verdant slopes,
To intercept the small meandering rills
Of upper hamlets: haughty trees, that sour
The shaded grass, that weaken thorn-set mounds,
And harbour villain crows, he rare allowed:
Only a slender tuft of useful ash,
And mingled beech and elm, securely tall,
The little smiling cottage warm embowered;
The little smiling cottage, where at eve   120
He meets his rosy children at the door,
Prattling their welcomes, and his honest wife,
With good brown cake and bacon slice, intent
To cheer his hunger after labour hard.
    Nor only soil, there also must be found
Felicity of clime, and aspect bland,
Where gentle sheep may nourish locks of price.
In vain the silken fleece on windy brows,
And northern slopes of cloud-dividing hills
Is sought, though soft Iberia [3] spreads her lap   130
Beneath their rugged feet, and names their heights
Biscayan or Segovian.   Bothnic realms,[4]
And dark Norwegian, with their choicest fields,

---

[1] A high ridge of hills near Worcester.
[2] People of Caermarthenshire in South Wales.
[3] Spain.
[4] Sweden and Finland, from Gulph of Bothnia.

Dingles, and dells, by lofty fir embowered,
In vain the bleaters court.   Alike they shun
Lybia's hot plains: what taste have they for groves
Of palm, or yellow dust of gold? no more
Food to the flock, than to the miser wealth,
Who kneels upon the glittering heap, and starves.
Even Gallic Abbeville the shining fleece,   140
That richly decorates her loom, acquires
Basely from Albion, by the ensnaring bribe,
The bait of avarice, which, with felon fraud,
For its own wanton mouth, from thousands steals.
   How erring oft the judgment in its hate,
Or fond desire!   Those slow-descending showers,
Those hovering fogs, that bathe our growing vales
In deep November (loathed by trifling Gaul,
Effeminate,) are gifts the Pleiads shed,
Britannia's handmaids.   As the beverage falls,   150
Her hills rejoice, her valleys laugh and sing.
   Hail noble Albion! where no golden mines,
No soft perfumes, nor oils, nor myrtle bowers,
The vigorous frame and lofty heart of man
Enervate: round whose stern cerulean brows
White-wingèd snow, and cloud, and pearly rain,
Frequent attend, with solemn majesty:
Rich queen of mists and vapours!   These thy sons
With their cool arms compress; and twist their nerves
For deeds of excellence and high renown.   160
Thus formed, our Edwards, Henrys, Churchills, Blakes,
Our Lockes, our Newtons, and our Miltons, rose.
   See! the sun gleams; the living pastures rise,
After the nurture of the fallen shower,
How beautiful!   How blue the ethereal vault,
How verdurous the lawns, how clear the brooks!
Such noble warlike steeds, such herds of kine,
So sleek, so vast; such spacious flocks of sheep,
Like flakes of gold illumining the green,
What other paradise adorn but thine,   170
Britannia? happy, if thy sons would know
Their happiness.   To these thy naval streams,
Thy frequent towns superb of busy trade,
And ports magnific add, and stately ships
Innumerous.   But whither strays my Muse?
Pleased, like a traveller upon the strand

Arrived of bright Augusta:[1] wild he roves
From deck to deck, through groves immense of masts;
'Mong crowds, bales, cars, the wealth of either Ind;
Through wharfs, and squares, and palaces, and domes,
In sweet surprise; unable yet to fix   181
His raptured mind, or scan in ordered course
Each object singly; with discoveries new
His native country studious to enrich.

    Ye shepherds, if your labours hope success,
Be first your purpose to procure a breed,
To soil and clime adapted.   Every soil
And clime, even every tree and herd, receives
Its habitant peculiar: each to each,
The Great Invisible, and each to all,   190
Through earth, and seas, and air, harmonious suits.
Tempestuous regions, Darwent's naked peaks,[2]
Snowdon[3] and blue Plynlymmon,[3] and the wide
Aerial sides of Cader-ydris[3] huge;
These are bestowed on goat-horned sheep, of fleece
Hairy and coarse, of long and nimble shank,
Who rove o'er bog or heath, and graze or brouse
Alternate, to collect, with due dispatch,
O'er the bleak wild, the thinly-scattered meal.
But hills of milder air, that gently rise   200
O'er dewy dales, a fairer species boast,
Of shorter limb, and frontlet more ornate;
Such the Silurian.   If thy farm extends
Near Cotswold downs, or the delicious groves
Of Symmonds, honoured through the sandy soil
Of elmy Ross,[4] or Devon's myrtle vales,
That drink clear rivers near the glassy sea;
Regard this sort, and hence thy sire of lambs
Select: his tawny fleece in ringlets curls;
Long swings his slender tail; his front is fenced   210
With horns Ammonian,[5] circulating twice
Around each open ear, like those fair scrolls
That grace the columns of the Ionic dome.
    Yet should thy fertile glebe be marly clay,
Like Melton pastures, or Tripontian fields,[6]

[1] London.   [2] The peaks of Derbyshire.
[3] High hills in North Wales.   [4] A town in Herefordshire.
[5] Jupiter Ammon was represented with ram's horns.
[6] The country between Rugby in Warwickshire and Lutterworth in
Leicestershire.

Where ever-gliding Avon's limpid wave
Thwarts the long course of dusty Watling-street;
That larger sort, of head defenceless, seek,
Whose fleece is deep and clammy, close and plain:
The ram short-limb'd, whose form compact describes
One level line along his spacious back;   221
Of full and ruddy eye, large ears, stretched head,
Nostrils dilated, breast and shoulders broad,
And spacious haunches, and a lofty dock.

    Thus to their kindred soil and air induced,
Thy thriving herd will bless thy skilful care,
That copies nature; who, in every change,
In each variety, with wisdom works,
And powers diversified of air and soil,
Her rich materials. Hence Sabæa's [1] rocks,   230
Chaldæa's marl, Ægyptus' watered loam,
And dry Cyrene's [2] sand, in climes alike,
With different stores supply the marts of trade.
Hence Zembla's icy tracts no bleaters hear;
Small are the Russian herds, and hard their fleece:
Of light esteem Germanic, far remote
From soft sea-breezes, open winters mild,
And summers bathed in dew: on Syrian sheep
The costly burden only loads their tails:
No locks Cormandel's, none Malacca's tribe   240
Adorn; but sleek of flix, and brown like deer,
Fearful and shepherdless, they bound along
The sands. No fleeces wave in torrid climes,
Which verdure boast of trees and shrubs alone.
Shrubs aromatic, caufee wild, or thea,
Nutmeg, or cinnamon, or fiery clove,
Unapt to feed the fleece. The food of wool
Is grass or herbage soft, that ever blooms
In temperate air, in the delicious downs
Of Albion, on the banks of all her streams.   250
    Of grasses are unnumbered kinds, and all
(Save where foul waters linger on the turf)
Salubrious. Early mark, when tepid gleams
Oft mingle with the pearls of summer showers,
And swell too hastily the tender plains:
Then snatch away thy sheep; beware the rot;
And with detersive bay-salt rub their mouths;

---

[1] Arabia.   [2] A ruined Grecian city in the north of Africa.

Or urge them on a barren bank to feed,
In hunger's kind distress, on tedded hay;
Or to the marish guide their easy steps,   260
If near thy tufted crofts the broad sea spreads.
Sagacious care foreacts: when strong disease
Breaks in, and stains the purple streams of health,
Hard is the strife of art: the coughing pest
From their green pastures sweeps whole flocks away.
    That dire distemper sometimes may the swain,
Though late, discern; when, on the lifted lid,
Or visual orb, the turgid veins are pale;
The swelling liver then her putrid store
Begins to drink: even yet thy skill exert,   270
Nor suffer weak despair to fold thy arms:
Again detersive salt apply, or shed
The hoary medicine o'er thy arid food.
    In cold stiff soils the bleaters oft complain
Of gouty ails, by shepherds termed the halt:
Those let the neighbouring fold or ready crook
Detain: and pour into their cloven feet
Corrosive drugs, deep-searching arsenic,
Dry alum, verdegrise, or vitriol keen.
But if the doubtful mischief scarce appears,   280
'Twill serve to shift them to a dryer turf,
And salt again: the utility of salt
Teach thy slow swains: redundant humours cold
Are the diseases of the bleating kind.
    The infectious scab, arising from extremes
Of want or surfeit, is by water cured
Of lime, or sodden stave-acre, or oil
Dispersive of Norwegian tar, renowned
By virtuous Berkeley,[1] whose benevolence
Explored its powers, and easy medicine thence   290
Sought for the poor: ye poor, with grateful voice,
Invoke eternal blessings on his head.
    Sheep also pleurisies and dropsies know,
Driven oft from nature's path by artful man,
Who blindly turns aside, with haughty hand,
Whom sacred instinct would securely lead.
But thou, more humble swain, thy rural gates
Frequent unbar, and let thy flocks abroad,
From lea to croft, from mead to arid field;

    [1] Bishop, whose treatise on tar water is well known.

Noting the fickle seasons of the sky. 300
Rain-sated pastures let them shun, and seek
Changes of herbage and salubrious flowers.
By their all-perfect Master inly taught,
They best their food and physic can discern;
For He, Supreme Existence, ever near,
Informs them.   O'er the vivid green observe
With what a regular consent they crop,
At every fourth collection to the mouth,
Unsavoury crow-flower; whether to awake
Languor of appetite with lively change, 310
Or timely to repel approaching ill,
Hard to determine.   Thou, whom nature loves,
And with her salutary rules entrusts,
Benevolent Mackenzie,[1] say the cause.
This truth howe'er shines bright to human sense;
Each strong affection of the unconscious brute,
Each bent, each passion of the smallest mite,
Is wisely given; harmonious they perform
The work of perfect reason, (blush, vain man)
And turn the wheels of nature's vast machine. 320

See that thy scrip have store of healing tar,
And marking pitch and raddle; nor forget
The sheers true-pointed, nor the officious dog,
Faithful to teach thy stragglers to return:
So may'st thou aid who lag along, or steal
Aside into the furrows or the shades,
Silent to droop; or who, at every gate
Or hillock, rub their sores and loosened wool.
But rather these, the feeble of thy flock,
Banish before the autumnal months: even age 330
Forbear too much to favour; oft renew,
And through thy field let joyous youth appear.

Beware the season of imperial love,
Who through the world his ardent spirit pours;
Even sheep are then intrepid: the proud ram
With jealous eye surveys the spacious field;
All rivals keep aloof, or desperate war
Suddenly rages; with impetuous force,
And fury irresistible, they dash
Their hardy frontlets; the wide vale resounds; 340

[1] Dr. Mackenzie, of Worcester, afterwards of Drumsugh, near Edinburgh;
we believe the same with Joshua Mackenzie, father of the "Man of Feeling."

The flock amazed stands safe afar; and oft
Each to the other's might a victim falls:
As fell of old, before that engine's sway,
Which hence ambition imitative wrought,
The beauteous towers of Salem to the dust.

    Wise custom, at the fifth or sixth return,
Or ere they've pass'd the twelfth of orient morn,
Castrates the lambkins: necessary rite,
Ere they be numbered of the peaceful herd.
But kindly watch whom thy sharp hand hath grieved,
In those rough months, that lift the turning year: 351
Not tedious in the office; to thy aid
Favonius hastens; soon their wounds he heals,
And leads them skipping to the flowers of May;
May, who allows to fold, if poor the tilth,
Like that of dreary, houseless, common fields,
Worn by the plough: but fold on fallows dry;
Enfeeble not thy flock to feed thy land:
Nor in too narrow bounds the prisoners crowd:
Nor ope the wattled fence, while balmy morn   360
Lies on the reeking pasture; wait till all
The crystal dews, impearled upon the grass,
Are touched by Phœbus' beams, and mount aloft,
With various clouds to paint the azure sky.

    In teasing fly-time, dank, or frosty days,
With unctuous liquids, or the lees of oil,
Rub their soft skins, between the parted locks;
Thus the Brigantes;[1] 'tis not idle pains:
Nor is that skill despised, which trims their tails,
Ere summer heats, of filth and tagged wool.   370
Coolness and cleanliness to health conduce.

    To mend thy mounds, to trench, to clear, to soil
Thy grateful fields, to medicate thy sheep,
Hurdles to weave, and cheerly shelters raise,
The vacant hours require: and ever learn
Quick ether's motions: oft the scene is turned;
Now the blue vault, and now the murky cloud,
Hail, rain, or radiance; these the moon will tell,
Each bird and beast, and these thy fleecy tribe:
When high the sapphire cope, supine they couch,   380
And chew the cud delighted; but, ere rain,
Eager, and at unwonted hour, they feed:

    [1] The inhabitants of Yorkshire.

Slight not the warning; soon the tempest rolls,
Scatt'ring them wide, close rushing at the heels
Of th' hurrying o'ertaken swains: forbear
Such nights to fold; such nights be theirs to shift
On ridge or hillock; or in homesteads soft,
Or softer cotes, detain them.   Is thy lot
A chill penurious turf, to all thy toils
Untractable?   Before harsh winter drowns   390
The noisy dykes, and starves the rushy glebe,
Shift the frail breed to sandy hamlets warm:
There let them sojourn, 'til gay Procne [1] skims
The thickening verdure, and the rising flowers.
And while departing Autumn all embrowns
The frequent-bitten fields; while thy free hand
Divides the tedded hay; then be their feet
Accustomed to the barriers of the rick,
Or some warm umbrage; lest, in erring fright,
When the broad dazzling snows descend, they run   400
Dispersed to ditches, where the swelling drift
Wide overwhelms: anxious, the shepherd swains
Issue with axe and spade, and, all abroad,
In doubtful aim explore the glaring waste;
And some, perchance, in the deep delve upraise,
Drooping, even at the twelfth cold dreary day,
With still continued feeble pulse of life;
The glebe, their fleece, their flesh, by hunger gnawed.
   Ah gentle shepherd! thine the lot to tend,
Of all, that feel distress, the most assailed,   410
Feeble, defenceless: lenient be thy care:
But spread around thy tenderest diligence
In flowery spring-time, when the new-dropt lamb,
Tottering with weakness by his mother's side,
Feels the fresh world about him; and each thorn,
Hillock, or furrow, trips his feeble feet:
O guard his meek sweet innocence from all
The innum'rous ills, that rush around his life!
Mark the quick kite, with beak and talons prone,
Circling the skies to snatch him from the plain;   420
Observe the lurking crows; beware the brake;
There the sly fox the careless minute waits;
Nor trust thy neighbour's dog, nor earth, nor sky;
Thy bosom to a thousand cares divide.

[1] Or Progne, the swallow.

Eurus oft flings his hail; the tardy fields
Pay not their promised food; and oft the dam
O'er her weak twins with empty udder mourns,
Or fails to guard, when the bold bird of prey
Alights, and hops in many turns around,
And tires her also turning: to her aid   430
Be nimble, and the weakest, in thine arms,
Gently convey to the warm cote, and oft,
Between the lark's note and the nightingale's,
His hungry bleating still with tepid milk:
In this soft office may thy children join,
And charitable habits learn in sport:
Nor yield him to himself, ere vernal airs
Sprinkle thy little croft with daisy flowers:
Nor yet forget him; life has rising ills:
Various as ether is the pastoral care: 440
Through slow experience, by a patient breast,
The whole long lesson gradual is attained,
By precept after precept, oft received
With deep attention: such as Nuceus [1] sings
To the full vale near Soare's [2] enamoured brook,
While all is silence: sweet Hincklean swain!
Whom rude obscurity severely clasps:
The Muse, howe'er, will deck thy simple cell
With purple violets and primrose flowers,
Well-pleased thy faithful lessons to repay.   450

  Sheep no extremes can bear: both heat and cold
Spread sores cutaneous; but, more frequent, heat:
The fly-blown vermin, from their woolly nest,
Press to the tortured skin, and flesh, and bone;
In littleness and number dreadful foes.
Long rains in miry winter cause the halt;
Rainy luxuriant summers rot your flock;
And all excess, even of salubrious food,
As sure destroys as famine or the wolf.
Inferior theirs to man's world-roving frame,   460
Which all extremes in every zone endures.

  With grateful heart, ye British swains, enjoy
Your gentle seasons and indulgent clime.
Lo! in the sprinkling clouds, your bleating hills
Rejoice with herbage, while the horrid rage

---

[1] Mr. Joseph Nutt, an apothecary at Hinckley.
[2] A river in Leicestershire.

Of winter irresistible o'erwhelms
The hyperborean tracts: his arrowy frosts,
That pierce through flinty rocks, the Lappian flies;
And burrows deep beneath the snowy world:
A drear abode, from rose-diffusing hours,   470
That dance before the wheels of radiant day,
Far, far remote; where, by the squalid light
Of fetid oil inflamed, sea-monster's spume,
Of fir-wood glaring in the weeping vault,
Twice three slow gloomy months, with various ills
Sullen he struggles; such the love of life!
His lank and scanty herds around him press,
As, hunger-stung, to gritty meal he grinds
The bones of fish, or inward bark of trees,
Their common sustenance. While ye, O swains,   480
Ye, happy at your ease, behold your sheep
Feed on the open turf, or crowd the tilth,
Where, thick among the greens, with busy mouths
They scoop white turnips: little care is yours;
Only, at morning hour, to interpose
Dry food of oats, or hay, or brittle straw,
The watery juices of the bossy root
Absorbing: or from noxious air to screen
Your heavy teeming ewes, with wattled fence
Of furze or copsewood, in the lofty field,   490
Which bleak ascends among the whistling winds.
Or, if your sheep are of Silurian breed,
Nightly to house them dry on fern or straw,
Silk'ning their fleeces. Ye, nor rolling hut,
Nor watchful dog, require; where never roar
Of savage tears the air, where careless night
In balmy sleep lies lulled, and only wakes
To plenteous peace. Alas! o'er warmer zones
Wild terror strides; there stubborn rocks are rent;
There mountains sink; there yawning caverns flame;
And fiery torrents roll impetuous down,   501
Proud cities deluging; Pompeian towers,
And Herculanean, and what riotous stood
In Syrian valley, where now the Dead Sea
'Mong solitary hills infectious lies.
   See the swift furies, famine, plague, and war,
In frequent thunders rage o'er neighbouring realms,
And spread their plains with desolation wide:

Yet your mild homesteads, ever-blooming, smile
Among embracing woods; and waft on high   510
The breath of plenty, from the ruddy tops
Of chimneys, curling o'er the gloomy trees,
In airy azure ringlets, to the sky.
Nor ye by need are urged, as Attic swains,
And Tarentine, with skins to clothe your sheep;
Expensive toil; howe'er expedient found
In fervid climates, while from Phœbus' beams
They fled to rugged woods and tangling brakes.
But those expensive toils are now no more;
Proud tyranny devours their flocks and herds: 520
Nor bleat of sheep may now, nor sound of pipe,
Soothe the sad plains of once sweet Arcady,
The shepherds' kingdom: dreary solitude
Spreads o'er Hymettus, and the shaggy vale
Of Athens, which, in solemn silence, sheds
Her venerable ruins to the dust.
    The weary Arabs roam from plain to plain,
Guiding the languid herd in quest of food;
And shift their little home's uncertain scene
With frequent farewell: strangers, pilgrims all, 530
As were their fathers.   No sweet fall of rain
May there be heard; nor sweeter liquid lapse
Of river, o'er the pebbles gliding by
In murmurs; goaded by the rage of thirst,
Daily they journey to the distant clefts
Of craggy rocks, where gloomy palms o'erhang
The ancient wells, deep sunk by toil immense,
Toil of the Patriarchs, with sublime intent
Themselves and long posterity to serve.
There, at the public hour of sultry noon,   540
They share the beverage, when to watering come,
And grateful umbrage, all the tribes around,
And their lean flocks, whose various bleatings fill
The echoing caverns: then is absent none,
Fair nymph or shepherd, each inspiring each
To wit, and song, and dance, and active feats;
In the same rustic scene, where Jacob won
Fair Rachel's bosom, when a rock's vast weight
From the deep dark-mouth'd well his strength removed,
And to her circling sheep refreshment gave.   550
    Such are the perils, such the toils of life,

In foreign climes. But speed thy flight, my Muse;
Swift turns the year; and our unnumbered flocks
On fleeces overgrown uneasy lie.

    Now, jolly swains, the harvest of your cares
Prepare to reap, and seek the sounding caves
Of high Brigantium,[1] where, by ruddy flames,
Vulcan's strong sons, with nervous arm, around
The steady anvil and the glaring mass,
Clatter their heavy hammers down by turns,   560
Flattening the steel: from their rough hands receive
The sharpened instrument, that from the flock
Severs the fleece. If verdant elder spreads
Her silver flowers; if humble daisies yield
To yellow crow-foot, and luxuriant grass,
Gay shearing-time approaches. First, howe'er,
Drive to the double fold, upon the brim
Of a clear river, gently drive the flock,
And plunge them one by one into the flood:
Plunged in the flood, not long the struggler sinks,   570
With his white flakes, that glisten through the tide;
The sturdy rustic, in the middle wave,
Awaits to seize him rising; one arm bears
His lifted head above the limpid stream,
While the full clammy fleece the other laves
Around, laborious, with repeated toil;
And then resigns him to the sunny bank,
Where, bleating loud, he shakes his dripping locks.

    Shear them the fourth or fifth return of morn,
Lest touch of busy fly-blows wound their skin: 580
Thy peaceful subjects without murmur yield
Their yearly tribute: 'tis the prudent part
To cherish and be gentle, while ye strip
The downy vesture from their tender sides.
Press not too close; with caution turn the points;
And from the head in regular rounds proceed:
But speedy, when ye chance to wound, with tar
Prevent the wingy swarm and scorching heat;
And careful house them, if the lowering clouds
Mingle their stores tumultuous: through the gloom   590
Then thunder oft with ponderous wheels rolls loud,
And breaks the crystal urns of heaven: adown

[1] The forges of Sheffield in Yorkshire, where the shepherds' shears and all edge-tools are made.

Falls streaming rain.   Sometimes among the steeps
Of Cambrian glades (pity the Cambrian glades)
Fast tumbling brooks on brooks enormous swell,
And sudden overwhelm their vanished fields;
Down with the flood away the naked sheep,
Bleating in vain, are borne, and straw-built huts,
And rifted trees, and heavy enormous rocks,
Down with the rapid torrent to the deep.   600
  At shearing-time, along the lively vales,
Rural festivities are often heard:
Beneath each blooming arbour all is joy
And lusty merriment: while on the grass
The mingled youth in gaudy circles sport,
We think the golden age again returned,
And all the fabled Dryades in dance.
Leering they bound along, with laughing air,
To the shrill pipe, and deep remurmuring cords
Of the ancient harp, or tabor's hollow sound.   610
  While the old apart, upon a bank reclined,
Attend the tuneful carol, softly mixed
With every murmur of the sliding wave,
And every warble of the feathered choir;
Music of paradise! which still is heard,
When the heart listens; still the views appear
Of the first happy garden, when content
To Nature's flowery scenes directs the sight.
Yet we abandon those Elysian walks,
Then idly for the lost delight repine: 620
As greedy mariners, whose desperate sails
Skim o'er the billows of the foaming flood,
Fancy they see the lessening shores retire,
And sigh a farewell to the sinking hills.
  Could I recall those notes which once the Muse
Heard at a shearing, near the woody sides
Of blue-topp'd Wreakin![1]   Yet the carols sweet,
Through the deep maze of the memorial cell,
Faintly remurmur.   First arose in song
Hoar-headed Damon, venerable swain,   630
The soothest shepherd of the flowery vale.
"This is no vulgar scene: no palace roof
Was e'er so lofty, nor so nobly rise
Their polished pillars, as these aged oaks,

[1] A high hill in Shropshire.

Which o'er our fleecy wealth and harmless sports
Thus have expanded wide their sheltering arms,
Thrice told an hundred summers. Sweet content,
Ye gentle shepherds, pillow us at night."

   "Yes, tuneful Damon, for our cares are short,
Rising and falling with the cheerful day,"   640
Colin replied, "and pleasing weariness
Soon our unaching heads to sleep inclines.
Is it in cities so? where, poets tell,
The cries of sorrow sadden all the streets,
And the diseases of intemperate wealth.
Alas, that any ills from wealth should rise!

   "May the sweet nightingale on yonder spray,
May this clear stream, these lawns, those snow-white
     lambs,
Which, with a pretty innocence of look,
Skip on the green, and race in little troops;   650
May that great lamp, which sinks behind the hill,
And streams around variety of lights,
Recall them erring: this is Damon's wish.

   "Huge Breaden's [1] stony summit once I climbed
After a kidling: Damon, what a scene!
What various views unnumber'd spread beneath!
Woods, towers, vales, caves, dells, cliffs, and torrent floods;
And here and there, between the spiry rocks,
The broad flat sea. Far nobler prospects these,
Than gardens black with smoke in dusty towns,   660
Where stenchy vapours often blot the sun:
Yet flying from his quiet, thither crowds
Each greedy wretch for tardy-rising wealth,
Which comes too late; that courts the taste in vain,
Or nauseates with distempers. Yes, ye rich,
Still, still be rich, if thus ye fashion life;
And piping, careless, silly shepherds we;
We silly shepherds, all intent to feed
Our snowy flocks, and wind the sleeky fleece."

   "Dream not, howe'er, our occupation mean,"   670
Damon replied, "while the Supreme accounts
Well of the faithful shepherd, ranked alike
With king and priest: they also shepherds are:
For so the All-seeing styles them, to remind
Elated man, forgetful of his charge.

  [1] A high hill on the borders of Montgomeryshire.

"But haste, begin the rites: see! purple Eve
Stretches her shadows: all ye nymphs and swains
Hither assemble.   Pleased with honours due,
Sabrina, guardian of the crystal flood,
Shall bless our cares, when she by moonlight clear,   68o
Skims o'er the dales, and eyes our sleeping folds:
Or in hoar caves, around Plynlymmon's brow,
Where precious minerals dart their purple gleams,
Among her sisters she reclines; the loved
Vaga, profuse of graces, Ryddol rough,
Blithe Ystwith, and Clevedoc [1] swift of foot;
And mingles various seeds of flowers and herbs
In the divided torrents, ere they burst
Through the dark clouds, and down the mountain roll,
Nor taint-worm shall infect the yeaning herds,   69o
Nor penny-grass, nor spearwort's poisonous leaf."
   He said: with light fantastic toe, the nymphs
Thither assembled, thither every swain;
And o'er the dimpled stream a thousand flowers,
Pale lilies, roses, violets, and pinks,
Mixed with the greens of burnet, mint, and thyme,
And trefoil, sprinkled with their sportive arms.
   Such custom holds along the irriguous vales,
From Wreakin's brow, to rocky Dolvoryn,[2]
Sabrina's early haunt, ere yet she fled   70o
The search of Guendolen, her stepdame proud,
With envious hate enraged.   The jolly cheer,
Spread on a mossy bank, untouched abides,
Till cease the rites: and now the mossy bank
Is gaily circled, and the jolly cheer
Dispersed in copious measure; early fruits,
And those of frugal store, in husk or rind;
Steeped grain, and curdled milk with dulcet cream
Soft tempered, in full merriment they quaff,
And cast about their gibes; and some apace   71o
Whistle to roundelays: their little ones
Look on delighted: while the mountain-woods,
And winding valleys, with the various notes
Of pipe, sheep, kine, and birds, and liquid brooks,
Unite their echoes: near at hand the wide
Majestic wave of Severn slowly rolls

[1] Rivers, the springs of which rise in the sides of Plynlymmon.
[2] A ruinous castle in Montgomeryshire, on the banks of the Severn.

Along the deep-divided glebe: the flood,
And trading bark with low contracted sail,
Linger among the reeds and copsy banks
To listen; and to view the joyous scene.   720

Book II

THE ARGUMENT

Introduction. Recommendation of mercifulness to animals. Of the winding of wool. Diversity of wool in the fleece: skill in the assorting of it; particularly among the Dutch. The uses of each sort. Severe winters pernicious to the fleece. Directions to prevent their effects. Wool lightest in common fields: inconveniencies of common fields. Vulgar errors concerning the wool of England: its real excellencies; and directions in the choice. No good wool in cold or wet pastures: yet all pastures improvable; exemplified in the drainage of Bedford level. Britain in ancient times not esteemed for wool. Countries esteemed for wool before the Argonautic expedition. Of that expedition, and its consequences. Countries afterwards esteemed for wool. The decay of arts and sciences in the barbarous ages: the revival, first at Venice. Countries noted for wool in the present times. Wool the best of all the various materials for clothing. The wool of our island, peculiarly excellent, is the combing wool. Methods to prevent its exportation. Apology of the author for treating this subject. Bishop Blaise, the inventor of wool-combing. Of the dyeing of wool. Few dyes the natural product of England: necessity of trade for importing them. The advantages of trade, and its utility in the moral world; exemplified in the prosperity and ruin of the elder Tyre.

Now of the severed lock begin the song,
With various numbers, through the simple theme
To win attention: this, ye shepherd swains,
This is a labour. Yet, O Wray, if thou
Cease not with skilful hand to point her way,
The lark-winged muse, above the grassy vale,
And hills, and woods, shall, singing, soar aloft;
And he, whom learning, wisdom, candour, grace,
Who glows with all the virtues of his sire,
Royston, approve, and patronise the strain.   10
    Through all the brute creation, none, as sheep,
To lordly man such ample tribute pay.
For him their udders yield nectareous streams;
For him the downy vestures they resign;
For him they spread the feast; ah! ne'er may he
Glory in wants which doom to pain and death

His blameless fellow creatures. Let disease,
Let wasted hunger, by destroying live;
And the permission use with trembling thanks,
Meekly reluctant: 'tis the brute beyond: 20
And gluttons ever murder, when they kill.
Even to the reptile every cruel deed
Is high impiety. Howe'er not all,
Not of the sanguinary tribe are all;
All are not savage. Come, ye gentle swains,
Like Brahma's healthy sons on Indus' bank,
Whom the pure stream and garden fruits sustain,
Ye are the sons of nature; your mild hands
Are innocent: ye, when ye shear, relieve.
Come, gentle swains, the bright unsullied locks   30
Collect; alternate songs shall soothe your cares,
And warbling music break from every spray.
Be faithful, and the genuine locks alone
Wrap round, nor alien flake, nor pitch enfold;
Stain not your stores with base desire to add
Fallacious weight; nor yet, to mimic those,
Minute and light, of sandy Urchinfield,[1]
Lessen, with subtle artifice, the fleece:
Equal the fraud. Nor interpose delay,
Lest busy ether through the open wool   4
Debilitating pass, and every film
Ruffle and sully with the valley's dust.
Guard too from moisture and the fretting moth
Pernicious: she, in gloomy shade concealed,
Her labyrinth cuts, and mocks the comber's care.
But in loose locks of fells she most delights,
And feeble fleeces of distempered sheep,
Whither she hastens, by the morbid scent
Allured; as the swift eagle to the fields
Of slaughtering war or carnage: such apart   5
Keep for their proper use. Our ancestors
Selected such, for hospitable beds
To rest the stranger, or the gory chief,
From battle or the chase of wolves returned.
    When many-coloured evening sinks behind
The purple woods and hills, and opposite
Rises, full-orbed, the silver harvest-moon,
To light the unwearied farmer, late afield

----

[1] The country about Ross in Herefordshire.

His scattered sheaves collecting; then expect
The artists, bent on speed, from populous Leeds,   60
Norwich, or Froome: they traverse every plain,
And every dale, where farm or cottage smokes:
Reject them not; and let the season's price
Win thy soft treasures: let the bulky wain
Through dusty roads roll nodding; or the bark,
That silently adown the cerule stream
Glides with white sails, dispense the downy freight
To copsy villages on either side,
And spiry towns, where ready Diligence,
The grateful burden to receive, awaits,   70
Like strong Briareus, with his hundred hands.
    In the same fleece diversity of wool
Grows intermingled, and excites the care
Of curious skill to sort the several kinds.
But in this subtle science none exceed
The industrious Belgians, to the work who guide
Each feeble hand of want: their spacious domes
With boundless hospitality receive
Each nation's outcasts: there the tender eye
May view the maimed, the blind, the lame, employed,
And unrejected age; even childhood there   81
Its little fingers turning to the toil
Delighted: nimbly, with habitual speed,
They sever lock from lock, and long, and short,
And soft, and rigid, pile in several heaps.
This the dusk hatter asks; another shines,
Tempting the clothier; that the hosier seeks;
The long bright lock is apt for airy stuffs;
But often it deceives the artist's care,
Breaking unuseful in the steely comb: 90
For this long spongy wool no more increase
Receives, while Winter petrifies the fields:
The growth of Autumn stops: and what though Spring
Succeeds with rosy finger, and spins on
The texture? yet in vain she strives to link
The silver twine to that of Autumn's hand.
Be then the swain advised to shield his flocks
From Winter's deadening frosts and whelming snows:
Let the loud tempest rattle on the roof,
While they, secure within, warm cribs enjoy,   100
And swell their fleeces, equal to the worth

Of clothed Apulian,[1] by soft warmth improved:
Or let them inward heat and vigour find,
By food of cole or turnip, hardy plants.
Besides, the lock of one continued growth
Imbibes a clearer and more equal dye.

But lightest wool is theirs, who poorly toil,
Through a dull round, in unimproving farms
Of common-field: enclose, enclose, ye swains;
Why will you joy in common-field, where pitch,   110
Noxious to wool, must stain your motley flock,
To mark your property? The mark dilates,
Enters the flake depreciated, defiled,
Unfit for beauteous tint: besides, in fields
Promiscuous held, all culture languishes;
The glebe, exhausted, thin supply receives;
Dull waters rest upon the rushy flats
And barren furrows: none the rising grove
There plants for late posterity, nor hedge
To shield the flock, nor copse for cheering fire;   120
And, in the distant village, every hearth
Devours the grassy sward, the verdant food
Of injured herds and flocks, or what the plough
Should turn and moulder for the bearded grain;
Pernicious habit, drawing gradual on
Increasing beggary and Nature's frowns.
Add too, the idle pilferer easier there
Eludes detection, when a lamb or ewe
From intermingling flocks he steals; or when,
With loosened tether of his horse or cow,   130
The milky stalk of the tall green-eared corn,
The year's slow-ripening fruit, the anxious hope
Of his laborious neighbour, he destroys.

There are, who over-rate our spongy stores,
Who deem that Nature grants no clime but ours,
To spread upon its fields the dews of heaven,
And feed the silky fleece; that card, nor comb,
The hairy wool of Gaul can e'er subdue,
To form the thread, and mingle in the loom,
Unless a thread from Britain swell the heap: 140
Illusion all; though of our sun and air
Not trivial is the virtue; nor their fruit,

---

[1] The shepherds of Apulia, Tarentum, and Attica used to clothe their
sheep with skins, to preserve and improve their fleeces.

Upon our snowy flocks, of small esteem:
The grain of brightest tincture none so well
Imbibes: the wealthy Gobelins [1] must to this
Bear witness, and the costliest of their looms.

And though, with hue of crocus or of rose,
No power of subtle food, or air, or soil,
Can dye the living fleece; yet 'twill avail
To note their influence in the tinging vase.   150
Therefore from herbage of old-pastured plains,
Chief from the matted turf of azure marl,
Where grow the whitest locks, collect thy stores.
Those fields regard not, through whose recent turf
The miry soil appears: not even the streams
Of Yare, or silver Stroud, can purify
Their frequent-sullied fleece; nor what rough winds,
Keen-biting on tempestuous hills, imbrown.

Yet much may be performed to check the force
Of Nature's rigour: the high heath, by trees   160
Warm sheltered, may despise the rage of storms:
Moors, bogs, and weeping fens, may learn to smile,
And leave in dykes their soon-forgotten tears.
Labour and art will every aim achieve
Of noble bosoms.   Bedford Level, [2] erst
A dreary pathless waste, the coughing flock
Was wont with hairy fleeces to deform;
And, smiling with her lure of summer flowers,
The heavy ox, vain-struggling, to ingulph;
Till one, of that high-honoured patriot name,   170
Russel, arose, who drained the rushy fen,
Confined the waves, bid groves and gardens bloom,
And through his new creation led the Ouze,
And gentle Camus, [3] silver-winding streams:
Godlike beneficence; from chaos drear
To raise the garden and the shady grove.

But see Ierne's moors and hideous bogs,
Immeasurable tract.   The traveller
Slow tries his mazy step on the yielding tuft,
Shuddering with fear: even such perfidious wilds,   180
By labour won, have yielded to the comb
The fairest length of wool.   See Deeping fens,
And the long lawns of Bourn.   'Tis art and toil
Gives Nature value, multiplies her stores,

[1] Flemings.   [2] In Cambridgeshire.   [3] The Cam.

Varies, improves, creates: 'tis art and toil
Teaches her woody hills with fruits to shine,
The pear and tasteful apple; decks with flowers
And foodful pulse the fields, that often rise,
Admiring to behold their furrows wave
With yellow corn.   What changes cannot toil,   190
With patient art, effect?   There was a time,
When other regions were the swain's delight,
And shepherdless Britannia's rushy vales,
Inglorious, neither trade nor labour knew,
But of rude baskets, homely rustic gear,
Woven of the flexile willow; till, at length,
The plains of Sarum opened to the hand
Of patient culture, and, o'er sinking woods,
High Cotswold showed her summits.   Urchinfield,
And Lemster's crofts, beneath the pheasant's brake, 200
Long lay unnoted.   Toil new pasture gives;
And, in the regions oft of active Gaul,
O'er lessening vineyards spreads the growing turf.

  In eldest times, when kings and hardy chiefs
In bleating sheepfolds met, for purest wool
Phœnicia's hilly tracts were most renowned,
And fertile Syria's and Judæa's land,
Hermon, and Seir, and Hebron's brooky sides:
Twice with the murex, crimson hue, they tinged
The shining fleeces: hence their gorgeous wealth;   210
And hence arose the walls of ancient Tyre.

  Next busy Colchis, bless'd with frequent rains,
And lively verdure (who the lucid stream
Of Phasis boasted, and a portly race
Of fair inhabitants) improved the fleece;
When, o'er the deep by flying Phryxus brought,
The famed Thessalian ram enriched her plains.

  This rising Greece with indignation viewed,
And youthful Jason an attempt conceived
Lofty and bold: along Peneus' banks,   220
Around Olympus' brows, the Muses' haunts,
He roused the brave to redemand the fleece.
Attend, ye British swains, the ancient song.
From every region of Ægea's shore
The brave assembled; those illustrious twins,
Castor and Pollux; Orpheus, tuneful bard!
Zetes and Calais, as the wind in speed;

Strong Hercules; and many a chief renown'd.
　　On deep Iolcos' sandy shore they throng'd,
Gleaming in armour, ardent of exploits;   230
And soon, the laurel cord and the huge stone
Up-lifting to the deck, unmoored the bark;
Whose keel, of wondrous length, the skilful hand
Of Argus fashioned for the proud attempt;
And in the extended keel a lofty mast
Up-raised, and sails full-swelling; to the chiefs
Unwonted objects; now first, now they learned
Their bolder steerage over ocean wave,
Led by the golden stars, as Chiron's art
Had marked the sphere celestial.　Wide abroad   240
Expands the purple deep: the cloudy isles,
Scyros and Scopelos and Icos rise,
And Halonesos: soon huge Lemnos heaves
Her azure head above the level brine,
Shakes off her mists, and brightens all her cliffs:
While they, her flattering creeks and opening bowers
Cautious approaching, in Myrina's port
Cast out the cabled stone upon the strand.
Next to the Mysian shore they shape their course,
But with too eager haste: in the white foam   250
His oar Alcides breaks; howe'er, not long
The chase detains; he springs upon the shore,
And, rifting from the roots a tapering pine,
Renews his stroke.　Between the threatening towers
Of Hellespont they ply the rugged surge,
Of Hero's and Leander's ardent love
Fatal: then smooth Propontis' widening wave,
That like a glassy lake expands, with hills;
Hills above hills, and gloomy woods, begirt.
And now the Thracian Bosphorus they dare,   260
Till the Symplegades, tremendous rocks,
Threaten approach; but they, unterrified,
Through the sharp-pointed cliffs and thundering floods
Cleave their bold passage: nathless by the crags
And torrents sorely shattered: as the strong
Eagle or vulture, in the entangling net
Involved, breaks through, yet leaves his plumes behind.
Thus, through the wide waves, their slow way they force
To Thynia's hospitable isle.　The brave
Pass many perils, and to fame by such   270

Experience rise.   Refreshed, again they speed
From cape to cape, and view unnumbered streams,
Halys, with hoary Lycus, and the mouths
Of Asparus and Glaucus, rolling swift
To the broad deep their tributary waves;
Till in the long-sought harbour they arrive
Of golden Phasis.   Foremost on the strand
Jason advanced: the deep capacious bay,
The crumbling terrace of the marble port,
Wondering he viewed, and stately palace-domes,   280
Pavilions proud of luxury: around,
In every glittering hall, within, without,
O'er all the timbrel-sounding squares and streets,
Nothing appeared but luxury, and crowds
Sunk deep in riot.   To the public weal
Attentive none he found: for he, their chief
Of shepherds, proud Æetes, by the name
Sometimes of king distinguished, 'gan to slight
The shepherd's trade, and turn to song and dance:
Even Hydrus ceased to watch; Medea's songs   290
Of joy and rosy youth and beauty's charms,
With magic sweetness lulled his cares asleep,
Till the bold heroes grasped the golden fleece.
Nimbly they winged the bark, surrounded soon
By Neptune's friendly waves: secure they speed
O'er the known seas, by every guiding cape,
With prosperous return.   The myrtle shores,
And glassy mirror of Iolcos' lake,
With loud acclaim received them.   Every vale,
And every hillock, touched the tuneful stops   300
Of pipes unnumbered, for the ram regained.

   Thus Phasis lost his pride: his slighted nymphs
Along the withering dales and pastures mourned;
The trade-ship left his streams; the merchant shunned
His desert borders; each ingenious art,
Trade, liberty, and affluence, all retired,
And left to want and servitude their seats;
Vile successors! and gloomy ignorance
Following, like dreary night, whose sable hand
Hangs on the purple skirts of flying day.   310

   Sithence, the fleeces of Arcadian plains,
And Attic, and Thessalian, bore esteem;
And those in Grecian colonies dispersed,

Caria, and Doris, and Ionia's coast,
And famed Tarentum, where Galesus' tide,
Rolling by ruins hoar of ancient towns,
Through solitary valleys seeks the sea.
Or green Altinum, by an hundred Alps
High-crowned, whose woods and snowy peaks aloft,
Shield her low plains from the rough northern blast. 320
Those too of Bætica's delicious fields,
With golden fruitage bless'd of highest taste,
What need I name?   The Turdetanian tract,
Or rich Coraxus, whose wide looms unrolled
The finest webs? where scarce a talent weighed
A ram's equivalent.   Then only tin
To late-improved Britannia gave renown.
    Lo! the revolving course of mighty Time,
Who loftiness abases, tumbles down
Olympus' brow, and lifts the lowly vale. 330
Where is the majesty of ancient Rome,
The throng of heroes in her splendid streets,
The snowy vest of peace, or purple robe,
Slow trailed triumphal?   Where the Attic fleece,
And Tarentine, in warmest littered cotes,
Or sunny meadows, clothed with costly care?
All in the solitude of ruin lost,
War's horrid carnage, vain ambition's dust.
    Long lay the mournful realms of elder fame
In gloomy desolation, till appeared 340
Beauteous Venetia, first of all the nymphs,
Who from the melancholy waste emerged:
In Adria's gulf her clotted locks she laved,
And rose another Venus: each soft joy,
Each aid of life, her busy wit restored;
Science revived, with all the lovely arts,
And all the graces.   Restituted trade
To every virtue lent his helping stores,
And cheered the vales around; again the pipe,
And bleating flocks, awaked the cheerful lawn. 350
    The glossy fleeces now of prime esteem
Soft Asia boasts, where lovely Casimere
Within a lofty mound of circling hills,
Spreads her delicious stores; woods, rocks, caves, lakes,
Hills, lawns, and winding streams; a region termed
The paradise of Indus.   Next, the plains

Of Lahor, by that arbour stretched immense,
Through many a realm, to Agra, the proud throne
Of India's worshipped prince, whose lust is law:
Remote dominions; nor to ancient fame   360
Nor modern known, till public-hearted Roe,
Faithful, sagacious, active, patient, brave,
Led to their distant climes adventurous trade.

   Add too the silky wool of Lybian lands,
Of Caza's bowery dales, and brooky Caus,
Where lofty Atlas spreads his verdant feet,
While in the clouds his hoary shoulders bend.

   Next proud Iberia glories in the growth
Of high Castile, and mild Segovian glades.

   And beauteous Albion, since great Edgar chased   370
The prowling wolf, with many a lock appears
Of silky lustre; chief, Siluria, thine;
Thine, Vaga, favoured stream; from sheep minute
On Cambria bred: a pound o'erweighs a fleece.
Gay Epsom's too, and Banstead's, and what gleams
On Vecta's [1] isle, that shelters Albion's fleet,
With all its thunders: or Salopian stores,
Those which are gathered in the fields of Clun:
High Cotswold also 'mong the shepherd swains
Is oft remembered, though the greedy plough   380
Preys on its carpet: he,[2] whose rustic Muse
O'er heath and craggy holt her wing displayed,
And sung the bosky bourns of Alfred's shrines,
Has favoured Cotswold with luxuriant praise.
Need we the levels green of Lincoln note,
Or rich Leicestria's marly plains, for length
Of whitest locks and magnitude of fleece
Peculiar, envy of the neighbouring realms?
But why recount our grassy lawns alone,
While even the tillage of our cultured plains,   390
With bossy turnip, and luxuriant cole,
Learns through the circling year their flocks to feed?

   Ingenious trade, to clothe the naked world,
Her soft materials, not from sheep alone,
From various animals, reeds, trees, and stones,
Collects sagacious: in Euboea's isle
A wondrous rock [3] is found, of which are woven
Vests incombustible: Batavia, flax;

---

[1] Isle of Wight.   [2] Drayton.   [3] The Asbestos.

Siam's warm marish yields the fissile cane;
Soft Persia, silk; Balasor's shady hills,   400
Tough bark of trees; Peruvian Pito, grass;
And every sultry clime the snowy down
Of cotton, bursting from its stubborn shell
To gleam amid the verdure of the grove.
With glossy hair of Thibet's shagged goat
Are light tiaras woven, that wreath the head,
And airy float behind: the beaver's flix
Gives kindliest warmth to weak enervate limbs,
When the pale blood slow rises through the veins.
Still shall o'er all prevail the shepherd's stores,   410
For numerous uses known: none yield such warmth,
Such beauteous hues receive, so long endure;
So pliant to the loom, so various, none.
   Wild rove the flocks, no burdening fleece they bear,
In fervid climes: Nature gives nought in vain.
Carmenian wool on the broad tail alone
Resplendent swells, enormous in its growth:
As the sleek ram from green to green removes,
On aiding wheels his heavy pride he draws,
And glad resigns it for the hatter's use.   420
   Even in the new Columbian world appears
The woolly covering: Apacheria's glades,
And Canses', [1] echo to the pipes and flocks
Of foreign swains.   While Time shakes down his sands,
And works continual change, be none secure:
Quicken your labours, brace your slackening nerves,
Ye Britons; nor sleep careless on the lap
Of bounteous Nature; she is elsewhere kind.
See Mississippi lengthen-on her lawns,
Propitious to the shepherds: see the sheep [2]   430
Of fertile Arica, [3] like camels formed,
Which bear huge burdens to the sea-beat shore,
And shine with fleeces soft as feathery down.
   Coarse Bothnic locks are not devoid of use;
They clothe the mountain carl, or mariner
Lab'ring at the wet shrouds, or stubborn helm,
While the loud billows dash the groaning deck.
All may not Stroud's or Taunton's vestures wear;

[1] Provinces in Louisiana, on the western side of the Mississippi.
[2] These sheep are called Guanacos.
[3] A province in Peru.

Nor what, from fleece Rataean,[1] mimic flower
Of rich Damascus: many a texture bright   440
Of that material in Prætorium [2] woven,
Or in Norvicum,[3] cheats the curious eye.
   If any wool peculiar to our isle
Is given by Nature, 'tis the comber's lock,
The soft, the snow-white, and the long-grown flake.
Hither be turned the public's wakeful eye,
This golden fleece to guard with strictest watch
From the dark hand of pilfering avarice,
Who, like a spectre, haunts the midnight hour
When Nature wide around him lies supine   450
And silent, in the tangles soft involved
Of death-like sleep: he then the moment marks,
While the pale moon illumes the trembling tide,
Speedy to lift the canvas, bend the oar,
And waft his thefts to the perfidious foe.
   Happy the patriot, who can teach the means
To check his frauds, and yet untroubled leave
Trade's open channels.   Would a generous aid
To honest toil, in Cambria's hilly tracts,
Or where the Lune [4] or Coker [5] wind their streams,   460
Be found sufficient?   Far, their airy fields,
Far from infectious luxury arise.
O might their mazy dales, and mountain sides,
With copious fleeces of Ierne shine,
And gulfy Caledonia, wisely bent
On wealthy fisheries and flaxen webs!
Then would the sister realms amid their seas,
Like the three Graces in harmonious fold,
By mutual aid enhance their various charms,
And bless remotest climes —— To this loved end   470
Awake, Benevolence; to this loved end,
Strain all thy nerves, and every thought explore.
Far, far away, whose passions would immure,
In your own little hearts, the joys of life;
(Ye worms of pride) for your repast alone,
Who claim all Nature's stores, woods, waters, meads,
All her profusion; whose vile hands would grasp
The peasant's scantling, the weak widow's mite,
And in the sepulchre of self entomb

---

[1] The fleeces of Leicestershire.   [2] Coventry.   [3] Norwich.
[4] A river in Cumberland.   [5] A river in Lancashire.

Whate'er ye can, whate'er ye cannot use.   480
Know, for superior ends the Almighty Power
(The Power, whose tender arms embrace the worm)
Breathes o'er the foodful earth the breath of life,
And forms us manifold; allots to each
His fair peculiar; wisdom, wit, and strength;
Wisdom, and wit, and strength, in sweet accord,
To aid, to cheer, to counsel, to protect,
And twist the mighty bond.   Thus feeble man,
With man united, is a nation strong;
Builds towery cities, satiates every want,   490
And makes the seas profound, and forests wild,
The gardens of his joys.   Man, each man's born
For the high business of the public good.

 For me, 'tis time to pray that men regard
Their occupations with an honest heart,
And cheerful diligence: like the useful bee,
To gather for the hive not sweets alone,
But wax, and each material; pleased to find
Whate'er may soothe distress, and raise the fallen
In life's rough race: oh, be it as my wish!   500
'Tis mine to teach the inactive hand to reap
Kind Nature's bounties, o'er the globe diffused.

 For this I wake the weary hours of rest;
With this desire the merchant I attend;
By this impelled the shepherd's hut I seek,
And, as he tends his flock, his lectures hear
Attentive, pleased with pure simplicity,
And rules divulged beneficent to sheep:
Or turn the compass o'er the painted chart,
To mark the ways of traffic; Volga's stream,   510
Cold Hudson's cloudy straits, warm Afric's cape,
Latium's firm roads, the Ptolemean fosse,
And China's long canals; those noble works,
Those high effects of civilising trade,
Employ me, sedulous of public weal:
Yet not unmindful of my sacred charge;
Thus also mindful, thus devising good,
At vacant seasons, oft: when evening mild
Purples the valleys, and the shepherd counts
His flock, returning to the quiet fold,   520
With dumb complacence: for religion, this,
To give our every comfort to distress,

And follow virtue with an humble mind;
This pure religion.   Thus, in elder time,
The reverend Blasius wore his leisure hours,
And slumbers, broken oft: till, filled at length
With inspiration, after various thought,
And trials manifold, his well-known voice
Gathered the poor, and o'er Vulcanian stoves,
With tepid lees of oil, and spiky comb,   530
Showed how the fleece might stretch to greater length,
And cast a glossier whiteness.   Wheels went round;
Matrons and maids with songs relieved their toils;
And every loom received the softer yarn.
What poor, what widow, Blasius, did not bless,
Thy teaching hand? thy bosom, like the morn,
Opening its wealth?   What nation did not seek,
Of thy new-modell'd wool the curious webs?

   Hence the glad cities of the loom his name
Honour with yearly festals: through their streets   540
The pomp, with tuneful sounds, and order just,
Denoting labour's happy progress, moves,
Procession slow and solemn: first the rout;
Then servient youth, and magisterial eld;
Each after each, according to his rank,
His sway, and office in the commonweal;
And to the board of smiling plenty's stores
Assemble, where delicious cates and fruits
Of every clime are piled; and with free hand,
Unsparing, each his appetite regales.   550
Toil only tastes the feast, by nerveless ease
Unrelished.   Various mirth and song resound;
And oft they interpose improving talk,
Divulging each to other knowledge rare,
Sparks, from experience that sometimes rise;
Till night weighs down the sense, or morning's dawn
Rouses to labour, man to labour born.

   Then the sleek brightening lock, from hand to hand,
Renews its circling course: this feels the card;
That in the comb admires its growing length;   560
This, blanched, emerges from the oily wave;
And that, the amber tint, or ruby, drinks.

   For it suffices not, in flowery vales,
Only to tend the flock and shear soft wool:
Gums must be stored of Guinea's arid coast;

Mexican woods, and India's brightening salts;
Fruits, herbage, sulphurs, minerals, to stain
The fleece prepared, which oil-imbibing earth
Of Wooburn blanches, and keen alum-waves
Intenerate. With curious eye observe,   570
In what variety the tribe of salts,
Gums, ores, and liquors, eye-delighting hues
Produce, abstersive or restringent; how
Steel casts the sable; how pale pewter, fused
In fluid spirit'ous, the scarlet dye;
And how each tint is made, or mix'd, or changed,
By mediums colourless: why is the fume
Of sulphur kind to white and azure hues,
Pernicious else: why no materials yield
Singly their colours, those except that shine   580
With topaz, sapphire, and cornelian rays:
And why, though Nature's face is clothed in green,
No green is found to beautify the fleece,
But what repeated toil by mixture gives.
    To find effects, while causes lie concealed,
Reason uncertain tries; howe'er, kind chance
Oft with equivalent discovery pays
Its wandering efforts: thus the German sage,
Diligent Drebet, o'er alchemic fire,
Seeking the secret source of gold, received   590
Of altered cochineal the crimson store.
Tyrian Melcartus thus (the first who brought
Tin's useful ore from Albion's distant isle,
And, for unwearied toils and arts, the name
Of Hercules acquired), when o'er the mouth
Of his attendant sheep-dog he beheld
The wounded murex strike a purple stain,
The purple stain on fleecy woofs he spread,
Which lured the eye, adorning many a nymph,
And drew the pomp of trade to rising Tyre.   600
    Our valleys yield not, or but sparing yield,
The dyer's gay materials. Only weld,
Or root of madder, here, or purple woad,
By which our naked ancestors obscured
Their hardy limbs, inwrought with mystic forms,
Like Egypt's obelisks. The powerful sun
Hot India's zone with gaudy pencil paints,
And drops delicious tints o'er hill and dale,

Which trade to us conveys.   Nor tints alone;
Trade to the good physician gives his balms;   610
Gives cheerful cordials to the afflicted heart;
Gives, to the wealthy, delicacies high;
Gives, to the curious, works of nature rare;
And when the priest displays, in just discourse,
Him, the all-wise Creator, and declares
His presence, power, and goodness, unconfined,
'Tis Trade, attentive voyager, who fills
His lips with argument.   To censure Trade,
Or hold her busy people in contempt,
Let none presume.   The dignity, and grace,   620
And weal of human life, their fountains owe
To seeming imperfections, to vain wants,
Or real exigencies; passions swift
Forerunning reason; strong contrarious bents,
The steps of men dispersing wide abroad
O'er realms and seas.   There, in the solemn scene,
Infinite wonders glare before their eyes,
Humiliating the mind enlarged; for they
The clearest sense of Deity receive
Who view the widest prospect of his works,   630
Ranging the globe with trade through various climes:
Who see the signatures of boundless love,
Nor less the judgment of Almighty Power,
That warns the wicked, and the wretch who 'scapes
From human justice: who astonished view
Etna's loud thunders and tempestuous fires;
The dust of Carthage; desert shores of Nile;
Or Tyre's abandoned summit, crowned of old
With stately towers; whose merchants, from their isles,
And radiant thrones, assembled in her marts;   640
Whither Arabia, whither Kedar, brought
Their shaggy goats, their flocks and bleating lambs:
Where rich Damascus piled his fleeces white,
Prepared, and thirsty for the double tint,
And flowering shuttle.   While the admiring world
Crowded her streets; ah! then the hand of pride
Sowed imperceptible his poisonous weed,
Which crept destructive up her lofty domes,
As ivy creeps around the graceful trunk
Of some tall oak.   Her lofty domes no more,   650
Not even the ruins of her pomp, remain;

Not even the dust they sank in; by the breath
Of the Omnipotent offended hurled
Down to the bottom of the stormy deep:
Only the solitary rock remains,
Her ancient site; a monument to those,
Who toil and wealth exchange for sloth and pride.

Book III

THE ARGUMENT

Introduction. Recommendation of labour. The several methods of spinning. Description of the loom, and of weaving. Variety of looms. The fulling-mill described, and the progress of the manufacture. Dyeing of cloth, and the excellence of the French in that art. Frequent negligence of our artificers. The ill consequences of idleness. County workhouses proposed; with a description of one. Good effects of industry exemplified in the prospect of Burstal and Leeds; and the cloth-market there described. Preference of the labours of the loom to other manufactures, illustrated by some comparisons. History of the art of weaving: its removal from the Netherlands, and settlement in several parts in England. Censure of those who would reject the persecuted and the stranger. Our trade and prosperity owing to them. Of the manufacture of tapestry, taught us by the Saracens. Tapestries of Blenheim described. Different arts procuring wealth to different countries. Numerous inhabitants, and their industry, the surest source of it. Hence a wish, that our country were open to all men. View of the roads and rivers through which our manufactures are conveyed. Our navigations not far from the seat of our manufactures: other countries less happy. The difficult work of Egypt in joining the Nile to the Red Sea; and of France attempting, by canals, a communication between the ocean and the Mediterranean. Such junctions may more easily be performed in England, and the Trent and Severn united to the Thames. Description of the Thames, and port of London.

PROCEED, Arcadian Muse; resume the pipe
Of Hermes, long disused, though sweet the tone,
And to the songs of Nature's choristers
Harmonious. Audience pure be thy delight,
Though few: for every note which virtue wounds,
However pleasing to the vulgar herd,
To the purged ear is discord. Yet too oft
Has false dissembling vice to amorous airs
The reed applied, and heedless youth allured:
Too oft, with bolder sound, inflamed the rage
Of horrid war. Let now the fleecy looms

10

Direct our rural numbers, as of old,
When plains and sheepfolds were the Muse's haunts.
  So thou, the friend of every virtuous deed
And aim, though feeble, shalt these rural lays
Approve, O Heathcote, whose benevolence
Visits our valleys; where the pasture spreads,
And where the bramble: and would justly act
True charity, by teaching idle want
And vice the inclination to do good,   20
Good to themselves, and in themselves to all,
Through grateful toil.   Even Nature lives by toil:
Beast, bird, air, fire, the heavens, and rolling worlds,
All live by action: nothing lies at rest,
But death and ruin: man is born to care;
Fashioned, improved by labour.   This of old,
Wise states observing, gave that happy law,
Which doomed the rich and needy, every rank,
To mutual occupation; and oft called
Their chieftains from the spade, or furrowing plough, 30
Or bleating sheepfold.   Hence utility
Through all conditions; hence the joys of health;
Hence strength of arm, and clear judicious thought;
Hence corn, and wine, and oil, and all in life
Delectable.   What simple Nature yields
(And Nature does her part) are only rude
Materials, cumbers on the thorny ground;
'Tis toil that makes them wealth; that makes the fleece,
(Yet useless, rising in unshapen heaps)
Anon, in curious woofs of beauteous hue,   40
A vesture usefully succinct and warm,
Or, trailing in the length of graceful folds,
A royal mantle.   Come, ye village nymphs,
The scattered mists reveal the dusky hills;
Gray dawn appears; the golden morn ascends,
And paints the glittering rocks and purple woods,
And flaming spires; arise, begin your toils;
Behold the fleece beneath the spiky comb
Drop its long locks, or, from the mingling card,
Spread in soft flakes, and swell the whitened floor.   50
   Come, village nymphs, ye matrons, and ye maids
Receive the soft material: with light step
Whether ye turn-around the spacious wheel,
Or, patient sitting, that revolve which forms

A narrower circle.   On the brittle work
Point your quick eye; and let the hand assist
To guide and stretch the gently-lessening thread:
Even, unknotted twine will praise your skill.

    A different spinning every different web
Asks from your glowing fingers: some require   60
The more compact, and some the looser wreath;
The last for softness, to delight the touch
Of chamber delicacy: scarce the cirque
Need turn-around, or twine the lengthening flake.

    There are, to speed their labour, who prefer
Wheels double-spoled, which yield to either hand
A several line: and many yet adhere
To the ancient distaff, at the bosom fixed,
Casting the whirling spindle as they walk:
At home or in the sheepfold, or the mart,   70
Alike the work proceeds.   This method still
Norvicum favours, and the Icenian towns: [1]
It yields their airy stuffs an apter thread.
This was of old, in no inglorious days,
The mode of spinning, when the Egyptian prince
A golden distaff gave that beauteous nymph,
Too beauteous Helen: no uncourtly gift
Then, when each gay diversion of the fair
Led to ingenious use.   But patient art,
That on experience works from hour to hour,   80
Sagacious, has a spiral engine [2] formed,
Which, on an hundred spoles, an hundred threads,
With one huge wheel, by lapse of water, twines,
Few hands requiring; easy-tended work,
That copiously supplies the greedy loom.

    Nor hence, ye nymphs, let anger cloud your brows;
The more is wrought, the more is still required:
Blithe o'er your toils, with wonted song, proceed:
Fear not surcharge; your hands will ever find
Ample employment.   In the strife of trade,   90
These curious instruments of speed obtain
Various advantage, and the diligent
Supply with exercise, as fountains sure,
Which ever-gliding feed the flowery lawn.
Nor, should the careful State, severely kind,

[1] The Iceni were the inhabitants of Suffolk.
[2] Paul's engine for cotton and fine wool.

In every province, to the house of toil
Compel the vagrant, and each implement
Of ruder art, the comb, the card, the wheel,
Teach their unwilling hands, nor yet complain.
Yours, with the public good, shall ever rise,   100
Ever, while o'er the lawns, and airy downs,
The bleating sheep and shepherd's pipe are heard;
While in the brook ye blanch the glistening fleece,
And the amorous youth, delighted with your toils,
Quavers the choicest of his sonnets, warmed
By growing traffic, friend to wedded love.

    The amorous youth with various hopes inflamed,
Now on the busy stage see him step forth,
With beating breast: high-honoured he beholds
Rich industry.   First, he bespeaks a loom: 110
From some thick wood the carpenter selects
A slender oak, or beech of glossy trunk,
Or saplin ash: he shapes the sturdy beam,
The posts, and treadles; and the frame combines.
The smith, with iron screws, and plated hoops,
Confirms the strong machine, and gives the bolt
That strains the roll.   To these the turner's lathe,
And graver's knife the hollow shuttle add.
Various professions in the work unite;
For each on each depends.   Thus he acquires   120
The curious engine, work of subtle skill;
Howe'er, in vulgar use around the globe
Frequent observed, of high antiquity
No doubtful mark: the adventurous voyager,
Tossed over ocean to remotest shores,
Hears on remotest shores the murmuring loom;
Sees the deep-furrowing plough, and harrowing field,
The wheel-moved wagon, and the discipline
Of strong-yoked steers.   What needful art is new?
    Next, the industrious youth employs his care   130
To store soft yarn; and now he strains the warp
Along the garden-walk, or highway side,
Smoothing each thread; now fits it to the loom,
And sits before the work: from hand to hand
The thready shuttle glides along the lines,
Which open to the woof, and shut, altern;
And ever and anon, to firm the work,
Against the web is driven the noisy frame,

That o'er the level rushes, like a surge,
Which, often dashing on the sandy beach,   140
Compacts the traveller's road: from hand to hand
Again, across the lines oft opening, glides
The thready shuttle, while the web apace
Increases, as the light of eastern skies,
Spread by the rosy fingers of the morn;
And all the fair expanse with beauty glows.

　　Or, if the broader mantle be the task,
He chooses some companion to his toil.
From side to side, with amicable aim,
Each to the other darts the nimble bolt,   150
While friendly converse, prompted by the work,
Kindles improvement in the opening mind.

　　What need we name the several kinds of looms?
Those delicate, to whose fair-coloured threads
Hang figured weights, whose various numbers guide
The artist's hand: he, unseen flowers, and trees,
And vales, and azure hills, unerring works.
Or that, whose numerous needles, glittering bright,
Weave the warm hose to cover tender limbs:
Modern invention: modern is the want.   160

　　Next, from the slackened beam the woof unrolled,
Near some clear sliding river, Aire or Stroud,
Is by the noisy fulling-mill received;
Where tumbling waters turn enormous wheels
And hammers, rising and descending, learn
To imitate the industry of man.

　　Oft the wet web is steeped and often raised,
Fast dripping, to the river's grassy bank;
And sinewy arms of men, with full-strained strength,
Wring out the latent water: then, up-hung   170
On rugged tenters, to the fervid sun
Its level surface, reeking, it expands;
Still brightening in each rigid discipline,
And gathering worth; as human life, in pains,
Conflicts, and troubles.　Soon the clothier's shears,
And burler's thistle, skim the surface sheen.
The round of work goes on, from day to day,
Season to season.　So the husbandman
Pursues his cares; his plough divides the glebe;
The seed is sown; rough rattle o'er the clods   180
The harrow's teeth; quick weeds his hoe subdues;

The sickle labours, and the slow team strains;
Till grateful harvest-home rewards his toils.

　　The ingenious artist, learn'd in drugs, bestows
The last improvement; for the unlabour'd fleece
Rare is permitted to imbibe the dye.
In penetrating waves of boiling vats
The snowy web is steeped, with grain of weld,
Fustic, or logwood, mixed, or cochineal,
Or the dark purple pulp of Pictish woad,　　　　　　　19
Of stain tenacious, deep as summer skies,
Like those that canopy the bowers of Stow
After soft rains, when birds their notes attune,
Ere the melodious nightingale begins.

　　From yon broad vase behold the saffron woofs
Beauteous emerge; from these the azure rise;
This glows with crimson; that the auburn holds;
These shall the prince with purple robes adorn;
And those the warrior mark, and those the priest.

　　Few are the primal colours of the art;　　　　　　　20
Five only; black, and yellow, blue, brown, red;
Yet hence innumerable hues arise.

　　That stain alone is good, which bears unchanged
Dissolving water's, and calcining sun's,
And thieving air's attacks.　How great the need,
With utmost caution to prepare the woof,
To seek the best-adapted dyes, and salts,
And purest gums! since your whole skill consists
In opening well the fibres of the woof
For the reception of the beauteous dye,　　　　　　　21
And wedging every grain in every pore,
Firm as the diamond in gold enchased.

　　But what the powers which lock them in the web;
Whether incrusting salts, or weight of air,
Or fountain-water's cold contracting wave,
Or all combined, it well befits to know.
Ah! wherefore have we lost our old repute?
And who inquires the cause, why Gallia's sons
In depth and brilliancy of hues excel?
Yet yield not, Britons; grasp in every art　　　　　　22
The foremost name.　Let others tamely view,
On crowded Smyrna's and Byzantium's strand,
The haughty Turk despise their proffered bales.

　　Now see, o'er vales, and peopled mountain-tops,

The welcome traders gathering every web,
Industrious, every web too few.   Alas!
Successless oft their industry, when cease
The loom and shuttle in the troubled streets;
Their motion stopp'd by wild intemperance,
Toil's scoffing foe, who lures the giddy rout,   230
To scorn their task-work, and to vagrant life
Turns their rude steps; while misery, among
The cries of infants, haunts their mouldering huts.

O when, through every province, shall be raised
Houses of labour, seats of kind constraint,
For those, who now delight in fruitless sports,
More than in cheerful works of virtuous trade,
Which honest wealth would yield, and portion due
Of public welfare?   Ho, ye poor, who seek,
Among the dwellings of the diligent,   240
For sustenance unearned; who stroll abroad
From house to house, with mischievous intent,
Feigning misfortune: Ho, ye lame, ye blind;
Ye languid limbs, with real want oppressed,
Who tread the rough highways, and mountains wild,
Through storms, and rains, and bitterness of heart;
Ye children of affliction, be compelled
To happiness: the long-wished daylight dawns,
When charitable rigour shall detain
Your step-bruised feet.   Even now the sons of trade,
Where'er the cultivated hamlets smile,   251
Erect the mansion: [1] here soft fleeces shine;
The card awaits you, and the comb, and wheel;
Here shroud you from the thunder of the storm;
No rain shall wet your pillow: here abounds
Pure beverage; here your viands are prepared;
To heal each sickness the physician waits,
And priest entreats to give your Maker praise.

Behold, in Calder's [2] vale, where wide around
Unnumbered villas creep the shrubby hills,   260
A spacious dome for this fair purpose rise.
High o'er the open gates, with gracious air,
Eliza's image stands.   By gentle steps
Up-raised, from room to room we slowly walk,
And view with wonder and with silent joy

---

[1] This alludes to the workhouses at Bristol, Birmingham, etc.
[2] A river in Yorkshire, which runs below Halifax, and passes by Wakefield.

The sprightly scene, where many a busy hand,
Where spoles, cards, wheels, and looms, with motion quick
And ever-murmuring sound, the unwonted sense
Wrap in surprise.   To see them all employed,
All blithe, it gives the spreading heart delight,   270
As neither meats, nor drinks, nor aught of joy
Corporeal, can bestow.   Nor less they gain
Virtue than wealth, while, on their useful works
From day to day intent, in their full minds
Evil no place can find.   With equal scale
Some deal abroad the well-assorted fleece;
These card the short, those comb the longer flake;
Others the harsh and clotted lock receive,
Yet sever and refine with patient toil,
And bring to proper use.   Flax too, and hemp,   280
Excite their diligence.   The younger hands
Ply at the easy work of winding yarn
On swiftly-circling engines, and their notes
Warble together, as a choir of larks:
Such joy arises in the mind employed.
Another scene displays the more robust,
Rasping or grinding rough Brazilian woods,
And what Campeachy's disputable shore
Copious affords to tinge the thirsty web;
And the Caribbee isles, whose dulcet canes   290
Equal the honeycomb.   We next are shown
A circular machine,[1] of new design,
In conic shape: it draws and spins a thread
Without the tedious toil of needless hands.
A wheel, invisible, beneath the floor,
To every member of the harmonious frame
Gives necessary motion.   One, intent,
O'erlooks the work: the carded wool, he says,
Is smoothly lapped around those cylinders,
Which, gently turning, yield it to yon cirque   30
Of upright spindles which, with rapid whirl,
Spin out in long extent an even twine.
     From this delightful mansion (if we seek
Still more to view the gifts which honest toil
Distributes) take we now our eastward course,
To the rich fields of Burstal.   Wide around

___
[1] A most curious machine, invented by Mr. Paul.   It is at present
contrived to spin cotton; but it may be made to spin fine carded wool.

Hillock and valley, farm and village, smile:
And ruddy roofs and chimney-tops appear,
Of busy Leeds, up-wafting to the clouds
The incense of thanksgiving: all is joy;   310
And trade and business guide the living scene,
Roll the full cars, adown the winding Aire
Load the slow-sailing barges, pile the pack
On the long tinkling train of slow-paced steeds.
As when a sunny day invites abroad
The sedulous ants, they issue from their cells
In bands unnumbered, eager for their work;
O'er high, o'er low, they lift, they draw, they haste
With warm affection to each other's aid;
Repeat their virtuous efforts, and succeed.   320
Thus all is here in motion, all is life:
The creaking wain brings copious store of corn:
The grazier's sleeky kine obstruct the roads;
The neat-dressed housewives, for the festal board
Crowned with full baskets, in the field-way paths
Come tripping on; the echoing hills repeat
The stroke of axe and hammer; scaffolds rise,
And growing edifices; heaps of stone,
Beneath the chisel, beauteous shapes assume
Of frieze and column.   Some, with even line,   330
New streets are marking in the neighbouring fields,
And sacred domes of worship.   Industry,
Which dignifies the artist, lifts the swain,
And the straw cottage to a palace turns,
Over the work presides.   Such was the scene
Of hurrying Carthage, when the Trojan chief
First viewed her growing turrets.   So appear
The increasing walls of busy Manchester,
Sheffield, and Birmingham, whose reddening fields
Rise and enlarge their suburbs.   Lo, in throngs,   340
For every realm, the careful factors meet,
Whispering each other.   In long ranks the bales,
Like war's bright files, beyond the sight extend.
Straight, ere the sounding bell the signal strikes,
Which ends the hour of traffic, they conclude
The speedy compact; and, well-pleased, transfer,
With mutual benefit, superior wealth
To many a kingdom's rent, or tyrant's hoard.
    Whate'er is excellent in art proceeds

From labour and endurance: deep the oak   350
Must sink in stubborn earth its roots obscure,
That hopes to lift its branches to the skies:
Gold cannot gold appear, until man's toil
Discloses wide the mountain's hidden ribs,
And digs the dusky ore, and breaks and grinds
Its gritty parts, and laves in limpid streams,
With oft-repeated toil, and oft in fire
The metal purifies: with the fatigue,
And tedious process of its painful works,
The lusty sicken, and the feeble die.   360
   But cheerful are the labours of the loom,
By health and ease accompanied: they bring
Superior treasures speedier to the State,
Than those of deep Peruvian mines, where slaves
(Wretched requital!) drink, with trembling hand,
Pale palsy's baneful cup.   Our happy swains
Behold arising, in their fattening flocks,
A double wealth; more rich than Belgium's boast,
Who tends the culture of the flaxen reed;
Or the Cathayan's, whose ignobler care   370
Nurses the silkworm; or of India's sons,
Who plant the cotton-grove by Ganges' stream.
Nor do their toils and products furnish more
Than gauds and dresses, of fantastic web,
To the luxurious: but our kinder toils
Give clothing to necessity; keep warm
The unhappy wanderer, on the mountain wild
Benighted, while the tempest beats around.
   No, ye soft sons of Ganges and of Ind,
Ye feebly delicate, life little needs   380
Your feminine toys, nor asks your nerveless arm
To cast the strong-flung shuttle, or the spear.
Can ye defend your country from the storm
Of strong invasion?   Can ye want endure
In the besieged fort, with courage firm?
Can ye the weather-beaten vessel steer,
Climb the tall mast, direct the stubborn helm,
Mid wild discordant waves, with steady course?
Can ye lead out to distant colonies,
The o'erflowings of a people, or your wrong'd   390
Brethren, by impious persecution driven,
And arm their breasts with fortitude to try

New regions; climes, though barren, yet beyond
The baneful power of tyrants?   These are deeds
To which their hardy labours well prepare
The sinewy arm of Albion's sons.   Pursue,
Ye sons of Albion, with unyielding heart,
Your hardy labours: let the sounding loom
Mix with the melody of every vale;
The loom, that long-renown'd, wide-envied gift   400
Of wealthy Flandria, who the boon received
From fair Venetia; she from Grecian nymphs;
They from Phenice, who obtained the dole
From old Ægyptus.   Thus, around the globe,
The golden-footed sciences their path
Mark, like the sun, enkindling life and joy;
And, followed close by ignorance and pride,
Lead day and night o'er realms.   Our day arose
When Alva's tyranny the weaving arts
Drove from the fertile valleys of the Scheld.   410
With speedy wing and scatter'd course, they fled,
Like a community of bees, disturbed
By some relentless swain's rapacious hand;
While good Eliza to the fugitives
Gave gracious welcome; as wise Ægypt erst
To troubled Nilus, whose nutritious flood
With annual gratitude enriched her meads.
Then, from fair Antwerp, an industrious train
Crossed the smooth channel of our smiling seas;
And in the vales of Cantium, on the banks   420
Of Stour alighted, and the naval wave
Of spacious Medway: some on gentle Yare
And fertile Waveney pitched; and made their seats
Pleasant Norvicum, and Colcestria's [1] towers:
Some to the Darent sped their happy way:
Berghem, and Sluys, and elder Bruges, chose
Antona's chalky plains, and stretched their tents
Down to Clausentum, and that bay supine
Beneath the shade of Vecta's cliffy isle.
Soon o'er the hospitable realm they spread,   430
With cheer revived; and in Sabrina's flood,
And the Silurian Tame, their textures blanched:
Not undelighted with Vigornia's spires,

[1] Colchester; those that follow are the old Latin names for districts,
wns, and rivers in England.

Nor those by Vaga's stream, from ruins raised
Of ancient Ariconium: nor less pleased
With Salop's various scenes; and that soft tract
Of Cambria, deep embayed, Dimetian land,
By green hills fenced, by ocean's murmur lulled;
Nurse of the rustic bard, who now resounds
The fortunes of the fleece; whose ancestors   440
Were fugitives from superstition's rage,
And erst from Devon thither brought the loom;
Where ivied walls of old Kidwelly's towers,
Nodding, still on their gloomy brows project
Lancastria's arms, embossed in mouldering stone.

    Thus then, on Albion's coast, the exiled band,
From rich Menapian towns and the green banks
Of Scheld alighted; and, alighting, sang
Grateful thanksgiving.   Yet, at times, they shift
Their habitations, when the hand of pride,   450
Restraint, or southern luxury, disturbs
Their industry, and urges them to vales
Of the Brigantes; where, with happier care
Inspirited, their art improves the fleece,
Which occupation erst, and wealth immense,
Gave Brabant's swarming habitants, what time
We were their shepherds only; from which state
With friendly arm they raised us: nathless some
Among our old and stubborn swains misdeemed,
And envied who enriched them; envied those,   460
Whose virtues taught the varletry of towns
To useful toil to turn the pilfering hand.

    And still, when bigotry's black clouds arise
(For oft they sudden rise in papal realms,)
They from their isle, as from some ark secure,
Careless, unpitying, view the fiery bolts
Of superstition and tyrannic rage,
And all the fury of the rolling storm,
Which fierce pursues the sufferers in their flight.
Shall not our gates, shall not Britannia's arms   470
Spread ever open to receive their flight?
A virtuous people, by distresses oft
(Distresses for the sake of truth endured)
Corrected, dignified; creating good
Wherever they inhabit: witness, all ye realms
Of either hemisphere, where commerce flows:

The important truth is stamped on every bale;
Each glossy cloth, and drape of mantle warm,
Receives the impression, every airy woof,
Cheyney, and baize, and serge, and alepine,   480
Tammy, and crape, and the long countless list
Of woollen webs; and every work of steel;
And that crystalline metal, blown or fused,
Limpid as water dropping from the clefts
Of mossy marble: not to name the aids
Their wit has given the fleece: now taught to link
With flax or cotton, or the silk-worm's thread,
And gain the graces of variety:
Whether to form the matron's decent robe,
Or the thin-shading trail of Agra's [1] nymphs;   490
Or solemn curtains, whose long gloomy folds
Surround the soft pavilions of the rich.
    They too the many-coloured arras taught
To mimic nature, and the airy shapes
Of sportive fancy: such as oft appear
In old mosaic pavements, when the plough
Up-turns the crumbling glebe of Weldon field;
Or that, o'ershadowed erst by Woodstock's bower,
Now graced by Blenheim, in whose stately rooms
Rise glowing tapestries, that lure the eye   500
With Marlb'rough's wars: here Schellenberg exults,
Behind surrounding hills of ramparts steep,
And vales of trenches dark; each hideous pass
Armies defend; yet on the hero leads
His Britons, like a torrent, o'er the mounds.
Another scene is Blenheim's glorious field,
And the red Danube.   Here, the rescued states
Crowding beneath his shield: there, Ramillies'
Important battle: next, the tenfold chain
Of Arleux burst, and the adamantine gates   510
Of Gaul flung open to the tyrant's throne.
A shade obscures the rest—Ah, then what power
Invidious from the lifted sickle snatched
The harvest of the plain?   So lively glows
The fair delusion, that our passions rise
In the beholding and the glories share

---

[1] There is woven at Manchester, for the East Indies, a very thin stuff,
f thread and cotton, which is cooler than the manufactures of that
ountry, where the material is only cotton.

Of visionary battle.   This bright art
Did zealous Europe learn of pagan hands,
While she assayed with rage of holy war
To desolate their fields: but old their skill: 52
Long were the Phrygians' picturing looms renowned;
Tyre also, wealthy seat of arts, excelled,
And elder Sidon, in the historic web.

    Far-distant Thibet in her gloomy woods
Rears the gay tent, of blended wool unwoven,
And glutinous materials: the Chinese
Their porcelain, Japan its varnish boasts.
Some fair peculiar graces every realm,
And each from each a share of wealth acquires.

    But chief by numbers of industrious hands   53
A nation's wealth is counted: numbers raise
Warm emulation: where that virtue dwells,
There will be traffic's seat; there will she build
Her rich emporium.   Hence, ye happy swains,
With hospitality inflame your breast,
And emulation: the whole world receive,
And with their arts, their virtues, deck your isle.
Each clime, each sea, the spacious orb of each,
Shall join their various stores, and amply feed
The mighty brotherhood; while ye proceed,   54
Active and enterprising, or to teach
The stream a naval course, or till the wild,
Or drain the fen, or stretch the long canal,
Or plough the fertile billows of the deep.
Why to the narrow circle of our coast
Should we submit our limits, while each wind
Assists the stream and sail, and the wide main
Wooes us in every port?   See Belgium build,
Upon the foodful brine, her envied power;
And, half her people floating on the wave,   55
Expand her fishy regions.   Thus our isle,
Thus only may Britannia be enlarged.—
But whither, by the visions of the theme
Smit with sublime delight, but whither strays
The raptured Muse, forgetful of her task?

    No common pleasure warms the generous mind,
When it beholds the labours of the loom;
How widely round the globe they are dispersed,
From little tenements by wood or croft,

Through many a slender path, how sedulous,   560
As rills to rivers broad, they speed their way
To public roads, to Fosse, or Watling-street,
Or Armine, ancient works; and thence explore,
Through every navigable wave, the sea
That laps the green earth round: through Tyne, and Tees,
Through Weare, and Lune, and merchandising Hull,
And Swale, and Aire whose crystal waves reflect
The various colours of the tinctured web;
Through Ken, swift rolling down his rocky dale,
Like giddy youth impetuous, then at Wick   570
Curbing his train, and, with the sober pace
Of cautious eld, meandering to the deep;
Through Dart, and sullen Exe, whose murmuring wave
Envies the Dune and Rother, who have won
The serge and kersie to their blanching streams;
Through Towy, winding under Merlin's towers,
And Usk, that frequent, among hoary rocks,
On her deep waters paints the impending scene,
Wild torrents, crags, and woods, and mountain snows.
The northern Cambrians, an industrious tribe,   580
Carry their labours on pigmean steeds,
Of size exceeding not Leicestrian sheep,
Yet strong and sprightly: over hill and dale
They travel unfatigued, and lay their bales
In Salop's streets, beneath whose lofty walls
Pearly Sabrina waits them with her barks,
And spreads the swelling sheet.   For nowhere far
From some transparent river's naval course
Arise and fall our various hills and vales,
Nowhere far distant from the masted wharf.   590
We need not vex the strong laborious hand
With toil enormous, as the Egyptian king,
Who joined the sable waters of the Nile,
From Memphis' towers to the Erythræan gulf:
Or as the monarch of enfeebled Gaul,
Whose will imperious forced an hundred streams,
Through many a forest, many a spacious wild,
To stretch their scanty trains from sea to sea,
That some unprofitable skiff might float
Across irriguous dales, and hollowed rocks.   600
    Far easier pains may swell our gentler floods,
And through the centre of the isle conduct

To naval union.　Trent and Severn's wave,
By plains alone disparted, woo to join
Majestic Thamis.　With their silver urns
The nimble-footed Naiads of the springs
Await upon the dewy lawn, to speed
And celebrate the union: and the light
Wood-nymphs; and those who o'er the grots preside,
Whose stores bituminous, with sparkling fires,　　610
In summer's tedious absence, cheer the swains,
Long sitting at the loom; and those besides,
Who crown, with yellow sheaves, the farmer's hopes;
And all the genii of commercial toil:
These on the dewy lawns await, to speed
And celebrate the union, that the fleece,
And glossy web, to every port around
May lightly glide along.　Even now behold,
Adown a thousand floods, the burdened barks,
With white sails glistening, through the gloomy woods
Haste to their harbours.　See the silver maze　　620
Of stately Thamis, ever chequered o'er
With deeply-laden barges, gliding smooth
And constant as his stream: in growing pomp,
By Neptune still attended, slow he rolls
To great Augusta's mart, where lofty trade,
Amid a thousand golden spires enthroned,
Gives audience to the world: the strand around
Close swarms with busy crowds of many a realm.
What bales, what wealth, what industry, what fleets!　630
Lo, from the simple fleece, how much proceeds.

Book IV

THE ARGUMENT

Our manufactures exported. Voyage through the Channel, and by
the coast of Spain. View of the Mediterranean. Decay of the Turkey
trade. Address to the factors there. Voyage through the Baltic. The
mart of Petersburg. The ancient channels of commerce to the Indies.
The modern course thither. Shores of Africa. Reflections on the slave-
trade. The Cape of Good Hope, and the eastern part of Africa. Trade
to Persia and Indostan, precarious through tyranny and frequent insur-
rections. Disputes between the French and English, on the coast of
Cormandel, censured. A prospect of the Spice-islands, and of China.
Traffic at Canton. Our woollen manufactures known at Pekin, by the
caravans from Russia. Description of that journey. Transition to the
western hemisphere. Voyage of Raleigh. The state and advantages
of our North American colonies. Severe winters in those climates: hence
the passage through Hudson's bay impracticable. Inquiries for an easier
passage into the Pacific Ocean. View of the coasts of South America,
and of those tempestuous seas. Lord Anson's expedition, and success
against the Spaniards. The naval power of Britain consistent with the
welfare of all nations. View of our probable improvements in traffic,
and the distribution of our woollen manufactures over the whole globe.

Now, with our woolly treasures amply stored,
Glide the tall fleets into the widening main,
A floating forest: every sail, unfurled,
Swells to the wind, and gilds the azure sky.
Meantime, in pleasing care, the pilot steers
Steady; with eye intent upon the steel,
Steady, before the breeze, the pilot steers:
While gaily o'er the waves the mounting prows
Dance, like a shoal of dolphins, and begin
To streak with various paths the hoary deep.   10
Batavia's shallow sounds by some are sought,
Or sandy Elb or Weser, who receive
The swain's and peasant's toil with grateful hand,
Which copious gives return: while some explore
Deep Finnic gulfs, and a new shore and mart,
The bold creation of that Kaisar's power,
Illustrious Peter! whose magnific toils
Repair the distant Caspian, and restore
To trade its ancient ports. Some Thanet's strand,
And Dover's chalky cliff, behind them turn.   20
Soon sinks away the green and level beach
Of Rumney marish, and Rye's silent port,
By angry Neptune closed, and Vecta's isle,
Like the pale moon in vapour, faintly bright.

An hundred opening marts are seen, are lost;
Devonia's hills retire, and Edgecombe mount,
Waving its gloomy groves, delicious scene.
Yet steady o'er the waves they steer: and now
The fluctuating world of waters wide
In boundless magnitude around them swells;   3○
O'er whose imaginary brim, nor towns,
Nor woods, nor mountain tops, nor aught appears,
But Phœbus' orb, refulgent lamp of light,
Millions of leagues aloft: heaven's azure vault
Bends over-head, majestic, to its base,
Uninterrupted clear circumference;
Till, rising o'er the flickering waves, the Cape
Of Finisterre, a cloudy spot appears.
Again, and oft, the adventurous sails disperse;
These to Iberia; others to the coast   4
Of Lusitania, the ancient Tharsis deemed
Of Solomon; fair regions, with the webs
Of Norwich pleased, or those of Manchester;
Light airy clothing for their vacant swains,
And visionary monks.   We in return
Receive Cantabrian steel and fleeces soft,
Segovian or Castilian, far renowned;
And gold's attractive metal, pledge of wealth,
Spur of activity, to good or ill
Powerful incentive; or Hesperian fruits,   5
Fruits of spontaneous growth, the citron bright,
The fig, and orange, and heart-cheering wine.
   Those ships, from ocean broad, which voyage through
The gates of Hercules,[1] find many seas
And bays unnumbered opening to their keels:
But shores inhospitable oft, to fraud
And rapine turned, or dreary tracts become
Of desolation.   The proud Roman coasts,
Fallen, like the Punic, to the dashing waves
Resign their ruins: Tiber's boasted flood,   6
Whose pompous moles o'erlooked the subject deep,
Now creeps along, through brakes and yellow dust,
While Neptune scarce perceives its murmuring rill:
Such are the effects, when virtue slacks her hand;
Wild nature back returns: along these shores
Neglected Trade with difficulty toils,

[1] The Straits of Gibraltar.

Collecting slender stores, the sun-dried grape,
Or capers from the rock, that prompt the taste
Of luxury.   Even Egypt's fertile strand,
Bereft of human discipline, has lost   70
Its ancient lustre: Alexandria's port,
Once the metropolis of trade, as Tyre,
And elder Sidon, as the Attic town,
Beautiful Athens, as rich Corinth, Rhodes,
Unhonoured droops.   Of all the numerous marts,
That in those glittering seas with splendour rose,
Only Byzantium, of peculiar site,
Remains in prosperous state; and Tripolis,
And Smyrna, sacred ever to the Muse.
     To these resort the delegates of trade,   80
Social in life, a virtuous brotherhood;
And bales of softest wool from Bradford looms,
Or Stroud, dispense; yet see, with vain regret,
Their stores, once highly prized, no longer now
Or sought, or valued: copious webs arrive,
Smooth-woven of other than Britannia's fleece,
On the thronged strand alluring; the great skill
Of Gaul, and greater industry, prevails;
That proud imperious foe.   Yet, ah—'tis not—
Wrong not the Gaul; it is the foe within,   90
Impairs our ancient mart: it is the bribe;
'Tis he who pours into the shops of trade
That impious poison: it is he who gains
The sacred seat of parliament by means
That vitiate and emasculate the mind;
By sloth, by lewd intemperance, and a scene
Of riot, worse than that which ruined Rome.
This, this the Tartar, and remote Chinese,
And all the brotherhood of life bewail.
     Meantime (while those, who dare be just, oppose   100
The various powers of many-headed Vice,)
Ye delegates of trade, by patience rise
O'er difficulties: in this sultry clime
Note what is found of use: the flix of goat,
Red-wool, and balm, and caufee's berry brown,
Or dropping gum, or opium's lenient drug;
Unnumbered arts await them: trifles oft,
By skilful labour, rise to high esteem.
Nor what the peasant, nor some lucid wave,

Pactolus, Simois, or Meander slow,   110
Renowned in story, with his plough upturns,
Neglect; the hoary medal, and the vase,
Statue and bust, of old magnificence
Beautiful reliques; oh, could modern time
Restore the mimic art, and the clear mien
Of patriot sages, Walsinghams, and Yorkes,
And Cecils, in long-lasting stone preserve!
But mimic art and nature are impaired—
Impaired they seem—or in a varied dress
Delude our eyes; the world in change delights: 120
Change then your searches, with the varied modes
And wants of realms.   Sabean frankincense
Rare is collected now: few altars smoke
Now in the idol fane: Panchaia views
Trade's busy fleets regardless pass her coast:
Nor frequent are the freights of snow-white woofs,
Since Rome, no more the mistress of the world,
Varies her garb, and treads her darkened streets
With gloomy cowl, majestical no more.
      See the dark spirit of tyrannic power.   130
The Thracian channel, long the road of trade
To the deep Euxine and its naval streams,
And the Mœotis, now is barred with chains,
And forts of hostile battlement: in aught
That joys mankind the arbitrary Turk
Delights not: insolent of rule, he spreads
Thraldom and desolation o'er his realms.
      Another path to Scythia's wide domains
Commerce discovers: the Livonian gulf
Receives her sails, and leads them to the port   140
Of rising Petersburg, whose splendid streets
Swell with the webs of Leeds: the Cossack there,
The Calmuc, and Mongolian, round the bales
In crowds resort, and their warmed limbs enfold,
Delighted; and the hardy Samoid,
Rough with the stings of frost, from his dark caves
Ascends, and thither hastes, ere winter's rage
O'ertake his homeward step; and they that dwell
Along the banks of Don's and Volga's streams;
And borderers of the Caspian, who renew   150
That ancient path to India's climes, which filled
With proudest affluence the Colchian state.

Many have been the ways to those renowned
Luxuriant climes of Indus, early known
To Memphis; to the port of wealthy Tyre;
To Tadmor, beauty of the wilderness,
Who down the long Euphrates sent her sails;
And sacred Salem, when her numerous fleets,
From Ezion-geber, passed the Arabian gulf.

But later times, more fortunate, have found,   160
O'er ocean's open wave a surer course,
Sailing the western coast of Afric's realms,
Of Mauritania, and Nigritian tracts,
And islands of the Gorgades, the bounds,
On the Atlantic brine, of ancient trade;
But not of modern, by the virtue led
Of Gama and Columbus.   The whole globe
Is now of commerce made the scene immense,
Which daring ships frequent, associated,
Like doves, or swallows, in the ethereal flood,   170
Or, like the eagle, solitary seen.

Some, with more open course, to Indus steer;
Some coast from port to port, with various men
And manners conversant; of the angry surge,
That thunders loud, and spreads the cliffs with foam,
Regardless, or the monsters of the deep,
Porpoise, or grampus, or the ravenous shark,
That chase their keels; or threatening rock o'erhead
Of Atlas old; beneath the threatening rocks,
Reckless, they furl their sails, and bartering take   180
Soft flakes of wool; for in soft flakes of wool,
Like the Silurian, Atlas' dales abound.

The shores of Sus inhospitable rise,
And high Bojador; Zara too displays
Unfruitful deserts; Gambia's wave in-isles
An oosy coast, and pestilential ills
Diffuses wide; behind are burning sands,
Adverse to life, and Nilus' hidden fount.

On Guinea's sultry strand, the drapery light
Of Manchester or Norwich is bestowed   190
For clear transparent gums and ductile wax
And snow-white ivory; yet the valued trade,
Along this barbarous coast, in telling wounds
The generous heart, the sale of wretched slaves;
Slaves by their tribes condemned, exchanging death

For life-long servitude; severe exchange!
These till our fertile colonies, which yield
The sugar-cane, and the Tobago-leaf,
And various new productions, that invite
Increasing navies to their crowded wharfs.   200

    But let the man, whose rough tempestuous hours
In this adventurous traffic are involved,
With just humanity of heart pursue
The gainful commerce: wickedness is blind:
Their sable chieftains may in future times
Burst their frail bonds, and vengeance execute
On cruel unrelenting pride of heart
And avarice.   There are ills to come of crimes.

    Hot Guinea too gives yellow dust of gold,
Which, with her rivers, rolls adown the sides   210
Of unknown hills, where fiery-wingèd winds,
And sandy deserts roused by sudden storms,
All search forbid: howe'er, on either hand
Valleys and pleasant plains, and many a tract
Deemed uninhabitable erst, are found
Fertile and populous: their sable tribes,
In shade of verdant groves and mountains tall,
Frequent enjoy the cool descent of rain,
And soft refreshing breezes: nor are lakes
Here wanting; those a sea-wide surface spread,   220
Which to the distant Nile and Senegal
Send long meanders: whate'er lies beyond,
Of rich or barren, ignorance o'ercasts
With her dark mantle.   Mon'motapa's coast
Is seldom visited; and the rough shore
Of Caffres, land of savage Hottentots,
Whose hands unnatural hasten to the grave
Their aged parents: what barbarity
And brutal ignorance, where social trade
Is held contemptible!   Ye gliding sails,   230
From these inhospitable gloomy shores
Indignant turn, and to the friendly Cape,
Which gives the cheerful mariner good hope
Of prosperous voyage, steer: rejoice to view,
What trade, with Belgian industry, creates,
Prospects of civil life, fair towns, and lawns,
And yellow tilth, and groves of various fruits,
Delectable in husk or glossy rind:

There the capacious vase from crystal springs
Replenish, and convenient store provide,   240
Like ants, intelligent of future need.
    See, through the fragrance of delicious airs,
That breathe the smell of balms, how traffic shapes
A winding voyage, by the lofty coast
Of Sofala, thought Ophir; in whose hills
Even yet some portion of its ancient wealth
Remains, and sparkles in the yellow sand
Of its clear streams, though unregarded now:
Ophirs more rich are found.   With easy course
The vessels glide; unless their speed be stopped   250
By dead calms, that oft lie on those smooth seas
While every zephyr sleeps: then the shrouds drop:
The downy feather on the cordage hung,
Moves not; the flat sea shines like yellow gold,
Fused in the fire; or like the marble floor
Of some old temple wide.   But where so wide,
In old or later time, its marble floor
Did ever temple boast as this, which here
Spreads its bright level many a league around?
At solemn distances its pillars rise,   260
Sofal's blue rocks, Mozambique's palmy steeps,
And lofty Madagascar's palmy shores,
Where various woods of beauteous vein and hue,
And glossy shells in elegance of form,
For Pond's rich cabinet, or Sloane's, are found.
Such calm oft checks their course, 'till this bright scene
Is brushed away before the rising breeze,
That joys the busy crew, and speeds again
The sail full-swelling to Socotra's isle,
For aloes famed; or to the wealthy marts   270
Of Ormus or Gombroon, whose streets are oft
With caravans and tawny merchants thronged,
From neighbouring provinces and realms afar;
And filled with plenty, though dry sandy wastes
Spread naked round; so great the power of trade!
    Persia few ports; more happy Indostan
Beholds Surat and Goa on her coasts,
And Bombay's wealthy isle and harbour famed,
Supine beneath the shade of cocoa groves.
But what avails, or many ports or few?   280
Where wild Ambition frequent from his lair

Starts up; while fell Revenge and Famine leads
To havoc, reckless of the tyrant's whip,
Which clanks along the valleys: oft in vain
The merchant seeks upon the strand, whom erst,
Associated by trade, he decked and clothed;
In vain, whom rage or famine has devoured,
He seeks; and with increased affection thinks
On Britain.   Still howe'er Bombaya's wharfs
Pile up blue indigo, and, of frequent use,   290
Pungent saltpetre, woods of purple grain,
And many-coloured saps from leaf or flower,
And various gums; the clothier knows their worth;
And wool resembling cotton, shorn from trees,
Not to the fleece unfriendly; whether mixed
In warp or woof, or with the line of flax,
Or softer silk's material: though its aid
To vulgar eyes appear not; let none deem
The fleece in any traffic unconcerned;
By every traffic aided; while each work   300
Of art yields wealth to exercise the loom,
And every loom employs each hand of art.
Nor is there wheel in the machine of trade,
Which Leeds, or Cairo, Lima, or Bombay,
Helps not with harmony to turn around,
Though all, unconscious of the union, act.
    Few the peculiars of Canara's realm,
Or sultry Malabar; where it behoves
The wary pilot, while he coasts their shores,
To mark o'er ocean the thick rising isles;   310
Woody Chaetta, Birter rough with rocks;
Green-rising Barmur, Mincoy's purple hills;
And the minute Maldivias, as a swarm
Of bees in summer, on a poplar's trunk
Clustering innumerable; these behind
His stern receding, o'er the clouds he views
Ceylon's grey peaks, from whose volcanoes rise
Dark smoke and ruddy flame, and glaring rocks
Darted in air aloft; around whose feet
Blue cliffs ascend, and aromatic groves,   320
In various prospect; Ceylon also deemed
The ancient Ophir.   Next Bengala's bay,
On the vast globe the deepest, while the prow
Turns northward to the rich disputed strand

Of Cormandel, where traffic grieves to see
Discord and Avarice invade her realms,
Portending ruinous war, and cries aloud,
"Peace, peace, ye blinded Britons, and ye Gauls;
Nation to nation is a light, a fire,
Enkindling virtue, sciences, and arts":   330
But cries aloud in vain.   Yet wise defence,
Against ambition's wide-destroying pride,
Madras erected, and Saint David's fort,
And those which rise on Ganges' twenty streams,
Guarding the woven fleece, Calcutta's tower,
And Maldo's and Patana's: from their holds
The shining bales our factors deal abroad,
And see the country's products, in exchange,
Before them heaped; cotton's transparent webs,
Aloes, and cassia, salutiferous drugs,   340
Alum, and lacque, and clouded tortoiseshell,
And brilliant diamonds, to decorate
Britannia's blooming nymphs.   For these, o'er all
The kingdoms round our draperies are dispersed,
O'er Bukor, Cabul, and the Bactrian vales,
And Casimere, and Atoc, on the stream
Of old Hydaspes, Porus' hardy realm;
And late-discovered Thibet, where the fleece,
By art peculiar is compressed and wrought
To threadless drapery, which in conic forms   350
Of various hues their gaudy roofs adorns.
   The keels, which voyage through Molucca's straits,
Amid a cloud of spicy odours sail,
From Java and Sumatra breathed, whose woods
Yield fiery pepper that destroys the moth
In woolly vestures: Ternate and Tidore
Give to the festal board the fragrant clove
And nutmeg, to those narrow bounds confined;
While gracious Nature, with unsparing hand,
The needs of life o'er every region pours.   360
   Near those delicious isles, the beauteous coast
Of China rears its summits.   Know ye not,
Ye sons of trade, that ever-flowery shore,
Those azure hills, those woods and nodding rocks?
Compare them with the pictures of your chart;
Alike the woods and nodding rocks o'erhang.
Now the tall glossy towers of porcelain,

And pillared pagods shine; rejoiced they see
The port of Canton opening to their prows,
And in the winding of the river moor.   370
    Upon the strand they heap their glossy bales,
And works of Birmingham in brass or steel,
And flint, and ponderous lead from deep cells raised,
Fit ballast in the fury of the storm,
That tears the shrouds and bends the stubborn mast:
These for the artists of the fleece procure
Various materials; and, for affluent life,
The flavoured tea and glossy painted vase;
Things elegant, ill-titled luxuries,
In temperance used, delectable and good.   380
They too from hence receive the strongest thread
Of the green silkworm.   Various is the wealth
Of that renowned and ancient land, secure
In constant peace and commerce; tilled to the height
Of rich fertility; where, thick as stars,
Bright habitations glitter on each hill
And rock and shady dale; even on the waves
Of copious rivers, lakes, and bordering seas,
Rise floating villages; no wonder, when,
In every province, firm and level roads,   390
And long canals, and navigable streams,
Ever with ease conduct the works of toil
To sure and speedy markets, through the length
Of many a crowded region, many a clime,
To the imperial towers of Cambalu,
Now Pekin, where the fleece is not unknown;
Since Calder's woofs, and those of Exe and Frome,
And Yare, and Avon slow, and rapid Trent,
Thither by Russic caravans are brought,
Through Scythia's numerous regions, waste and wild,
Journey immense! which to the attentive ear   401
The Muse in faithful notes shall brief describe.
    From the proud mart of Petersburg, erewhile
The watery seat of desolation wide,
Issue these trading caravans, and urge,
Through dazzling snows, their dreary trackless road;
By compass steering oft, from week to week,
From month to month; whole seasons view their toils.
Neva they pass, and Kesma's gloomy flood,
Volga, and Don, and Oka's torrent prone,   410

Threatening in vain; and many a cataract,
In its fall stopp'd, and bound with bars of ice.
  Close on the left unnumbered tracts they view
White with continual frost; and on the right
The Caspian lake, and ever-flowery realms,
Though now abhorred, behind them turn, the haunt
Of arbitrary rule, where regions wide
Are destined to the sword; and on each hand
Roads hung with carcases, or under foot
Thick strown; while, in their rough bewildered vales, 420
The blooming rose its fragrance breathes in vain,
And silver fountains fall, and nightingales
Attune their notes, where none are left to hear.
  Sometimes o'er level ways, on easy sleds,
The generous horse conveys the sons of trade;
And ever and anon the docile dog;
And now the light rein-deer with rapid pace
Skims over icy lakes; now slow they climb
Aloft o'er clouds, and then adown descend
To hollow valleys, till the eye beholds   430
The roofs of Tobol, whose hill-crowning walls
Shine like the rising moon through watery mists:
Tobol, the abode of those unfortunate
Exiles of angry state, and thralls of war;
Solemn fraternity! where carl, and prince,
Soldier, and statesman, and uncrested chief,
On the dark level of adversity
Converse familiar; while, amid the cares
And toils for hunger, thirst, and nakedness,
Their little public smiles, and the bright sparks   440
Of trade are kindled: trade arises oft,
And virtue, from adversity and want:
Be witness, Carthage, witness, ancient Tyre,
And thou, Batavia, daughter of distress.
This, with his hands, which erst the truncheon held,
The hammer lifts; another bends and weaves
The flexile willow; that the mattock drives:
All are employed; and by their works acquire
Our fleecy vestures.   From their tenements,
Pleased and refreshed, proceeds the caravan   450
Through lively-spreading cultures, pastures green,
And yellow tillages in opening woods:
Thence on, through Narim's wilds, a pathless road

They force, with rough entangling thorns perplexed;
Land of the lazy Ostiacs, thin dispersed,
Who, by avoiding, meet the toils they loathe,
Tenfold augmented; miserable tribe,
Void of commercial comforts: who, nor corn,
Nor pulse, nor oil, nor heart-enlivening wine,
Know to procure; nor spade, nor scythe, nor share,   460
Nor social aid: beneath their thorny bed
The serpent hisses, while in thickets nigh
Loud howls the hungry wolf.   So on they fare,
And pass by spacious lakes begirt with rocks,
And azure mountains; and the heights admire
Of white Imaus, whose snow-nodding crags
Frighten the realms beneath, and from their urns
Pour mighty rivers down, the impetuous streams
Of Oby, Irtis, and Jenisca swift,
Which rush upon the northern pole, upheave   470
Its frozen seas, and lift their hills of ice.
　　These rugged paths and savage landscapes passed,
A new scene strikes their eyes: among the clouds
Aloft they view what seems a chain of cliffs,
Nature's proud work; that matchless work of art,
The wall of Sina, by Chihoham's power
In earliest times erected.   Warlike troops
Frequent are seen in haughty march along
Its ridge, a vast extent, beyond the length
Of many a potent empire; towers and ports,   480
Three times a thousand, lift their brows
At equal spaces, and in prospect 'round,
Cities, and plains, and kingdoms overlook.
　　At length the gloomy passage they attain
Of its deep vaulted gates, whose opening folds
Conduct at length to Pekin's glittering spires,
The destined mart, where joyous they arrive.
　　Thus are the textures of the fleece conveyed
To Sina's distant realm, the utmost bound
Of the flat floor of stedfast earth; for so   490
Fabled antiquity, ere peaceful trade
Informed the opening mind of curious man.
　　Now to the other hemisphere, my Muse,
A new world found, extend thy daring wing.
Be thou the first of the harmonious Nine
From high Parnassus, the unwearied toils

Of industry and valour, in that world
Triumphant, to reward with tuneful song.
   Happy the voyage, o'er the Atlantic brine,
By active Raleigh made, and great the joy,   500
When he discerned above the foamy surge
A rising coast, for future colonies,
Opening her bays and figuring her capes,
Even from the northern tropic to the pole.
No land gives more employment to the loom,
Or kindlier feeds the indigent; no land
With more variety of wealth rewards
The hand of labour: thither, from the wrongs
Of lawless rule the freeborn spirit flies;
Thither affliction, thither poverty,   510
And arts and sciences: thrice happy clime,
Which Britain makes the asylum of mankind.
   But joy superior far his bosom warms,
Who views those shores in every culture dressed;
With habitations gay, and numerous towns,
On hill and valley; and his countrymen
Formed into various states, powerful and rich,
In regions far remote: who from our looms
Take largely for themselves, and for those tribes
Of Indians, ancient tenants of the land,   520
In amity conjoined, of civil life
The comforts taught, and various new desires,
Which kindle arts, and occupy the poor,
And spread Britannia's flocks o'er every dale.
   Ye, who the shuttle cast along the loom,
The silkworm's thread inweaving with the fleece,
Pray for the culture of the Georgian tract,
Nor slight the green savannahs, and the plains
Of Carolina, where thick woods arise
Of mulberries, and in whose watered fields   530
Up springs the verdant blade of thirsty rice.
Where are the happy regions, which afford
More implements of commerce, and of wealth?
   Fertile Virginia, like a vigorous bough
Which overshades some crystal river, spreads
Her wealthy cultivations wide around,
And, more than many a spacious realm, rewards
The fleecy shuttle: to her growing marts
The Iroquese, Cheroques, and Oubacks, come,

And quit their feathery ornaments uncouth   540
For woolly garments; and the cheers of life,
The cheers, but not the vices, learn to taste.
Blush, Europeans, whom the circling cup
Of luxury intoxicates; ye routs,
Who for your crimes have fled your native land;
And ye voluptuous idle, who in vain
Seek easy habitations, void of care:
The sons of nature, with astonishment
And detestation, mark your evil deeds:
And view, no longer awed, your nerveless arms,   550
Unfit to cultivate Ohio's banks.
    See the bold emigrants of Accadie,[1]
And Massachuset, happy in those arts,
That join the politics of trade and war,
Bearing the palm in either; they appear
Better exemplars; and that hardy crew,
Who, on the frozen beach of Newfoundland,
Hang their white fish amid the parching winds:
The kindly fleece, in webs of Duffield woof,
Their limbs benumbed enfolds with cheerly warmth,
And frieze of Cambria, worn by those who seek,   561
Through gulfs and dales of Hudson's winding bay,
The beaver's fur, though oft they seek in vain,
While winter's frosty rigour checks approach,
Even in the fiftieth latitude.   Say why
(If ye, the travelled sons of commerce, know)
Wherefore lie bound their rivers, lakes, and dales,
Half the sun's annual course, in chains of ice?
While the Rhine's fertile shore, and Gallic realms,
By the same zone encircled, long enjoy   570
Warm beams of Phœbus, and, supine, behold
The plains and hillocks blush with clustering vines.
    Must it be ever thus? or may the hand
Of mighty labour drain their gusty lakes,
Enlarge the brightening sky, and, peopling, warm
The opening valleys, and the yellowing plains?
Or rather shall we burst strong Darien's chain,
Steer our bold fleets between the cloven rocks,
And through the great Pacific every joy
Of civil life diffuse?   Are not her isles   580
Numerous and large?   Have they not harbours calm,

[1] Or Acadia.   For their sad story see Longfellow's *Evangeline*.

Inhabitants, and manners? haply, too,
Peculiar sciences, and other forms
Of trade, and useful products, to exchange
For woolly vestures?   'Tis a tedious course
By the Antarctic circle: nor beyond
Those sea-wrapt gardens of the dulcet reed,
Bahama and the Caribbee, may be found
Safe mole or harbour, till on Falkland's isle
The standard of Britannia shall arise.   590
Proud Buenos Ayres, low-couched Paraguay,
And rough Corrientes, mark with hostile eye
The labouring vessel: neither may we trust
The dreary naked Patagonian land,
Which darkens in the wind.   No traffic there,
No barter for the fleece.   There angry storms
Bend their black brows, and, raging, hurl around
Their thunders.   Ye adventurous mariners,
Be firm; take courage from the brave.   'Twas there
Perils and conflicts inexpressible   600
Anson, with steady undespairing breast,
Endured, when o'er the various globe he chased
His country's foes.   Fast-gathering tempests roused
Huge Ocean, and involved him: all around
Whirlwind, and snow, and hail, and horror: now,
Rapidly, with the world of waters, down
Descending to the channels of the deep,
He viewed the uncovered bottom of the abyss;
And now the stars, upon the loftiest point
Tossed of the sky-mixed surges.   Oft the burst   610
Of loudest thunder, with the dash of seas
Tore the wild-flying sails and tumbling masts;
While flames, thick-flashing, in the gloom revealed
Ruins of decks and shrouds, and sights of death.
    Yet on he fared, with fortitude his cheer,
Gaining, at intervals, slow way beneath
Del Fuego's rugged cliffs, and the white ridge,
Above all height, by opening clouds revealed,
Of Montegorda, and inaccessible
Wreck-threatening Staten-land's o'erhanging shore,   620
Enormous rocks on rocks, in ever-wild
Posture of falling; as when Pelion, reared
On Ossa, and on Ossa's tottering head
Woody Olympus, by the angry gods

Precipitate on earth were doomed to fall.
  At length, through every tempest, as some branch,
Which from a poplar falls into a loud
Impetuous cataract, though deep immersed,
Yet reascends, and glides, on lake or stream,
Smooth through the valleys: so his way he won   630
To the serene Pacific, flood immense,
And reared his lofty masts, and spread his sails.
  Then Paita's walls, in wasting flames involved,
His vengeance felt, and fair occasion gave
To show humanity and continence,
To Scipio's not inferior.   Then was left
No corner of the globe secure to pride
And violence: although the far-stretched coast
Of Chili, and Peru, and Mexico,
Armed in their evil cause; though fell disease,   640
Un'bating labour, tedious time, conspired,
And heat inclement, to unnerve his force;
Though that wide sea, which spreads o'er half the world,
Denied all hospitable land or port;
Where, seasons voyaging, no road he found
To moor, no bottom in the abyss, whereon
To drop the fastening anchor; though his brave
Companions ceased, subdued by toil extreme;
Though solitary left in Tinian's seas,
Where never was before the dreaded sound   650
Of Britain's thunder heard; his wave-worn bark
Met, fought, the proud Iberian, and o'ercame.
So fare it ever with our country's foes.
  Rejoice, ye nations, vindicate the sway
Ordained for common happiness.   Wide o'er
The globe terraqueous let Britannia pour
The fruits of plenty from her copious horn.
What can avail to her, whose fertile earth
By ocean's briny waves are circumscribed,
The armèd host, and murdering sword of war,   660
And conquest o'er her neighbours?   She ne'er breaks
Her solemn compacts, in the lust of rule:
Studious of arts and trade, she ne'er disturbs
The holy peace of states.   'Tis her delight
To fold the world with harmony, and spread
Among the habitations of mankind
The various wealth of toil, and what her fleece,

To clothe the naked, and her skilful looms,
Peculiar give.   Ye too rejoice, ye swains;
Increasing commerce shall reward your cares.   670
A day will come, if not too deep we drink
The cup which luxury on careless wealth,
Pernicious gift, bestows; a day will come,
When, through new channels sailing, we shall clothe
The Californian coast, and all the realms
That stretch from Anian's straits to proud Japan;
And the green isles, which on the left arise
Upon the glassy brine, whose various capes
Not yet are figured on the sailor's chart:
Then every variation shall be told   680
Of the magnetic steel; and currents marked,
Which drive the heedless vessel from her course.
   That portion too of land, a tract immense,
Beneath the Antarctic spread, shall then be known,
And new plantations on its coast arise.
Then rigid winter's ice no more shall wound
The only naked animal; but man
With the soft fleece shall everywhere be clothed.
The exulting Muse shall then, in vigour fresh,
Her flight renew.   Meanwhile, with weary wing,   690
O'er ocean's wave returning, she explores
Siluria's flowery vales, her old delight,
The shepherd's haunts, where the first springs arise
Of Britain's happy trade, now spreading wide,
Wide as the Atlantic and Pacific seas,
Or as air's vital fluid o'er the globe.

GRONGAR HILL [1]

SILENT nymph, with curious eye!
Who, the purple evening, lie
On the mountain's lonely van,
Beyond the noise of busy man,
Painting fair the form of things,
While the yellow linnet sings;
Or the tuneful nightingale

[1] In South Wales.

Charms the forest with her tale;
Come with all thy various hues,
Come, and aid thy sister Muse;   10
Now while Phœbus riding high
Gives lustre to the land and sky!
Grongar Hill invites my song,
Draw the landscape bright and strong;
Grongar, in whose mossy cells
Sweetly-musing Quiet dwells;
Grongar, in whose silent shade,
For the modest Muses made,
So oft I have, the even still,
At the fountain of a rill,   20
Sate upon a flowery bed,
With my hand beneath my head;
And strayed my eyes o'er Towy's flood,
Over mead and over wood,
From house to house, from hill to hill,
'Till Contemplation had her fill.
    About his chequered sides I wind,
And leave his brooks and meads behind,
And groves, and grottos where I lay,
And vistas shooting beams of day: 30
Wider and wider spreads the vale,
As circles on a smooth canal:
The mountains round, unhappy fate!
Sooner or later, of all height,
Withdraw their summits from the skies,
And lessen as the others rise:
Still the prospect wider spreads,
Adds a thousand woods and meads,
Still it widens, widens still,
And sinks the newly-risen hill.   40
    Now I gain the mountain's brow,
What a landscape lies below!
No clouds, no vapours intervene,
But the gay, the open scene
Does the face of Nature show,
In all the hues of heaven's bow!
And, swelling to embrace the light,
Spreads around beneath the sight.
    Old castles on the cliffs arise,
Proudly towering in the skies!   50

Rushing from the woods, the spires
Seem from hence ascending fires!
Half his beams Apollo sheds
On the yellow mountain-heads!
Gilds the fleeces of the flocks:
And glitters on the broken rocks!
   Below me trees unnumbered rise,
Beautiful in various dyes:
The gloomy pine, the poplar blue,
The yellow beech, the sable yew,   60
The slender fir that taper grows,
The sturdy oak with broad-spread boughs.
And beyond the purple grove,
Haunt of Phillis, queen of love!
Gaudy as the opening dawn,
Lies a long and level lawn,
On which a dark hill, steep and high,
Holds and charms the wandering eye!
Deep are his feet in Towy's flood,
His sides are cloth'd with waving wood,   70
And ancient towers crown his brow,
That cast an awful look below;
Whose ragged walls the ivy creeps,
And with her arms from falling keeps;
So both a safety from the wind
On mutual dependence find.
   'Tis now the raven's bleak abode;
'Tis now the apartment of the toad;
And there the fox securely feeds;
And there the poisonous adder breeds,   80
Concealed in ruins, moss and weeds,
While, ever and anon, there falls
Huge heaps of hoary mouldered walls.
Yet Time has seen, that lifts the low,
And level lays the lofty brow,
Has seen this broken pile complete,
Big with the vanity of state;
But transient is the smile of fate!
A little rule, a little sway,
A sunbeam in a winter's day,   90
Is all the proud and mighty have
Between the cradle and the grave.
   And see the rivers how they run,

Through woods and meads; in shade and sun,
Sometimes swift, sometimes slow,
Wave succeeding wave, they go
A various journey to the deep,
Like human life to endless sleep!
Thus is Nature's vesture wrought,
To instruct our wandering thought;　　　　100
Thus she dresses green and gay,
To disperse our cares away.

　　Ever charming, ever new,
When will the landscape tire the view!
The fountain's fall, the river's flow,
The woody valleys, warm and low;
The windy summit, wild and high,
Roughly rushing on the sky!
The pleasant seat, the ruined tower,
The naked rock, the shady bower;　　　　110
The town and village, dome and farm,
Each give each a double charm,
As pearls upon an Æthiop's arm.

　　See on the mountain's southern side,
Where the prospect opens wide,
Where the evening gilds the tide;
How close and small the hedges lie!
What streaks of meadows cross the eye!
A step methinks may pass the stream,
So little distant dangers seem;　　　　120
So we mistake the future's face,
Eyed through hope's deluding glass;
As yon summits soft and fair,
Clad in colours of the air,
Which to those who journey near,
Barren, brown, and rough appear;
Still we tread the same coarse way,
The present 's still a cloudy day.

　　O may I with myself agree,
And never covet what I see:　　　　130
Content me with an humble shade,
My passions tamed, my wishes laid;
For while our wishes wildly roll,
We banish quiet from the soul:
'Tis thus the busy beat the air;
And misers gather wealth and care.

Now, even now, my joys run high,
As on the mountain-turf I lie;
While the wanton Zephyr sings,
And in the vale perfumes his wings;   140
While the waters murmur deep;
While the shepherd charms his sheep;
While the birds unbounded fly,
And with music fill the sky,
Now, even now, my joys run high.

Be full, ye courts, be great who will;
Search for peace with all your skill:
Open wide the lofty door,
Seek her on the marble floor,
In vain you search, she is not there;   150
In vain ye search the domes of Care!
Grass and flowers Quiet treads,
On the meads, and mountain-heads,
Along with Pleasure, close allied,
Ever by each other's side:
And often, by the murmuring rill,
Hears the thrush, while all is still,
Within the groves of Grongar Hill.

THE RUINS OF ROME

A POEM

Aspice murorum moles, præruptaque saxa,
 Obrutaque horrenti vasta theatra situ:
Hæc sunt *Roma*.   Viden' velut ipsa cadavera tantæ
 Urbis adhuc spirent imperiosa minas?

                                        JANUS VITALIS.

ENOUGH of Grongar, and the shady dales
Of winding Towy, Merlin's fabled haunt,
I sung inglorious.   Now the love of arts,
And what in metal or in stone remains
Of proud antiquity, through various realms
And various languages and ages famed,
Bears me remote, o'er Gallia's woody bounds,
O'er the cloud-piercing Alps remote; beyond

The vale of Arno purpled with the vine,
Beyond the Umbrian and Etruscan hills,   10
To Latium's wide champagne, forlorn and waste,
Where yellow Tiber his neglected wave
Mournfully rolls.   Yet once again, my Muse,
Yet once again, and soar a loftier flight;
Lo the resistless theme, imperial Rome!

    Fallen, fallen, a silent heap; her heroes all
Sunk in their urns; behold the pride of pomp,
The throne of nations fallen; obscured in dust;
Even yet majestical: the solemn scene
Elates the soul, while now the rising sun   20
Flames on the ruins in the purer air
Towering aloft, upon the glittering plain,
Like broken rocks, a vast circumference;
Rent palaces, crushed columns, rifted moles,
Fanes rolled on fanes, and tombs on buried tombs.

    Deep lies in dust the Theban obelisk,
Immense along the waste; minuter art,
Glyconian [1] forms, or Phidian, subtly fair,
O'erwhelming; as the immense Leviathan
The finny brood, when near Ierne's shore   30
Out-stretched, unwieldy, his island length appears,
Above the foamy flood.   Globose and huge,
Grey-mouldering temples swell, and wide o'ercast
The solitary landscape, hills and woods,
And boundless wilds; while the vine-mantled brows
The pendant goats unveil, regardless they
Of hourly peril, though the clefted domes
Tremble to every wind.   The pilgrim oft
At dead of night, 'mid his oraison hears
Aghast the voice of time, disparting towers,   40
Tumbling all precipitate down-dashed,
Rattling around, loud thundering to the moon:
While murmurs soothe each awful interval
Of ever-falling waters; shrouded Nile,
Eridanus, and Tiber with his twins,
And palmy Euphrates; [2] they with dropping locks,
Hang o'er their urns, and mournfully among
The plaintive-echoing ruins pour their streams.

    Yet here adventurous in the sacred search

[1] Glycon, Phidias, Grecian sculptors.
[2] Fountains at Rome adorned with the statues of those rivers.

Of ancient arts, the delicate of mind, 50
Curious and modest, from all climes resort,
Grateful society! with these I raise,
The toilsome step up the proud Palatine,
Through spiry cypress groves, and towering pine,
Waving aloft o'er the big ruin's brows,
On numerous arches reared; and frequent stopped,
The sunk ground startles me with dreadful chasm,
Breathing forth darkness from the vast profound
Of aisles and halls, within the mountain's womb.
Nor these the nether works; all these beneath, 60
And all beneath the vales and hills around,
Extend the caverned sewers, massy, firm,
As the Sibylline grot beside the dead
Lake of Avernus; such the sewers huge,
Whither the great Tarquinian genius dooms
Each wave impure; and proud with added rains,
Hark how the mighty billows lash their vaults,
And thunder; how they heave their rocks in vain!
Though now incessant time has rolled around
A thousand winters o'er the changeful world, 70
And yet a thousand since, the indignant floods
Roar loud in their firm bounds, and dash and swell,
In vain; conveyed to Tiber's lowest wave.
   Hence, over airy plains, by crystal founts,
That weave their glittering waves with tuneful lapse,
Among the sleeky peebles, agate clear,
Cerulian ophite, and the flowery vein
Of orient jasper, pleased I move along,
And vases bossed and huge inscriptive stones,
And intermingling vines; and figured nymphs, 80
Floras and Chloes of delicious mould,
Cheering the darkness; and deep empty tombs,
And dells, and mouldering shrines, with old decay
Rustic and green, and wide-embowering shades,
Shot from the crooked clefts of nodding towers;
A solemn wilderness! With error sweet,
I wind the lingering step, where'er the path
Mazy conducts me, which the vulgar foot
O'er sculptures maimed has made; Anubis, Sphinx,
Idols of antique guise, and hornèd Pan, 90
Terrific, monstrous shapes! preposterous gods,
Of Fear and Ignorance, by the sculptor's hand

Hewn into form, and worshipped; as even now
Blindly they worship at their breathless mouths [1]
In varied appellations: men to these
(From depth to depth in darkening error fallen)
At length ascribed the inapplicable name.

    How doth it please and fill the memory
With deeds of brave renown, while on each hand
Historic urns and breathing statues rise,   100
And speaking busts! Sweet Scipio, Marius stern,
Pompey superb, the spirit-stirring form
Of Cæsar raptured with the charm of rule
And boundless fame; impatient for exploits,
His eager eyes upcast, he soars in thought
Above all height: and his own Brutus see,
Desponding Brutus, dubious of the right,
In evil days, of faith, of public weal
Solicitous and sad. Thy next regard
Be Tully's graceful attitude; upraised,   110
His out-streched arm he waves, in act to speak
Before the silent masters of the world,
And Eloquence arrays him.   There behold
Prepared for combat in the front of war
The pious brothers; jealous Alba stands
In fearful expectation of the strife,
And youthful Rome intent: the kindred foes
Fall on each other's neck in silent tears;
In sorrowful benevolence embrace—
Howe'er, they soon unsheathed the flashing sword,   120
Their country calls to arms; now all in vain
The mother clasps the knee, and even the fair
Now weeps in vain; their country calls to arms.
Such virtue Clelia, Cocles, Manlius, roused;
Such were the Fabii, Decii; so inspired
The Scipios battled, and the Gracchi spoke:
So rose the Roman state. Me now, of these
Deep-musing, high ambitious thoughts inflame
Greatly to serve my country, distant land,
And build me virtuous fame; nor shall the dust   130
Of these fallen piles with shew of sad decay
Avert the good resolve, mean argument,
The fate alone of matter.——Now the brow

[1] Several statues of the Pagan gods have been converted into images
of saints.

We gain enraptured; beauteously distinct [1]
The numerous porticos and domes upswell,
With obelisks and columns interposed,
And pine, and fir, and oak: so fair a scene
Sees not the dervise from the spiral tomb
Of ancient Chammos, while his eye beholds
Proud Memphis' reliques o'er the Egyptian plain: 140
Nor hoary hermit from Hymettus' brow,
Though graceful Athens, in the vale beneath,
Along the windings of the Muse's stream,
Lucid Ilyssus, weeps her silent schools,
And groves, unvisited by bard or sage.
Amid the towery ruins, huge, supreme,
The enormous amphitheatre behold,
Mountainous pile! o'er whose capacious womb
Pours the broad firmament its varied light;
While from the central floor the seats ascend 150
Round above round, slow-widening to the verge,
A circuit vast and high; nor less had held
Imperial Rome and her attendant realms,
When, drunk with rule, she willed the fierce delight,
And oped the gloomy caverns, whence out-rushed
Before the innumerable shouting crowd
The fiery, madded, tyrants of the wilds,
Lions and tigers, wolves and elephants,
And desperate men, more fell. Abhorr'd intent!
By frequent converse with familiar death, 160
To kindle brutal daring apt for war;
To lock the breast, and steel the obdurate heart
Amid the piercing cries of sore distress
Impenetrable.—But away thine eye;
Behold yon steepy cliff; the modern pile
Perchance may now delight, while that, revered [2]
In ancient days, the page alone declares,
Or narrow coin through dim cerulean rust.
The fane was Jove's, its spacious golden roof
O'er thick-surrounding temples beaming wide 170
Appeared as when above the morning hills,
Half the round sun ascends; and towered aloft,
Sustained by columns huge, innumerous
As cedars proud on Canaan's verdant heights

---

[1] From the Palatine hill one sees most of the remarkable antiquities.
[2] The Capitol.

Darkening their idols, when Astarte lured
Too prosperous Israel from his living strength.
  And next regard yon venerable dome,
Which virtuous Latium, with erroneous aim
Raised to her various deities, and named
Pantheon; plain and round; of this our world   180
Majestic emblem; with peculiar grace,
Before its ample orb, projected stands
The many-pillared portal; noblest work
Of human skill: here, curious architect,
If thou assay'st, ambitious, to surpass
Palladius, Angelus, or British Jones,
On these fair walls extend the certain scale,
And turn the instructive compass: careful mark
How far in hidden art the noble plain
Extends, and where the lovely forms commence   190
Of flowing sculpture: nor neglect to note
How range the taper columns, and what weight
Their leafy brows sustain: fair Corinth first
Boasted their order which Callimachus
(Reclining studious on Æsopus' banks
Beneath an urn of some lamented nymph)
Haply composed; the urn with foliage curled
Thinly concealed, the chapiter informed.
  See the tall obelisks, from Memphis old,
One stone enormous each, or Thebes conveyed;   200
Like Albion's spires they rush into the skies.
And there the temple, where the summoned state [1]
In deep of night convened: even yet methinks
The veh'ment orator in rent attire
Persuasion pours, ambition sinks her crest;
And lo the villain, like a troubled sea
That tosses up her mire! Ever disguised,
Shall treason walk? shall proud oppression yoke
The neck of virtue?   Lo the wretch, abashed,
Self-betrayed Catiline! O liberty,   210
Parent of happiness, celestial born;
When the first man became a living soul,
His sacred genius thou; be Britain's care;
With her secure, prolong thy loved retreat;
Thence bless mankind; while yet among her sons,
Even yet there are, to shield thine equal laws,

[1] The temple of Concord, where the senate met on Catiline's conspiracy.

Whose bosom kindle at the sacred names
Of Cecil, Raleigh, Walsingham, and Drake.
May others more delight in tuneful airs;
In masque and dance excel; to sculptured stone   220
Give with superior skill the living look;
More pompous piles erect, or pencil soft
With warmer touch the visionary board:
But thou, thy nobler Britons teach to rule;
To check the ravage of tyrannic sway;
To quell the proud; to spread the joys of peace
And various blessings of ingenious trade.
Be these our arts; and ever may we guard,
Ever defend thee with undaunted heart,
Inestimable good; who giv'st us Truth,   230
Arrayed in every charm: whose hand benign
Teaches unwearied toil to clothe the fields,
And on his various fruits inscribes the name
Of Property: O nobly hailed of old
By thy majestic daughters, Judah fair,
And Tyrus and Sidonia, lovely nymphs,
And Libya bright, and all enchanting Greece,
Whose numerous towns and isles and peopled seas,
Rejoiced around her lyre: the heroic note
(Smit with sublime delight) Ausonia caught,   240
And planned imperial Rome.   Thy hand benign
Reared up her towery battlements in strength;
Bent her wide bridges o'er the swelling stream
Of Tuscan Tiber; thine those solemn domes
Devoted to the voice of humbler prayer;
And thine those piles undecked, capacious, vast,[1]
In days of dearth where tender Charity
Dispensed her timely succours to the poor.
Thine too those musically-falling founts
To slake the clammy lip; adown they fall,   250
Musical ever; while from yon blue hills
Dim in the clouds, the radiant aqueducts
Turn their innumerable arches o'er
The spacious desert, brightening in the sun,
Proud and more proud, in their august approach:
High o'er irriguous vales and woods and towns,
Glide the soft whispering waters in the wind,
And here united pour their silver streams

[1] The public granaries.

Among the figured rocks, in murmuring falls,
Musical ever. These thy beauteous works: 260
And what beside felicity could tell
Of human benefit: more late the rest;
At various times their turrets chanced to rise,
When impious tyranny vouchsafed to smile.

    Behold by Tiber's flood, where modern Rome [1]
Couches beneath the ruins: there of old
With arms and trophies gleamed the field of Mars:
There to their daily sports the noble youth
Rushed emulous; to fling the pointed lance;
To vault the steed; or with the kindling wheel   270
In dusty whirlwinds sweep the trembling goal;
Or wrestling, cope with adverse swelling breasts,
Strong grappling arms, closed heads, and distant feet;
Or clash the lifted gauntlets: there they formed
Their ardent virtues: lo the bossy piles,
The proud triumphal arches: all their wars,
Their conquests, honours, in the sculptures live.
And see from every gate those ancient roads,
With tombs high-verged, the solemn paths of Fame:
Deserve they not regard? O'er whose broad flints   280
Such crowds have rolled, so many storms of war!
Such trains of consuls, tribunes, sages, kings!
So many pomps! so many wondering realms!
Yet still through mountains pierced, o'er valleys raised,
In even state, to distant seas around,
They stretch their pavements. Lo the fane of Peace,
Built by that prince, who to the trust of power [2]
Was honest, the delight of human kind.
Three nodding aisles remain; the rest an heap
Of sand and weeds; her shrines, her radiant roofs,   290
And columns proud, that from her spacious floor,
As from a shining sea, majestic rose
An hundred foot aloft, like stately beech
Around the brim of Dion's glassy lake,
Charming the mimic painter: on the walls
Hung Salem's sacred spoils; the golden board,
And golden trumpets, now concealed, entombed
By the sunk roof.—O'er which in distant view
The Etruscan mountains swell, with ruins crowned

---

[1] Modern Rome stands chiefly on the old Campus Martius.
[2] Begun by Vespasian, and finished by Titus.

Of ancient towns; and blue Soracte spires,   300
Wrapping his sides in tempests.   Eastward hence,
Nigh where the Cestian pyramid divides [1]
The mouldering wall, behold yon fabric huge,
Whose dust the solemn antiquarian turns,
And thence, in broken sculptures cast abroad,
Like Sybil's leaves, collects the builder's name
Rejoiced, and the green medals frequent found
Doom Caracalla to perpetual fame:
The stately pines, that spread their branches wide
In the dun ruins of its ample halls,[2]   310
Appear but tufts; as may whate'er is high
Sink in comparison, minute and vile.

  These, and unnumbered, yet their brows uplift,
Rent of their graces; as Britannia's oaks
On Merlin's mount, or Snowdon's rugged sides,
Stand in the clouds, their branches scattered round,
After the tempest; Mausoleums, Cirques,
Naumachias,[3] Forums: Trajan's column tall,
From whose low base the sculptures wind aloft,
And lead through various toils, up the rough steep,   320
Its hero to the skies: and his dark tower [4]
Whose execrable hand the city fired,
And while the dreadful conflagration blazed,
Played to the flames; and Phœbus' lettered dome; [5]
And the rough reliques of Carinæ's street,
Where now the shepherd to his nibbling sheep
Sits piping with his oaten reed; as erst
There piped the shepherd to his nibbling sheep,
When the humble roof Anchises' son explored
Of good Evander, wealth-despising king,   330
Amid the thickets: so revolves the scene;
So Time ordains, who rolls the things of pride
From dust again to dust.   Behold that heap
Of mouldering urns (their ashes blown away,
Dust of the mighty) the same story tell;
And at its base, from whence the serpent glides

[1] The tomb of Cestius, partly within and partly without the walls, near which lie Keats and Shelley.
[2] The baths of Caracalla, a vast ruin, in which Shelley wrote his *Prometheus Unbound*.
[3] Large erections for representing naval engagements. One built by Augustus was capable of containing fifty ships.
[4] Nero's.
[5] The Palatine library.

Down the green desert street, yon hoary monk
Laments the same, the vision as he views,
The solitary, silent, solemn scene,
Where Cæsars, heroes, peasants, hermits lie,   340
Blended in dust together; where the slave
Rests from his labours; where the insulting proud
Resigns his power; the miser drops his hoard;
Where human folly sleeps.—There is a mood,
(I sing not to the vacant and the young)
There is a kindly mood of melancholy,
That wings the soul, and points her to the skies;
When tribulation clothes the child of man,
When age descends with sorrow to the grave,
'Tis sweetly-soothing sympathy to pain,   350
A gently wakening call to health and ease.
How musical! when all-devouring Time,
Here sitting on his throne of ruins hoar,
While winds and tempests sweep his various lyre,
How sweet thy diapason, Melancholy!
Cool evening comes; the setting sun displays
His visible great round between yon towers,
As through two shady cliffs; away, my Muse,
Though yet the prospect pleases, ever new
In vast variety, and yet delight   360
The many-figured sculptures of the path
Half beauteous, half effaced; the traveller
Such antique marbles to his native land
Oft hence conveys; and every realm and state
With Rome's august remains, heroes and gods,
Deck their long galleries and winding groves;
Yet miss we not the innumerable thefts,
Yet still profuse of graces teems the waste.

Suffice it now the Esquilian mount to reach
With weary wing, and seek the sacred rests   370
Of Maro's humble tenement; a low
Plain wall remains; a little sun-gilt heap,
Grotesque and wild: the gourd and olive brown
Weave the light roof; the gourd and olive fan
Their amorous foliage, mingling with the vine,
Who drops her purple clusters through the green.
Here let me lie, with pleasing fancy soothed:
Here flowed his fountain; here his laurels grew;
Here oft the meek good man, the lofty bard

Framed the celestial song, or social walked   380
With Horace and the ruler of the world:
Happy Augustus! who, so well inspired,
Couldst throw thy pomps and royalties aside,
Attentive to the wise, the great of soul,
And dignify thy mind.   Thrice glorious days,
Auspicious to the Muses!   Then revered,
Then hallowed was the fount, or secret shade,
Or open mountain, or whatever scene
The poet chose to tune the ennobling rhyme
Melodious; even the rugged sons of war,   390
Even the rude hinds revered the Poet's name:
But now—another age, alas! is ours——
Yet will the Muse a little longer soar,
Unless the clouds of care weigh down her wing,
Since Nature's stores are shut with cruel hand,
And each aggrieves his brother: since in vain
The thirsty pilgrim at the fountain asks
The o'erflowing wave—Enough—the plaint disdain.—
      See'st thou yon fane [1]? even now incessant time
Sweeps her low mouldering marbles to the dust;   400
And Phœbus' temple, nodding with its woods,
Threatens huge ruin o'er the small rotund.
'Twas there beneath a fig-tree's umbrage broad,
The astonished swains with reverend awe beheld
Thee, O Quirinus, and thy brother-twin,
Pressing the teat within a monster's grasp,
Sportive; while oft the gaunt and rugged wolf
Turned her stretched neck and formed your tender limbs:
So taught of Jove, even the fell savage fed
Your sacred infancies, your virtues, toils,   410
The conquests, glories, of the Ausonian state,
Wrapp'd in their sacred seeds.   Each kindred soul,
Robust and stout, ye grapple to your hearts,
And little Rome appears.   Her cots arise,
Green twigs of osier weave the slender walls,
Green rushes spread the roofs; and here and there
Opens beneath the rock the gloomy cave.
Elate with joy Etruscan Tiber views
Her spreading scenes enamelling his waves,
Her huts and hollow dells, and flocks and herds,   420
And gathering swains; and rolls his yellow car

[1] The temple of Romulus and Remus under Mount Palatine.

To Neptune's court with more majestic train.
　　Her speedy growth alarmed the states around
Jealous; yet soon by wondrous virtue won,
They sink into her bosom.　From the plough
Rose her dictators; fought, o'ercame, returned,
Yes, to the plough returned, and hailed their peers;
For then no private pomp, no household state,
The public only swelled the generous breast.
Who has not heard the Fabian heroes sung?　　　　　430
Dentatus' scars, or Mutius' flaming hand?
How Manlius saved the capitol? the choice
Of steady Regulus?　As yet they stood,
Simple of life; as yet seducing wealth
Was unexplored, and shame of poverty
Yet unimagined—Shine not all the fields
With various fruitage? murmur not the brooks
Along the flowery valleys?　They, content,
Feasted at Nature's hand, indelicate,
Blithe, in their easy taste; and only sought　　　　　440
To know their duties; that their only strife,
Their generous strife, and greatly to perform.
They through all shapes of peril and of pain,
Intent on honour, dared in thickest death
To snatch the glorious deed.　Nor Trebia quell'd,
Nor Thrasymene, nor Cannæ's bloody field,
Their dauntless courage; storming Hannibal
In vain the thunder of the battle rolled,
The thunder of the battle they returned
Back on his Punic shores; till Carthage fell,　　　　450
And danger fled afar.　The city gleamed
With precious spoils: alas prosperity!
Ah baneful state! yet ebbed not all their strength
In soft luxurious pleasures; proud desire
Of boundless sway, and feverish thirst of gold,
Roused them again to battle.　Beauteous Greece,
Torn from her joys, in vain with languid arm
Half raised her rusty shield; nor could avail
The sword of Dacia, nor the Parthian dart;
Nor yet the car of that famed British chief,　　　　460
Which seven brave years beneath the doubtful wing
Of victory dreadful rolled its griding wheels
Over the bloody war: the Roman arms
Triumphed, till Fame was silent of their foes.

And now, the world unrivalled they enjoyed
In proud security: the crested helm,
The plated greave and corslet hung unbraced;
Nor clanked their arms, the spear and sounding shield,
But on the glittering trophy to the wind.

Dissolved in ease and soft delights they lie,   470
'Till every sun annoys, and every wind
Has chilling force, and every rain offends:
For now the frame no more is girt with strength
Masculine, nor in lustiness of heart
Laughs at the winter storm and summer beam,
Superior to their rage: enfeebling vice
Withers each nerve, and opens every pore
To painful feeling: flowery bowers they seek
(As ether prompts, as the sick sense approves)
Or cool Nymphean grots, or tepid baths   480
(Taught by the soft Ionians); they, along
The lawny vale, of every beauteous stone,
Pile in the roseate air with fond expense:
Through silver channels glide the vagrant waves,
And fall on silver beds crystalline down,
Melodious murmuring; while luxury
Over their naked limbs, with wanton hand,
Sheds roses, odours, sheds unheeded bane.

Swift is the flight of wealth; unnumbered wants,
Brood of voluptuousness, cry out aloud   490
Necessity, and seek the splendid bribe.
The citron board, the bowl embossed with gems,
And tender foliage wildly wreathed around
Of seeming ivy, by that artful hand,
Corinthian Thericles; whate'er is known
Of rarest acquisition; Tyrian garbs,
Neptunian Albion's high testaceous food,
And flavoured Chian wines with incense fumed
To slake Patrician thirst: for these, their rights
In the vile streets they prostitute to sale;   500
Their ancient rights, their dignities, their laws,
Their native glorious freedom.   Is there none,
Is there no villain, that will bind the neck
Stretched to the yoke? they come, the market throngs.
But who has most by fraud or force amassed?
Who most can charm corruption with his doles?
He be the monarch of the state; and lo!

Didius, vile usurer, through the crowd he mounts,[1]
Beneath his feet the Roman eagle cowers,
And the red arrows fill his grasp uncouth.   510
O Britons, O my countrymen, beware,
Gird, gird your hearts; the Romans once were free,
Were brave, were virtuous.—Tyranny howe'er
Deigned to walk forth awhile in pageant state
And with licentious pleasures fed the rout,
The thoughtless many: to the wanton sound
Of fifes and drums they danced, or in the shade
Sung Cæsar, great and terrible in war,
Immortal Cæsar! lo, a god, a god,
He cleaves the yielding skies!   Cæsar meanwhile   520
Gathers the ocean pebbles; or the gnat
Enraged pursues; or at his lonely meal
Starves a wide province; tastes, dislikes, and flings
To dogs and sycophants: a god, a god!
The flowery shades and shrines obscene return.

But see along the north the tempest swell
O'er the rough Alps, and darken all their snows!
Sudden the Goth and Vandal, dreaded names!
Rush as the breach of waters, whelming all
Their domes, their villas; down the festive piles,   530
Down fall their Parian porches, gilded baths,
And roll before the storm in clouds of dust.

Vain end of human strength, of human skill,
Conquest, and triumph, and domain, and pomp,
And ease and luxury!   O luxury,
Bane of elated life, of affluent states,
What dreary change, what ruin is not thine?
How doth thy bowl intoxicate the mind!
To the soft entrance of thy rosy cave
How dost thou lure the fortunate and great!   540
Dreadful attraction! while behind thee gapes
The unfathomable gulf where Asshur lies
O'erwhelmed, forgotten; and high-boasting Cham;
And Elam's haughty pomp; and beauteous Greece;
And the great queen of earth, imperial Rome.

---

[1] Didius Julianus, who bought the empire.

THE COUNTRY WALK

THE morning's fair, the lusty Sun
With ruddy cheek begins to run;
And early birds, that wing the skies,
Sweetly sing to see him rise.
    I am resolved, this charming day,
In the open field to stray;
And have no roof above my head,
But that whereon the gods do tread.
Before the yellow barn I see
A beautiful variety   10
Of strutting cocks, advancing stout,
And flirting empty chaff about,
Hens, ducks, and geese, and all their brood,
And turkeys gobbling for their food;
While rustics thrash the wealthy floor,
And tempt them all to crowd the door.
    What a fair face does Nature show!
Augusta, wipe thy dusty brow;
A landscape wide salutes my sight,
Of shady vales, and mountains bright;   20
And azure heavens I behold,
And clouds of silver and of gold.
And now into the fields I go,
Where thousand flaming flowers glow;
And every neighbouring hedge I greet,
With honeysuckles smelling sweet.
Now o'er the daisy meads I stray,
And meet with, as I pace my way,
Sweetly shining on the eye,
A rivulet, gliding smoothly by;   30
Which shows with what an easy tide
The moments of the happy glide.
Here, finding pleasure after pain,
Sleeping, I see a wearied swain,
While his full scrip lies open by,
That does his healthy food supply.
    Happy swain, sure happier far
Than lofty kings and princes are!
Enjoy sweet sleep, which shuns the crown,
With all its easy beds of down.   40

The Sun now shows his noontide blaze,
And sheds around me burning rays.
A little onward, and I go
Into the shade that groves bestow;
And on green moss I lay me down
That o'er the root of oak has grown;
Where all is silent, but some flood
That sweetly murmurs in the wood;
But birds that warble in the sprays,
And charm e'en silence with their lays. 50

O powerful Silence, how you reign
In the poet's busy brain!
His numerous thoughts obey the calls
Of the tuneful waterfalls,
Like moles, whene'er the coast is clear,
They rise before thee without fear,
And range in parties here and there.

Some wildly to Parnassus wing,
And view the fair Castalian spring;
Where they behold a lonely well, 60
Where now no tuneful Muses dwell;
But now and then a slavish hind
Paddling the troubled pool they find.

Some trace the pleasing paths of joy,
Others the blissful scene destroy;
In thorny tracks of sorrow stray,
And pine for Clio far away.
But stay—methinks her lays I hear,
So smooth! so sweet! so deep! so clear!
No, 'tis not her voice, I find, 70
'Tis but the echo stays behind.

Some meditate ambition's brow,
And the black gulf that gapes below:
Some peep in courts, and there they see
The sneaking tribe of Flattery.
But, striking to the ear and eye,
A nimble deer comes bounding by;
When rushing from yon rustling spray,
It made them vanish all away.

I rouse me up, and on I rove, 80
'Tis more than time to leave the grove.
The Sun declines, the evening breeze
Begins to whisper through the trees:

And, as I leave the sylvan gloom,
As to the glare of day I come,
An old man's smoky nest I see,
Leaning on an aged tree:
Whose willow walls, and furzy brow,
A little garden sway below.
Through spreading beds of blooming green,   90
Matted with herbage sweet and clean,
A vein of water limps along,
And makes them ever green and young.
Here he puffs upon his spade,
And digs up cabbage in the shade:
His tatter'd rags are sable brown,
His beard and hair are hoary grown:
The dying sap descends apace,
And leaves a withered hand and face.

   Up Grongar hill I labour now,   100
And reach at last his bushy brow.
Oh, how fresh, how pure the air!
Let me breathe a little here;
Where am I, Nature?   I descry
Thy magazine before me lie!
Temples!—and towns!—and towers!—and woods!
And hills!—and vales!—and fields!—and floods!
Crowding before me, edged around
With naked wilds, and barren ground.

   See, below, the pleasant dome,   110
The poet's pride, the poet's home,
Which the sunbeams shine upon,
To the even, from the dawn.
See her woods, where Echo talks,
Her gardens trim, her terrace walks,
Her wildernesses, fragrant brakes,
Her gloomy bowers, and shining lakes,
Keep, ye gods, this humble seat,
For ever pleasant, private, neat.

   See yonder hill, uprising steep,   120
Above the river slow and deep:
It looks from hence a pyramid,
Beneath a verdant forest hid;
On whose high top there rises great,
The mighty remnant of a seat,
An old green tower, whose batter'd brow

Frowns upon the vale below.
   Look upon that flowery plain,
How the sheep surround their swain,
How they crowd to hear his strain!   130
All careless with his legs across,
Leaning on a bank of moss,
He spends his empty hours at play,
Which fly as light as down away.
   And there behold a bloomy mead,
A silver stream, a willow shade,
Beneath the shade a fisher stand,
Who, with the angle in his hand,
Swings the nibbling fry to land.
   In blushes the descending Sun   140
Kisses the streams, while slow they run;
And yonder hill remoter grows,
Or dusky clouds do interpose.
The fields are left, the labouring hind
His weary oxen does unbind;
And vocal mountains, as they low,
Re-echo to the vales below;
The jocund shepherds piping come,
And drive the herd before them home;
And now begin to light their fires,   150
Which send up smoke in curling spires:
While with light heart all homeward tend,
To Abergasney [1] I descend.
   But, oh! how bless'd would be the day,
Did I with Clio pace my way,
And not alone and solitary stray!

THE INQUIRY

Ye poor little sheep, ah! well may ye stray,
While sad is your shepherd, and Clio away!
Tell where have you been, have you met with my love,
On the mountain, or valley, or meadow, or grove?
Alas-aday, no—Ye are stray'd, and half dead;
Ye saw not my love, or ye all had been fed.

[1] The name of a seat belonging to the author's brother.

Oh, Sun, did you see her?—ah! surely you did:
'Mong what willows, or woodbines, or reeds, is she hid?
Ye tall whistling pines, that on yonder hill grow,
And o'erlook the beautiful valley below,   10
Did you see her a-roving in wood or in brake?
Or bathing her fair limbs in some silent lake?

Ye mountains, that look on the vigorous East,
And the North, and the South, and the wearisome West,
Pray tell where she hides her—you surely do know—
And let not her lover pine after her so.

Oh, had I the wings of an eagle, I'd fly
Along with bright Phœbus all over the sky;
Like an eagle look down, with my wings wide display'd,
And dart in my eyes at each whispering shade: 20
I'd search every tuft in my diligent tour,
I'd unravel the woodbines, and look in each bower,
Till I found out my Clio, and ended my pain,
And made myself quiet, and happy again.

EPISTLES

TO A FAMOUS PAINTER

Delightful partner of my heart,
Master of the loveliest art!
How sweet our senses you deceive,
When we, a gazing throng, believe!
Here flows the Po—the Minis there,
Winding about with sedgy hair;
And there the Tiber's yellow flood,
Beneath a thick and gloomy wood;
And there Darius' broken ranks
Upon the Granic's bloody banks,   10
Who bravely die, or basely run
From Philip's all-subduing son;
And there the wounded Porus, brought
(The bravest man that ever fought)
To Alexander's tent, who eyes
His dauntless visage as he lies
In death's most painful agonies.

    To me reveal thy heavenly art,
To me thy mysteries impart.
As yet I but in verse can paint,   20
And to the idea colour faint
What to the open eye you show,
Seeming nature's living glow:
The beauteous shapes of objects near,
Or distant ones confus'd in air;
The golden eve, the blushing dawn,
Smiling on the lovely lawn!
And pleasing views of checker'd glades,
And rivers winding through the shades,
And sunny hills—and pleasant plains,   30
And groups of merry nymphs and swains.
Or some old building, hid with grass,

Rearing sad its ruin'd face,
Whose columns, friezes, statues, lie
The grief and wonder of the eye!
Or swift adown a mountain tall
A foaming cataract's sounding fall,
Whose loud roaring stuns the ear
Of the wandering traveller;
Or a calm and quiet bay,   40
And a level shining sea;
Or surges rough, that froth and roar,
And, angry, dash the sounding shore;
And vessels toss'd, and billows high,
And lightning flashing from the sky;
Or that which gives me most delight,
The fair idea (seeming sight!)
Of warrior fierce, with shining blade,
Or orator, with arms display'd,
Tully's engaging air and mien   50
Declaiming against Catiline;
Or fierce Achilles towering high
Above his foes, who round him die.
    Or Hercules, with lion's hide,
And knotty cudgel, thrown aside,
Lifting Antæus high in air,
Who in his gripe expires there.
    Or Sisyphus, with toil and sweat,
And muscles strain'd striving to get
Up a steep hill a ponderous stone,   60
Which near the top recoils, and rolls impetuous down;
Or beauteous Helen's easy air,
With head reclin'd, and flowing hair;
Or comely Paris, gay and young,
Moving with gallant grace along!
These you can do—I but advance
In a florid ignorance,
And say to you, who better know,
You should design them so and so.

TO AARON HILL, ESQ.

ON HIS POEM CALLED "GIDEON"

[Those lines in this poem marked with inverted commas are taken out of
the poem called *Gideon*.]

TELL me, wondrous friend, where were you
   When Gideon was your lofty song!
Where did the heavenly spirit bear you,
   When your fair soul reflected strong
     Gideon's actions, as they shined
     Bright in the chambers of your mind!
Say, have you trod Arabia's spicy vales,
   Or gathered bays beside Euphrates' stream,
Or lonely sung with Jordan's water-falls,
   While heavenly Gideon was your sacred theme?   10
Or have you many ages given
   To close retirement and to books!
And held a long discourse with Heaven,
   And noticed Nature in her various looks!
Full of inspiring wonder and delight,
   Slow read I Gideon with a greedy eye,
Like a pleased traveller that lingers sweet
     On some fair and lofty plain
     Where the sun does brightly shine,
And glorious prospects all around him lie.   20
On Gideon's pages beautifully shine,
   Surprising pictures rising to my sight,
With all the life of colours and of line,
     And all the force of rounding shade and light,
     And all the grace of something more divine!
High on a hill, beneath an oak's broad arm,
   I see a youth divinely fair,
"Pensive he leans his head on his left hand;
   His smiling eye sheds sweetness mixed with awe,
His right hand, with a milk-white wand, some figure seems
       to draw!   30
   A nameless grace is scatter'd through his air,
And o'er his shoulders loosely flows his amber-colour'd hair!"
   Above, with burning blush the morning glows,
   The waking world all fair before him lies;
   "Slow from the plain the melting dews,

   To kiss the sunbeams, climbing, rise," etc.
  Methinks the grove of Baal I see,
   In terraced stages mount up high,
And wave its sable beauties in the sky.
   "From stage to stage, broad steps of half-hid stone,   40
With curling moss and blady grass o'ergrown,
Lead awful——
        Down in a dungeon deep,
Where through thick walls, oblique the broken light
From narrow loopholes quivers to the sight,
     With swift and furious stride,
Close-folded arms, and short and sudden starts,
The fretful prince, in dumb and sullen pride,
Revolves escape——"
  Here in red colours glowing bold   50
   A warlike figure strikes my eye!
The dreadful sudden sight his foes behold
Confounded so, they lose the power to fly;
"Backening they gaze at distance on his face,
Admire his posture, and confess his grace;
His right hand grasps his planted spear," etc.
Alas! my Muse, through much good-will, you err:
And we the mighty author greatly wrong;
   To gather beauties here and there,
    As but a scatter'd few there were,   60
While every word 's a beauty in his song!

TO MR. SAVAGE

SON OF THE LATE EARL RIVERS

Sink not, my friend, beneath misfortune's weight,
Pleased to be found intrinsically great.
Shame on the dull, who think the soul looks less,
Because the body wants a glittering dress.
It is the mind's for ever bright attire,
The mind's embroidery, that the wise admire!
That which looks rich to the gross vulgar eyes
Is the fop's tinsel which the grave despise.
Wealth dims the eyes of crowds, and while they gaze,
The coxcomb 's ne'er discovered in the blaze!   10

As few the vices of the wealthy see,
So virtues are concealed by poverty.
   Earl Rivers!—In that name how wouldst thou shine?
Thy verse how sweet! thy fancy how divine!
Critics and bards would, by their worth, be awed,
And all would think it merit to applaud.
But thou hast nought to please the vulgar eye,
No title hast, nor what might titles buy.
Thou wilt small praise, but much ill-nature find,
Clear to thy errors, to thy beauties blind;   20
And if, though few, they any faults can see,
How meanly bitter will cold censure be!
But, since we all, the wisest of us, err,
Sure 'tis the greatest fault to be severe.
   A few, however, yet expect to find,
Among the misty millions of mankind,
Who proudly stoop to aid an injured cause,
And o'er the sneer of coxcombs force applause,
Who, with felt pleasure, see fair Virtue rise,
And lift her upwards to the beckoning prize!   30
Or mark her labouring in the modest breast,
And honour her the more, the more depress'd.
   Thee, Savage, these (the justly great) admire,
Thee, quickening judgment's phlegm with fancy's fire!
Thee, slow to censure, earnest to commend,
An able critic, but a willing friend.

TO A FRIEND IN TOWN [1]

1 HAVE my friends in the town, in the gay busy town,
     Forgot such a man as John Dyer?
  Or heedless despise they, or pity the clown,
     Whose bosom no pageantries fire?

2 No matter, no matter—content in the shades—
     (Contented?—why every thing charms me)
  Fall in tunes all adown the green steep, ye cascades,
     Till hence rigid Virtue alarms me.

[1] Among the poems of Mr. Savage, there is one to Mr. Dyer, in answer
to his from the country.

3 Till Outrage arises, or Misery needs
   The swift, the intrepid avenger;   10
Till sacred Religion or Liberty bleeds,
   Then mine be the deed and the danger.

4 Alas! what a folly, that wealth and domain
   We heap up in sin and in sorrow!
Immense is the toil, yet the labour how vain!
   Is not life to be over to-morrow?

5 Then glide on my moments, the few that I have,
   Smooth-shaded, and quiet, and even;
While gently the body descends to the grave,
   And the spirit arises to Heaven.   20

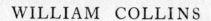

WILLIAM COLLINS

WILLIAM COLLINS (1721–1759)

Verses in *Gentleman's Magazine*, Jan. and Oct., 1739.
Persian Eclogues, 1742 (reprinted as Oriental Eclogues, 1759).
Odes, 1746.
Odes in Dodsley's *Museum*, 1746 and '49.
Works, 1765.   Edition by Dyce in 1827.
Criticism: Johnson, *Lives of the Poets*.
Langhorne, in edition of Works, 1765.

PREFACE

IT is with the writings of mankind, in some measure, as with their complexions or their dress, each nation hath a peculiarity in all these, to distinguish it from the rest of the world.

The gravity of the Spaniard, and the levity of the Frenchman, are as evident in all their productions as in their persons themselves; and the stile of my countrymen is as naturally strong and nervous, as that of an Arabian or Persian is rich and figurative.

There is an elegancy and wildness of thought which recommends all their compositions; and our genius's are as much too cold for the entertainment of such sentiments, as our climate is for their fruits and spices. If any of these beauties are to be found in the following eclogues, I hope my reader will consider them as an argument of their being original. I received them at the hands of a merchant, who had made it his business to enrich himself with the learning, as well as the silks and carpets of the Persians. The little information I could gather concerning their author, was, that his name was Mahamed, and that he was a native of Tauris.

It was in that city that he died of a distemper fatal in those parts, whilst he was engag'd in celebrating the victories of his favourite monarch, the Great Abbas. As to the eclogues themselves, they give a very just view of the miseries, and inconveniences, as well as the felicities that attend one of the finest countries in the East.

The time of the writing them was probably in the beginning of Sha Sultan Hosseyn's reign, the successor of Sefi or Solyman the Second.

Whatever defects, as, I doubt not, there will be many, fall under the reader's observation, I hope his candour will incline him to make the following reflections:

That the works of Orientals contain many peculiarities, and that thro' defect of language few European translators can do them justice.

SONNET

[Written 1739: first published over the signature "Delicatulus" in the *Gentleman's Magazine*, October 1739.]

WHEN Phœbe form'd a wanton smile,
  My soul! it reach'd not here!
Strange, that thy peace, thou trembler, flies
  Before a rising tear!

From midst the drops, my love is born,
  That o'er those eyelids rove:
Thus issued from a teeming wave
  The fabled queen of love.

ECLOGUE THE FIRST

SELIM; OR, THE SHEPHERD'S MORAL

Scene: a valley near Bagdat.   Time: the morning

YE Persian maids, attend your poet's lays,
And hear how shepherds pass their golden days:
Not all are blest, whom Fortune's hand sustains
With wealth in courts, nor all that haunt the plains:
Well may your hearts believe the truths I tell,
'Tis virtue makes the bliss, where'er we dwell.

Thus Selim sung; by sacred Truth inspir'd;
No praise the youth, but her's alone desir'd:
Wise in himself, his meaning songs convey'd
Informing morals to the shepherd maid,   10
Or taught the swains that surest bliss to find,
What groves nor streams bestow, a virtuous mind.

When sweet and od'rous, like an eastern bride,
The radiant morn resum'd her orient pride,
When wanton gales, along the valleys play,
Breathe on each flow'r, and bear their sweets away:
By Tigris' wand'rer wav*es he sate, and sung
This useful lesson for the fair and young.

Ye Persian dames, he said, to ye belong,
Well may they please, the morals of my song;   20
No fairer maids, I trust, than ye are found,
Grac'd with soft arts, the peopled world around!
The morn that lights you, to your loves supplies
Each gentler ray delicious to your eyes:
For ye those flow'rs her fragrant hands bestow,
And yours the love that kings delight to know.
Yet think not these, all beauteous as they are,
The best kind blessings Heav'n can grant the fair!
Who trust alone in beauty's feeble ray,

345

Balsora's [1] pearls have more of worth, than they;　　30
Drawn from the deep, they sparkle to the sight,
And all-unconscious shoot a lust'rous light:
Such are the maids, and such the charms they boast,
By sense unaided, or to virtue lost.
Self-flattering sex! your hearts believe in vain
That love shall blind, when once he fires the swain;
Or hope a lover by your faults to win,
As spots on ermin beautify the skin:
Who seeks secure to rule, be first her care
Each softer virtue that adorns the fair,　　40
Each tender passion man delights to find,
The lov'd perfections of a female mind.

Blest were the days, when Wisdom held her reign,
And shepherds sought her on the silent plain,
With Truth she wedded in the secret grove,
The fair-eyed Truth, and daughters bless'd their love.

O haste, fair maids, ye Virtues come away,
Sweet Peace and Plenty lead you on your way!
The balmy shrub, for ye shall love our shore,
By Ind' excell'd or Araby no more.　　50

Lost to our fields, for so the Fates ordain,
The dear deserters shall return again.
O come, thou Modesty, as they decree,
The rose may then improve her blush by thee.
Here make thy court amidst our rural scene,
And shepherd-girls shall own thee for their queen.
With thee be Chastity, of all afraid,
Distrusting all, a wise suspicious maid;
But man the most; not more the mountain doe
Holds the swift falcon for her deadly foe.　　60
Cold is her breast, like flow'rs that drink the dew,
A silken veil conceals her from the view.
No wild desires amidst thy train be known,
But Faith, whose heart is fix'd on one alone:
Desponding Meekness with her down-cast eyes,
And friendly Pity full of tender sighs;
And Love the last: By these your hearts approve,
These are the virtues that must lead to love.

[1] The gulph of that name, famous for the pearl-fishery.

Thus sung the swain, and eastern legends say,
The maids of Bagdat verify'd the lay: 70
Dear to the plains, the Virtues came along,
The shepherds lov'd, and Selim bless'd his song.

ECLOGUE THE SECOND

HASSAN; OR, THE CAMEL DRIVER

Scene: the desart. Time: mid-day

In silent horror o'er the desart-waste
The driver Hassan with his camels past.
One cruise of water on his back he bore,
And his light scrip contain'd a scanty store:
A fan of painted feathers in his hand,
To guard his shaded face from scorching sand.
The sultry sun had gain'd the middle sky,
And not a tree, and not an herb was nigh.
The beasts, with pain, their dusty way pursue,
Shrill roar'd the winds, and dreary was the view! 10
With desp'rate sorrow wild th' affrighted man
Thrice sigh'd, thrice strook his breast, and thus began:
Sad was the hour, and luckless was the day,
When first from Schiraz' walls I bent my way.

Ah! little thought I of the blasting wind,
The thirst or pinching hunger that I find!
Bethink thee, Hassan, where shall thirst assuage,
When fails this cruise, his unrelenting rage?
Soon shall this scrip its precious load resign,
Then what but tears and hunger shall be thine? 20

Ye mute companions of my toils, that bear
In all my griefs a more than equal share!
Here, where no springs, in murmurs break away,
Or moss-crown'd fountains mitigate the day:
In vain ye hope the green delights to know,
Which plains more blest, or verdant vales bestow.
Here rocks alone, and tasteless sands are found,
And faint and sickly winds for ever howl around.
Sad was the hour, and luckless was the day,
When first from Schiraz' walls I bent my way. 30

Curst be the gold and silver which persuade
Weak men to follow far-fatiguing trade.
The lilly-peace outshines the silver store,
And life is dearer than the golden ore.
Yet money tempts us o'er the desart brown,
To ev'ry distant mart, and wealthy town:
Full oft we tempt the land, and oft the sea,
And are we only yet repay'd by thee?
Ah! why was ruin so attractive made,
Or why fond man so easily betray'd?   40
Why heed we not, whilst mad we haste along,
The gentle voice of Peace, or Pleasure's song?
Or wherefore think the flow'ry mountain's side,
The fountain's murmurs, and the valley's pride,
Why think we these less pleasing to behold,
Than dreary desarts, if they lead to gold?
    Sad was the hour, and luckless was the day,
    When first from Schiraz' walls I bent my way.

O cease, my fears! all frantic as I go,
When thought creates unnumber'd scenes of woe,   50
What if the lion in his rage I meet!
Oft in the dust I view his printed feet:
And fearful! oft, when Day's declining light
Yields her pale empire to the mourner Night,
By hunger rous'd, he scours the groaning plain,
Gaunt wolves and sullen tygers in his train:
Before them Death with shrieks directs their way,
Fills the wild yell, and leads them to their prey.
    Sad was the hour, and luckless was the day,
    When first from Schiraz' walls I bent my way.   60

At that dead hour the silent asp shall creep,
If ought of rest I find, upon my sleep:
Or some swoln serpent twist his scales around,
And wake to anguish with a burning wound.
Thrice happy they, the wise contented poor,
From lust of wealth, and dread of death secure;
They tempt no desarts, and no griefs they find;
Peace rules the day, where Reason rules the mind.
    Sad was the hour, and luckless was the day,
    When first from Schiraz' walls I bent my way.   70

O hapless youth! for she thy love hath won,
The tender Zara, will be most undone!
Big swell'd my heart, and own'd the pow'rful maid,
When fast she dropt her tears, as thus she said:
"Farewel the youth whom sighs could not detain,
Whom Zara's breaking heart implor'd in vain;
Yet as thou go'st, may ev'ry blast arise,
Weak and unfelt as these rejected sighs!
Safe o'er the wild, no perils mayst thou see,
No griefs endure, nor weep, false youth, like me."   80
O let me safely to the Fair return,
Say with a kiss, she must not, shall not mourn.
Go teach my heart, to lose its painful fears,
Recall'd by Wisdom's voice, and Zara's tears.

He said, and call'd on Heav'n to bless the day,
When back to Schiraz' walls he bent his way.

ECLOGUE THE THIRD

ABRA; OR, THE GEORGIAN SULTANA

Scene: a forest.   Time: the evening

In Georgia's land, where Tefflis' tow'rs are seen,
In distant view along the level green,
While ev'ning dews enrich the glitt'ring glade,
And the tall forests cast a longer shade,
Amidst the maids of Zagen's peaceful grove,
Emyra sung the pleasing cares of love.

Of Abra first began the tender strain,
Who led her youth, with flocks upon the plain:
At morn she came those willing flocks to lead,
Where lillies rear them in the wat'ry mead;   10
From early dawn the live-long hours she told,
'Till late at silent eve she penn'd the fold.
Deep in the grove beneath the secret shade,
A various wreath of od'rous flow'rs she made:

Gay-motley'd pinks [1] and sweet junquils [1] she chose,
The violet-blue, that on the moss-bank grows;
All-sweet to sense, the flaunting rose was there;
The finish'd chaplet well-adorn'd her hair.

    Great Abbas chanc'd that fated morn to stray,
By love conducted from the chace away;   20
Among the vocal vales he heard her song,
And sought the vales and echoing groves among:
At length he found, and woo'd the rural maid,
She knew the monarch, and with fear obey'd.
    Be ev'ry youth like Royal Abbas mov'd,
    And ev'ry Georgian maid like Abra lov'd.

    The royal lover bore her from the plain,
Yet still her crook and bleating flock remain:
Oft as she went, she backward turn'd her view,
And bad that crook, and bleating flock adieu.   30
Fair happy maid! to other scenes remove,
To richer scenes of golden pow'r and love!
Go leave the simple pipe, and shepherd's strain,
With love delight thee, and with Abbas reign.
    Be ev'ry youth like Royal Abbas mov'd,
    And ev'ry Georgian maid like Abra lov'd.

    Yet midst the blaze of courts she fix'd her love,
On the cool fountain, or the shady grove;
Still with the shepherd's innocence her mind
To the sweet vale, and flow'ry mead inclin'd,   40
And oft as Spring renew'd the plains with flow'rs,
Breath'd his soft gales, and led the fragrant hours,
With sure return she sought the sylvan scene,
The breezy mountains, and the forests green.
Her maids around her mov'd, a duteous band!
Each bore a crook all-rural in her hand:
Some simple lay, of flocks and herds they sung,
With joy the mountain, and the forest rung.
    Be ev'ry youth like Royal Abbas mov'd,
    And ev'ry Georgian maid like Abra lov'd.   50

---

[1] That these flowers are found in very great abundance in some of the
provinces of Persia; see the *Modern History* of the ingenious Mr. Salmon.

And oft the royal lover left the care,
And thorns of state, attendant on the fair:
Oft to the shades and low-roof'd cots retir'd,
Or sought the vale where first his heart was fir'd;
A russet mantle, like a swain, he wore,
And thought of crowns and busy courts no more.
  Be ev'ry youth like Royal Abbas mov'd,
  And ev'ry Georgian maid like Abra lov'd.

Blest was the life, that Royal Abbas led:
Sweet was his love, and innocent his bed.   60
What if in wealth the noble maid excel;
The simple shepherd girl can love as well.
Let those who rule on Persia's jewell'd throne,
Be fam'd for love, and gentlest love alone:
Or wreath, like Abbas, full of fair renown,
The lover's myrtle, with the warrior's crown.

Oh happy days! the maids around her say,
Oh haste, profuse of blessings, haste away!
  Be ev'ry youth, like Royal Abbas, moved,
  And ev'ry Georgian maid, like Abra, lov'd.   70

ECLOGUE THE FOURTH

AGIB AND SECANDER; OR, THE FUGITIVES

Scene: a mountain in Circassia.   Time: midnight

IN fair Circassia, where to love inclin'd,
Each swain was blest, for ev'ry maid was kind!
At that still hour, when awful midnight reigns,
And none, but wretches, haunt the twilight plains;
What time the moon had hung her lamp on high,
And past in radiance, thro' the cloudless sky:
Sad o'er the dews, two brother shepherds fled,
Where wild'ring fear and desp'rate sorrow led.
Fast as they prest their flight, behind them lay
Wide ravag'd plains, and valleys stole away.   10
Along the mountain's bending sides they ran,
Till faint and weak Secander thus began.

SECANDER

O stay thee, Agib, for my feet deny,
No longer friendly to my life, to fly.
Friend of my heart, O turn thee and survey,
Trace our sad flight thro' all its length of way!
And first review that long-extended plain,
And yon wide groves, already past with pain!
Yon ragged cliff, whose dang'rous path we try'd,
And last this lofty mountain's weary side!   20

AGIB

Weak as thou art, yet hapless must thou know
The toils of flight, or some severer woe!
Still as I haste, the tartar shouts behind,
And shrieks and sorrows load the sad'ning wind:
In rage of heart, with ruin in his hand,
He blasts our harvests, and deforms our land.
Yon citron grove, whence first in fear we came,
Droops its fair honours to the conqu'ring flame:
Far fly the swains, like us, in deep despair,
And leave to ruffian bands their fleecy care.   30

SECANDER

Unhappy land, whose blessings tempt the sword,
In vain, unheard, thou call'st thy Persian lord!
In vain, thou court'st him, helpless to thine aid,
To shield the shepherd, and protect the maid,
Far off in thoughtless indolence resign'd,
Soft dreams of love and pleasure sooth his mind:
'Midst fair Sultanas lost in idle joy,
No wars alarm him, and no fears annoy.

AGIB

Yet these green hills, in summer's sultry heat,
Have lent the monarch oft a cool retreat,   40
Sweet to the sight is Zabran's flow'ry plain,
And once by maids and shepherds lov'd in vain!
No more the virgins shall delight to rove,
By Sargis' banks or Irwan's shady grove:
On Tarkie's mountain catch the cooling gale,
Or breathe the sweets of Aly's flow'ry vale:

Fair scenes! but ah no more with peace possest,
With ease alluring, and with plenty blest.
No more the shepherds whit'ning seats appear,
Nor the kind products of a bounteous year;   50
No more the dale with snowy blossoms crown'd,
But ruin spreads her baleful fires around.

SECANDER

In vain Circassia boasts her spicy groves,
For ever fam'd for pure and happy loves:
In vain she boasts her fairest of the fair,
Their eyes' blue languish, and their golden hair!
Those eyes in tears, their fruitless grief must send,
Those hairs the Tartar's cruel hand shall rend.

AGIB

Ye Georgian swains that piteous learn from far
Circassia's ruin, and the waste of war: 60
Some weightier arms than crooks and staves prepare,
To shield your harvests, and defend your fair:
The Turk and Tartar like designs pursue,
Fix'd to destroy, and stedfast to undo.
Wild as his land, in native deserts bred,
By lust incited, or by malice led,
The villain-Arab, as he prowls for prey,
Oft marks with blood and wasting flames the way;
Yet none so cruel as the Tartar foe,
To death inur'd, and nurst in scenes of woe.   70

He said, when loud along the vale was heard
A shriller shriek, and nearer fires appear'd:
Th' affrighted shepherds thro' the dews of night
Wide o'er the moon-light hills, renew'd their flight.

TO SIR THOMAS HANMER

SIR,

WHILE, own'd by you, with smiles the Muse surveys
Th' expected triumph of her sweetest lays:
While, stretch'd at ease, she boasts your guardian aid,
Secure, and happy in her sylvan shade:
Excuse her fears, who scarce a verse bestows,
In just remembrance of the debt she owes;
With conscious awe she hears the critic's fame,
And blushing hides her wreath at Shakespear's name.

Long slighted Fancy, with a mother's care,
Wept o'er his works, and felt the last despair.   10
Torn from her head, she saw the roses fall,
By all deserted, tho' admir'd by all.
"And oh!" she cry'd, "shall Science still resign
Whate'er is Nature's, and whate'er is mine?
Shall Taste and Art, but shew a cold regard,
And scornful pride reject th' unletter'd bard?
Ye myrtled nymphs, who own my gentle reign,
Tune the sweet lyre, and grace my airy train!
If, where ye rove, your searching eyes have known
One perfect mind, which judgment calls its own: 20
There ev'ry breast its fondest hopes must bend,
And ev'ry Muse with tears await her friend."

'Twas then fair Isis from her stream arose,
In kind compassion of her sister's woes.
'Twas then she promis'd to the mourning maid
Th' immortal honours, which thy hands have paid:
"My best-lov'd son (she said) shall yet restore
Thy ruin'd sweets, and Fancy weep no more."

Each rising art by slow gradation moves,
Toil builds on toil, and age on age improves.   30
The Muse alone unequal dealt her rage,
And grac'd with noblest pomp her earliest stage.
Preserv'd thro' time, the speaking scenes impart
Each changeful wish of Phædra's tortur'd heart:
Or paint the curse, that mark'd the Theban's [1] reign,
A bed incestuous, and a father slain.

[1] The Œdipus of Sophocles.

Line after line, our pitying eyes o'erflow,
Trace the sad tale, and own another's woe.

To Rome remov'd, with equal pow'r to please,
The comic Sisters kept their native ease.
With jealous fear declining Greece beheld 40
Her own Menander's art almost excell'd!
But ev'ry Muse essay'd to raise in vain
Some labour'd rival of her tragic strain;
Illissus' laurels, tho' transferr'd with toil,
Droop'd their fair leaves, nor knew th' unfriendly soil.

When Rome herself, her envy'd glories dead,
No more imperial, stoop'd her conquer'd head:
Luxuriant Florence chose a softer theme,
While all was peace, by Arno's silver stream. 50
With sweeter notes th' Etrurian vales complain'd,
And arts reviving told—a Cosmo reign'd.
Their wanton lyres the bards of Provence strung,
Sweet flow'd the lays, but love was all they sung.
The gay description could not fail to move,
For, led by Nature, all are friends to love.

But Heav'n, still rising in its works, decreed
The perfect boast of time should last succeed.
The beauteous union must appear at length,
Of Tuscan fancy, and Athenian strength: 60
One greater Muse Eliza's reign adorn,
And ev'n a Shakespear to her fame be born!

Yet ah! so bright her morning's op'ning ray,
In vain our Britain hop'd an equal day!
No second growth the Western Isle could bear,
At once exhausted with too rich a year.
Too nicely Johnson knew the critic's part;
Nature in him was almost lost in Art.
Of softer mold the gentle Fletcher came,
The next in order, as the next in name. 70
With pleas'd attention 'midst his scenes we find
Each glowing thought, that warms the female mind;
Each melting sigh, and ev'ry tender tear,
The lover's wishes and the virgin's fear.

His [1] ev'ry strain the Loves and Graces own;
But stronger Shakespear felt for man alone:
Drawn by his pen, our ruder passions stand
Th' unrivall'd picture of his early hand.

    With gradual steps, and slow, exacter France
Saw Art's fair empire o'er her shores advance: 80
By length of toil, a bright perfection knew,
Correctly bold, and just in all she drew.
Till late Corneille from Epick Lucan [2] brought
The full expression, and the Roman thought;
And classic judgment gain'd to sweet Racine
The temp'rate strength of Maro's chaster line.

    But wilder far the British laurel spread,
And wreaths less artful crown our poet's head.
Yet he alone to ev'ry scene could give
Th' historian's truth, and bid the manners live.   90
Wak'd at his call I view, with glad surprize,
Majestic forms of mighty monarchs rise.
There Henry's trumpets spread their loud alarms
And laurel'd conquest waits her hero's arms.
Here gentler Edward claims a pitying sigh,
Scarce born to honours, and so soon to die!
Yet shall thy throne, unhappy infant, bring
No beam of comfort to the guilty king?
The time shall come, when Glo'ster's heart shall bleed [3]
In life's last hours, with horror of the deed: 100
When dreary visions shall at last present
Thy vengeful image, in the midnight tent:
Thy hand unseen the secret death shall bear,
Blunt the weak sword, and break th' oppressive spear.

    Where'er we turn, by fancy charm'd, we find
Some sweet illusion of the cheated mind.
Oft, wild of wing, she calls the soul to rove
With humbler Nature, in the rural grove;
Where swains contented own the quiet scene,
And twilight fairies tread the circled green: 110

---

  [1] Their characters are thus distinguished by Mr. Dryden.
  [2] The favourite author of the elder Corneille.

  [3] Tempus erit Turno, magno cum optaverit emptum
    Intactum Pallanta, etc.

Drest by her hand, the woods and vallies smile,
And spring diffusive decks th' enchanted isle.

O blest in all that genius gives to charm,
Whose morals mend us, and whose passions warm!
Oft let my youth attend thy various page,
Where rich invention rules th' unbounded stage.
There ev'ry scene the poet's warmth may raise,
And melting music find the softest lays.
O might the Muse with equal ease persuade,
Expressive picture, to adopt thine aid!   120
Some pow'rful Raphael shou'd again appear,
And Arts consenting fix their empire here.

Methinks ev'n now I view some fair design,
Where breathing Nature lives in ev'ry line:
Chaste, and subdu'd, the modest colours lie,
In fair proportion to th' approving eye.—
And see, where Antony [1] lamenting stands
In fixt distress, and spreads his pleading hands!
O'er the pale corse the warrior seems to bend,
Deep sunk in grief, and mourns his murther'd friend!
Still as they press, he calls on all around,   131
Lifts the torn robe, and points the bleeding wound.

But who is he,[2] whose brows exalted bear
A rage impatient, and a fiercer air?
Ev'n now, his thoughts with eager vengeance doom
The last sad ruin of ungrateful Rome.
Till, slow-advancing o'er the tented plain,
In sable weeds, appear the kindred-train:
The frantic mother leads their wild despair,
Beats her swoln breast, and rends her silver hair.   140
And see he yields! . . . the tears unbidden start,
And conscious Nature claims th' unwilling heart!
O'er all the man conflicting passions rise,
Rage grasps the sword, while pity melts the eyes.

Thus, gen'rous critic, as thy bard inspires,
The sister arts shall nurse their drooping fires;
Each from his scenes her stores alternate bring,
Spread the fair tints, or wake the vocal string:

[1] See the tragedy of *Julius Cæsar*.
[2] Coriolanus.   See Mr. Spence's dialogues on the *Odyssey*.

Those Sibyl-leaves, the sport of ev'ry wind,
(For poets ever were a careless kind)   150
By thee dispos'd, no farther toil demand,
But, just to Nature, own thy forming hand.

So spread o'er Greece, th' harmonious whole unknown,
Ev'n Homer's numbers charm'd by parts alone.
Their own Ulysses scarce had wander'd more,
By winds and waters cast on ev'ry shore:
When, rais'd by fate, some former Hanmer join'd
Each beauteous image of the tuneful mind:
And bad, like thee, his Athens ever claim,
A fond alliance, with the poet's name.   160

OXFORD, *December* 3,
     1743.

ODE TO PITY

O THOU, the friend of man assign'd,
With balmy hands his wounds to bind,
     And charm his frantic woe:
When first distress with dagger keen
Broke forth to waste his destin'd scene,
     His wild unsated foe!

II

By Pella's bard,[1] a magic name,
By all the griefs his thought could frame,
     Receive my humble rite:
Long, Pity, let the nations view   10
Thy sky-worn robes of tend'rest blue,
     And eyes of dewy light!

III

But wherefore need I wander wide
To old Illissus' distant side,
     Deserted stream, and mute?
Wild Arun[2] too has heard thy strains,
And Echo, 'midst my native plains,
     Been sooth'd by Pity's lute.

[1] Euripides, of whom Aristotle pronounces, on a comparison of him with Sophocles, that he was the greater master of the tender passions ἦν τραγικώτερος.
[2] The River Arun runs by the village in Sussex, where Otway had his birth.

IV

There first the wren thy myrtles shed
On gentlest Otway's infant head,
   To him thy cell was shown;   20
And while he sung the female heart,
With youth's soft notes unspoil'd by art,
   Thy turtles mix'd their own.

V

Come, Pity, come, by Fancy's aid,
Ev'n now my thoughts, relenting maid,
   Thy temple's pride design:
Its southern site, its truth compleat
Shall raise a wild enthusiast heat,
   In all who view the shrine.   30

VI

There picture's toils shall well relate,
How chance, or hard involving fate,
   O'er mortal bliss prevail:
The buskin'd Muse shall near her stand,
And sighing prompt her tender hand,
   With each disastrous tale.

VII

There let me oft, retir'd by day,
In dreams of passion melt away,
   Allow'd with thee to dwell:
There waste the mournful lamp of night,   40
Till, virgin, thou again delight
   To hear a British shell!

ODE TO FEAR

THOU, to whom the world unknown
With all its shadowy shapes is shown;
Who see'st appall'd th' unreal scene,
While Fancy lifts the veil between:
   Ah Fear! Ah frantic Fear!
   I see, I see thee near.
I know thy hurried step, thy haggard eye!
Like thee I start, like thee disorder'd fly,

For lo what Monsters in thy train appear!
Danger, whose limbs of giant mold   10
What mortal eye can fix'd behold?
Who stalks his round, an hideous form,
Howling amidst the midnight storm,
Or throws him on the ridgy steep
Of some loose hanging rock to sleep:
And with him thousand phantoms join'd,
Who prompt to deeds accurs'd the mind:
And those, the fiends, who near allied,
O'er Nature's wounds, and wrecks preside;
Whilst Vengeance, in the lurid air,   20
Lifts her red arm, expos'd and bare:
On whom that rav'ning brood of fate,[1]
Who lap the blood of sorrow, wait;
Who, Fear, this ghastly train can see,
And look not madly wild, like thee?

EPODE

In earliest Greece to thee with partial choice,
    The grief-full Muse addrest her infant tongue;
The maids and matrons, on her awful voice,
    Silent and pale in wild amazement hung.

Yet he, the bard [2] who first invok'd thy name,   30
    Disdain'd in Marathon its pow'r to feel:
For not alone he nurs'd the poet's flame,
    But reach'd from Virtue's hand the patriot's steel.

But who is he whom later garlands grace,
    Who left a-while o'er Hybla's dews to rove,
With trembling eyes thy dreary steps to trace,
    Where thou and Furies shar'd the baleful grove?

Wrapt in thy cloudy veil th' incestuous queen [3]
    Sigh'd the sad call [4] her son and husband hear'd,
When once alone it broke the silent scene,   40
    And he the wretch of Thebes no more appear'd.

---

[1] Alluding to the Κύνας ἀφύκτους of Sophocles. See the *Electra*.
[2] Æschylus. [3] Jocasta.
     [4] οὐδ' ἔτ' ὠρώρει βοή,
'Ην μὲν σιωπῇ, φθέγμα δ' ἐξαίφνης τινὸς
Θώϋξεν αὐτόν, ὥστε πάντας ὀρθίας
Στῆσαι φόβῳ δείσαντας ἐξαίφνης τρίχας.
       See the *Œdip. Colon.* of Sophocles.

O Fear, I know thee by my throbbing heart,
   Thy with'ring pow'r inspir'd each mournful line,
Tho' gentle Pity claim her mingled part,
   Yet all the thunders of the scene are thine!

ANTISTROPHE

Thou who such weary lengths hast past,
Where wilt thou rest, mad nymph, at last?
Say, wilt thou shroud in haunted cell,
Where gloomy Rape and Murder dwell?
Or, in some hollow'd seat,   50
'Gainst which the big waves beat,
Hear drowning sea-men's cries in tempests brought!
Dark pow'r, with shudd'ring meek submitted thought
Be mine, to read the visions old,
Which thy awak'ning bards have told:
And lest thou meet my blasted view,
Hold each strange tale devoutly true;
Ne'er be I found, by thee o'eraw'd,
In that thrice-hallow'd eve abroad,
When ghosts, as cottage-maids believe,   60
Their pebbled beds permitted leave,
And Gobblins haunt from fire, or fen,
Or mine, or flood, the walks of men!
  O thou whose spirit most possest
The sacred seat of Shakespear's breast!
By all that from thy prophet broke,
In thy divine emotions spoke:
Hither again thy fury deal,
Teach me but once like him to feel:
His cypress wreath my meed decree,   70
And I, O Fear, will dwell with thee!

ODE TO SIMPLICITY

I

O THOU by Nature taught,
   To breathe her genuine thought,
In numbers warmly pure, and sweetly strong:
   Who first on mountains wild,
   In Fancy loveliest child,
Thy babe, or Pleasure's, nurs'd the pow'rs of song!

II

Thou, who with hermit heart
Disdain'st the wealth of art,
And gauds, and pageant weeds, and trailing pall:
    But com'st a decent maid   10
    In Attic robe array'd,
O chaste unboastful nymph, to thee I call!

III

By all the honey'd store
On Hybla's thymy shore,
By all her blooms, and mingled murmurs dear,
    By her,[1] whose love-lorn woe
    In ev'ning musings slow
Sooth'd sweetly sad Electra's poet's ear:

IV

By old Cephisus deep,
Who spread his wavy sweep   20
In warbled wand'rings round thy green retreat,
    On whose enamel'd side
    When holy Freedom died
No equal haunt allur'd thy future feet.

V

O sister meek of Truth,
To my admiring youth,
Thy sober aid and native charms infuse!
    The flow'rs that sweetest breathe,
    Tho' beauty cull'd the wreath,
Still ask thy hand to range their order'd hues.   30

VI

While Rome could none esteem
But Virtue's patriot theme,
You lov'd her hills, and led her laureate band:
    But staid to sing alone
    To one distinguish'd throne,
And turn'd thy face, and fled her alter'd land.

---

[1] The ἀηδών, or nightingale, for which Sophocles seems to have entertain'd a peculiar fondness.

VII

No more, in hall or bow'r,
The passions own thy pow'r,
Love, only love her forceless numbers mean:
For thou hast left her shrine,   40
Nor olive more, nor vine,
Shall gain thy feet to bless the servile scene.

VIII

Tho' taste, tho' genius bless,
To some divine excess,
Faints the cold work till thou inspire the whole;
What each, what all supply,
May court, may charm our eye,
Thou, only thou can'st raise the meeting soul!

IX

Of these let others ask,
To aid some mighty task,   50
I only seek to find thy temp'rate vale:
Where oft my reed might sound
To maids and shepherds round,
And all thy sons, O Nature, learn my tale.

ODE ON THE POETICAL CHARACTER

As once, if not with light regard,
I read aright that gifted bard,
(Him whose school above the rest
His loveliest Elfin queen has blest.)
One, only one, unrival'd fair,[1]
Might hope the magic girdle wear,
At solemn turney hung on high,
The wish of each love-darting eye;

Lo! to each other nymph in turn applied,
As if, in air unseen, some hov'ring hand,
Some chaste and angel-friend to virgin-fame   10
With whisper'd spell had burst the starting band,

[1] Florimel. See Spenser, Leg. 4th.

It left unblest her loath'd dishonour'd side;
    Happier hopeless fair, if never
    Her baffled hand with vain endeavour
Had touch'd that fatal zone to her denied!

Young Fancy thus, to me divinest name,
    To whom, prepar'd and bath'd in Heav'n,
    The cest of amplest pow'r is giv'n:
    To few the God-like gift assigns,   20
    To gird their blest prophetic loins,
And gaze her visions wild, and feel unmix'd her flame!

II

The band, as fairy legends say,
Was wove on that creating day,
When he, who call'd with thought to birth
Yon tented sky, this laughing earth,
And drest with springs, and forests tall,
And pour'd the main engirting all,
Long by the lov'd Enthusiast woo'd,
Himself in some diviner mood,   30
Retiring, sate with her alone,
And plac'd her on his saphire throne,
The whiles, the vaulted shrine around,
Seraphic wires were heard to sound,
Now sublimest triumph swelling,
Now on love and mercy dwelling;
And she, from out the veiling cloud,
Breath'd her magic notes aloud:
And thou, thou rich-hair'd youth of morn,
And all thy subject life was born!   40
The dang'rous passions kept aloof,
Far from the sainted growing woof:
But near it sate ecstatic Wonder,
List'ning the deep applauding thunder:
And Truth, in sunny vest array'd,
By whose the tarsel's eyes were made;
All the shad'wy tribes of Mind,
In braided dance their murmurs join'd,
And all the bright uncounted Pow'rs
Who feed on Heav'n's ambrosial flow'rs.   50
Where is the bard, whose soul can now
Its high presuming hopes avow?

Where he who thinks, with rapture blind,
This hallow'd work for him design'd?

III

High on some cliff, to Heav'n up-pil'd,
Of rude access, of prospect wild,
Where, tangled round the jealous steep,
Strange shades o'erbrow the valleys deep,
And holy genii guard the rock,
Its gloomes embrown, its springs unlock,   60
While on its rich ambitious head,
An Eden, like his own, lies spread.
I view that oak, the fanciest glades among,
By which as Milton lay, his ev'ning ear,
From many a cloud that drop'd ethereal dew,
Nigh spher'd in Heav'n its native strains could hear:
On which that ancient Trump he reach'd was hung;
    Thither oft his glory greeting,
    From Waller's myrtle shades retreating,
With many a vow from Hope's aspiring tongue,   70
My trembling feet his guiding steps pursue;
    In vain—such bliss to one alone,
    Of all the sons of soul was known,
    And Heav'n, and Fancy, kindred pow'rs,
    Have now o'erturn'd th' inspiring bow'rs,
Or curtain'd close such scene from ev'ry future view.

ODE

[Written in the beginning of the year 1746.]

I

How sleep the brave, who sink to rest,
By all their country's wishes blest!
When Spring, with dewy fingers cold,
Returns to deck their hallow'd mold,
She there shall dress a sweeter sod,
Than Fancy's feet have ever trod.

II

By fairy hands their knell is rung,
By forms unseen their dirge is sung;

There Honour comes, a pilgrim grey,
To bless the turf that wraps their clay, 10
And Freedom shall a-while repair,
To dwell a weeping hermit there!

ODE TO MERCY

[Written in 1746.]

STROPHE

O THOU, who sit'st a smiling bride
By Valour's arm'd and awful side,
Gentlest of sky-born forms, and best ador'd:
Who oft with songs, divine to hear,
Win'st from his fatal grasp the spear,
And hid'st in wreaths of flow'rs his bloodless sword!
Thou who, amidst the deathful field,
By Godlike chiefs alone beheld,
Oft with thy bosom bare art found,
Pleading for him the youth who sinks to ground: 10
See, Mercy, see, with pure and loaded hands,
Before thy shrine my country's genius stands,
And decks thy altar still, tho' pierc'd with many a wound!

ANTISTROPHE

When he whom ev'n our joys provoke,
The Fiend of Nature join'd his yoke,
And rush'd in wrath to make our isle his prey;
Thy form, from out thy sweet abode,
O'ertook him on his blasted road,
And stop'd his wheels, and look'd his rage away.

I see recoil his sable steeds, 20
That bore him swift to salvage deeds,
Thy tender melting eyes they own;
O maid, for all thy love to Britain shown,
Where Justice bars her iron tow'r,
To thee we build a roseate bow'r,
Thou, thou shalt rule our queen, and share our monarch's
throne!

ODE TO LIBERTY

STROPHE

WHO shall awake the Spartan fife,
And call in solemn sounds to life,
The youths, whose locks divinely spreading,
  Like vernal hyacinths in sullen hue,
At once the breath of Fear and Virtue shedding,
  Applauding Freedom lov'd of old to view?
What new Alcæus,[1] fancy-blest,
Shall sing the sword, in myrtles drest,
  At Wisdom's shrine a-while its flame concealing,
(What place so fit to seal a deed renown'd?)   10
Till she her brightest lightnings round revealing,
It leap'd in glory forth, and dealt her prompted wound!
    O Goddess, in that feeling hour,
  When most its sounds would court thy ears,
    Let not my shell's misguided pow'r,[2]
  E'er draw thy sad, thy mindful tears.
No, Freedom, no, I will not tell,
How Rome, before thy weeping face,
With heaviest sound, a giant-statue, fell,
Push'd by a wild and artless race,   20
From off its wide ambitious base,
When Time his northern sons of spoil awoke,
  And all the blended work of strength and grace,
  With many a rude repeated stroke,
And many a barb'rous yell, to thousand fragments broke.

---

[1] Alluding to that beautiful fragment of Alcæus.

    Ἐν μύρτου κλαδὶ τὸ ξίφος φορήσω,
    Ὥσπερ Ἁρμόδιος καὶ Ἀριστογείτων.
    Φίλταθ' Ἁρμόδι, οὔπω τέθνηκας,
    Νήσοις δ' ἐν Μακάρων σέ φασιν εἶναι.
    Ἐν μύρτου κλαδὶ τὸ ξίφος φορήσω,
    Ὥσπερ Ἁρμόδιος καὶ Ἀριστογείτων,
    Ὅτ' Ἀθηναίης ἐν θυσίαις
    Ἄνδρα τύραννον Ἵππαρχον ἐκαινέτην.
    Ἀεὶ σφῶν κλέος ἔσσεται κατ' αἶαν,
    Φίλταθ' Ἁρμόδι, καὶ Ἀριστογείτων.

[2] Μὴ μὴ ταῦτα λέγωμες, ἃ δάκρυον ἤγαγε Δηοῖ.

             Callimach. Ὕμνος εἰς Δήμητρα.

EPODE

II

Yet ev'n, where'er the least appear'd,
Th' admiring world thy hand rever'd;
Still 'midst the scatter'd states around,
Some remnants of her strength were found;
They saw by what escap'd the storm,   30
How wond'rous rose her perfect form;
How in the great the labour'd whole,
Each mighty master pour'd his soul!
For sunny Florence, seat of Art,
Beneath her vines preserv'd a part,
Till they,[1] whom Science lov'd to name,
(O who could fear it?) quench'd her flame.
And lo, an humbler relick laid
In jealous Pisa's olive shade!
See small Marino [2] joins the theme,   40
Tho' least, not last in thy esteem:
Strike, louder strike th' ennobling strings
To those,[3] whose merchant sons were kings;
To him,[4] who deck'd with pearly pride,
In Adria weds his green-hair'd bride;
Hail port of glory, wealth, and pleasure,
Ne'er let me change this Lydian measure:
Nor e'er her former pride relate,
To sad Liguria's [5] bleeding state.
Ah no! more pleas'd thy haunts I seek,   50
On wild Helvetia's [6] mountains bleak:
(Where, when the favor'd of thy choice,
The daring archer heard thy voice;
Forth from his eyrie rous'd in dread,
The rav'ning eagle northward fled.)
Or dwell in willow'd meads more near,
With those to whom thy stork [7] is dear:
Those whom the rod of Alva bruis'd,

[1] The family of the Medici.   [2] The little republic of San Marino.
[3] The Venetians.   [4] The Doge of Venice.
[5] Genoa.   [6] Switzerland.
[7] The Dutch, amongst whom there are very severe penalties for those who are convicted of killing this bird. They are kept tame in almost all their towns, and particularly at the Hague, of the arms of which they make a part. The common people of Holland are said to entertain a superstitious sentiment, that if the whole species of them should become extinct, they should lose their liberties.

Whose crown a British queen[1] refus'd!
The Magic works, thou feel'st the strains, 60
One holier name alone remains;
The perfect spell shall then avail,
Hail nymph, ador'd by Britain, hail!

ANTISTROPHE

Beyond the measure vast of thought,
The works, the wizzard Time has wrought!
  The Gaul, 'tis held of antique story,
Saw Britain link'd to his now adverse strand,[2]
  No sea between, nor cliff sublime and hoary,
He pass'd with unwet feet thro' all our land.
  To the blown Baltic then, they say, 70
  The wild waves found another way,
Where Orcas howls, his wolfish mountains rounding;
  Till all the banded west at once 'gan rise,
A wide wild storm ev'n Nature's self confounding,
  With'ring her giant sons with strange uncouth surprise.
    This pillar'd earth so firm and wide,
      By winds and inward labors torn,
    In thunders dread was push'd aside,
      And down the should'ring billows born.
And see, like gems, her laughing train, 80
  The little isles on ev'ry side,
Mona,[3] once hid from those who search the main,
  Where thousand elfin shapes abide,
And Wight who checks the west'ring tide,
  For thee consenting Heav'n has each bestow'd,
A fair attendant on her sov'reign pride:
  To thee this blest divorce she ow'd,
For thou hast made her vales thy lov'd, thy last abode!

[1] Queen Elizabeth.
[2] This tradition is mention'd by several of our old historians. Some naturalists too have endeavour'd to support the probability of the fact, by arguments drawn from the correspondent disposition of the two opposite coasts. I don't remember that any poetical use has been hitherto made of it.
[3] There is a tradition in the Isle of Man, that a mermaid becoming enamour'd of a young man of extraordinary beauty, took an opportunity of meeting him one day as he walked on the shore, and open'd her passion to him, but was receiv'd with a coldness, occasion'd by his horror and surprize at her appearance. This, however, was so misconstrued by the sea-lady, that in revenge for his treatment of her, she punish'd the whole island, by covering it with a mist, so that all who attempted to carry on any commerce with it, either never arriv'd at it, but wander'd up and down the sea, or were on a sudden wreck'd upon its cliffs.

SECOND EPODE

Then too, 'tis said, an hoary pile,
'Midst the green navel of our isle,   90
Thy shrine in some religious wood,
O soul-enforcing Goddess stood!
There oft the painted native's feet,
Were wont thy form celestial meet:
Tho' now with hopeless toil we trace
Time's backward rolls, to find its place;
Whether the fiery-tressed Dane,
Or Roman's self o'erturn'd the fane,
Or in what Heav'n-left age it fell,
'Twere hard for modern song to tell.   100
Yet still, if truth those beams infuse,
Which guide at once, and charm the Muse,
Beyond yon braided clouds that lie,
Paving the light-embroider'd sky:
Amidst the bright pavilion'd plains,
The beauteous Model still remains.
There happier than in islands blest,
Or bow'rs by spring or Hebe drest,
The chiefs who fill our Albion's story,
In warlike weeds, retir'd in glory,   110
Hear their consorted Druids sing
Their triumphs to th' immortal string.
  How may the poet now unfold
What never tongue or numbers told?
How learn delighted, and amaz'd,
What hands unknown that fabric rais'd?
Ev'n now before his favor'd eyes,
In Gothic pride it seems to rise!
Yet Græcia's graceful orders join,
Majestic thro' the mix'd design;   120
The secret builder knew to chuse,
Each sphere-found gem of richest hues:
Whate'er heav'n's purer mold contains,
When nearer suns emblaze its veins;
There on the walls the Patriot's sight,
May ever hang with fresh delight,
And, grav'd with some prophetic rage,
Read Albion's fame thro' ev'ry age.
  Ye forms divine, ye laureate band,

That near her inmost altar stand!   130
Now sooth her, to her blissful train
Blithe Concord's social form to gain:
Concord, whose myrtle wand can steep
Ev'n Anger's blood-shot eyes in sleep:
Before whose breathing bosom's balm,
Rage drops his steel, and storms grow calm;
Her let our sires and matrons hoar
Welcome to Britain's ravag'd shore,
Our youths, enamour'd of the fair,
Play with the tangles of her hair,   140
Till in one loud applauding sound,
The nations shout to her around,
O how supremely art thou blest,
Thou, Lady, thou shalt rule the West!

ODE, TO A LADY ON THE DEATH OF COLONEL ROSS IN THE ACTION OF FONTENOY

[Written in May 1745, and addressed to Miss Elizabeth Goddard of
Harting in Sussex.   First published in Dodsley's *Museum*, 7 June, 1746.]

I

WHILE, lost to all his former mirth,
Britannia's genius bends to earth,
    And mourns the fatal day:
While stain'd with blood he strives to tear
Unseemly from his sea-green hair
    The wreaths of chearful May:

II

The thoughts which musing pity pays,
And fond remembrance loves to raise,
    Your faithful hours attend:
Still Fancy to herself unkind,   10
Awakes to grief the soften'd mind,
    And points the bleeding friend.

III

By rapid Scheld's descending wave
His country's vows shall bless the grave,
    Where'er the youth is laid:

That sacred spot the village hind
With ev'ry sweetest turf shall bind,
        And peace protect the shade.

IV

Blest youth, regardful of thy doom,
Aërial hands shall build thy tomb,   20
        With shadowy trophies crown'd:
Whilst Honor bath'd in tears shall rove
To sigh thy name thro' ev'ry grove,
        And call his heros round.

V

The warlike dead of ev'ry age,
Who fill the fair recording page,
        Shall leave their sainted rest:
And, half-reclining on his spear,
Each wond'ring Chief by turns appear,
        To hail the blooming guest.   30

VI

Old Edward's sons, unknown to yield,
Shall croud from Cressy's laurell'd field,
        And gaze with fix'd delight:
Again for Britain's wrongs they feel,
Again they snatch the gleamy steel,
        And wish th' avenging fight.

VII

But lo where, sunk in deep despair,
Her garments torn, her bosom bare,
        Impatient Freedom lies!
Her matted tresses madly spread,   40
To ev'ry sod, which wraps the dead,
        She turns her joyless eyes.

VIII

Ne'er shall she leave that lowly ground,
Till notes of triumph bursting round
        Proclaim her reign restor'd:
Till William seek the sad retreat,
And bleeding at her sacred feet,
        Present the sated sword.

IX

If, weak to sooth so soft an heart,
These pictur'd glories nought impart,
    To dry thy constant tear: 50
If yet, in sorrow's distant eye,
Expos'd and pale thou see'st him lie,
    Wild war insulting near:

X

Where'er from time thou court'st relief,
The Muse shall still, with social grief,
    Her gentlest promise keep:
Ev'n humble Harting's cottag'd vale
Shall learn the sad repeated tale,
    And bid her shepherds weep.   60

ODE TO EVENING

If ought of oaten stop, or pastoral song,
May hope, O pensive Eve, to soothe thine ear,
    Like thy own brawling springs,
    Thy springs, and dying gales,
O Nymph reserv'd, while now the bright-hair'd sun
Sits in yon western tent, whose cloudy skirts,
    With brede ethereal wove,
    O'erhang his wavy bed:
Now air is hush'd, save where the weak-ey'd bat,
With short shrill shriek flits by on leathern wing,   10
    Or where the beetle winds
    His small but sullen horn,
As oft he rises 'midst the twilight path,
Against the pilgrim born in heedless hum:
    Now teach me, maid compos'd,
    To breathe some soften'd strain,
Whose numbers stealing thro' thy darkning vale,
May not unseemly with its stillness suit,
    As musing slow, I hail
    Thy genial lov'd return!   20
For when thy folding star arising shews

His paly circlet, at his warning lamp
    The fragrant Hours, and Elves
    Who slept in buds the day,
And many a Nymph who wreaths her brows with sedge,
And sheds the fresh'ning dew, and lovelier still,
    The pensive Pleasures sweet
    Prepare thy shadowy car.
Then let me rove some wild and heathy scene,
Or find some ruin 'midst its dreary dells,   30
    Whose walls more awful nod
    By thy religious gleams.
Or if chill blustring winds, or driving rain,
Prevent my willing feet, be mine the hut,
    That from the mountain's side,
    Views wilds, and swelling floods,
And hamlets brown, and dim-discover'd spires,
And hears their simple bell, and marks o'er all
    Thy dewy fingers draw
    The gradual dusky veil.   40
While Spring shall pour his show'rs, as oft he wont,
And bathe thy breathing tresses, meekest Eve!
    While Summer loves to sport,
    Beneath thy ling'ring light:
While sallow Autumn fills thy lap with leaves,
Or Winter yelling thro' the troublous air,
    Affrights thy shrinking train,
    And rudely rends thy robes.
So long regardful of thy quiet rule,
Shall Fancy, Friendship, Science, smiling Peace,   50
    Thy gentlest influence own,
    And love thy fav'rite name!

ODE TO PEACE

I

O THOU, who bad'st thy turtles bear
Swift from his grasp thy golden hair,
    And sought'st thy native skies:
When War, by vultures drawn from far,
To Britain bent his iron car,
    And bad his storms arise!

II

Tir'd of his rude tyrannic sway,
Our youth shall fix some festive day,
    His sullen shrines to burn:
But thou who hear'st the turning spheres,   10
What sounds may charm thy partial ears,
    And gain thy blest return!

III

O Peace, thy injur'd robes up-bind,
O rise, and leave not one behind
    Of all thy beamy train:
The British lion, goddess sweet,
Lies stretch'd on earth to kiss thy feet,
    And own thy holier reign.

IV

Let others court thy transient smile,
But come to grace thy western isle,   20
    By warlike Honour led!
And, while around her ports rejoice,
While all her sons adore thy choice,
    With him for ever wed!

THE MANNERS: AN ODE

[Possibly written about the time that Collins left Oxford, 1744.]

FAREWELL, for clearer ken design'd,
The dim-discover'd tracts of mind:
Truths which, from action's paths retir'd,
My silent search in vain requir'd!
No more my sail that deep explores,
No more I search those magic shores,
What regions part the world of soul,
Or whence thy streams, Opinion, roll:
If e'er I round such fairy field,
Some pow'r impart the spear and shield,   10
At which the wizzard Passions fly,
By which the giant Follies die!

Farewell the porch, whose roof is seen,
Arch'd with th' enlivening olive's green:
Where Science, prank'd in tissued vest,
By Reason, Pride, and Fancy drest,
Comes like a bride so trim array'd,
To wed with Doubt in Plato's shade!

Youth of the quick uncheated sight,
Thy walks, Observance, more invite!   20
O thou, who lov'st that ampler range,
Where life's wide prospects round thee change,
And with her mingling sons ally'd,
Throw'st the prattling page aside:
To me in converse sweet impart,
To read in man the native heart,
To learn, where Science sure is found,
From Nature as she lives around:
And gazing oft her mirror true,
By turns each shifting image view!   30
Till meddling Art's officious lore,
Reverse the lessons taught before,
Alluring from a safer rule,
To dream in her enchanted school;
Thou Heav'n, whate'er of great we boast,
Hast blest this social science most.

Retiring hence to thoughtful cell,
As Fancy breathes her potent spell,
Not vain she finds the charmful task,
In pageant quaint, in motley mask,   40
Behold before her musing eyes,
The countless Manners round her rise;
While ever varying as they pass,
To some Contempt applies her glass:
With these the white rob'd Maids combine,
And those the laughing Satyrs join!
But who is he whom now she views,
In robe of wild contending hues?
Thou by the passions nurs'd, I greet
The comic sock that binds thy feet!   50
O Humour, thou whose name is known
To Britain's favor'd isle alone:
Me too amidst thy band admit,
There where the young-eyed healthful Wit,
(Whose jewels in his crisped hair

Are plac'd each other's beams to share,
Whom no delights from thee divide)
In laughter loos'd attends thy side!
      By old Miletus [1] who so long
Has ceas'd his love-inwoven song: 60
By all you taught the Tuscan maids,
In chang'd Italia's modern shades:
By him,[2] whose Knight's distinguish'd name
Refin'd a nation's lust of fame;
Whose tales ev'n now, with echos sweet,
Castilia's Moorish hills repeat:
Or him,[3] whom Seine's blue nymphs deplore,
In watchet weeds on Gallia's shore,
Who drew the sad Sicilian maid,
By virtues in her sire betray'd: 70
      O Nature boon, from whom proceed
Each forceful thought, each prompted deed;
If but from thee I hope to feel,
On all my heart imprint thy seal!
Let some retreating cynic find,
Those oft-turn'd scrolls I leave behind,
The Sports and I this hour agree,
To rove thy scene-full world with thee!

THE PASSIONS: AN ODE FOR MUSIC

WHEN Music, heav'nly maid, was young,
While yet in early Greece she sung,
The Passions oft to hear her shell,
Throng'd around her magic cell,
Exulting, trembling, raging, fainting,
Possest beyond the Muse's painting;
By turns they felt the glowing mind,
Disturb'd, delighted, rais'd, refin'd.
Till once, 'tis said, when all were fir'd,
Fill'd with fury, rapt, inspir'd,   10
From the supporting myrtles round,
They snatch'd her instruments of sound,

[1] Alluding to the Milesian tales, some of the earliest romances.
[2] Cervantes.
[3] Monsieur Le Sage, author of the incomparable adventures of Gil Blas
de Santillane, who died in Paris in the year 1745.

And as they oft had heard a-part
Sweet lessons of her forceful art,
Each, for madness rul'd the hour,
Would prove his own expressive pow'r.

First Fear his hand, its skill to try,
   Amid the chords bewilder'd laid,
And back recoil'd he knew not why,
   Ev'n at the sound himself had made.   20

Next Anger rush'd, his eyes on fire,
   In lightnings own'd his secret stings,
In one rude clash he struck the lyre,
   And swept with hurried hand the strings.

With woful measures wan Despair
   Low sullen sounds his grief beguil'd,
A solemn, strange, and mingled air,
   'Twas sad by fits, by starts 'twas wild.

But thou, O Hope, with eyes so fair,
   What was thy delightful measure?   30
Still it whisper'd promis'd pleasure,
   And bad the lovely scenes at distance hail!

Still would her touch the strain prolong,
   And from the rocks, the woods, the vale,
She call'd on Echo still thro' all the song;
   And, where her sweetest theme she chose,
   A soft responsive voice was heard at ev'ry close,
And Hope enchanted smil'd, and wav'd her golden hair.
And longer had she sung,—but with a frown,
   Revenge impatient rose,   40
He threw his blood-stain'd sword in thunder down,
   And with a with'ring look,
   The war-denouncing trumpet took,
And blew a blast so loud and dread,
Were ne'er prophetic sounds so full of woe.
   And ever and anon he beat
   The doubling drum with furious heat;
And tho' sometimes each dreary pause between,
   Dejected Pity at his side,
   Her soul-subduing voice applied,   50
Yet still he kept his wild unalter'd mien,
While each strain'd ball of sight seem'd bursting from his head.

Thy numbers, Jealousy, to nought were fix'd,
   Sad proof of thy distressful state,
Of diff'ring themes the veering song was mix'd,
   And now it courted Love, now raving call'd on Hate.

With eyes up-rais'd, as one inspir'd,
Pale Melancholy sate retir'd,
And from her wild sequester'd seat,
In notes by distance made more sweet,   60
Pour'd thro' the mellow horn her pensive soul:
   And dashing soft from rocks around,
   Bubbling runnels join'd the sound;
Thro' glades and glooms the mingled measure stole,
Or o'er some haunted stream with fond delay,
   Round an holy calm diffusing,
   Love of peace, and lonely musing,
In hollow murmurs died away.
But O how alter'd was its sprightlier tone!
When Chearfulness, a nymph of healthiest hue,   70
   Her bow a-cross her shoulder flung,
   Her buskins gem'd with morning dew,
Blew an inspiring air, that dale and thicket rung,
   The hunter's call to Faun and Dryad known!
   The oak-crown'd Sisters, and their chast-ey'd Queen,
   Satyrs and sylvan boys were seen,
   Peeping from forth their alleys green;
Brown Exercise rejoic'd to hear,
   And Sport leapt up, and seiz'd his beechen spear.

Last came Joy's ecstatic trial,   80
He with viny crown advancing,
   First to the lively pipe his hand addrest,
But soon he saw the brisk awak'ning viol,
   Whose sweet entrancing voice he lov'd the best.
   They would have thought who heard the strain,
   They saw in Tempe's vale her native maids,
   Amidst the festal sounding shades,
To some unwearied minstrel dancing,
   While as his flying fingers kiss'd the strings,
   LOVE fram'd with Mirth, a gay fantastic round,   90
   Loose were her tresses seen, her zone unbound,
   And HE amidst his frolic play,
   As if he would the charming air repay,
   Shook thousand odours from his dewy wings.

O Music, sphere-descended maid,
Friend of pleasure, Wisdom's aid,
Why, Goddess, why to us deny'd?
Lay'st thou thy antient lyre aside?
As in that lov'd Athenian bow'r,
You learn'd an all-commanding pow'r,   100
Thy mimic soul, O nymph endear'd,
Can well recall what then it heard.
Where is thy native simple heart,
Devote to Virtue, Fancy, Art?
Arise as in that elder time,
Warm, energic, chaste, sublime!
Thy wonders in that God-like age,
Fill thy recording Sister's page—
'Tis said, and I believe the tale,
Thy humblest Reed could more prevail,   110
Had more of strength, diviner rage,
Than all which charms this laggard age,
Ev'n all at once together found,
Cæcilia's mingled world of sound—
O bid our vain endeavors cease,
Revive the just designs of Greece,
Return in all thy simple state!
Confirm the tales her sons relate!

TO
GEORGE LYTTLETON, ESQ.
THIS
ODE
IS INSCRIB'D BY
THE AUTHOR

ODE ON THE DEATH OF MR. THOMSON

[*The scene of the following stanzas is suppos'd to lie on the Thames near Richmond.*]

I

IN yonder grave a DRUID lies
    Where slowly winds the stealing wave!
The year's best sweets shall duteous rise
    To deck it's POET's sylvan grave!

II

In yon deep bed of whisp'ring reeds
    His airy harp [1] shall now be laid,
That he, whose heart in sorrow bleeds
    May love thro' life the soothing shade.

III

Then maids and youths shall linger here,
    And while it's sounds at distance swell,   10
Shall sadly seem in Pity's ear
    To hear the WOODLAND PILGRIM's knell.

IV

REMEMBRANCE oft shall haunt the shore
    When THAMES in summer-wreaths is drest,
And oft suspend the dashing oar
    To bid his gentle spirit rest!

V

And oft as EASE and HEALTH retire
    To breezy lawn, or forest deep,
The friend shall view yon whit'ning spire, [2]
    And 'mid the varied landschape weep.   20

VI

But thou, who own'st that earthy bed,
    Ah! what will ev'ry dirge avail?
Or tears, which LOVE and PITY shed
    That mourn beneath the gliding sail!

VII

Yet lives there one, whose heedless eye
    Shall scorn thy pale shrine glimm'ring near?
With him, sweet bard, may FANCY die,
    And JOY desert the blooming year.

VIII

But thou, lorn STREAM, whose sullen tide
    No sedge-crown'd SISTERS now attend,
Now waft me from the green hill's side   30
    Whose cold turf hides the buried FRIEND!

---

[1] The harp of Æolus, of which see a description in the *Castle of Indolence.*
[2] Richmond Church.

IX

And see, the fairy valleys fade,
    Dun Night has veil'd the solemn view!
—Yet once again, dear parted SHADE
    Meek NATURE'S CHILD again adieu!

X

The genial meads assign'd to bless
    Thy life, shall mourn thy early doom,
Their hinds, and shepherd-girls shall dress
    With simple hands thy rural tomb.   40

XI

Long, long, thy stone and pointed clay
    Shall melt the musing BRITON'S eyes,
O! VALES, and WILD WOODS, shall HE say
    In yonder grave YOUR DRUID lies!

A SONG FROM SHAKESPEAR'S CYMBELINE

SUNG BY GUIDERUS AND ARVIRAGUS OVER FIDELE,
SUPPOS'D TO BE DEAD

[See page 278 of the seventh volume of Theobald's edition of Shakespear.]

I

To fair FIDELE'S grassy tomb
    Soft maids, and village hinds shall bring
Each op'ning sweet, of earliest bloom,
    And rifle all the breathing spring.

II

No wailing ghost shall dare appear
    To vex with shrieks this quiet grove:
But shepherd lads assemble here,
    And melting virgins own their love.

III

No wither'd witch shall here be seen,
    No goblins lead their nightly crew:
The female fays shall haunt the green,
    And dress thy grave with pearly dew!   10

IV

The redbreast oft at ev'ning hours
    Shall kindly lend his little aid:
With hoary moss, and gather'd flow'rs,
    To deck the ground where thou art laid.

V

When howling winds, and beating rain,
    In tempests shake the sylvan cell:
Or midst the chace on ev'ry plain,
    The tender thought on thee shall dwell.   20

VI

Each lonely scene shall thee restore,
    For thee the tear be duly shed:
Belov'd, till life could charm no more;
    And mourn'd, till Pity's self be dead.

AN ODE ON THE POPULAR SUPERSTITIONS OF THE HIGHLANDS OF SCOTLAND

CONSIDERED AS THE SUBJECT OF POETRY

[Written about 1749 and first printed with interpolations by the editor in the *Transactions* of the Royal Society of Edinburgh, I. ii, § ii, p. 63.]

H——, thou return'st from Thames, whose Naiads long
    Have seen thee ling'ring, with a fond delay,
Mid those soft friends, whose hearts, some future day,
    Shall melt, perhaps, to hear thy tragic song.
Go, not unmindful of that cordial youth,
    Whom, long endear'd, thou leav'st by Lavant's side;
Together let us wish him lasting truth,
    And joy untainted with his destin'd bride,
Go! nor regardless, while these numbers boast
    My short-liv'd bliss, forget my social name;   10
But think far off how, on the southern coast,
    I met thy friendship with an equal flame!
Fresh to that soil thou turn'st, whose ev'ry vale

Shall prompt the poet, and his song demand:
To thee thy copious subjects ne'er shall fail;
    Thou need'st but take the pencil to thy hand,
And paint what all believe who own thy genial land.

II

There must thou wake perforce thy Doric quill,
    'Tis Fancy's land to which thou sett'st thy feet;
Where still, 'tis said, the fairy people meet   20
    Beneath each birken shade on mead or hill.
There each trim lass that skims the milky store
    To the swart tribes their creamy bowl allots;
By night they sip it round the cottage-door,
    While airy minstrels warble jocund notes.
There every herd, by sad experience, knows
    How, wing'd with fate, their elf-shot arrows fly;
When the sick ewe her summer food foregoes,
    Or, stretch'd on earth, the heart-smit heifers lie.
Such airy beings awe th' untutor'd swain: 30
    Nor thou, though learn'd, his homelier thoughts neglect;
Let thy sweet muse the rural faith sustain:
    These are the themes of simple, sure effect,
That add new conquests to her boundless reign,
And fill, with double force, her heart-commanding strain.

III

Ev'n yet preserv'd, how often may'st thou hear,
    Where to the pole the Boreal mountains run,
Taught by the father to his list'ning son
    Strange lays, whose power had charm'd a SPENCER'S ear.
At ev'ry pause, before thy mind possest,   40
    Old RUNIC bards shall seem to rise around,
With uncouth lyres, in many-coloured vest,
    Their matted hair with boughs fantastic crown'd:
Whether thou bid'st the well-taught hind repeat
    The choral dirge that mourns some chieftain brave,
When ev'ry shrieking maid her bosom beat,
    And strew'd with choicest herbs his scented grave;
Or whether, sitting in the shepherd's shiel,
    Thou hear'st some sounding tale of war's alarms;
When, at the bugle's call, with fire and steel,   50
    The sturdy clans pour'd forth their bony swarms,
And hostile brothers met to prove each other's arms.

IV

'Tis thine to sing, how framing hideous spells
  In Sky's lone isle the gifted wizzard seer,
Lodged in the wintry cave with ———,
  Or in the depth of Uist's dark forests dwells:
How they, whose sight such dreary dreams engross,
  With their own visions oft astonish'd droop,
When o'er the wat'ry strath or quaggy moss
  They see the gliding ghosts unbodied troop.   60
Or if in sports, or on the festive green,
  Their ——— glance some fated youth descry,
Who, now perhaps in lusty vigour seen
  And rosy health, shall soon lamented die.
For them the viewless forms of air obey,
  Their bidding heed, and at their beck repair.
They know what spirit brews the stormful day,
  And heartless, oft like moody madness stare
To see the phantom train their secret work prepare.

[25 lines lost.]

VI

What though far off, from some dark dell espied
  His glimm'ring mazes cheer th' excursive sight,
Yet turn, ye wand'rers, turn your steps aside,
  Nor trust the guidance of that faithless light;
For watchful, lurking 'mid th' unrustling reed,
  At those mirk hours the wily monster lies,   100
And listens oft to hear the passing steed,
  And frequent round him rolls his sullen eyes,
If chance his savage wrath may some weak wretch surprise.

VII

Ah, luckless swain, o'er all unblest indeed!
  Whom late bewilder'd in the dank, dark fen,
Far from his flocks and smoking hamlet then!
  To that sad spot ———————:
On him enrag'd, the fiend, in angry mood,
  Shall never look with pity's kind concern,
But instant, furious, raise the whelming flood   110
  O'er its drown'd bank, forbidding all return.
Or, if he meditate his wish'd escape
  To some dim hill that seems uprising near,

To his faint eye the grim and grisly shape,
    In all its terrors clad, shall wild appear.
Meantime, the wat'ry surge shall around him rise,
    Pour'd sudden forth from ev'ry swelling source,
What now remains but tears and hopeless sighs?
    His fear-shook limbs have lost their youthly force,
And down the waves he floats, a pale and breathless corse.

VIII

For him, in vain, his anxious wife shall wait,   121
    Or wander forth to meet him on his way;
For him, in vain, at to-fall of the day,
    His babes shall linger at th' unclosing gate!
Ah, ne'er shall he return! Alone, if night
    Her travell'd limbs in broken slumbers steep,
With dropping willows drest, his mournful sprite
    Shall visit sad, perchance, her silent sleep:
Then he, perhaps, with moist and wat'ry hand,
    Shall fondly seem to press her shudd'ring cheek,   130
And with his blue swoln face before her stand,
    And, shiv'ring cold, these piteous accents speak:
Pursue, dear wife, thy daily toils pursue
    At dawn or dusk, industrious as before;
Nor e'er of me one hapless thought renew,
    While I lie welt'ring on the ozier'd shore,
Drown'd by the KAELPIE's wrath, nor e'er shall aid thee more!

IX

Unbounded is thy range; with varied stile
    Thy muse may, like those feath'ry tribes which spring
From their rude rocks, extend her skirting wing   140
    Round the moist marge of each cold Hebrid isle,
To that hoar pile which still its ruin shows:
    In whose small vaults a pigmy-folk is found,
Whose bones the delver with his spade upthrows,
    And culls them, wond'ring, from the hallow'd ground!
Or thither where beneath the show'ry west
    The mighty kings of three fair realms are laid:
Once foes, perhaps, together now they rest.
    No slaves revere them, and no wars invade:
Yet frequent now, at midnight's solemn hour,   150

The rifted mounds their yawning cells unfold,
And forth the monarchs stalk with sov'reign pow'r
  In pageant robes, and wreath'd with sheeny gold,
And on their twilight tombs aerial council hold.

X

But O! o'er all, forget not KILDA's race,
  On whose bleak rocks, which brave the wasting tides,
Fair Nature's daughter, Virtue, yet abides.
  Go, just, as they, their blameless manners trace!
Then to my ear transmit some gentle song
  Of those whose lives are yet sincere and plain,   160
Their bounded walks the rugged cliffs along,
  And all their prospect but the wintry main.
With sparing temp'rance, at the needful time,
  They drain the sainted spring, or, hunger-prest,
Along th' Atlantic rock undreading climb,
  And of its eggs despoil the solan's nest.
Thus blest in primal innocence they live,
  Suffic'd and happy with that frugal fare
Which tasteful toil and hourly danger give.
  Hard is their shallow soil, and bleak and bare;   170
Nor ever vernal bee was heard to murmur there!

XI

Nor need'st thou blush, that such false themes engage
  Thy gentle mind, of fairer stores possest;
For not alone they touch the village breast,
  But fill'd in elder time th' historic page,
There SHAKESPEARE's self, with ev'ry garland crown'd,
  In musing hour, his wayward sisters found,
And with their terrors drest the magic scene.
From them he sung, when mid his bold design,
  Before the Scot afflicted and aghast,   180
The shadowy kings of BANQUO's fated line,
  Through the dark cave in gleamy pageant past.
Proceed, nor quit the tales which, simply told,
  Could once so well my answ'ring bosom pierce;
Proceed, in forceful sounds and colours bold
  The native legends of thy land rehearse;
To such adapt thy lyre and suit thy powerful verse.

XII

In scenes like these, which, daring to depart
　From sober truth, are still to nature true,
　And call forth fresh delight to fancy's view,   190
　　Th' heroic muse employ'd her TASSO's art!
How have I trembled, when at TANCRED's stroke,
　Its gushing blood the gaping cypress pour'd;
When each live plant with mortal accents spoke,
　And the wild blast up-heav'd the vanish'd sword!
How have I sat, when pip'd the pensive wind,
　To hear his harp, by British FAIRFAX strung.
Prevailing poet, whose undoubting mind
　Believ'd the magic wonders which he sung!
Hence at each sound imagination glows;   200
Hence his warm lay with softest sweetness flows;
　Melting it flows, pure, num'rous, strong and clear,
And fills th' impassion'd heart, and wins th' harmonious ear.

XIII

All hail, ye scenes that o'er my soul prevail,
　Ye ——— friths and lakes which, far away,
Are by smooth ANNAN fill'd, or past'ral TAY,
　Or DON's romantic springs, at distance, hail!
The time shall come when I, perhaps, may tread
　Your lowly glens, o'erhung with spreading broom,
Or o'er your stretching heaths by fancy led: 210
Then will I dress once more the faded bow'r,
　Where JOHNSON sat in DRUMMOND's ——— shade;
Or crop from Tiviots dale each ———,
　And mourn on Yarrow's banks ———.
Meantime, ye pow'rs, that on the plains which bore
　The cordial youth, on LOTHIAN's plains attend,
Where'er he dwell, on hill, or lowly muir,
　To him I lose, your kind protection lend,
And, touch'd with love like mine, preserve my absent friend.

WRITTEN ON A PAPER, WHICH CONTAINED A PIECE
    OF BRIDE CAKE, GIVEN TO THE AUTHOR BY
    A LADY

[First (?) published in Pearch's Collection, vol. ii, ed. 2, 1770.]

YE curious hands, that hid from vulgar eyes,
    By search profane shall find this hallow'd cake,
With Virtue's awe forbear the sacred prize,
    Nor dare a theft for Love and Pity's sake!

This precious relick, form'd by magic power
    Beneath the shepherd's haunted pillow laid,
Was meant by Love to charm the silent hour,
    The secret present of a matchless maid.

The Cyprian queen, at Hymen's fond request,
    Each nice ingredient chose with happiest art;   10
Fears, sighs, and wishes of th' enamour'd breast,
    And pains that please are mixt in every part.

With rosy hand the spicy fruit she brought
    From Paphian hills, and fair Cythera's isle;
And temper'd sweet with these the melting thought,
    The kiss ambrosial and the yielding smile.

Ambiguous looks, that scorn and yet relent,
    Denials mild, and firm unalter'd truth,
Reluctant pride, and amorous faint consent,
    And meeting ardours, and exulting youth.   20

Sleep, wayward God! hath sworn while these remain,
    With flattering dreams to dry his nightly tear,
And chearful Hope, so oft invok'd in vain,
    With fairy songs shall sooth his pensive ear.

If bound by vows to Friendship's gentle side,
    And fond of soul, thou hop'st an equal grace,
If youth or maid thy joys and griefs divide,
    O much intreated, leave this fatal place.

Sweet Peace, who long hath shunn'd my plaintive day,
    Consents at length to bring me short delight,   30
Thy careless steps may scare her doves away,
    And Grief with raven note usurp the night.

WILLIAM COLLINS

SONG

THE SENTIMENTS BORROWED FROM SHAKESPEARE

[Perhaps written at Winchester in 1739. Printed anonymously in *The Public Advertiser*, 7 March, 1788, but it seems to have been first included among Collins's works in Anderson's *Poets*. Dyce printed it as the work of Collins on the authority of Thomas Parke.]

YOUNG Damon of the vale is dead,
  Ye lowland hamlets moan,
A dewy turf lies o'er his head,
  And at his feet a stone.

His shroud, which Death's cold damps destroy,
  Of snow-white threads was made,
All mourn'd to see so sweet a boy
  In earth for ever laid.

Pale pansies o'er his corpse were plac'd,
  Which, pluck'd before their time,
Bestrew'd the boy, like him to waste,
  And wither in their prime.

But will he ne'er return, whose tongue
  Could tune the rural lay?
Ah, no! his bell of peace is rung,
  His lips are cold as clay.

They bore him out at twilight hour,
  The youth belov'd so well:
Ah me! how many a true-love show'r
  Of kind remembrance fell!

Each maid was woe—but Lucy chief,
  Her grief o'er all was tried;
Within his grave she drop'd in grief,
  And o'er her lov'd-one died.

MADE AT THE TEMPLE PRESS LETCHWORTH IN GREAT BRITAIN